ENERGY ANALYSIS AND POLICY

SELECTED WORKS

Mohan Munasinghe

Foreword by Robert Pindyck

Introduction by Rajendra Pachauri

Butterworths

London Boston Singapore Sydney Toronto Wellington

First published 1990

© Butterworth & Co (Publishers) Ltd, 1990

British Library Cataloguing in Publication Data

Munasinghe, Mohan 1945–
    Energy analysis and policy: selected works.
    1. Energy resources
    I. Title
    333.79

ISBN 0-408-05634-7

Library of Congress Cataloging-in-Publication Data

Munasinghe, Mohan, 1945–
    Energy analysis and policy: selected works/
Mohan Munasinghe; foreword by Robert S. Pindyck;
introduction by Rajendra K. Pachauri.
       p.   cm.
    Includes bibliographical references.
    ISBN 0-408-05634-7:
    1. Energy policy—Developing countries. 2. Energy
consumption—Developing countries. 3. Energy
development—Developing countries. I. Title.
    HD9502.D442M84   1989
    333.79′09172′4—dc20
                                89-25254
                                    CIP

Printed and bound by Hartnolls Ltd, Bodmin, Cornwall

To Sria

This collection of essays and its companion publication entitled *Electric Power Economics* are being issued to commemorate the receipt of two awards by Mohan Munasinghe, for:

(a) exceptional contributions to energy literature and research, from the International Association for Energy Economics, USA (1987);
(b) outstanding research and applications in power and energy system analysis and pricing, from the Latin America and Caribbean Conference on Electric Power and Energy (1988).

These twin volumes are published with the compliments and felicitations of the following:

Bulletin of Indonesian Economic Studies
Energy Economics
Energy Journal (publication of the International Association for
    Energy Economics)
Energy Policy
Energy Systems and Policy
IEE Review (publication of the Institution of Electrical
    Engineers, UK)
IEEE Transactions on Power Apparatus and Systems (publication of
    the Institute of Electrical and Electronic Engineers, USA)
International Journal of Ambient Energy
International Journal of Electrical Power and Energy Systems
Journal of Consumer Research
Journal of Development Economics
Journal of Energy and Development
Natural Resources Forum
Natural Resources Journal
Pacific and Asian Journal of Energy
Pakistan Economic and Social Review
Power Engineering Journal (publication of the Institution of
    Electrical Engineers, UK)
Proceedings of the IEEE (publication of the Institute of
    Electrical and Electronic Engineers, USA)
Rand Journal of Economics (formerly *Bell Journal of Economics*)
SLEMA Journal (publication of the Sri Lanka Energy Managers
    Association)

CONTENTS

FIGURES

TABLES

FOREWORD

There are few sectors of an economy that are as important as the energy sector. The rapid changes in energy prices that have occurred during the past two decades have had a major impact on economic growth, employment and inflation in virtually every country of the world. The oil price shocks of 1974 and 1979-80 have made us actually aware of how dependent macroeconomic policy and performance are on the evolution of world energy markets, and how critical the design of a sound energy policy is to economic performance.

This is particularly the case in developing countries. The economies of energy exporting countries like Mexico and Indonesia, and energy importing countries like Turkey and Sri Lanka, are in their own ways heavily dependent on what happens to world energy prices. These countries have found that their economies are vulnerable to sudden and unexpected energy price changes, and have had to design and implement strategies to reduce this vulnerability. Well designed policies for the management of domestic energy markets -- policies that minimize market distortions, that price fuels at their true marginal social value, and that promote efficiency in both production and consumption -- are likewise of critical importance. And energy investment decisions -- for example in electric power generation and transmission, and oil and gas development -- have become riskier and require much more careful analysis.

This has made the analysis of energy markets and design of energy policy an area of utmost importance for economists and planners. Few people have contributed more to this area than Mohan Munasinghe, whose research contributions have spanned most of the issues raised above. He has, both figuratively and literally, "written the book" on virtually every major aspect of electricity economics, including pricing, demand forecasting, investment analysis and system reliability. He has also "written the book" on energy sector analysis, forecasting and policy design for developing countries. His research on energy economics, the numerous books and articles that he has authored or co-authored, and the extensive lectures and seminars that he has given around the world, have done much to promote a better understanding of energy markets and a more sensible design of energy policies. His work at the World Bank, and for several years as Senior Energy Advisor to the President of Sri Lanka, also have done much to put this understanding into practice.

This book pulls together fourteen of Mohan's recent papers on energy economics and policy. It is "vintage Munasinghe", spanning a broad range of issues, but treating each in depth and with great insight, and with a writing style that is clear and accessible. The chapters range from the "macro" (Chapter 2, on "Integrated National Energy Planning in Developing Countries"), to the "micro" (Chapter 10, on "Non-conventional Energy Project Analysis"). They cover demand (Chapter 8, on "Energy Demand Analysis and Forecasting") and supply (Chapter 11 on "Energy Project Analysis and Planning"). They deal with traditional fuels (Chapter 12, on "Biomass Management Policy"), and commercial energy (Chapter 13, on "Rural-Industrial Energy and Fossil Fuel Issues"). And finally, they address basic problems such as energy pricing, demand management and conservation, investment policy, and energy research and development.

Together, the chapters of this book provide a clear and comprehensive overview of the diversity of problems we face in analyzing energy markets and designing sound energy policies. The chapters also provide a good understanding of how careful analysis can be used to obtain rational and workable solutions to these problems. Given the importance of these issues to our economic well being, this book is bound to have a wide and appreciative audience.

Robert S Pindyck
Mitsubishi Bank Professor of Applied Economics
Sloan School, Massachusetts Institute of Technology
Cambridge, Massachusetts

ACKNOWLEDGEMENTS

I am deeply indebted to all the colleagues and friends, too numerous to mention here, who have contributed so generously to my intellectual development over the years. Special mention should be made of those who helped to co-author the various works that provide the basis for several chapters in this volume, as indicated in the relevant footnotes.

I am most grateful and privileged also, to have the Foreword contributed by one of the foremost international scholars and authorities in the field, Robert Pindyck, and the Introduction prepared by another world renowned energy expert and researcher, Rajendra Pachauri. Finally, many thanks are owed especially to Chitrupa Fernando, as well as to Mark Bernstein, Jayant Sathaye, Susantha Perera and the staff of Butterworths for assistance in reviewing, compiling and editing this volume.

INTRODUCTION[1]

Writing an introduction to the works of a great author is similiar perhaps to introducing a distinguished speaker to an audience eager to listen to the star of the evening and not one bit interested in the drabness of the introduction. In preparing this short text, therefore, I feel uncomfortably sandwiched between a lucid and effective Foreword by a distinguished economist -- Professor Robert Pindyck -- and the rich creation of Professor Mohan Munasinghe based on years of thought, analysis and insightful probing into the energy problems facing the world. However, since I have the honor of contributing the introduction to this admirable piece of work, I shall attempt to do full justice to my task.

Before I get into the substance of the enormous range of subjects covered by Mohan, I must pay adequate tribute to the professional *par excellence* in him. Each one of us has memories of that one great teacher who, through his brilliance and mastery of the subject, could explain the most complex of ideas and analyses in the simplest terms. Professor Munasinghe's writings are typically those of that great teacher -- covering the most intricate and difficult issues with the facility and ease of a master.

The other general impression which I have gathered from the valuable material contained in this volume relates to the great industry, zeal, and dedication of the man. Most of us hold talks and lectures at many training programs and workshops, but I have run into very few who do not follow the general practice of putting a few things together at the last minute and presenting a rehash of what they have been saying for the past several years. Often the applause that one receives at the end of such a talk lulls one into a feeling of false accomplishment, tempting one to repeat the process at the next opportunity. One gains a facility with words and delivery, which over time becomes a substitute for profound analysis and original thinking. It is apparent from the lectures delivered by Professor Munasinghe, some of which are included in this book, that he treats each such event as a professsional challenge and as an opportunity to produce a work of original scholarship and rigorous analysis. Herein lies his strength, which undoubtedly is evidence of his dedication to perfection.

The material presented in this volume has general relevance to energy analysts and policymakers throughout the world, but has a special appeal for those dealing with this area in the developing countries. This Third World emphasis reflects not only the author's own interests and concerns, but has merit of its own, since the developing countries face unprecedented challenges in the energy sector, which can only be met through analysis and innovation of the highest order.

The most difficult challenge facing Third World countries lies in the growing demand for finance that those dealing with energy sector decisions have to contend with. This challenge results not only from a rapid increase in demand for energy, and therefore, for supply capacity, but also from the growing capital intensity of the energy supply industry. The problems to be solved are, therefore, manifold.

Firstly, energy sector organizations in the developing countries must achieve economic efficiency in their investment decisions and operations through the practice of rational economic principles. Secondly, supply capacity enhancement must be

---

[1] The opinions expressed herein are those of the author, and do not necessarily represent the views of any organization or institution.

integrated with approaches for management of demand, so that overall resources for development are utilized in an optimal fashion with explicit inclusion of efficiency objectives. Thirdly, the imperatives of growth require that the development of the energy sector must take place in a manner such that the welfare of society is maximized, particularly in respect of economic disparities that exist between rich and poor in the Third World.

The chapters of this volume address these questions and provide a framework whereby analysts and policymakers can pursue integrated energy planning and policymaking in accordance with the overall objectives of growth and equity.

The first chapter in the book deals with energy economics in developing countries, and examines the complex problem of adapting economic theory to practice in an environment where market forces and mechanisms often do not operate at all, or function under distortions which are not easy to remove in view of various social, political and organizational constraints. The value of this chapter (which is an edited version of Munasinghe's acceptance speech on the occasion of receiving the annual IAEE Award for Excellence in 1987), lies in the fact that policymakers often dismiss sound economic theory for being too far removed from reality. On the other hand, many theorists denigrate institutional arrangements in such situations as totally unsuitable for the implementation of rational economic principles, and contend that unless existing institutions and organizations are dismantled, sound economic theory cannot be applied. Mohan bridges the gap between these two extremes and one emerges with a greater understanding after reading his analysis irrespective of whether the reader prefers one or the other viewpoint.

The second and third chapters are classic works published concurrently in 1980, in which Munasinghe brought together his research of the late 1970's, to develop an original and comprehensive framework for energy pricing, planning, policy analysis, and implementation in the developing countries. In the second chapter, the principles of integrated national energy planning are set out, clearly. Here, not only are non-conventional forms of energy included in the exposition, but also traditional fuels -- a vital part of energy consumption in many developing countries. This chapter is particularly valuable, because planning for different forms of energy remains oftentimes fragmented in most countries, both developed and developing.

The concept of integrated energy planning is relatively new and came into focus only when substitution possibilities became more attractive economically, in the wake of the first oil price shock of 1973-74. Earlier, electric utilities, oil companies, coal suppliers, and the nuclear power establishment generally followed their own isolated attempts at energy planning. Notwithstanding the inclusion of a few variables such as the price of substitute fuels that entered into their demand functions, very little was done to evaluate fuel choices within an integrated framework.

In those countries where energy planning is based on the free interplay of market forces, there is still no integrated energy planning, even though governments may have prepared documents and future scenarios utilizing an integrated approach. In the developing countries, where a large share of energy sector decisions is still centralized in the hands of the government, the integration of different energy forms within an overall framework is essential not only for ensuring balanced economic growth, but also for minimizing overall costs of energy and use.

Munasinghe has done valuable work in the field of energy pricing. His writings are not only quoted frequently, but several of his arguments are utilized extensively by researchers, policymakers and analysts. I find his 1980 paper on "Energy Pricing: An Integrated Framework" perhaps the most valuable contribution in this volume, difficult as it is to separate out one from so many excellent chapters. It is really in this chapter that, through a simple but rigorous approach, the author presented a novel framework linking energy prices with other economic variables, and analyzed the structure of energy prices and their influence on economic activities and vice versa.

Perhaps greater harm has been done in the long run by policymakers round the world who deviate from an integrated energy pricing framework than from any other set of energy related decisions. Unfortunately, a regime of irrational prices is very difficult to alter. Even more difficult is the prospect of changing opinions and positions on energy pricing when they have been developed over time through a restricted view of the role of prices in an economic system. Munasinghe's chapter in this book presents an excellent picture of how pricing decisions should be promulgated, if economic welfare is to be maximized. He has adopted a framework that is concurrently logical, easily understood and yet rigorous.

The fourth chapter dealing with integrated national energy planning using microcomputers is an interesting exposition of how he successfully implemented, while serving as the Senior Energy Advisor to the President of Sri Lanka, many of the principles and analytical techniques he had developed earlier. I recall the presentation of this paper in a one week workshop dealing with this subject in September 1985, at which I had the pleasure of being the Technical Chairman of the workshop organized by the the UN DTCD. Mohan's was one of the few papers that addressed the challenges of applying the use of models within a Third World organizational and institutional milieu which may not be entirely conducive to energy modelling. Often, researchers who have developed energy models get carried away in their presentations by the technical excitement of the model itself, divorced from the environment within which these models are to be used.

Of course, 1985 was a period when interest in microcomputers and the development of microcomputer-based software was not as widely prevalent as it is today. The subsequent four years witnessed an enormous explosion of energy modelling activities and applications of models dealing with energy and other forms of natural resource use. Nevertheless, Munasinghe's presentation contains benefits for all those interested in the subject at this time, particularly since the organizational problems in the use of energy models and many of the questions dealing with the decisionmaking process are as valid today as they were when he carried out his work.

The next five essays dealing with energy strategies for oil importing developing countries (1984), energy demand management and conservation (1978), national energy policy implementation in Sri Lanka (1983), energy demand analysis and forecasting (1983), and energy project evaluation and planning (1982), are all subjects that form an essential part of the energy planning and analysis process. The merit of the material presented again lies in a very practical approach based on rational economic principles. Typically, there is widespread interest in energy conservation possibilities in several developing countries, but little is known on how energy conservation goals and objectives can be built into overall planning strategies. Mohan's analysis is illuminating because it deals with particular energy using sectors, specific types of end uses, and problems of behavioral change. As exemplified in Chapter 6, he had made key contributions over a decade ago, towards establishing a sound analytical and practical basis for the energy efficiency, demand management and conservation programmes that have become the accepted practice in the environmentally-conscious 1980s. The references to the situation in Sri Lanka and other countries add a case study dimension and practical flavour to energy management strategies and approaches.

The chapter on energy demand analysis and forecasting is an extremely useful summary and can be used essentially as a manual by anyone who wishes to analyze energy demand and make projections for the future. The simplicity and clarity of presentation of methodologies is refreshing. While it does not examine in detail, some sophisticated econometric techniques that have been employed widely in recent years -- such as the translog production function -- it is a very useful guide for anyone who wishes to study energy demand for simple and direct application, especially in an operating environment where data is scarce.

Of the remaining chapters in the book that I have not specifically mentioned, I would like to single out the chapters dealing with non-conventional energy project analysis (1983), rural energy issues and supply options (1986) and bioenergy management policy (1979). These three chapters have particular relevance to the developing countries, and their strength lies in the consideration that the author has provided to non-conventional subjects within a conventional framework. Generally, this is where the gap lies in the process of policy formulation and energy planning for renewables in most developing countries.

Unfortunately, even in those nations where vigorous non-conventional energy programs are being pursued, the path followed is one of isolation from conventional energy development. There is as much a gap between organizations and institutions in this regard as there is in methodologies of planning. Conventional energy projects are often pursued on the basis of routine accounting and financial principles; whereas advocates of non-conventional energy pursue a technology-driven approach where economic questions are often wished away as inconvenient and irrelevant. Yet, within a national planning framework, economic rationality has to govern the development of non-conventional energy use, just as conventional energy forms have to contend with questions of resource depletion, environmental costs and other social costs which are either hidden or minimized by analysts pushing thermal power plants, refineries or large hydro projects. Munasinghe provides a valuable framework to bridge this gap.

The final two chapters dealing with energy issues in Thailand (1979) and energy research and development in the developing countries (1983), once again demonstrate the breadth of the author's coverage and interests in the energy field. In the same spirit, I wish to end this introduction by suggesting that Munasinghe direct his energies even more widely -- to some of the environmental implications of energy policy analysis and planning -- not because it is currently fashionable to do so, but in the interests of ensuring that energy choices in the future fully account for environmental costs and benefits. In my own experience I have found that a whole range of issues such as the setting of environmental standards, the estimation of environmental costs and benefits, and environmental impact analysis are still dealt with in an arbitrary manner. Yet the environmental implications of energy supply and use are immense and continue to grow in magnitude and implication.

Knowing Mohan Munasinghe's ability and wide interests as a researcher, I am certain that some of these questions are already receiving his attention. Regardless of what Munasinghe writes in the coming months and years, I eagerly await his upcoming works and know that the many thousands of his readers share this feeling. It has been an education and pleasure to read this present volume, and an honour to write the introduction for it. No monopolist can derive a higher economic rent.

Rajendra K. Pachauri
President, International Association for Energy Economics and
Director, Tata Energy Research Institute
Delhi, India

ENERGY ECONOMICS IN DEVELOPING COUNTRIES: ANALYTICAL FRAMEWORK AND PROBLEMS OF APPLICATION[1]

1.1 Introduction

The pervasive and vital role of energy in national economies indicates that the identification of energy issues, and energy policy analysis and implementation are important areas of study. While the softening of world oil prices which began in 1986 has provided some relief to the economies of oil importing nations, energy related problems still preoccupy the minds of decisionmakers in most developing countries. Thus, the availability of adequate energy resources at a reasonable cost remains a vital precondition for continued economic growth, while most of the key energy issues identified during the past decade persist. Typically, developing country energy investments still account for about 25 percent of total public capital expenditures, while this figure is around 50% in some nations -- particularly in Latin America. Furthermore, oil importers are spending an average of 15-20 percent of export earnings on petroleum imports, and serious fuelwood shortages and deforestation problems continue unabated -- especially in Africa and Asia.

Following the first international oil crisis of 1973, the rapidly increasing costs of all forms of energy, led by the world oil price, stimulated the development of new analytical tools and policies. Indeed, much of this success may be attributed to the discipline of energy economics, and the increasing recognition received by our profession reflects the valuable contributions made by many distinguished researchers and colleagues in the field. It is a privilege to briefly set out in this paper, my views on the progress made in recent years, and its impact on energy decisionmaking and implementation in the developing countries. Unfortunately, limitations of space and time prevent full justice being done to the considerable literature available.

Central to the success of the energy economics approach has been the concept of economic value of scarce resources. The economic numeraire has provided the basis on which alternative uses of various resources might be evaluated, facilitating the tradeoff between energy and other more traditional inputs such as capital and labour, as well as among the different forms of energy themselves. Furthermore, economic efficiency in both energy supply and use is a practical benchmark. Thus, the economic costs of deviating from efficient policies, to meet sociopolitical and other goals, may be used to assess the desirability of such options.

Several important lessons have been learned by both energy analysts and policymakers, during the last 10-15 years. First the importance of an integrated approach to energy analysis, and more systematic exploration of energy-macroeconomic links, emerged. Furthermore, while policy analysis and

---

[1] Edited version of award acceptance plenary address delivered at the IAEE International Conference held in Calgary, Canada, in July 1987; and subsequently published in *The Energy Journal*, vol.9, January 1988, pp.1-19.

formulation at the national level might be centralised, the effective implementation of policy requires the maximum use of decentralised market forces and institutions. Second, the need became apparent, for greater coordination between energy supply and demand options, and better use of demand management and conservation. Third, the more disaggregate analysis of both supply and demand within the energy sector offered greater opportunities for inter-fuel substitution in specific uses. Fourth, the analytical and modelling tools for energy subsector planning became more sophisticated, particularly in their treatment of uncertainty, reliability and supply quality. Fifth, greater practical reliance was placed on economic principles, such as marginal costing and shadow pricing in the developing countries, rather than relying on engineering and financial analysis alone.

1.2   Framework for Integrated National Energy Planning (INEP), Policy Analysis and Implementation

Energy decisions cannot be made in isolation. The complexity of energy-economic interactions indicate that energy sector investment planning, pricing and management should be carried out on an integrated basis, e.g., within a integrated national energy planning (INEP) framework which helps analyse the whole range of energy issues and policy options over a long period of time.

Energy planning, broadly interpreted, denotes a series of steps or procedures by which the myriad of interactions involved in the production and use of all forms of energy may be studied and understood within an explicit analytical framework. Planning techniques range from simple manual methods to sophisticated computer modelling. The complexity of energy problems and the enhanced capability of low cost microcomputers, has led to increasing reliance on the latter approach. Energy policy analysis is the systematic investigation of the impact of specific energy policies or policy packages on the economy and society, at all levels. Energy supply and demand management involves the use of a selected set of policies and policy instruments, to achieve desirable national objectives.

An important goal of developing countries must be to upgrade the quality of energy planning, policy analysis and management. However, the word planning, whether applied to the national economy or the energy sector in particular, need not imply some rigid framework along the lines of centralized or fully planned economies. Planning, whether by design or neglect, takes place even in the so-called market economies. Furthermore, while the energy planning, policy analysis and formulation may require centralised coordination, policy implementation is most effectively carried out using decentralised mechanisms and market forces, as discussed later in this paper.

In energy planning and policy analysis, the principal emphasis is on the detailed and comprehensive analysis of the energy sector, its linkages with the rest of the economy, and the main interactions within the various energy subsectors themselves. In the industrialised nations, the complex and intricate relationships between the various economic sectors, and the prevalence of private market decisions, make policy analysis a difficult task. In the developing countries, substantial levels of market distortions, shortages of foreign exchange as well as human and financial resources, larger numbers of poor households whose basic needs have to be met, greater emphasis on rural energy problems, and relative paucity of energy and other data, add to the already complicated problems faced by energy analysts everywhere.

In order to better understand the nature of decisionmaking in the energy sector, we begin by identifying below, some of the broad goals of energy policy as seen from the national perspective. (See Chapter 2 for the original development of the INEP concept).

National Policy Objectives

The broad rationale underlying all national level planning and policymaking is the need to ensure the best use of scarce resources, in order to further socio-economic development efforts and improve the quality of life of citizens. Energy planning must also be part of, and closely integrated with overall economic planning and policy analysis, to meet many specific, inter- related and frequently conflicting national objectives. Specific goals might include: (a) ensuring economic efficiency in the supply and use of all forms of energy, to maximize growth -- other efficiency related objectives are energy conservation and elimination of wasteful consumption, and saving scarce foreign exchange; (b) raising sufficient revenues from energy sales, to finance sector development; (c) meeting the basic energy needs of the poor, and income redistribution; (d) diversifying supply, reducing dependence on foreign sources, and meeting national security requirements; (e) contributing to development of special regions (particularly rural or remote areas), and priority sectors of the economy; (f) price stability; (g) preserving the environment; and so on.

Scope of INEP

The INEP concept may be represented by a hierarchical framework (see Figure 2.1 in Chapter 2), with reference to which the scope of integrated national energy planning, policy analysis, and supply-demand management may be clarified. At the most aggregate level, it is clearly recognized that energy is but one sector of the whole economy. Therefore, energy planning requires analysis of the links between the energy sector and the rest of the economy. The range of macroeconomic policy options from long term structural adjustments to short term stabilization programs, will have significant impacts on the energy decisions. More specific links between the energy sector and the rest of the economy include energy sector inputs such as capital, labour, raw material and environmental resources (eg. clean air, water or space), as well as energy outputs such as electricity, petroleum products, or wood fuel, and the impact on the economy of various energy policies.

The second conceptual level of INEP treats the energy sector as a separate entity composed of sub-sectors such as electricity, petroleum products and so on. This permits detailed analysis, with special emphasis on interactions among the different energy sub-sectors, substitution possibilities, and the resolution of any resulting policy conflicts such as competition between natural gas, oil and coal for electricity production; woodfuel and kerosene for cooking; or diesel and gasoline for transportation.

The third and most disaggregate level pertains to planning within each of the energy sub-sectors. Thus, for example, the electricity subsector must determine its own demand forecast and long-term investment programs; the woodfuel sub-sector its consumption projections and detailed plans for reafforestation, harvesting of timber, and so on. It is at this lowest hierarchical level that most of the detailed formulation, planning, and implementation of energy schemes are carried out.

In practice, the three levels of INEP merge and overlap considerably. Energy-environmental interactions that tend to cut across all the levels need to be incorporated into the analysis -- to the extent possible. In view of the growing concern about protecting the environment, some of the salient issues are discussed in the next section. Finally, spatial disaggregation also may be required, especially in large or diverse countries. The INEP process should result in the development of a flexible and constantly updated energy strategy which can meet the national goals discussed earlier. Such a national energy strategy, of which the optimal investment program and pricing policy are important elements, may be implemented through a set of energy supply and demand management policies and programs that effectively use decentralized policy instruments and market forces, as described below.

In the recent past, analytical advances have been made in implementing hierarchical modelling with a policy focus. Earlier energy models sought to encompass the entire scope of energy planning within a single framework. However, recent work has been based on a modular hierarchical system along the lines of the INEP concept. The efficacy of this analytical approach has been proven in recent applications.

Policy Instruments

To achieve the desired national goals the policy instruments available to third world governments, for optimal energy management include; (a) physical controls; (b) technical methods; (c) direct investments or investment-inducing policies; (d) education and promotion; (e) pricing, taxes, subsidies and other financial incentives; and (f) reforms in market organization, regulatory framework and institutional structure. Since these tools are interrelated, their use should be closely coordinated for maximum effect.

Physical controls are most useful in the short-run when there are unforeseen shortages of energy. All methods of limiting consumption by physical means such as load shedding, or rotating power cuts in the electricity sub-sector, reducing or rationing the supply of gasoline or banning the use of motor cars during specified periods, are included in this category. Use of physical controls as long-run policy tools, however, is generally undesirable because of severe economic consequences. Technical means are used to manage both the supply of and demand for energy, and include determination of the most efficient means of producing a given form of energy (e.g., choice of the least-cost or cheapest mix of fuels for supplying power) and disseminating higher efficiency energy conversion devices.

Investment policies have a major effect on both energy supply and consumption patterns in the long run. The electrification of new areas, extension of natural gas distribution networks, and building of new power plants based on more readily available fuels such as coal, are some examples of such policies. The policy tool of education and promotion can help to improve the energy supply situation through efforts to make citizens aware of cost-effective ways to reduce energy consumption, the energy use implications of specific appliances or vehicles, and the scope for economically beneficial tradeoffs between savings on recurrent energy costs and capital expenditures required to realise such savings.

Pricing is politically sensitive, but a most effective means of demand management and in view of its importance, pricing policy is discussed in more detail in the next section. Taxation and subsidies are useful policy instruments that can also profoundly affect energy consumption patterns in the long run. For example, the imposition of duties or taxes on oil powered motors and the subsidization of electric motors may cause a significant shift from petroleum-based products to electricity, where such a substitution is desirable from the national perspective.

Finally, the potential for policy reforms to improve market organization and promote greater efficiency in the energy sector, is the subject of increasing scrutiny in many third world countries, as well as the development community. This theme is also more fully developed later.

We conclude this section by noting that the chief constraints which limit effective policy formulation and implementation are: (a) poor institutional framework; (b) insufficient manpower and other resources; (c) weak analytical tools; (d) inadequate policy instruments; (e) lack of political will; and (f) other constraints such as low incomes, and economic distortions.

1.3   Economic Efficiency and Energy–Environmental Interactions

The foregoing discussion has helped to establish a wider basis for energy planning and policy analysis using the principles of energy economics. As indicated earlier, it is the concept of the economic value of scarce resources that ties this analysis together, and permits the decisionmaker to focus on policy alternatives, involving tradeoffs arising from the deployment and use of otherwise non-comparable sets of inputs and outputs (including energy). Thus energy economics is helpful in developing energy policies that permit the economy to produce and consume energy more efficiently, thereby maximizing net output and growth.

It is convenient to recall here that the specific prerequisites for economic efficiency include both:

(a)   efficient consumption of energy, by providing efficient price signals that ensure optimal energy use and resource allocation; and

(b)   efficient production of energy, by ensuring the least-cost supply mix through the optimization of investment planning and energy system operation.

During recent decades, the efficient and optimal use of our global natural resource base, including air, land and water, has emerged as an area of particular concern. Since there has been much discussion also about the key role that *energy efficiency* and *energy conservation* might play in mitigating *environmental costs*, it is useful first to examine how these topics relate to *economic efficiency*. Specific issues dealing with the formulation and implementation of economically efficient energy policies are presented in the subsequent sections of this chapter.

Major environmental issues vary widely, particularly in terms of scale or magnitude of impact, but most are linked to energy use and are demanding increasing attention from energy analysts. First, there are the truly global problems such as the potential worldwide warming due to increasing accumulation of greenhouse gases like carbon dioxide and methane in the atmosphere, high altitude ozone depletion because of excessive release of chlorofluorocarbons used mainly in referigeration devices, pollution of the oceanic and marine environment by oil spills and other wastes, and overdepletion of certain animal and mineral resources.

Second in scale are the transnational issues like acid rain or radioactive fallout in one european country due to fossil-fuel or nuclear emissions in a neighbouring nation, and excessive downstream siltation of river water in Bangladesh due to deforestation of watersheds and soil erosion in nearby Nepal. Third, one might identify national and regional effects, for example those involving the Amazon basin in Brazil, or the Mahaweli basin in Sri Lanka. Finally, there are more localised and project specific problems like the complex environmental and social impacts of a specific hydroelectric or multipurpose dam.

While environmental and natural resource problems of any kind are a matter for serious concern, those that fall within the national boundaries of a given country are inherently easier to deal with from the viewpoint of policy implementation. Such issues that fall within the energy sector must be addressed within the national policymaking framework. Meanwhile, driven by strong pressures arising from far-reaching potential consequences of global issues like atmospheric greenhouse gas accumulation, significant efforts are being made in the areas of not only scientific analysis, but also international cooperation mechanisms to implement mitigatory measures.

Given this background, we discuss next some of the principal points concerning energy use and economic efficiency -- the same points are explained more rigorously in Appendix A1.1. In many countries, especially those in the developing world, inappropriate policies have encouraged wasteful and unproductive uses of some forms of energy. In such cases, better energy management could lead to improvements in economic efficiency (higher value of net output produced), energy efficiency (higher value of net output per unit of energy used), energy conservation (reduced absolute amount of energy used), and environmental protection (reduced energy related environmental costs). While such a result fortuitously satisfies all four goals, the latter are not always mutually consistent. For example, in some developing countries where the existing levels of per capita energy consumption are very low and certain types of energy use are uneconomically constrained, it may become necessary to promote more energy consumption in order to raise net output (thereby increasing economic efficiency). There are also instances where it may be possible to increase energy efficiency while decreasing energy conservation.

Despite the above complications, our basic conclusion remains valid -- that the economic efficiency criterion which helps us maximize the value of net output from all available scarce resources in the economy (including energy), should effectively subsume purely energy oriented objectives such as energy efficiency and energy conservation. Furthermore, the costs arising from energy-related adverse environmental impacts may be included (to the extent possible) in the energy economics analytical framework, to determine how much energy use and net output that society should be willing to forego, in order to abate or mitigate environmental damage. The existence of the many other national policy objectives indicated in Section 1.2 -- including social goals that are particularly relevant in the case of low income populations -- will complicate the decisionmaking process even further, as explained in subsequent sections.

We may conclude briefly, that while the energy required for economic development will continue to grow in the developing countries, in the short to medium run there is generally considerable scope for most of them to practice better energy management, thereby both increasing net output and using their energy resources more efficiently. In the medium to long run, it will become possible for developing countries to adopt newer and more advanced (energy efficient) technologies that are now emerging in the industrialized world, thus enabling their transformed economies to produce even more output using less energy.

1.4 Pricing Policy

In the past, energy prices in most countries were determined mainly on the basis of socio-political considerations, and financial or accounting criteria such as earning sufficient sales revenues to meet operating and investment costs. More recently however, there has been increasing emphasis on the use of economic principles in order to encourage more efficient consumption and production of energy.

While economic efficiency is a useful starting point for price setting, a number of other national goals (indicated earlier) must be also met. Since these criteria are often in conflict with one another, an effective integrated energy pricing policy should be flexible enough to accommodate tradeoffs among them. Thus in the first stage, a set of prices based on the marginal opportunity costs (MOC) of supply, is determined, to meet the strict economic efficiency objective. In practice, it is easier to begin the optimal pricing procedure from MOC, because supply costs are generally well defined (using techno-economic considerations). In the second stage of price setting, the MOC based efficient prices are adjusted to meet the other goals of pricing policy.

The energy pricing issues which are presented in this section are discussed more comprehensively in Chapter 5.

Strictly Efficient Energy Prices

For a typical nontraded form of energy like electricity, MOC is the long run marginal cost (LRMC) of supply from the power system. LRMC is estimated using the economic opportunity costs or shadow prices for inputs to the power sector (like capital, labor, and fuel), instead of purely financial costs. This approach facilitates efficient utilization of capacity to meet peak demands, with price structures that vary with the marginal costs of serving demands: by different consumer categories; in different seasons; at different hours of the day; by different voltage levels; and in different geographical areas. In particular, with an appropriate choice of the peak period, structuring the LRMC-based tariffs by time-of-day generally leads to the conclusion that peak consumers should pay both capacity and energy costs, whereas off-peak consumers need to pay only the energy costs. Similarly, analysis of LRMC by voltage level usually indicates that the lower the service voltage, the greater the costs imposed on the system by consumers.

Contemporary ideas in electric power pricing, such as spot pricing, take account of the dynamics of instantaneous demand and the fact that the MOC also changes dynamically as the generation mix is adjusted to meet shifts in demand. These concepts have great potential for improving economic efficiency, particularly in the case of large power consumers, though formidable implementation constraints remain.

For tradable fuels like crude oil, and fuels that are substitutes for tradables at the margin, the international or border prices (c.i.f. price of imports or f.o.b. price of exports) are appropriate indicators of MOC. Fuels such as gas or coal could be treated as tradables or nontradables, depending on the specific circumstances. The MOC of depletable, nontraded energy sources will include an economic rent or "user cost", in addition to the marginal costs of production. Generally, MOC of depletables will depend on demand conditions, stock of resources, and opportunities for substitution or trade, all of which could vary with time. The economic value of traditional fuels (like biomass) are the most difficult to determine, because in many cases the relevant markets are not well defined. However, they may be valued indirectly, in terms of savings on alternative commercial fuels like kerosene, the opportunity cost of labour for gathering fuelwood, or the external costs of deforestation and erosion.

In summary, the efficient price for nontraded energy is the opportunity cost of inputs used to produce it plus a user cost where relevant, while MOC for traded fuels is the import or export price. Thus strictly efficient prices will signal to the consumer, the economic costs of resources used or alternative benefits foregone, resulting from increased energy use. MOC may need to be modified because of second-best considerations on the demand side, if prices elsewhere in the economy do not reflect marginal costs -- especially when this applies to close energy substitutes or complements in specific applications. The rather simplified marginal cost rule also needs to be adapted, to accommodate the dynamics of shifts in supply and demand over time, capital indivisibilities, uncertainty and reliability considerations.

Adjustments to Meet Nonefficiency Criteria

In this section, we examine how strictly efficient energy prices need to be modified to arrive at a practically implementable price structure that also meets the nonefficiency objectives mentioned earlier.

The purely financial goals most often encountered relate to meeting the revenue requirements of the sector, and are often embodied in criteria such as some target financial rate of return on assets, or an acceptable contribution toward the future investment program. In principle, for state-owned energy suppliers, the most efficient solution would be to set the price at the efficient level, and to rely on government to subsidize losses or tax away surpluses. In practice, some measure of financial autonomy and self-sufficiency is an important institutional goal. Because of the premium that is placed on public funds, a pricing policy that results in continual failure to achieve minimum financial targets would rarely be acceptable. The converse case, where efficient pricing would result in financial surpluses well in excess of traditional revenue targets, may be politically unpopular, especially for a public enterprise. In either circumstance, changes in revenues have to be achieved by adjusting the efficient prices.

It is intuitively clear that discriminating between the various consumer categories, so that the greatest divergence from the marginal opportunity cost-based price occurs for the consumer group with the lowest price elasticity of demand, and vice versa, will result in the smallest deviations from the "optimal" levels of consumption consistent with a strict efficiency pricing regime. In many countries the necessary data for the analysis of demand by consumer categories is rarely available, so rule-of- thumb methods of determining the appropriate tariff structure have to be adopted. However, if marginal costs are greater than average costs, the fiscal implications should be exploited to the full. Thus, electric power tariffs (especially in a developing country) constitute a practical means of raising public revenues in a manner that is generally consistent with the economic efficiency objective, at least for the bulk of the consumers who are not subsidized; at the same time they help supply basic energy needs to low-income groups. Cross subsidization is often used also in the petroleum subsector, where high prices for gasoline, based on efficiency, externality, and conservation considerations, may be used to finance subsidies on kerosene for poor households or diesel for transport.

Next, we consider the income distributional objective. Sociopolitical or equity arguments are often advanced in favor of subsidized prices or "lifeline" rates for energy, especially where the costs of energy consumption are high relative to the incomes of poor households. Economic reasoning based on externality effects may also be used to support subsidies; for example, cheap kerosene to reduce excessive firewood use and limit deforestation, erosion, and so on. To prevent leakages and abuse of such subsidies, energy suppliers must act as discriminating monopolists. Targeting specific consumer classes such as poor households, and limiting the cheap price only to a minimum block of consumption, are easiest to implement, for metered forms of energy like gas or electricity. Other means of discrimination, such as rationing, licensing, etc., may also be required, but are difficult to apply effectively.

In practice, the magnitude of the minimum consumption has to be carefully determined, to avoid subsidizing relatively affluent consumers; it should be based on acceptable criteria for identifying "low-income" groups and reasonable estimates of their basic energy requirements. The subsidized price level relative to the efficient price may be determined on the basis of the poor consumer's income level in relation to some critical consumption level or poverty threshold. The financial requirements of the energy sector would also be considered in determining the magnitude of the subsidy.

As indicated earlier, there are several additional political, and social considerations that may be adequate justification for departing from a strict efficient pricing policy. The decision to provide commercial energy like kerosene or electricity in a remote rural area (which often entails subsidies), could be made on completely noneconomic grounds. Typical reasons of a general sociopolitical nature include maintaining a viable regional industrial or agricultural base, stemming rural to urban migration, or alleviating local political discontent. Similarly, uniform nationwide energy prices are a political necessity in many countries, although this policy may, for example, imply subsidization of consumers in remote rural areas (where supply costs are high) by energy users in urban centers. However, the full economic benefits of such a course of action may sometimes be greater than the apparent costs of the divergence between actual and efficient price levels. Again this possibility is likely to be much more significant in a developing country than in a developed one, not only because of the high cost of energy relative to incomes in the former, but also because the available administrative or fiscal machinery to redistribute incomes is frequently ineffective.

The conservation objective (to reduce dependence on imported energy, improve the trade balance, and so on) usually runs counter to subsidy arguments. Therefore, it may be necessary to restrict cheap energy to productive economic sectors that need to be strengthened while in the case of the basic energy needs of households, the energy price could be sharply increased for consumption beyond appropriate minimum levels. In other cases, conservation of one fuel may require a subsidy on the price of another energy substitute. For example, cheap kerosene might be required, especially in rural areas, to reduce excessive fuelwood consumption and thus help to prevent the adverse environmental consequences of deforestation and erosion.

It is particularly difficult to raise prices to anywhere near the efficient levels where low incomes and a tradition of subsidized energy have increased consumer resistance. In practice, price changes have to be gradual, in view of the costs that may be imposed on those who have already incurred expenditures on energy using equipment and made other decisions, while expecting little or no change in traditional energy pricing policies. At the same time, a steady price rise will prepare consumers for high future energy prices.

Finally, owing to the practical difficulties of metering, price discrimination, and billing, and the need to avoid confusing consumers, the pricing structure may have to be simplified. Thus, the number of customer categories, rating periods, consumption blocks, and so on, will have to be limited. Electricity and gas offer the greatest possibilities for structuring. The degree of sophistication of metering depends among other things, on the net benefits of metering and on problems of installation and maintenance. For electricity or gas, different charges for various consumption blocks may be effectively applied with conventional metering. However, for liquid fuels like kerosene, subsidized or discriminatory pricing would usually require schemes involving rationing and coupons, and could lead to leakage and abuses.

1.5   Supply Efficiency[2]

We recall that efficient energy pricing based on marginal costs assumes that the energy supply system is already optimally planned and operated. This makes good sense from even a purely practical point of view -- thus an inefficient supplier that is routinely permitted to pass on excessively high costs to consumers, under the umbrella of marginal cost pricing, will have very little incentive to reduce costs and produce nore efficiently. There are also solid analytical reasons for insisting on supply efficiency as a prerequisite to efficient pricing. We begin by discussing the power subsector, where the analysis is particularly sophisticated, and then generalise the results to other energy subsectors.

Optimal Reliability and Traditional Least Cost Planning

Recent theoretical work has emphasized that the optimal conditions for price and capacity levels must be simultaneously satisfied to maximize the net social benefits of electricity consumption. In this context, determining the optimal capacity level is equivalent to establishing the optimal level of reliability, since capacity additions do improve the reliability level. We may summarize simply, the complex analysis underlying the joint optimality conditions, as follows. The optimal price is the marginal cost of supply. Simultaneously, the optimal reliability (capacity) level is defined by the point at which the marginal cost of increasing reliability is exactly equal to the corresponding increase in marginal benefits to consumers because of improved supply quality.

In brief, this approach indicates that for a given price structure, an optimal long-run investment plan and a corresponding range of reliability levels may be determined which maximize net social benefits of energy consumption, and thus reflect the national viewpoint. This reliability (or capacity) optimization model subsumes rather than replaces the conventional least cost criterion. In the conventional approach to power system design and planning, costs are minimized subject to supplying the load at some (arbitrarily) given reliability level. Since the forecast demand is assumed to be fixed in this case, consumption benefits are also constant. Therefore, cost minimization (or the least cost criterion) is equivalent to maximization of net benefits. With the new approach, it is possible to determine, rather than assume the optimal reliability level, by explicitly maximizing the net benefits of energy use. A social cost-benefit model is used to evaluate the inherent trade- off between the increase in energy system supply costs required to achieve a higher level of reliability, and the corresponding increase in consumer benefits, including the cost savings due to reduced supply shortages. It is possible to then design the supply system to meet the forecast

---

[2] See Chapter 8 and also the companion volume: *Electric Power Economics*, for a more detailed treatment of energy supply related issues.

load, subject to the new reliability requirement, using the traditional least-cost planning techniques. This would permit the application of existing sophisticated least cost system planning models and techniques.

As discussed earlier, the process of extracting energy resources and converting them into end-use energy forms, often imposes a heavy environmental burden. Thus, explicit consideration of environmental effects is now well within the purview of the energy sector planner, who can influence environmental impacts by choice of supply technology, fuel type, and mitigating measures adopted. The above analytical framework for investment choice and policy may be readily modified to take account of environmental effects, by incorporating an environmental cost term in the expression for the net benefits of energy production and consumption (see also section 1.3 and Appendix A1.1). Then, the decision rule for maximizing net benefits would be the minimization of total costs -- now consisting of the system and outage costs together with a new environmental cost term. Thus, one of the main challenges facing energy analysts is the more accurate identification and quantitative estimation of such environmental costs (and benefits). The use of appropriate regulatory measures and financial tools such as pollution taxes also will play an increasingly important role in the future.

The contemporary ideas of reliability differentiation and priority service, though related more to the demand side, take these concepts a step further by recognising that customers differ in their willingness-to-pay for reliability. Thus, welfare could be increased by supplying customers (and charging them) according to the reliability level they desire, rather than using a universal reliability level as at present. However, practical implementation is subject to the same constraints that apply to spot pricing.

We note that reliability optimization may be generalized for application in other energy subsectors. For example, in oil and gas investment planning, the costs due to gasoline queues, lack of furnace oil, or gas for domestic and industrial use may be traded off against the supply costs of augmenting storage capacity or delivery capability. Clearly, these additional considerations would modify the marginal costs of energy supply and thus affect optimal pricing policies.

Because of greater uncertainties in the present global scene, including unforeseen changes in energy demand, fuel prices, technology, environmental constraints, interest rates, and trade and economic conditions, minimizing risk is playing a more important role in modelling. Thus, decisionmakers in developing countries are now paying increasing attention to risk diversifying energy policy options that are robust over a wide range of exogenous scenarios, rather than adopting purely cost minimizing, deterministic but risky solutions that were more appropriate for the narrower band of possibilities which existed in the past.

Finally, we note that supply efficiency requires optimal operation of energy systems (in addition to optimal investment planning), which in turn implies that plant performance, loss levels, etc. are also optimised.

Efficient Operation of Enterprises

Unfortunately, the performance of energy supplying institutions in many developing countries has deteriorated drastically in the past few years. Problems that have plagued these institutions include: the inability to raise prices to meet revenue requirements, weak planning, inefficient operation and inadequate maintenance, high losses, low supply quality and frequent shortages, poor management, excessive staffing and low salaries, poor staff morale and performance, excessive government interference, etc. Concurrently, there has been a shift towards large monolithic state owned energy enterprises in the developing countries. This trend has been based on reasons such as: scale economies, improved coordination, reduced reserve margins, nationalisation and elimination of foreign ownership. Although some of this rationale is still valid, new options for improving enterprise efficiency are being increasingly explored.

Of the difficulties plaguing developing country energy enterprises, undue government interference in organizational and operational matters may be the most pervasive. Such interference, which has resulted in loss of management autonomy, is at least partly responsible for the other problems mentioned above. In order to address these difficulties, an important principle must be recognised -- that given the complexity of energy problems and the scarcity of resources and managerial talent in developing countries, each set of issues should be dealt with by that level of decisionmaking and management best suited to analyzing the difficulty and implementing the solution. This hierarchical approach corresponds closely to the INEP concept developed earlier.

Thus, political decisionmakers, senior government officials and ministry level staff would do better by focussing on critical macroeconomic and energy sector strategy and policy, in order to determine global expectations of energy sector performance. The senior management of the enterprise, appropriately buffered by an independent board of directors, could then conduct their daily operations free from government interference, to meet the overall national policy objectives and targets within regulatory guidelines. As far as possible, the enterprise management should be assured of continuity at the top, even in the face of political changes. Decisionmakers should discuss with the power enterprise management, any relevant national goals, especially the extent to which government finds it necessary to trade off efficient pricing and investment policies against broader sociopolitical objectives. While the enterprise is provided wider autonomy, it would now become more accountable in terms of performance measured against an agreed set of specific objectives and monitored indicators.

Major changes in enterprise management may be required, to mirror changes in the external environment discussed above. The enterprise's organizational structure may be inadequate. Administrative and financial controls might be loose. Management can be timid and lacking in objectives. There should be sufficiently comprehensive management reporting and information systems which address each level of management and ensure accountability. Long range planning and economic analysis responsibilities need to be clearly defined and assigned. Commercial forms of accounting must be instituted to help in assessing performance and making decisions. Billing and collection of receivables often need to be improved. Finally, decentralisation of administration, and technical, operational, and commercial activity must keep pace with the increasing size of the enterprise.

Once again, the fundamental principle that will help to address these problems is delegation of authority. Very often, in developing country power utilities, the senior management attempts to deal with all problems, and trivial issues often get more attention than critical ones. Provided that middle-level managers could be adequately trained and made accountable, senior managers could (by appropriate delegation of tasks) free themselves to deal with higher level policy. This process would then be repeated down to the lowest working levels. Obviously, staff training and education, and performance incentives at all levels and stages of career would play a critical role in ensuring the success of such an approach.

1.6 Sector Organization and Financing

The natural monopoly characteristics of some energy enterprise functions, as well as the perceived national interest to use these companies as a general policy tool, are in many countries accepted as sufficient reasons for maintaining large public sector monopoly organisations. Nevertheless, the observed problems inherent in stimulating management of developing country monopoly enterprises to be cost conscious, innovative, and responsive to consumer needs, indicates a need for more fundamental change. It could be worthwhile to consider trading off some of the perceived economies of scale in some energy enterprises for other organisational and regulatory structures which provide a greater inherent incentives for management efficiency and consumer responsiveness.

Decentralization Options

The options for decentralization, variations in ownership and corresponding regulatory changes, are numerous. Options for private and cooperative ownership of energy enterprises could include both local and foreign participation as well as joint ventures. As long as a given regulatory framework prevails, it can be argued that the form of ownership alone (private or public) may not necessarily affect operating efficiency. The main point is that, to the extent possible, the introduction of competitive market forces should be encouraged such as by full or partial divestiture of some government owned enterprises. A first step could be for government-owned energy enterprises to competitively contract out activities or functions better handled by others. Obvious areas which many companies already subcontract on the basis of competitive bidding, include civil works and plant construction. Some energy companies have even subcontracted on a competitive basis, the development of local retail and distribution networks, reaping benefits such as lower costs and greater programming flexibility (brought about partly by a reduction in problems associated with public sector labor unions, work rules and general 'featherbedding').

There are also opportunities for decentralization on a spatial basis. For example, larger countries can, and sometimes do, choose to have independent regional power grids. Power or gas distribution companies could be separated by municipality, with perhaps limited overlap in some fringe franchise areas, and have the right to purchase from various suppliers, when feasible. If private participation were allowed, one advantage might be that at least the large energy consumers could also be legitimate shareholders who would be concerned not only with service efficiency but also with the financial viability of the company.

Power generation also has potential for efficiency improvements through divestiture. While the bulk power transmission and distribution functions might be regarded as having more natural monopoly carrier type characteristics in most developing countries, this is not so with generation. In fact, there is substantial scope for competition in power generation with independent (perhaps foreign-owned enclave) producers (or cogenerators) selling to a central grid (or common carrier), as in the case of large industrial cogeneration. For example, in the USA the Public Utilities Regulatory Policies Act of 1978 (PURPA) specifically encourages small privately owned suppliers to generate electricity in various ways for sale to the public grid. As a result there are now a large number of small companies producing and selling electricity presumably at costs below those incurred by some large utilities through conventional generation. Similar laws have been passed elsewhere and are beginning to impact.

In fact, with appropriate legislation allowing the break up of national or regional power monopolies and with innovative contractual arrangements, greater scope for cogeneration and free generation might be encouraged. The advantage to the power company would be a de-emphasis on large lumpy capital-intensive projects together with the fact that the cogeneration and free generation companies would put up all or part of the capital and be paid only out of revenues from power sold at guaranteed prices. For larger enclave generation facilities (perhaps peat, coal, or nuclear), the concept would be that a foreign investor put up the plant, mobilise equity and other financing, operate and maintain the plant for an agreed period, and be repaid out of power sold at guaranteed prices convertible in foreign currency.

Financial Options

Developing countries are turning increasingly to more innovative financing options, most of which have been used in the industrialised countries. Some of the financial instruments that are now being studied in third world nations, include:

1) Non-recourse and limited recourse financing (or project specific financing);
2) Leasing of individual pieces of equipment or whole plants, by local or foreign investors;
3) Private ownership or operation of energy producing or distributing facilities;
4) Counter trade, involving barter type exchange of specific export goods for energy imports;
5) Developing financial instruments to finance local costs, often involving the creation of new financial intermediaries;
6) Revenue bonds, with yields tied to enterprise profitability;
7) Tax-exempt bonds; and
8) Sale of energy futures, that encourage large users to seek more stable longer term price contracts.

The Multilateral Investment Guarantee Agency (MIGA), recently created by the World Bank, could also play a key role in the future. It will seek to promote the flow of international capital to developing countries, by providing guarantees (on a fee basis), against the following non-commercial forms of risk:

1) Transfer risk, arising from host government restrictions against convertibility and transfer of foreign exchange;
2) Loss risk, resulting from legislative or administrative action (or omission) of the host government that leads to loss of ownership, control, or benefits;
3) Contract repudiation risk, when the outside investor has no recourse to an adequate forum, faces undue delays, or is unable to enforce a favourable judgement; and
4) War and civil disturbance risk.

1.7   Conclusions

We see that our understanding of energy problems, both from the analytical and practical points of view, have improved significantly since the early 1970's. Energy economics has developed from a fledgling discipline to a well recognised one during this same period, and in the process continues to make a valuable contribution to the management of energy problems, especially in the developing countries. The central concepts of opportunity costs and economic value have provided the numeraire on the basis of which integrated national energy policies could be developed, and alternative options concerning the use of scarce resources might be traded off. The economic efficiency objective provides a practical benchmark against which other goals and objectives can be conveniently evaluated.

At the same time, important energy and environmental issues still await resolution, and the tools of energy economics will continue to help us analyse, understand and address these problems.

Appendix A1.1   Economic Efficiency, Energy Needs and Environmental Costs

As explained in the main text, the application of the principles of economic efficiency to both the supply and use of energy can help us to increase the net value of output produced by economic activities. Thus, economic efficiency relates to the efficient use of all scarce resources (including energy), to maximize net output. At the same time, we may define energy efficiency as the value of net output per unit of input energy, while energy conservation refers to an absolute reduction in energy use.

Consider a discrete economic activity that uses a single form of energy (such as electricity). Figure A1.1 indicates the relationship between energy needs (Q) and the value of net output or net benefits (Y) realized through this activity. The curve Y represents the value of economic outputs minus the total costs of all inputs, including energy and quantifiable environment related costs (but specifically excluding environmental externality costs that are not internalized in the economic calculus). We assume the application of existing technology to both the supply and use of energy. Environmental damages not explicitly included already in Y are indicated by the curve C, which increases with rising energy production.

In the case of many developing countries, a typical economic activity might operate at point A, because of poor policies -- especially energy prices that are subsidized below marginal opportunity costs (see Section 1.4), inefficient energy supplying or using equipment and processes, and institutional weaknesses, that lead to the excessive and wasteful energy use. Thus, there is ample scope to move from A towards the maximum of the Y curve at B, through more effective energy management resulting from the pursuit of rational policy options and measures (discussed later in this chapter, and also in Chapters 6 and 7). We note that this movement will increase net output from Y_1 to Y_M while decreasing the energy required from Q_1 to Q_M.

The foregoing example could be generalized by interpreting Y as the net output of an enterprise, city, region, nation, or the whole world, and including other forms of energy within Q. The environmental damage function C also would have to be reinterpreted correspondingly (e.g., if Y represented world GNP, then C would include the adverse global effects of greenhouse gas emissions). In these more complex cases, it would be necessary to recognize changes in the structure of multiple economic activities as well as shifts among different forms of energy, but the basic arguments presented below would not be affected. Thus, the movement from A to B would involve improvements in economic efficiency (greater net output), energy efficiency (higher net output per unit of energy), energy conservation (reduced energy requirement), and environmental costs (reduced damage to the environment), thereby simultaneously satisfying all these criteria. However, such a favourable congruence may not result in every case, as explained below.

In some instances, especially where excessive constraints and high prices unduly discourage energy use, economic activity might be confined to the point S. Clearly, in this case improved energy policies and management could increase net output in the direction of B, but at the expense of reduced energy efficiency and conservation, and higher environmental costs. By contrast, an increase in energy efficiency and further energy savings would be realized only by moving in the opposite direction, from S to F -- at which point net output per unit of energy (Y_2/Q_2) is maximized (i.e., the line OF is a tangent to the Y curve), but net output and economic efficiency have declined. In other words, the pursuit of energy efficiency and conservation goals, without relating these to economic efficiency, may sometimes lead to undesirable reductions in net output and overall economic welfare (see also Figure 6.1 and the discussion in Section 6.1 of Chapter 6). For example, a specific energy conservation project would be economically justified only after a rigorous cost-benefit analysis which proved that the gains from energy savings and other benefits would exceed all costs - - including the costs of foregone energy use.

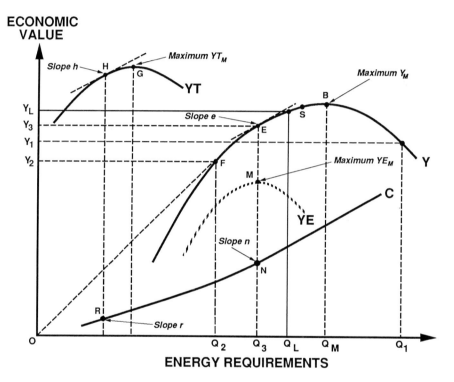

Figure A1.1:   Relationships Between Economic Efficiency, Energy Requirements and Environmental Costs

Notes: At point B, $(\partial Y/\partial Q) = 0$ and Y is maximized.

At point F, (Y_2/Q_2) is maximized and OF is tangent to the Y curve.

At point M, $(\partial YE/\partial Q) = 0$ and YE is maximized. Also $(\partial Y/\partial Q) = (\partial C/\partial Q)$; or equivalently, slope e = slope n.

At point G, $(\partial YT/\partial Q) = 0$ and YT is maximized.

At point H, $(\partial YT/\partial Q) = (\partial C/\partial Q)$; or equivalently, slope h = slope r.

Now, we define an environmentally adjusted net output curve: $YE = Y - C$. Further movement along the Y curve, from B to E, will bring us to the maximum of the YE curve, at point M. In this situation, the slope (e) of the Y curve is exactly equal to the slope (n) of the C curve (see Figure A1.1). Although the (unadjusted) net output, Y, has declined from Y_M to Y_3, society is better off at point E because the environmentally adjusted net output, YE_M, is maximised. If the shape of the environmental damage function C is not well defined -- which is often the case -- it may become necessary to mandate maximum acceptable physical levels for degradation of the environment (e.g., limits on emission levels for power plants), which in turn will constrain energy use to Q_L and net output to Y_L. The limit Q_L generally might embody not only known environmental pollution effects arising from energy production, but also an insurance component related to the risk of less well defined catastrophic, but low probability events (such as nuclear plant accidents or dam failures), as well as the attitudes of society towards such events.

Next, consider the same economic activity, but now allowing for technological improvements in both the supply and use of energy (see Section 6.2 in Chapter 6 for details). The net output curve YT for such a technologically advanced economy, is shifted to the left -- indicating that higher levels of net output are possible with lower energy inputs. In this case, even if we ignore environmental costs, reaching the maximum net output YT_M at point G (which is greater than the levels that were previously attainable), requires less energy than before. Finally, if we adjust YT for environmental costs C and then maximize the resulting net output, the environmentally optimal operating point lies at H, where the slope (h) of the YT curve equals the slope (r) of the C curve.

Chapter 2

INTEGRATED NATIONAL ENERGY PLANNING (INEP) IN DEVELOPING COUNTRIES[1]

2.1   Introduction

In recent years, decision makers in an increasing number of countries have realized that energy sector planning should be carried out on an integrated basis within the framework of a national energy master plan which determines energy policy, ranging from short-term supply and demand management decisions to long-term planning. However, in practice investment planning and pricing are still carried out on an ad hoc and at best partial or subsector basis. Thus typically, electricity and oil subsector planning have traditionally been carried out independently of each other as well as other energy subsectors. As long as energy was cheap such partial approaches were acceptable, but lately, with the international oil price acting as the messenger of rising energy costs, significant fluctuations in relative fuel prices, and sudden energy shortages, the advantages of an integrated energy policy have become evident.

In this chapter the importance of co-ordinated energy planning is emphasized, with particular reference to the interrelationships among the policies adopted in various energy subsectors such as electric power (including hydro, nuclear, geothermal, oil, and coal fired sources), petroleum, natural gas, coal, non-conventional (solar, bio-gas, mini-hydro) and traditional fuels (woodfuel, bagasse, or vegetable residue). The scope and objectives of integrated national energy planning, the policy tools available, and constraints particular to the developing countries are discussed next. The energy planning process is outlined thereafter, while the problems of implementing the resulting policy conclusions are examined in the final section.

2.2   Scope and Objectives of Energy Planning, Policy Tools and Constraints

We begin by discussing what is meant by integrated energy planning in the developing country context. The broad rationale underlying INEP is the need for an energy master plan (EMP) that will make the best use of energy resources, promote socio-economic development and improve the welfare and quality of life of citizens. Therefore energy planning is an essential part of overall economic planning, and should be carried out and implemented in close coordination with the latter. However, in energy planning, the principal emphasis is on the detailed and disaggregate analysis

---

[1] Edited version of a paper presented at the seminar on Energy in Sri Lanka, held in Colombo, Sri Lanka, in January 1980; and subsequently published in *Natural Resources Forum*, vol.4, August 1980, pp. 359-73.

of the energy sector, with due regard for the main interactions within the sector itself, as well as the rest of the economy.

Scope and Levels of Planning

The scope of integrated national energy planning (INEP) may be clarified by examining the hierarchical framework depicted in Figure 2.1. At the highest and most aggregate level, it should be clearly recognized that the energy sector is a part of the whole economy. Therefore, energy planning requires analysis of the links between the energy sector and the rest of the economy. Such links include the input requirements of the energy sector such as capital, labour and raw materials as well as energy outputs such as electricity, petroleum products, woodfuel and so on, and the impact on the economy of policies concerning availability of supply, energy prices, taxes and so on, in relation to national objectives. Since energy permeates the whole economy, the energy sector is much more extensive than other sectors such as agriculture or industry. In this respect, the energy sector is like the "financial sector," with energy acting as the physical counterpart of money.

The second level of INEP treats the energy sector as a separate entity composed of subsectors such as electricity, petroleum products and so on. This permits detailed analysis of the sector with special emphasis on interactions among the different energy subsectors, substitution possibilities, and the resolution of any resulting policy conflicts, such as competition between kerosene and electricity for lighting, or woodfuel and kerosene for cooking. The third and most disaggregate level pertains to planning within each of the energy subsectors. Thus, for example, the electricity subsector must determine its own demand forecast and long-term investment programme, the woodfuel subsector must develop consumption projections and detailed plans for reforestation, harvesting of timber and so on.

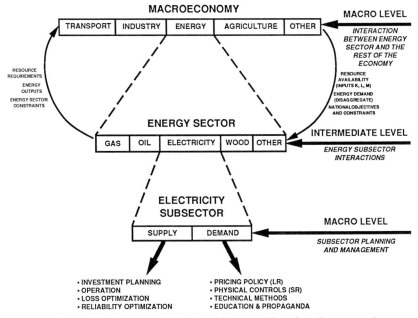

Figure 2.1: Integrated National Energy Planning Framework

Integrated energy planning permits the development of a coherent set of policies which meet the needs of many interrelated and often conflicting national objectives. These objectives include: determining the detailed energy needs of the economy to achieve growth and development targets; choosing the mix of energy sources to meet future energy requirements in the cheapest way possible; conserving energy resources and eliminating wasteful consumption; diversifying and reducing dependance on foreign sources; supplying basic energy needs of the poor; saving scarce foreign exchange and reducing the trade deficit; priority development of special regions or sectors of the economy; raising sufficient revenues to finance energy sector development; ensuring continuity of supply and price stability; preservation of the environment, and so on.

Policy Tools and Constraints

To achieve the desired objectives, the policy tools available to the government for optimal supply-demand planning and management include: physical controls; technical methods (including research and development); education and propaganda; and pricing. Since these tools are interrelated, their use should be closely co-ordinated for maximum effect. Physical controls are most useful in the short-term when there are unforeseen shortages of energy. All methods of physically limiting consumption such as load shedding and rotating power cuts in the electricity subsector, as well as reducing the supply of gasoline or banning the use of automobiles during some periods, are included in this category. Technical means applied to the supply of energy include the determination of the most efficient means of producing a given form of energy, choice of the cheapest mix of fuels, research and development of substitute fuels such as wood-alcohol for gasoline, and so on. Technology may be used also to influence energy demand, for example, by introducing higher efficiency energy conversion devices such as better stoves for woodfuel. The policy tools of education and propaganda can help to improve the energy supply situation through efforts to make citizens aware of environmental concerns, and demand for energy may also be reduced by an effective programme of public education for energy conservation.

Pricing is a very important policy tool, especially in the long run (a detailed presentation of energy pricing in an integrated framework is provided in Chapter 3). As will be discussed later, an important criterion for price setting is that it should reflect the cost of supply. However, we note that energy supply systems, including electricity generation, transmission and distribution, oil and gas wells and pipelines, coal mines, forests and so on usually require large capital investments; such projects also involve long lead times and have long lifetimes. Therefore once the investment decision is made (usually on the basis of the conventional least-cost method of supplying a given fuel type, with due regard for interfuel substitution possibilities), the country is effectively locked into a certain supply pattern for many years. Therefore, prices should be related to costs of supply, based on the long-term horizon of planning. On the demand side also, energy conversion devices, such as automobiles, gas stoves, electric appliances, machines and so on, are expensive relative to average income levels (especially in the developing countries), and have relatively long lifetimes. Therefore, once they have purchased certain items of equipment, the ability of consumers to change their energy usage patterns in response to changes in relative fuel prices, is very limited in the short run.

The price of a particular form of energy, say gasoline, can be used most effectively as a two-way signal. Thus for economically efficient allocation of scarce resources both within the energy sector and between it and the rest of the economy, the energy producer, that is, the government, must establish an appropriate price based on the optimal economic cost of supply, the marginal opportunity cost. This indicates to the consumer the true resource cost to the economy of making energy available to him. At the same time the consumer's willingness to pay indicates to the supplier, the value placed on energy by users.

In the developing countries there are generally additional constraints on energy policy. For example, there may be severe market distortions due to taxes, import duties, subsidies and externalities which cause market (or financial) prices to diverge substantially from the true economic opportunity costs (or shadow prices). Therefore, on the grounds of economic efficiency alone we have to use shadow prices instead of financial costs in making both the investment and energy pricing decisions. Then there are often severe income disparities and social considerations which require subsidized energy prices and rationing to meet the basic energy needs of poor consumers. Finally, there could be many additional considerations including future investment requirements, financial viability and autonomy of the energy sector, and regional development needs, as well as socio-political, legal and other constraints, affecting the policy decision.

2.3   Developing the Energy Master Plan (EMP)

As explained earlier, INEP is the process through which it is possible to achieve the goal of the energy master plan. Since both the means and the end are closely interlinked, describing the INEP procedure will provide a better understanding of the EMP. In the previous section the three hierarchical levels which define the scope of INEP were described: analysis of interactions between the energy sector and the rest of the economy; interactions among different subsectors within the energy sector; and activities within each energy subsector. Next we will discuss the hierarchy of time horizons which must be considered in INEP, the short, medium and long-term, and also outline the problems of uncertainty, before describing the INEP procedure.

Planning Horizons and Uncertainty

In the short-term, with a time scale of about one year, national energy planning is most useful for supply-demand management decisions to meet unforeseen problems. If past planning had been successful, short-term energy management would be free of problems as a part of the continuing evolution of the longer term energy strategy. However, when sudden difficulties occur (for example, unavailability of hydroelectric power following a drought or shortages of petroleum-based fuels), contingency plans including physical rationing, price surcharges and so on must be set in motion to minimize any adverse effect on the development effort.

Energy planning for the medium term is more flexible because there is sufficient time to make significant policy changes within the approximately two to ten-year time horizon involved. In particular, the most important decisions include the planning, evaluation and implementation of energy projects, for example, building a new thermal power station or gas pipeline; pricing, inter-fuel substitution and conservation policies. Long-term energy planning horizons, which generally extend at least ten to twenty years, involve the most fundamental strategies of all. Typically, a variety of alternative scenarios are examined. These might include the choice of greater or lesser energy intensive patterns of economic development, gradual changeover from dependence on some energy sources to others as the former become unavailable, optimum energy supply development programmes (usually consisting of a series of individual projects, such as long range electric power system expansion planning), and others.

It should be noted that while the distinction between long, medium and short-term planning is convenient for conceptual and analytical purposes, in practice there are no sharp dividing lines among the three categories. There is a hierarchical relationship involved in which the short-term decisions and medium term policies should merge as smoothly and consistently as possible with the long run strategy. However, the longer the planning horizon, the more uncertain the data and projections.

All forms of planning must deal with the problem of uncertainty. However, uncertainty raises greater difficulties in energy planning because of the sector's widespread interaction with the rest of the economy and vulnerability to international events. Specific problems of uncertainty are caused by: the long planning horizon for energy investment decisions, long lead times required for energy resource development, and danger of resultant "lock-in" effects; incomplete knowledge of the national energy resource base, and the possibility of finding oil, gas, coal and so on in the future; changes in the patterns of energy use; changes in the technology of energy supply and end-use; and variations in energy prices.

Therefore, it is important for several alternative planning scenarios or assumptions regarding the future to be considered during the INEP process described next. Energy policies should be flexible, relying on a variety of energy sources, and using the full range of policy instruments for demand management. Finally, the planning process should be dynamic and continuous, with all data, assumptions and analyses being constantly revised using the most recent information.

Socio-economic Background

The INEP procedure itself may be broken down as shown in Figure 2.2 into the following steps: Socio-economic background and national objectives; energy demand analysis; energy supply analysis: energy balance; policy formulation and impact analysis. It should be noted that these divisions are conceptual, and in practice there will be considerable overlap among them.

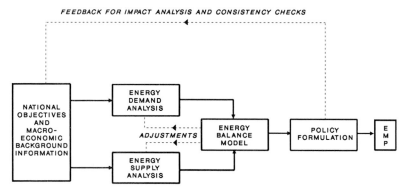

Figure 2.2: Basic Steps in Implementing INEP

The first and last steps examine broad relationships with the rest of the economy, corresponding to the highest hierarchical level discussed earlier. Thus in the first step, national priorities and objectives, as well as the overall evolution of the economic background, say over the next twenty years, must be examined. Typical questions that should addressed concern economic targets like the desired growth rate of the GNP, as well as socio-political considerations such as the minimum levels of energy to be provided to disadvantaged groups to meet their basic needs, and special requirements for development of depressed regions or rural areas. Information is also required on the energy intensity of future socio-economic development plans, for example, whether rapid industrialization will occur, or whether agricultural growth will entail significant use of energy intensive fertilizers and mechanization. A related set of questions concerns technically and socially feasible inter-fuel substitution possibilities and policies, such as encouraging or discouraging households to switch from traditional non-commercial fuels such as woodfuel to commercial fuels such as kerosene or gas; electrification of railways versus greater reliance on road transport; and so on. Finally, projections are needed for future availability and prices of fuels like crude oil or coal on the world market; for availability of financial resources for energy imports or development of domestic energy sources; and for development of relevant new technologies and non-conventional sources such as solar, biogas and mini-hydro.

Supply and Demand Analyses

The second through fourth steps relate mainly to the lower levels in the INEP hierarchy shown in Figure 2.1, that is, energy sector and subsector planning. It should be noted that these stages in INEP will be strongly influenced by the information and assumptions from the preceding step. While these steps deal with forecasts spanning the full long-term horizon of INEP (20 years), medium and short-term projections should be developed within the same consistent framework. The principal objective of energy demand analysis is to determine future requirements by type of fuel and by consumer category (or type of usage). Past and present energy usage patterns must be analysed in detail relative to other factors such as prices, incomes, levels of economic activity, supply constraints, and stocks of energy using equipment. These results and information on possible changes in future usage patterns form the basis for forecasting the structure of national energy demands. In general, the energy requirements of productive sectors of the economy may be analyzed on the basis of the technological relationships and production functions underlying these activities. However, a thorough analysis of household energy demand, particularly for traditional fuels which often constitute the bulk of the fuel supply, will require comprehensive surveys and economic studies (see Chapters 8 and 11).

Energy supply analysis involves the systematic determination of all possible future energy supply options, disaggregated by energy subsector. First, past and present data on energy resources and production, imports and exports, generation, storage, refining, transportation, distribution and retailing, financial and manpower requirements, costs and output prices must be examined. Then this information together with projections of fuel resource development projects and programmes, energy subsector output capabilities, capacity to import and export, application of new technologies and non-conventional sources, financial, manpower and organizational resources must be combined to provide detailed forecasts of the availability of the different forms of energy.

Energy Balance

Supply-demand balancing consists basically of assigning specific energy sources to corresponding uses. A simple but typical matrix for doing this is shown in Figure 2.3 where the columns represent energy sources and the rows indicate energy uses -- including losses in processing, refining, transportation and retailing (for details see Ramsdell and Walton 1979). Examination of past and present energy balances allows the energy analyst to determine the evolution of supply and demand within a comprehensive framework, the bottlenecks that exist, and how supply and demand has adjusted to constraints. Next, supply-demand balances must be developed for future years. Projected energy shortages and surpluses by fuel type and usage category must be reconciled, for example, by increasing or decreasing energy imports or exports, inter-fuel substitution (where technically and socially feasible), augmenting domestic conventional and non-conventional energy sources, reducing demand through pricing, rationing and physical controls. Thus, some of these equilibrating measures will require going back to earlier steps to re-adjust the supply and demand analyses and forecasts.

Policy Formulation and EMP

The series of four steps described above will yield a set of energy policies for management of supply and demand which ensure that future national energy requirements are satisfied. Since there are many different policy combinations there will be several alternative packages or sets of policies involving the basic policy tools described earlier (physical controls, technical methods, education and propaganda, and pricing). The final step consists of formulating these alternative policy packages and then testing them for their impact on the rest of the economy.

At this stage, certain consistency checks must be made. Thus, the consequences of some energy policies may imply violation of other national objectives or assumptions regarding the evolution of the economy; the strategy may entail unacceptably high balance of payments deficits for energy imports or draining of financial resources from sectors like agriculture, or drastically curtailing the energy supply of those sectors, thus infringing on other priorities set by the government. If some of these basic objectives or background data are changed as a result of tradeoffs, then the steps must be repeated using the new assumptions. Thus, the INEP process permits dynamic consistency checks through iterative feedback, as summarized in Figure 2.2.

Finally, the set of energy policies which are consistent with broad national goals and which best satisfy future energy needs may be selected by the decisionmakers. This policy package, and the associated set of supply and demand forecasts and balances constitute the energy master plan (EMP).

Unit : terajoules

Commodities / Transactions	Hard Coal Lignite & Peat (1)	Briquettes & Cokes (2)	Crude, Petroleum & NGL (3)	Light Petroleum Products (4)	Heavy Petroleum Products (5)	Other Petroleum Products (6)	LPG & Other Petroleum Gases (7)	Natural Gas (8)	Derived Gases (9)	Nuclear, Hydro and Geothermal Electricity — Conventional Fuel Equivalent (10)	Nuclear, Hydro and Geothermal Electricity — Physical Energy Input (11)	Electricity (12)	Total Commercial Energy — Conventional Fuel Equivalent (13)	Total Commercial Energy — Physical Energy Input (14)	Traditional Fuels (15)	Total Energy — Conventional Fuel Equivalent (16)	Total Energy — Physical Energy Input (17)
1 Production of Primary Energy																	
2 Imports																	
3 Exports																	
4 Marine/Aviation Bunkers																	
5 Stock Change																	
6 Total Energy requirements																	
7 Energy Converted																	
8 Briquetting Plants																	
9 Coke Ovens and Coke Plants																	
10 Gasworks																	
11 Blast Furnaces																	
12 Petroleum Refineries																	
13 NGL Processing Plants																	
14 Electric Power Plants																	
15 Heating Plants																	
16 Other Conversion industries																	
17 Net Transfers																	
18 Consumption by Energy Sector																	
19 Losses in Transport & Distribution																	
20 Consumption for Non-energy Uses																	
21 Statistical Differences																	
22 Final Consumption																	
23 By Industry and Construction																	
24 Iron & Steel Industry																	
25 Chemical Industry																	
26 Other Industry & Construction																	
27 By Transport																	
28 Road																	
29 Rail																	
30 Air																	
31 Inland & Coastal Waterways																	
32 By Household & other Consumers																	
33 Households																	
34 Agriculture																	
35 Other Consumers																	

Figure 2.3: Typical Energy Balance Sheet

2.4   Problems of Implementation

In this section we discuss problems associated with practical implementation of INEP and execution of EMP, once it has been determined. These difficulties may be examined in two convenient categories: data collection and analysis; and institutional structure and manpower needs.

Data Collection and Analysis

INEP can be carried out at different levels of sophistication depending on data availability and the capability to analyse this information utilizing computer facilities, skilled manpower and so on. In countries where these constraints are severe, and especially when there has been little prior experience in energy planning even in individual subsectors, INEP may have to be implemented progressively.

For example, the first phase might consist of energy planning at a relatively uncomplicated level. A basic socio-economic accounting matrix (or small input-output table) might be used to generate information regarding the economic background. Similarly, simple time trend projections could be used for energy supply and demand forecasts (with judicious assumptions where data is unavailable, particularly with respect to traditional fuels). The energy balance might consist of a basic table like Figure 2.3, with reliance on direct policies such as increasing oil imports or shedding electrical load (power cuts) to make equilibrating adjustments. Thus the initial version of the EMP would consist of simple supply and demand projections and a straightforward set of policies, with little scope for impact analysis or iteration. In brief, such a first attempt at INEP would rely principally on physically based data, extrapolation of past trends in energy supply and demand (assuming for lack of better information, that energy resources and technology, consumer behaviour, external factors and so on would essentially continue unchanged), very basic consistency checks in the energy balance, and relatively uncomplicated policy analysis.

At this stage it is worthwhile stressing the importance of data collection and analysis in the INEP procedure. Therefore, building a good energy data base is an important requirement of INEP. In particular, the data should, as far as possible, be easy to gather, accurate, convenient to manipulate and analyse, internally consistent, relevant to policy work, compatible with the work of other sectors in the economy, and consistent with internationally accepted standards. Since the quality of data across subsectors is likely to be uneven, attention should be focused early on the weaker areas (availability and usage of traditional fuels), to avoid distorting the energy balance. A simple data base might be a set of tables, while a more sophisticated version would involve a computerized data bank. While basic data (by energy subsector) may be in diverse physical units (e.g., kilowatt-hours of electricity, barrels of oil, tons of coal, of wood, etc.), it is important to reduce them to a common energy unit for comparison, and preparation of the energy balance. Commonly used basic energy units include the Joule, tonne of oil equivalent and ton of coal equivalent. It should also be made clear whether the energy is in gross or net terms, that is of electricity delivered to the consumer, or litres of fuel oil burned at a thermal power station before accounting for efficiency of conversion and losses.

Even the first version of an EMP based on a simple INEP procedure can be used very effectively. First, at the very least, it provides a consistent and comprehensive approach to solving national energy problems which is superior to the traditional uncoordinated planning by subsector. Second, by focusing on data needs and analysis, it permits the authorities to identify areas where information is poor, data collection and organization must be improved, manpower and analytical skills have to be built up, and so on. Third, it forces energy planners to relate the process to explicit objectives and policies. More generally, INEP and the EMP facilitate the recognition of key energy issues, and help to resolve these problems in a consistent way. The identification of such issues and the formulation of policies to solve them (or establishing guidelines to study them further before deciding on appropriate policies), is one of the most important goals of INEP. Typical energy related issues might include: data problems (as discussed earlier); manpower and organizational needs; conservation; imports and exports and dependence on foreign sources; environmental degradation; pricing; investment and financing; and shortages and rationing.

Once experience has been gained and skills built up by working with the simplified INEP procedure, more sophisticated approaches may be developed. Thus, a multi-sector macro-economic model could be used to establish the socio-economic background, including analysis of several alternative scenarios which take uncertainty into account. These might include high versus low economic growth rate, more versus less energy intensive growth, or high versus low costs of energy imports and exports. (When values are attached to goods and services in the economy, shadow prices which represent true economic opportunity costs should be used. The use of shadow prices in the energy sector is described in Chapters 4 & 11).

The supply and demand projections could also be more complex, using multiple correlation techniques to include the effects of economic variables like price and income, and to capture the impact of policy induced changes in energy and supply patterns such as a programme to promote LPG and discourage use of kerosene. The energy balance could be expanded to include additional sub-categories of supply and demand, details of losses in extraction, refining, conversion, transportation and so on.

Ultimately a sophisticated computerized energy modelling system might be developed, that would incorporate the effects of many items of physical, economic and behavioural information, and government policies (see Figure 2.4). These models generally fall into two broad categories. The first, the optimization model, in which some form of objective function (that is, a mathematical expression which embodies the required goal), is optimized subject to technical, economic and behavioural relationships, as well as physical and policy constraints. One such function might be the minimization of the costs of meeting total energy needs. The second is the simulation model, in which alternative scenarios are explored in a self-consistent framework, subject to constraints. Optimization models usually yield a well-defined optimal EMP, whereas with simulation models, the policymaker has to choose from among the alternative simulated scenarios. Thus, simulation models allow more flexibility with respect to adjustments based on expert judgement and incorporation of considerations which cannot be quantified in the model - a situation which may be more relevant in developing countries. It is important that such a model be calibrated and tuned by testing it using historical data, so that it provides an accurate representation of the energy sector.

Policy impact analysis and feedback is also facilitated by using a computerized energy model, which could interface with the macro-economic model. A more complex set of national objectives could be formulated, and explicit trade-offs among them explored. In summary, as data and analytical capability improve, the INEP procedure may be progressively upgraded with greater payoffs in improved energy sector planning and supply-demand management. This gradual and pragmatic approach to implementation of the INEP framework is demonstrated in the Sri Lanka case study in Chapter 4.

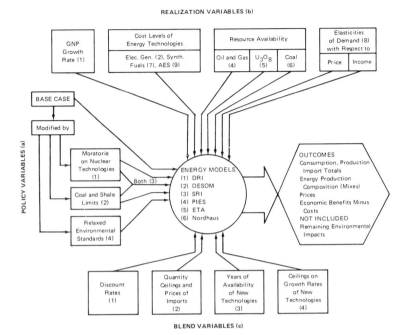

Figure 2.4: Compressed View of the Interrelationships Among the Driving Variables and Outcomes of Six U.S. Energy Models

Institutional Structure and Manpower Needs

The major organizational problem in most countries is the one referred to in the first paragraph of this paper. It is the fact that energy subsector institutions such as the electricity authority, petroleum authority, forestry department and so on are scattered among many different ministries and pursue their own policies with very little coordination. Ideally, a single energy ministry or authority should control all energy producing organizations and determine energy policy. In practice, this solution may be difficult to implement quickly because individuals and organizations may not wish to change the existing situation.

In some countries, particularly small ones with limited skilled manpower resources, locating a fledgling energy planning group within an established subsector institution (for example, the electricity authority), may be the only realistic short-term alternative. However, this is rarely a desirable long-term solution, especially if it strengthens the bias and dominance of the subsector agency or becomes a heavy burden on it. Implanting an energy planning cell within an existing national economic planning body may also be possible, and this would facilitate coordination between the energy and other sectors. However, this is likely to result in dilution of energy related responsibilities and may reduce the effectiveness of energy policy, especially if planning itself is perceived mainly as a paper exercise that is rarely implemented.

A step-wise approach in reorganizing the energy sector may often be more desirable. For example, an energy council or board which brings together representatives of all energy suppliers and major users might be constituted initially to coordinate national energy planning. This body could have a secretariat which would form the nucleus of the network for data collection and analysis, to begin implementing INEP.

Once the advantages of coordinating the energy plan become evident, a central energy authority (CEA) or ministry of energy (MOE) might be set up which would have full control over the energy sector. The CEA concept is modeled on the lines of a central bank, because the pervasive role of energy makes it the physical counterpart of money. Therefore, the CEA should be an autonomous body with maximum authority. The alternative approach of an MOE would be more conventional.

Whichever institution is established, two general points should be emphasized. Firstly, because of the importance of energy, the CEA or MOE should have direct access to the head of state and be able to invoke his authority, to bring other ministries or institutions into line. Secondly, the CEA or MOE should be primarily concerned with energy planning and policymaking, including in particular the gathering and analysis of energy data, and review of major decisions relating to pricing, investment and energy usage. Execution of energy policy, day-to-day operations, preparation of subsector investment or pricing programmes, routine paper work and so on should be left to the line agencies in the various subsectors themselves, for example, electricity authority, forestry department, and so on. Involvement of the CEA or MOE in these functions would soon transform it into a huge bureaucracy and drastically reduce its effectiveness. While a CEA could be set up independently with specific safeguards against this danger, an MOE is more likely to become bureaucratized, especially in countries where many existing ministries are still influenced by administrative procedures with roots stretching back to the colonial period. Therefore, it would be worthwhile to set up a separate group or institute for planning and policy within the MOE, which would act as a driving force.

Those carrying out INEP should be drawn from as many other government departments and institutions as possible, to represent a wide variety of viewpoints and skills. This would help develop a balanced approach to INEP and also maintain links with other sectors and institutions without which INEP could become an abstract theoretical exercise. In particular, the commercial energy subsectors should not be allowed to dominate the traditional fuel subsector.

The balanced development of energy planning skills both at the management and technical level is important. The underlying theme should be self-reliance in energy planning, because the final responsibility for INEP should rest on local staff and policymakers. Although in many cases it may be necessary to rely on foreign experts or consultants to initiate the process and play an advisory role, the training of local counterparts and the goal of eventual transition to completely national staffing should have a high priority. At the same time, because both technical and economic knowledge in the energy area tends to change rapidly, energy planners should have good, up-to-date library and documentation facilities, as well as ready access to international conferences, training courses, and meetings. Finally, if salary levels are inadequate, it will be rather difficult to recruit and retain personnel with energy related skills.

References

Ramsdell, A. and K. Walton, "Basic Energy Statistics: A Global Perspective", in *Workshop on Energy Data of Developing Countries, Proceedings: Volume 1*, International Energy Agency, Paris, 1979, pp.33-44.

Chapter 3

ENERGY PRICING: AN INTEGRATED FRAMEWORK[1]

3.1 Introduction

In recent years, decisionmakers in an increasing number of countries have realized that energy sector investment planning and pricing should be carried out on an integrated basis, e.g., within the framework of a national energy master plan that determines energy policy, ranging from short-run supply-demand management to long-run planning. However, in practice investment planning and pricing are still carried out on an ad hoc and at best partial or subsector basis. Thus, electricity and oil subsector planning have traditionally been carried out independent of each other as well as independent of other energy subsectors. As long as energy was cheap, such partial and uncoordinated approaches and the resulting policy inconsistencies and economic losses were acceptable, but lately, with higher energy costs, changes in relative fuel prices, and substitution possibilities, the advantages of an integrated energy policy have become more evident.

In this chapter the importance of coordinated energy planning and pricing will be emphasized, with particular reference to the interrelationships among the pricing policies adopted in various energy subsectors such as electric power, petroleum, natural gas, coal, and traditional fuels (e.g., firewood, crop residues, and dung). Nonconventional sources can also be fitted into this framework. We will focus on the LDC context where, generally, higher levels of market distortion, shortages of foreign exchange and resources for development, larger numbers of poor households whose basic needs must be met, greater reliance on traditional fuels, and relative paucity of energy data add to already complicated problems faced by energy planners in the developed countries. We will also touch on the chief investment issues to the extent that they strongly influence pricing policy.

Before developing an integrated framework for power and energy pricing, it is necessary to briefly discuss what is meant by integrated national energy planning and policy analysis (see also Chapter 1). The broad underlying rationale is to make the best use of energy resources to promote socioeconomic development and improve citizen's welfare and quality of life. Therefore energy planning is an essential part of overall national economic planning, and should be carried out and implemented in close coordination with the latter. However, in energy planning, the principal emphasis is on the comprehensive and disaggregate analysis of the energy sector, with due regard for the main interactions with the rest of the economy. In a strictly technical sense, the energy planner's role might be confined to seeking the least-cost method of meeting future energy requirements. However, energy planning also includes a variety of other objectives, including reducing dependence of foreign sources, supplying basic energy needs of the poor, reducing the trade and foreign exchange deficit, priority development of special regions or sectors of the economy, raising

---

[1] Edited version of a paper published in *The Energy Journal*, vol.1, July 1980, pp.1-30.

sufficient revenues to finance energy sector development (at least partially), ensuring continuity of supply and price stability, preserving the environment, and so on.

In general, energy planning requires analysis at the following three hierarchical levels in relation to fundamental national objectives: (1) links between the energy sector and the rest of the economy; (2) interactions between different subsectors within the energy sector; and (3) activities in each individual energy subsector. The steps involved in the planning procedure usually include supply and demand analyses and forecasting, energy balancing, policy formulation, and impact analysis, to meet short-, medium-, and long-range goals. Initially, these activities, may be carried out at a relatively simple level; later, as data and local analytical capabilities improve, more sophisticated techniques, including computer modeling, may be implemented. This institutional structure should also be rationalized by setting up a central energy authority (CEA), or ministry of energy, with its principal focus on energy planning and policymaking. The execution of policy and day-to-day operations, would remain the responsibility of the electricity utilities or petroleum corporations that already exist in practically all countries.

3.2   Scope and Objectives of Pricing

To put pricing in proper context, we note that it is only one of the policy tools available for optimal supply-demand planning and management; others include physical controls, technical methods (including research and development), and education and propaganda. Since these tools are interrelated, their use should be well coordinated (a more detailed analysis of coordinated energy demand management and conservation, and policy instruments is provided in Chapter 6). Physical controls are more effective in the short-run when there are unforeseen shortages of energy. All methods of physically limiting consumption are included in this category, such as load shedding and rotating power cuts in the electricity subsector, as well as reducing the supply gasoline or banning the use of motor cars during some periods. Technical means on the supply side include the least cost or cheapest means of producing a given form of energy, the best mix of fuels, and research and development of substitute fuels such as wood-alcohol for gasoline; on the demand side, they include introducing higher efficiency energy conversion devices, such as better stoves for woodfuel. Education and propaganda on the supply side include efforts to make citizens aware of external diseconomies such as pollution, and supportive of reforestation schemes to preserve the environment; on the demand side, they include public education for energy conservation.

Pricing is a very important tool, especially in the long-run. As discussed below, the pricing and investment decisions should be closely related. However, energy supply systems -- e.g., electricity generation, transmission, and distribution; oil and gas wells and pipelines; coal mines; and forests -- usually require large capital investments with long lead times and lifetimes. Therefore, once the investments decision is made, usually on the basis of the conventional least-cost method of meeting demand by subsector, with due regard for interfuel substitution possibilities, there is a lock-in effect with respect to supply. Thus prices should be related to the long-run planning horizon. On the demand side also, energy conversion devices (e.g., motor cars, gas stoves, electric appliances, and machines) are expensive relative to average income levels and have relatively long lifetimes, thus limiting consumer's ability to respond in the short run to changes in relative fuel prices.

The objectives of energy pricing are closely related to goals of energy planning, but they are more specific. First, the economic growth objective requires that pricing policy should promote economically efficient allocation of resources, both within the energy sector and between it and the rest of the economy. In general terms, this implies that future energy use would be at optimal levels, with the price (or the consumer's willingness to pay) for the marginal unit of energy used reflecting the incremental resource cost of supply to the national economy. Relative fuel prices should also influence the pattern of consumption in the direction of the optimal or least-cost mix of energy sources required to meet future demand. Distortions and constraints in the economy necessitate the use of shadow prices and economic second-best adjustments, as described in the next section.

Second, the social objective recognizes every citizen's basic right to be supplied with certain minimum energy needs. Given the existence of significant numbers of poor consumers and also wide disparities of income, this implies subsidized prices, at least for low-income consumers.

Third, government would be concerned with financial objectives relating to the viability and autonomy of the energy sector. This would usually be effected by pricing policies that permit institutions (typically, government-owned) in the different energy subsectors to earn a fair rate of return on assets and to self-finance an acceptable portion of the investments required to develop future energy resources.

Fourth, energy conservation is also an objective of pricing policy. While prevention of unnecessary waste is an important goal, other reasons often underlie the desire to conserve certain fuels. These include the desire for greater independence from foreign sources (e.g., oil imports) and deforestation and erosion problems.

Fifth, we recognize a number of additional objectives, such as the need for price stability, to prevent shocks to consumers from large price fluctuations, and the need for simplicity in energy pricing structures, to avoid confusing the public and to simplify metering and billing.

Finally, there are other specific objectives, such as promoting regional development (e.g., rural electrification) or specific sectors (e.g., export-oriented industries), and other sociopolitical, legal, and environmental constraints.

In summary, therefore, price is most effective as a long-run policy tool. From the viewpoint of economic efficiency, the price indicates the consumer's willingness to pay and the use-value of energy; to the consumers, it signals the present and future opportunity costs of supply that draws on various energy sources.

We conclude this section with a brief review of the pervasive role that most governments play in the pricing of commercial energy resources, and the relative neglect of issues relating to traditional forms of energy. Governments exercise direct influence, usually through the ownership of energy sources or price controls. Indirect influences occur through such means as taxes, import duties, subsidies, market quotas, taxes on energy-using equipment, and government-guided investments in energy resources.

In practically all developing countries, the electric utility is government-owned. In oil and gas production, refining, and distribution, as well as in coal mining, both public and private organizations operate, often side by side. However, irrespective of the form of ownership, all governments exercise some form of wholesale or retail price control, usually at several levels, including during production, during refining, after transport or transmission, and so on. Income and excise taxes are also levied from both public and private energy sector companies.

Generally, certain fuels in specific uses tend to be subsidized, although leakages and abuses of subsidies by non-targeted consumer groups also occur. Thus kerosene for lighting and cooking, rural electricity for lighting and agricultural pumping, and diesel fuel for transportation commonly qualify for subsidies. Cross-subsidies exist between different fuels, user groups, and geographic regions; therefore high-priced gasoline may finance the subsidy on kerosene, industrial electricity users may subsidize household consumers, and a uniform national pricing policy usually implies subsidization of energy users in remote areas by those living in urban centers. The principal problem associated with subsidies is that the energy producer may not be able to raise sufficient revenues to finance investment to meet expanding demand, or even to maintain existing facilities, and thus shortages eventually result. Furthermore, cross-subsidies give consumers the wrong price signals, with consequent misallocation of investments.

Import and export duties, excise taxes, and sales taxes are levied, often by several levels of government from federal to municipal, at various stages in the production, processing, distribution, and retailing chain. In many developing countries, the combined levies are several hundred percent of the original product price for some items, and negative or close to zero for others. Several less obvious methods, such as property taxes, water rights and user charges, and franchise fees are also used to influence energy use. Energy prices are also affected by the wide range of royalty charges, profit sharing schemes, and exploration agreements that are made, for the development of oil and gas resources, between governments and multinational companies.

Other policy instruments are often used to reinforce pricing policies, such as quotas on imported or scarce forms of energy, coupled with high prices. Conservation regulations may affect depletion rates for oil and gas, while availability of hydropower from some multipurpose dams may be subordinate to the use of water for irrigation or river navigation. Many special policies involving tax holidays and concession, import subsidies, export bonuses, government loans or grants, high taxes on large automobiles, etc., are also used to affect energy use.

The traditional fuels subsector has been relatively neglected because transactions involving these forms of energy are usually of a noncommercial nature. However, there is growing acceptance of the coordinated use of indirect methods such as displacement of fuelwood used in cooking by subsidizing kerosene and LPG, increasing the supply of fuelwood by reforestation programs and effective distribution of charcoal, enforcing stiffer penalties for illegal felling of trees, and proper watershed management.

3.3   Economic Framework

Because the objectives mentioned above are often not mutually consistent, a realistic integrated energy pricing structure must be flexible enough to permit tradeoffs among them. To allow this flexibility, the formulation of energy pricing policy must be carried out in two stages. In the first stage, a set of prices that strictly meets the economic efficiency objective is determined, based on a consistent and rigorous framework. The second stage consists of adjusting these efficient prices (established in the first step), to meet all the other objectives. The latter procedure is more ad hoc, with the extent of the adjustments being determined by the relative importance attached to the different objectives. In the rest of this section, we discuss the importance of shadow pricing and develop the economic framework that permits the efficient pricing of energy. The second stage adjustments due to noneconomic factors are discussed in the next section.

Shadow pricing theory has been developed mainly for use in the cost-benefit analysis of projects (Little and Mirrlees 1974, Squire and Van der Tak 1975). However, since investment decisions in the energy sector are closely related to the pricing of energy outputs, for consistency the same shadow pricing framework should be used in both instances (Munasinghe 1979b). Shadow prices are used instead of market prices (or private financial costs), to represent the true economic opportunity costs of resources -- see also Chapter 9.

In the idealized world of perfect competition, the interaction of atomistic profit-maximizing producers and atomistic utility-maximizing consumers yields market prices that reflect the correct economic opportunity costs, and scarce resources including energy will be efficiently allocated. However, in the real world, distortions may result from monopoly practices, external economies and diseconomies (which are not internalized in the private market), interventions in the market process through taxes, import duties, and subsidies, etc., and these distortions cause market prices for goods and services to diverge substantially from their shadow prices or true economic opportunity costs. Therefore, shadow prices must be used in investment and output pricing decisions to ensure the economically efficient use of resources. Moreover, if there are large income disparities, we will see later that even these "efficient" shadow prices must be further adjusted, especially to achieve socially equitable energy pricing policies for serving poor households.

It is important to realize that lack of data, time, and manpower resources, particularly in the LDC context, will generally preclude the analysis of a full economy-wide model when energy-related decision are made. This holistic or general equilibrium analysis is conceptually important. For example, the efficient shadow price of a given resource may be represented by the change in value of aggregate national consumption or output, due to a small change in the availability of that resource. However in practice, the partial approach shown in Figure 3.1 may be used, where key linkages and resource flows between the energy sector and the rest of the economy, as well as interactions among different energy subsectors, are selectively identified and analyzed, using appropriate shadow prices such as the opportunity cost of capital, shadow wage rate, and marginal opportunity cost for different fuels (Munasinghe 1979b). Surprisingly valuable results may be obtained from relatively simple models and assumptions.

To clarify the basic concepts involved in optimal energy pricing, we first analyze a relatively simple model. Next the effects of more complex features are examined, including short-run versus long-run dynamic considerations, capital indivisibilities, joint output cost allocation, quality of supply, and price feedback effects on demand. The process of establishing the efficient economic price in a given energy subsector may be conveniently analyzed in two steps (see Appendix A3.1 for details). First, the marginal opportunity cost (MOC) or shadow price of supply must be determined. Second, this value has to be further adjusted to compensate for demand-side effects arising from distortions in the prices of other goods, including other energy substitutes. From a practical viewpoint, an optimal pricing procedure that begins with MOC is easier to implement, because supply costs are generally well-defined (from technological-economic considerations), whereas data on the demand curve are relatively poor.

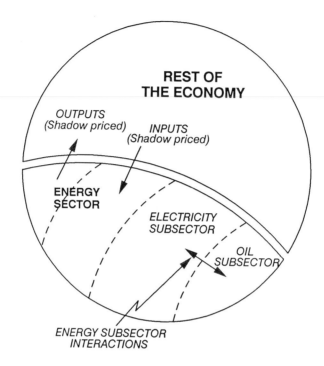

Figure 3.1: Partial Equilibrium Framework for Energy Pricing

Suppose that the marginal opportunity cost of supply in a given energy subsector is the curve MOC(Q) shown in Figure 3.2. For a typical nontraded item like electricity, MOC that is generally upward sloping is calculated by first shadow pricing the inputs to the power sector and then estimating both the level and structure of marginal supply costs (MSC) based on a long-run system expansion program -- in this particular sector MSC is represented by the long run marginal cost, LRMC (Munasinghe 1979a). For tradable items like crude oil and for fuels that are substitutes for tradables at the margin, the international or border prices of the tradeables (i.e., c.i.f. price of imports or f.o.b. price of exports, with adjustments for internal transport and handling costs) are appropriate indicators of MOC -- the use of these border prices does not require the assumption of free trade, but does imply that the numeraire for shadow pricing is uncommitted foreign exchange (see Chapter 9). For most developing countries, such import or export MOC curves will generally be flat or perfectly elastic. Other fuels such as coal and natural gas could treated either way, depending on whether they are tradables or nontraded. A nontraded item is generally characterized by a domestic supply price that lies above the f.o.b. price of exports but below the c.i.f. price of imports. The MOC of nonrenewable, nontraded energy sources will generally include a "user cost" or economic rent component, in addition to the marginal cost of production. The economic values of traditional fuels are the most difficult to determine, because in many cases there is no established market. However, as discussed later, they may be valued indirectly on the basic of the savings they allow on alternative fuels such as kerosene, the opportunity costs of labor for gathering firewood, and/or the external costs of deforestation and erosion.

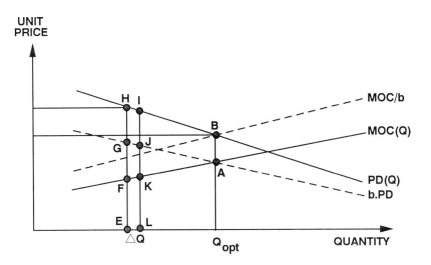

Figure 3.2: Efficient Pricing with Shadow Prices

Thus, for a nontraded form of energy, MOC is the opportunity cost of inputs used to produce it plus a user cost where relevant, while for a tradable fuel or a substitute, MOC represents the marginal foreign exchange cost of imports or the marginal export earnings foregone. In each case, MOC measures the shadow-priced economic value of alternative output foregone because of increased consumption of a given form of energy. After identifying the correct supply curve, we next examine demand-side effects, especially second best corrections that capture interactions between different energy subsectors. This second step is just as important as the first one, and therefore it will be examined in some detail.

In Figure 3.2, the market-priced demand curve for the form of energy under consideration is given by the curve PD(Q), which is the consumer's willingness to pay. Consider a small increment of consumption ΔQ at the market price level p. The traditional optimal pricing approach attempts to compare the incremental benefit of consumption due to ΔQ, (i.e. the area between the demand curve and x-axis), with the corresponding supply cost, (i.e. the area between the supply curve and x-axis). However, since MOC is shadow priced, PD must also be transformed into a shadow-priced curve to make the comparison valid. This is done by taking the increment of expenditure p.ΔQ and asking what is the shadow-priced marginal cost of resources used up elsewhere in the economy if the amount p.ΔQ (in market prices) is devoted to alternative consumption (and/or investment).

Suppose that the shadow cost of this alternative pattern of expenditure is $b(p.\Delta Q)$, where b is called a conversion factor. Then the transformed PD curve, which represents the shadow costs of alternative consumption foregone, is given by PD(Q); in Figure 3.2, it is assumed that $b < 1$. Thus at the price p, incremental benefits EGJL exceed incremental costs EFKL. The optimal consumption level is Q_{opt}, where the MOC and b.PD curves cross, or equivalently where a new pseudo-supply curve MOC/b and the market demand curve PD intersect. The optimal or efficient selling price to be charged to consumers (because they react only along the market demand curve PD, rather than the shadow-priced curve b.PD) will be p_e = MOC/b at the actual market clearing point B. At this level of consumption, the shadow costs and benefits of marginal consumption are equal, that is, MOC = b.PD. Since b depends on user specific consumption patterns, different values of the efficient price p_e may be derived for various consumer categories, all based on the same value of MOC. We clarify the foregoing by considering several specific practical examples.

First, suppose that all the expenditure $(p.\Delta Q)$ is used to purchase a substitute fuel; that is, assume complete substitution. Then the conversion factor b is the relative distortion or ratio of the shadow price to market price of this other fuel. Therefore p_e = MOC/b represents a specific second-best adjustment to the MOC of the first fuel, to compensate for the distortion in the price of the substitute fuel. For example, MOC_{EL} could represent the long-run marginal cost of rural electricity (for lighting), and the substitute fuel could be imported kerosene. Suppose that the (subsidized) domestic market price of kerosene is set at one-half its import (border) price for sociopolitical reasons. Then b=2, and the efficient selling price of electricity p_e = $MOC_{EL}/2$. This analysis ignores differences in the quality of the two fuels, and the capital costs of conversion equipment such as light bulbs, kerosene lamps, and partial substitution effects -- a more refined analysis of substitution possibilities would have to incorporate these additional considerations. It would be misleading, however, to then attempt to justify the subsidized kerosene price on the basis of comparison with the newly calculated low price of electricity, p_e. Such circular reasoning is far more likely to occur when pricing policies in different energy subsectors are uncoordinated, rather than in an integrated pricing framework. We note that all these energy sector subsidies must be carefully targeted to avoid leakages and abuses, as discussed later.

Next, consider a less specific case in which the amount $(p.\Delta Q)$ is used to buy an average basket of goods. If the consumer is residential, b would be the ratio of the shadow price to the market price of the household's market basket (here, b is also called the consumption conversion factor). The most general case would be when the consumer was unspecified, or detailed information on consumer categories was unavailable, so that b would be the standards conversion factor (SCF), which is the ratio of the official exchange rate (OER) to the shadow exchange rate (SER). With the foreign exchange numeraire, we convert domestic priced values into shadow-priced equivalents by application of the SCF to the former. This is conceptually the inverse of the traditional practice of multiplying foreign currency costs by the SER (instead of the OER) to convert to the domestic priced equivalent.

The use of the SCF for b represents a global second-best correction for the divergence between market and shadow prices, averaged throughout the economy. For example, suppose the border price of imported diesel is 4 pesos per liter (i.e., US$ 0.20 per liter, converted at the OER of 20 pesos per US$). Let the appropriate SER that reflects the average level of import duties and export subsidies be 25 pesos per US$. Therefore SCF = OER/SER = 0.8, and the appropriate strictly efficient selling price of diesel is p_e = 4/0.8 = 5 pesos per liter.

3.4   Extensions of the Basic Model

The analysis so far has been static. However, in many instances the situation with regard to the availability of a given energy source, interfuel substitution possibilities, and so on tends to vary over time, thus leading to disequilibrium in certain fuel markets, and divergence of the short-run price from the long-run optimal price. This aspect is illustrated below by means of an example that shows how the optimal depletion rate and time path for MOC of a domestic nonrenewable resource will be affected by varying demand conditions, especially tradability, extent of reserves, and substitution possibilities.

In Figure 3.3, the international energy price that acts as the benchmark is assumed to rise steadily in real terms, along the path BE. Suppose that the present-day marginal supply cost (MSC) (including extraction costs, and additional transport and environmental costs, etc., where appropriate) of a domestic energy source such as coal lies below the thermal equivalency price of an internationally traded fuel (e.g., petroleum of high-quality coal), as indicated by points A and B. Thermal equivalents are defined as the unit quantities of two substitutable fuels that provide the same useful energy output in a given use (i.e., including the efficiency of conversion). We note that the choice between the energy forms would depend on the quality of the final heat output, capital and handling costs of conversion, and so on, but to simplify the analysis here we abstract from these problems and compare the fuels only on the basis of unit price.

Let us initially examine two polar extremes based on simple, intuitively appealing arguments. First, if the reserves are practically infinite and the use of this fuel at the margin will not affect exports or substitution for imports of traded fuels, then the MOC of the domestic energy source in the long run would continue to be based on the marginal supply cost, that is, along the path AC, which is upward sloping to allow for increases in real factor costs or extraction costs. On the other hand, suppose there is a ready export market for the indigenous resource, or substitution possibilities with respect to imported fuels. In this case the marginal use of this resource will reduce export earnings or increase the import bill for the international fuels in the short run, because the reserves are small or output capacity is limited. Then, the marginal opportunity cost would tend to follow the path AD and rise quickly toward parity with the international energy price.

The actual situation is likely to fall between these two extremes, thus yielding alternative price such as AFE or AGHE. Here, the initial use of the resource has no marginal impact on exports or import substitution, but there is gradual depletion of finite domestic reserves over time, and eventual transition to higher-priced fuels in the future. For a given volume of reserves, the rate of depletion of the domestic energy source will be greater and the time to depletion will be shorter if its price is maintained low (i.e., on the path AGHE) for as long as possible rather than when the price rises steadily (i.e. along path AFE). The macroeconomic consequences of the path AGHE are also more undesirable because of the sudden price increase at the point of transition, when the domestic resource is exhausted. In practice the price path may well be determined by noneconomic factors. For example, the price of newly discovered gas or coal may have to be kept low for some years to capture the domestic market and displace the use of imported liquid fuels (which continue to be subsidized for political reasons). In general, the desire to keep energy prices low as long as possible must be balanced against the need to avoid a large price shock in the future.

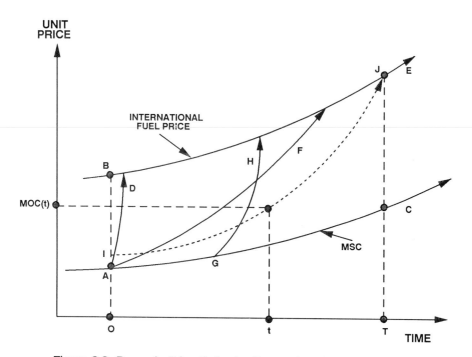

Figure 3.3: Dynamic Price Paths for Domestic Exhaustible Energy

The preceding discussion is more useful for oil-importing or energy deficit LDCs. In the case of major oil exporters, the ability to influence the world market price and to determine the rate of resource depletion provides greater flexibility. Significant foreign exchange surpluses and limited capacity to absorb investment imply decreased attractiveness of marginal export earnings coupled with the need to conserve oil resources. There is also greater ability to subsidize domestic oil consumption to meet basic needs and to accelerate economic development by increasing investment and expanding nonoil gross domestic product (Samii 1979).

More rigorous dynamic models, which maximize the net economic benefits of energy consumption over a long period, have been developed to determine the optimal price path and depletion rate; however, these models depend on factors such as the social discount rate, the size of reserves, the growth of demand, and the cost and time lag needed to develop a backstop technology (which could replace the international energy price as the upper bound on price). Uncertainties in future supply and demand -- such as the possibility of discovering new energy resources or technologies -- add to the complexities of dynamic analysis. The classical argument was developed by Hotelling in 1931 (for details see Appendix A3.2). This approach indicates that the rate of increase in the optimal rent (or difference between price and marginal extraction cost) for the resource should equal the rate of return on capital (r). In our shadow pricing framework, r would be the social discount rate or "accounting rate of interest" (ARI).

The foregoing implies that the optimal path of MOC would be IJE in Figure 3.3, defined at any time t by

$$MOC(t) = MSC(t) + JL/(1+r)^{T-t}$$

where JL is the rent at the time of depletion T. Thus MOC consists of the current marginal costs of extraction, transport, environmental degradation, and so on (MSC), plus the appropriately discounted "user cost" or foregone surplus benefits of future consumption (JL). As T approaches infinity, IJ would tend toward AC, which is the infinite reserves case, while as T falls to zero, IJ would approximate AD more closely, corresponding to the case of very small reserves and rapid transition to the expensive fuel.

We now consider another type of dynamic effect due to the growth of demand from year 0 to year 1, which leads to an outward shift in the market demand curve from PD_0 to PD_1 as shown in Figure 3.4. Assuming that the correct market clearing price p_0 was prevailing in year 0, excess demand equal GK will occur in year 1. Ideally, the supply should be increased to Q_1, and the new optimal market clearing price established at p_1. However, the available information concerning the demand curve PD_1 may be incomplete, making it difficult to locate the point L.

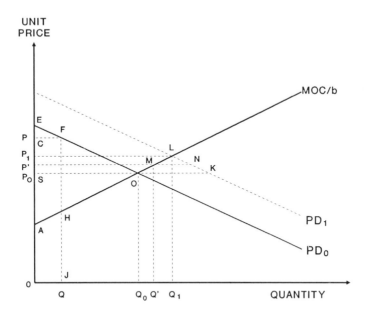

Figure 3.4: Dynamic Effects due to Demand Curve Shifts

Fortunately, the technical-economic relationships underlying the production function or known international prices usually permit the marginal opportunity cost curve to be determined more accurately. Therefore, as a first step, the supply may be increased to an immediate level Q', at the price p'. Observation of the excess demand MN indicates that both the supply and, if necessary, also the marginal cost price should be further increased. Conversely, if we overshoot L and end up in a situation of excess supply, then it may be necessary to wait until the growth of demand catches up with the oversupply. In this interactive manner, it is possible to move along the MOC curve toward the optimal market clearing point. As we approach it, note that the optimum is also shifting with demand growth, and therefore we may never hit this moving target. However, the basic guideline of pegging the price to the marginal opportunity cost of supply and expanding output until the market clears, is still valid.

Next, we examine the practical complications raised by price feedback effects. Typically, a long-range demand forecast is made assuming some given future evolution of prices, a least-cost investment program is determined to meet this demand, and optimal prices are computed on the basis of the latter. However, if the estimated optimal price that is to be imposed on consumers is significantly different from the original assumption regarding the evolution of prices, then the first-round price estimates must be fed back into the model to revise the demand forecast and repeat the calculation.

In theory, this iterative procedure could be repeated until future demand, prices, and MOC estimates become mutually self-consistent. In practice, uncertainties in price elasticities of demand and other data may dictate a more pragmatic approach in which the MOC would be used to devise prices after only one iteration. The behavior of demand is then observed over some time period and the first round prices are revised to move closer to the optimum, which may itself have shifted as described earlier.

When MOC is based on marginal production costs, the effect of capital indivisibilities or lumpiness of investments causes difficulties in many energy subsectors. Thus, owing to economies of scale, investments for electric power systems, gas production and transport, oil refining, coal mining, reafforestation, and so on tend to be large and long-lived. As shown in Figure 3.5, suppose that in year 0 the maximum supply capacity is QM_1, while the optimal price and output combination (p_0, Q_0) prevails, corresponding to demand curve D_0 and the short-run marginal cost curve SRMC (e.g., variable, operating, and maintenance costs).

As demand grows from D_0 to D_1 over time and the limit of existing capacity is reached, the price must be increased to p_1 to clear the market -- that is, "price rationing" occurs. When the demand curve has shifted to D_2 and the price is p_2, capacity is increased to QM_2. However, as soon as the capacity increment is completed and becomes a sunk cost, price should fall to the old trend of SRMC -- for example, p_3 is the optimal price corresponding to demand D_3. Generally, the large price fluctuations during this process will be disruptive and unacceptable to consumers. This practical problem may be avoided by adopting a long-run marginal cost (LRMC) approach, which provides the required price stability while retaining the basic principle of matching willingness to pay and incremental supply costs. Essentially, the future capital costs of a single project or an investment program are distributed over the stream of output expected during the lifetime of this plant. For example, capital costs could be annualized at the appropriate social discount rate and divided by the annual output, or an average incremental cost approach could be used (Munasinghe 1979a). This average investment cost per unit of incremental output is added to variable cost (SRMC), to yield LRMC, as shown in Figure 3.5. If continued demand growth is expected, consumers' initial willingness to pay a price equal to the annual equivalent LRMC is assumed to imply willingness to do so over the lifetime of the asset.

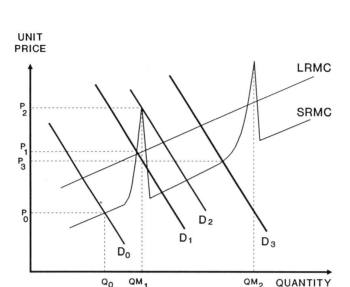

Figure 3.5: The Effect of Capital Indivisibilities on Price

Exceptions to the LRMC rule may lead to efficiency gains in certain cases. If substantial excess supply capacity exists, it could be appropriate to temporarily use SRMC (including both variable and user costs) as a basis for pricing to specific consumers. However, SRMC priced supplies must be decreased as LRMC priced demand grows, and the temporary users of low-priced supplies should not be permitted to become a permanent burden, e.g., an interruptible load in electric power systems.

Another method of allocating capacity costs, known as peak load pricing, is particularly relevant for electricity and also natural gas. The basic peak load pricing model shown in Figure 3.6 has two demand curves; for example, D_{pk} could represent the peak demand during the x daylight and evening hours of the day when electric loads are large, while D_{op} would indicate the off- peak demand during the remaining (24-x) hours when loads are light. The marginal cost curve is simplified assuming a single type of plant with the fuel, operating, and maintenance costs given by the constant a, and the incremental cost of capacity given by the constant b. The static diagram has been drawn to indicate that the pressure on capacity arises due to peak demand D_{pk}, while the off-peak demand D_{op} does not infringe on the capacity limit QM. The optimal pricing rule now has two parts corresponding to two distinct rating periods (i.e., differentiated by the time of day):

peak period price $\quad p_{pk} = a + b$

off-peak period price $\ p_{op} = a$

The logic of this simple result is that peak period users, who are the cause of capacity additions, should bear full responsibility for the capacity costs as well as fuel, operating, and maintenance costs, while off-peak consumers pay only the latter costs. Peak load pricing can also be applied in different seasons of the year[2]. More sophisticated peak load pricing models indicate that in an optimally planned system, marginal capacity costs should be allocated in proportion to marginal shortage costs during two or more different rating periods. If the peak period is too narrowly defined, peak load pricing may shift the peak to another rating period; this would be an extreme case of price feedback effects, which were discussed earlier.

Related problems of allocating joint costs arise in other energy subsectors as well -- an example is the allocation of capacity costs of natural gas, or of refinery costs among different petroleum products. The former may be treated like the electricity case. For oil products, the light refinery cuts that are tradable, such as kerosene, gasoline, and diesel, have benchmark international prices. However, other items like heavy residual oils may have to be treated like nontradables. Furthermore, associated gas that may be flared at the refinery is often assumed to have a low MOC, although subsequent storage and handling for use as LPG will add to the costs. A more complicated approach would be to use a programming model of a refinery to solve the dual problem as a means of determining shadow prices of distillates.

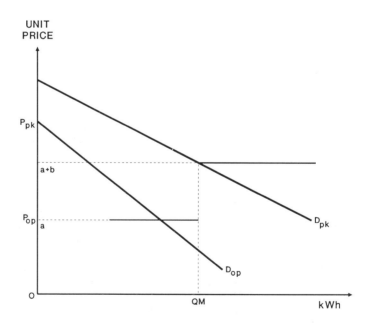

Figure 3.6: Peak Load Pricing Model

A more general aspect of the capacity constraint, which encompasses peak load pricing, is that energy prices have to be structured. For example, the MOC shown in Figure 3.2 may vary by the type of consumer, geographic location, time and level of consumption, voltage level (for electricity), and so on. These values of MOC then have to be modified to reflect demand-side considerations (as discussed earlier). Therefore, the economically efficient prices in a given energy subsector may exhibit considerable structuring.

The interrelated issues of supply and demand uncertainty, safety margins, and shortage costs also raise complications. We first illustrate this issue using electricity as an example, and then generalize the results for the other subsectors. Thus the least-cost system expansion plan to meet an electricity demand forecast is generally determined assuming some (arbitrary) target level of system reliability -- e.g., loss-of-load probability (LOLP), reserve margin, etc. Therefore, marginal costs depend on the target reliability level, when in fact economic theory suggests that reliability should also be treated as a variable to be optimized, and both price and capacity (or equivalently, reliability) levels should be optimized simultaneously. The optimal price is the marginal cost price as described earlier, while the optimal reliability level is achieved when the marginal cost of capacity additions (to improve the reserve margin) are equal to the expected value of economic cost savings to consumers due to electricity supply shortages averted by those capacity increments. These considerations lead to a more generalized approach to system expansion planning, as shown below (Munasinghe 1980a).

Consider a simple expression for the net benefits (NB) of electricity consumption, which is to be maximized:

$$NB(D,R) = TB(D) - SC(D,R) - OC(D,R)$$

where TB = total benefits of consumption if there were no outages; SC = supply costs (i.e., system costs); OC = outage costs (i.e., costs to consumers of supply shortages); D = demand; and R = reliability.

In the traditional approach to system planning (i.e., least-cost system expansion planning), both D and R are exogenously fixed, and therefore NB is maximized when SC is minimized. However, if R is treated as a variable,

$$\frac{d(NB)}{dR} = -\frac{\partial(SC+OC)}{\partial R} + \frac{\partial(TB-SC-OC)}{\partial D} \cdot \frac{\partial D}{\partial R} = 0$$

is the necessary first-order maximization condition.

Assuming $\partial D/\partial R = 0$, we have:

$$\partial(SC)/\partial R = -\partial(OC)/\partial R$$

Therefore, as described earlier, reliability should be increased by adding to capacity until the above condition is satisfied. An alternative way of expressing this result is that since TB is independent of R, NB is maximized when total costs, TC = (SC + OC), are minimized. The above criterion effectively subsumes the traditional system planning rule of minimizing only the system costs. The emphasis on outage costs requires greater effort to measure these costs (Munasinghe and Gellerson 1979, Munasinghe 1980b).

We note that this approach may be generalized for application in other energy subsectors. Thus while sophisticated measures of reliability like LOLP do not exist outside the power subsector, the concept of minimizing total costs to society is still relevant. For example, in oil and gas investment planning, the cost of shortages due to gasoline queues, lack of furnace oil, or gas for domestic and industrial use may be traded off against the supply costs of increased storage capacity and greater delivery capability incurred by augmenting surface transport or pipeline systems. The latter case could form the basis for raising fuel prices, vehicle licensing fees, road user charges, parking charges, and so on in a large metropolis, relative to rural areas. Clearly, these additional considerations would modify the marginal costs of energy supply and thus effect optimal pricing policies.

Finally, externalities, especially environmental considerations, have to be included as far as possible in the determination of efficient energy prices. For example, if the building of a new hydroelectric dam results in the flooding of land that had recreational or agricultural value, or if urban transportation growth leads to congestion and air pollution, these costs should be reflected in MOC. While such externality costs may, in certain cases, be quite difficult to quantify, they may already be included (at least partially) on the supply side, in terms of measures taken to avoid environmental degradation, for example, the cost of pollution control equipment at an oil refinery or coal-burning electricity plant, or the cost of landscaping strip-mined land.

Estimation of environmental costs is most problematic in the case of noncommercial or traditional energy sources such as woodfuel, where marginal opportunity costs could be based (when appropriate) on the externality costs of deforestation, erosion, loss of watershed, and so on. Other measures of the economic value of traditional fuel would include the opportunity cost of labor required to collect woodfuel, or the cost savings from displaced substitute fuels such as kerosene and LPG.

3.5   Adjusting Efficient Prices to Meet Other Objectives

Once efficient energy prices have been determined, the second stage of pricing must be carried out to meet social, financial, political, and other constraints.

We note that efficient energy prices deviate from the prices calculated on the basis of financial costs, because shadow prices are used instead of the market prices. This is done to correct for distortions in the economy. Therefore, the constraints that force further departures from efficient prices (in the second stage of the pricing procedure) may also be considered as distortions that impose their own shadow values on the calculation (Munasinghe 1979a).

Subsidized Prices and Lifeline Rates

Sociopolitical or equity arguments are often advanced in favor of subsidized prices or "lifeline" rates for energy, especially where the costs of energy consumption are high relative to the incomes of poor households. Economic reasoning based on externality effects may also be used to support subsidies, for example cheap kerosene to reduce excessive firewood use and prevent deforestation, erosion, and so on. To prevent leakages and abuse of such subsidies, energy suppliers must act as discriminating monopolists. Targeting specific consumer classes (for example, poor households) and limiting the cheap price only to a minimum block of consumption are easiest to achieve, in practice, for metered forms of energy like gas or electricity. Other means of discrimination such as rationing and licensing may also be required -- for example, a minimum ration of cheap kerosene for households, or a special license for trucks using subsidized diesel oil and a ban on diesel-driven passenger cars. All these complex and interrelated issues require detailed analysis.

The concept of a subsidized "social" block, or "lifeline" rate, for low-income consumers has another important economic rationale, based on the income redistribution argument. We clarify this point with the aid of Figure 3.7, which shows the respective demand curves for energy AB and GH of low (I_1) and average (I_2) income domestic users, the social tariff p_s over the minimum consumption block 0 to Q_{min}, and the efficient price level p_e. All tariff levels are in domestic market prices. If the actual price $p = p_e$, the average household will be consuming at the "optimal" level Q_2, but the poor household will not be able to afford the service.

If increased benefits accruing to the poor have a high social value, then, although in nominal domestic prices the point A lies below p_e, the consumer surplus portion ABF multiplied by an appropriate social weight w could be greater than the shadow price of supply (see Appendix A3.1 for details). The adoption of the block tariff shown in Figure 3.7, consisting of the lifeline rate p_s, followed by the full tariff p_e, helps capture the consumer surplus of the poor user but does not affect the optimal consumption pattern of the average consumer. This ignores the income effect due to reduced expenditure by the average consumer for the first block of consumption (up to Q_{min}).

In practice, the magnitude Q_{min} has to carefully determined, to avoid subsidizing relatively well-off consumers; it should be based on acceptable criteria for identifying "low-income" groups and reasonable estimates of their minimum consumption levels (e.g., sufficient to supply basic energy requirements for the household). The level'of p_s relative to the efficient price may be determined on the basis of the poor consumer's income level relative to some critical consumption level, as shown in the appendix. The financial requirements of the energy sector would also be considered in determining p_s and Q_{min}. This approach may be reinforced by an appropriate supply policy (e.g., subsidized house connections for electricity and special supply points for kerosene).

Financial Viability

The financial constraints most often encountered relate to meeting the revenue requirements of the sector, and are often embodied in criteria such as some target financial rate of return on assets, or an acceptable rate of contribution toward the future investment program. In principle, for state-owned energy suppliers, the most efficient solution would be to set the price at the efficient level, and to rely on government to subsidize losses or tax surpluses exceeding sector financial needs. In practice, some measure of financial autonomy and self-sufficiency is an important goal for the sector. Because of the premium that is placed on public funds, a pricing policy that results in failure to achieve minimum financial targets for continued operation of the sector would rarely be acceptable. The converse and more typical case, where efficient pricing would result in financial surpluses well in excess of traditional revenue targets, may be politically unpopular, especially for an electric utility. Therefore in either case, changes in revenues have to be achieved by adjusting the efficient prices.

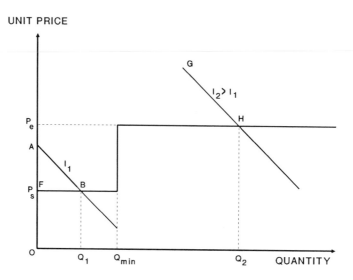

Figure 3.7: Economic Basis for the Social or Lifeline Rate

It is intuitively clear that price discrimination between the various consumer categories should aim for the greatest divergence from the marginal opportunity cost-based price for the consumer group with the lowest price elasticity of demand, and vice versa, because this will result in the smallest deviations from the "optimal" levels of consumption consistent with a strict efficiency pricing regime (Baumol and Bradford 1970). In many countries the necessary data for the analysis of demand by consumer categories is rarely available, so rule-of-thumb methods of determining the appropriate tariff structure have to be adopted. However, if the energy subsector exhibits increasing costs (i.e., if marginal costs are greater than average costs), the fiscal implications should be exploited to the full. Thus, for example, electric power tariffs (especially in a developing country) constitute a practical means of raising public revenues in a manner that is generally consistent with the economic efficiency objective, at least for the bulk of the consumers who are not subsidized; at the same time they help supply basic energy needs to low-income groups. Similar arguments may be made in the petroleum subsector, where high prices for gasoline, based on efficiency, externality, and conservation arguments, may be used to cross-subsidize the "poor man's" fuel -- kerosene, or diesel used for transportation. However, a number of undesirable side effects may follow, such as the practice of mixing gasoline with kerosene and the substitution of diesel for gasoline. The income distribution effects may also be perverse, with the relatively wealthy diverting cheap kerosene or diesel for use in vehicles or in industry.

Other Considerations

There are several additional economic, political, and social considerations that may be adequate justification for departing from a strict efficient pricing policy. The decision to provide commercial energy like kerosene or electricity in a remote rural area (which often also entails subsidies because the beneficiaries are not able to pay the full price based on high unit costs), could be made on completely noneconomic grounds, e.g., for general sociopolitical reasons such as maintaining a viable regional industrial or agricultural base, stemming rural to urban migration, or alleviating local political discontent. Similarly, uniform nationwide energy prices are a political necessity in many countries, although this policy may, for example, imply subsidization of consumers in remote rural areas (where energy transport costs are high) by energy users in urban centers. However, the full economic benefits of such a course of action may be must greater than the apparent efficiency costs that arise from any divergence between actual and efficient price levels. Again this possibility is likely to be much more significant in a developing country than in a developed one, not only because of the high cost of energy relative to incomes in the former, but also because the available administrative or fiscal machinery to redistribute incomes (or to achieve regional or industrial development objectives by other means) is frequently ineffective.

The conservation objective (to reduce dependence on imported energy, improve the trade balance, and so on) usually runs counter to subsidy arguments. Therefore, it may be necessary to restrict cheap energy to productive economic sectors that need to be strengthened, while in the case of the basic energy needs of households, the energy price could be sharply increased for consumption beyond appropriate minimum levels. In other cases, conservation and subsidized energy prices may consistent. For example, cheap kerosene might be required, especially in rural areas, to reduce excessive woodfuel consumption and thus prevent deforestation and erosion.

It is particularly difficult to raise prices anywhere near the efficient levels where low income and a tradition of subsidized energy have increased consumer resistance. In practice, price changes have to be gradual, in view of the costs that may be imposed on those who have already incurred expenditures on energy using equipment and made other decisions, while expecting little or no change in traditional energy pricing policies. At the same time, a steady price rise will prepare consumers for high future energy prices. The efficiency costs of a gradual price increase can be seen as an implicit shadow value placed on the social benefits that result from this policy.

Finally, owing to the practical difficulties of metering, price discrimination, and billing, and the need to avoid confusing consumers, the pricing structure may have to be simplified. Thus, the number of customer categories, rating periods, consumption blocks, and so on, will have to be limited. Electricity and gas offer the greatest possibilities for structuring. The degree of sophistication of metering depends among other things, on the net benefits of metering and on problems of installation and maintenance. In general, various forms of peak electricity pricing (i.e., using maximum demand or time-of-day metering) would be particularly applicable to large-, medium-, and high-voltage industrial and commercial consumers. However, for very poor consumers receiving a subsidized rate of electricity, a simple current limiting device may suffice, because the cost of even simple kWh metering may exceed the net benefit (which equal the savings in supply costs due to reduced consumption, less the decrease in consumption benefits). For electricity or gas, different charges for various consumption blocks may be effectively applied with conventional metering. However, for liquid fuels like kerosene, subsidized or discriminatory pricing would usually require schemes involving rationing and coupons, and could lead to leakage and abuses.

3.6 Summary and Conclusions

The recent past has been characterized by higher real costs of energy and fluctuations in relative fuel prices. This article has emphasized the importance of comprehensive energy planning, especially an integrated approach to energy pricing, due to the confusion arising from the often conflicting nature of national objectives, from the complexity of energy policy tools currently in use, including pricing, physical controls, technical methods, and public education, and from the many types of energy sources that may be used in a variety of applications.

Energy policymakers in developing countries face special difficulties, such as high levels of market distortion, shortages of foreign exchange and investment funds, large numbers of poor customers whose basic energy needs must be met, and relatively greater usage of traditional fuels, in addition to the energy issues found in industrialized countries. Thus, an integrated pricing framework must begin with a clear statement of national objectives, and must provide a method for trading off among mutually contradictory goals. Important linkages between the energy sector and the rest of the economy, as well as interactions between and activities within different energy subsectors, must be analyzed using shadow prices, essentially within a partial equilibrium framework. For consistency, the shadow pricing methodology used for pricing energy sector outputs must be the same as the one used to make investment decisions. Special attention must also be paid to the hitherto neglected area of traditional fuels.

Energy pricing structures, disaggregated by energy subsector, are derived in two stages. First, the shadow-priced marginal opportunity cost (MOC) of a given form of energy is determined, based essentially on supply-side considerations. For a tradable form of energy, an appropriate measure of MOC would be the marginal cost of imports or export earnings foregone, with adjustments for local transport and handling costs. For nontraded fuels, MOC would be the marginal supply cost, plus a user cost component (in the case of nonrenewable resources). Next, demand-side effects including distortions in the prices of other goods, especially substitute fuels, are used to derive from the MOC the strictly efficient energy price level p_e. In practice, this basic theoretical framework may be extended to cover dynamic effects relating to both supply and demand uncertainty, shortage costs, and externalities.

In the second stage of the pricing procedure, the efficient price (p_e) is further adjusted to yield a realistic pricing structure that meets social-subsidy considerations, sector financial requirements, and other practical constraints such as the need to change prices gradually, simplicity of price structure for metering and billing, and so on.

Direct pricing policies are usually inapplicable in the traditional fuels subsector, due the lack of well-developed markets for these forms of energy. Therefore, indirect methods -- including augmentation of supply, the appropriate pricing of substitute fuels, improvements in the efficiency of woodfuel energy conversion, and punitive measures for excessive use -- must be used in close coordination.

Appendix A3.1   Model for Optimal Energy Pricing Using Shadow Prices

In this appendix, a general expression for the socially optimal price in the subsector for energy type A is developed based on shadow prices, to compensate for distortions in the economy. Starting from the general equation, results for optimal energy pricing are derived for cases that reflect the following:

1. a perfectly competitive economy (classical result)
2. efficient prices, including economic second best considerations.
3. subsidized social prices or lifeline rates for poor consumers.

The supply and demand for a form of energy A is shown in Figure A3.1, where S is the supply curve represented by the marginal cost of supply (evaluated at domestic market prices), and D is the corresponding demand curve for a specific consumer. Starting with the initial combination of price and consumption (p,Q), consider the impact of a small price reduction (dp), and the resultant increase in demand (dQ), on the net social benefits of energy A consumption.

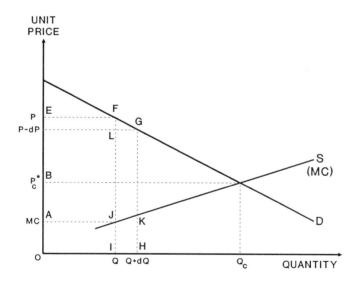

Figure A3.1: Supply and Demand in Energy Subsector A

Before evaluating the net social benefit of this price change, let us define the shadow pricing framework. First, suppose we calculate the marginal cost of supply MC without shadow pricing, i.e., in market prices. Then a_p is defined as the energy A conversion factor (ACF), which transforms MC into the corresponding real economic resource cost, i.e., with correct shadow pricing, the marginal opportunity cost is MOC = $(a_p MC)$. Second, we assign a specific social weight W_c to each marginal unit of consumption (valued in market prices) of a given individual i in the economy. For example, if this user of energy A is poor, the corresponding social weight may be much larger than for a rich customer, to reflect society's emphasis on the increased consumption of low-income groups. Third, if the given individual's consumption of goods and services other than in the energy A subsector (valued in market prices) increases by one unit, then the shadow-priced marginal cost of economic resources used (or the shadow cost to the economy) is b_i.

As a result of the price reduction, the consumer is using dq units more of energy A, which has a market value of (p.dQ) (i.e., area IFGH). However, the consumer's income has increased by the amount pQ-(p-dP).(Q+dQ), and assuming none of it is saved, this individual's consumption of other goods and services will increase by the amount (Qdp-pdQ), also valued in market prices (i.e., area BEFG minus area IFGH). Therefore, the consumer's total consumption -- that is, energy A plus other goods -- will increase by the net amount (Q.dp) in market prices. This is the traditional increase in consumer surplus benefits. The shadow value of this increased consumption is W_c.(Q.dp) where W_c is the social weight appropriate to this consumer's income/consumption level.

Next, consider the resource costs of these changes in consumption. The shadow cost of increasing the supply of energy A is (a_p.MC.dQ) (i.e., a_p times area IJKH), and the resources used up to provide the other additional goods consumed b_c.(Qdp-pdQ), where a_p is the conversion factor for energy A, and b_c is the conversion factor for other goods consumed by this consumer. Finally, the income change of the producer of energy A (if any) must also be considered, but this effect may be ignored if we assume quite plausibly that the producer is the government.

The total increase in net social benefits due to the energy A price decrease is given by:

$$dNB = W_c(p.dQ) - a_p(MC.dQ) + (W_c-b_c).(Q.dp-p.dQ)$$

Therefore:

$$dNB/dp = Q[((W_c-b_c) + n.b_c) - n.a_p.(MC/p)]$$

where $n = (p.dQ/Q.dp)$ is the elasticity of demand (magnitude). The necessary first-order condition for maximizing net social benefits, in the limit, is $d(NB)/dp = 0$. This yields the optimal price level:

$$\hat{p} = a_p.MC/[b_c + (W_c - b_c)/n] \qquad (A3.1)$$

This expression may be reduced to a more familiar form, by making some simplifying assumptions.

Case 1: Perfectly competitive economy where market prices and shadow prices are the same, and income transfer effects are ignored, i.e., no social weighting.

Therefore, $a_p = W_c = b_c = 1$, and equation (A3.1) reduces to

$$\hat{p}_c = MC \qquad (A3.2)$$

This is the classical marginal cost pricing result, where net social benefits are maximized when price is set equal to marginal cost at the market clearing point (p_c, Q_c) in Figure A3.1.

Case 2: Income transfer effects ignored, because the marginal social benefit of consumption is equal to the marginal cost to the economy of providing this consumption.

Therefore, $W_c = b_c$, and equation (A3.1) becomes

$$p_e = (a_p.MC)/b_c = MOC/b_c \qquad (A3.3)$$

This is the optimal efficient price that emphasizes the efficient allocation of resources and neglects income distributional considerations.

As mentioned earlier, the marginal opportunity cost of energy A (MOC) may usually be evaluated in a straightforward manner (e.g., the international border price for a tradeable fuel, or, in the case of a nontradable like electricity, by applying the appropriate shadow prices to the least cost mix of technically determined inputs used in production). However, the conversion factor b_c depends crucially on the type of consumer involved.

For residential consumers, b_c represents the consumption conversion factor (CCF), which reflects the resource cost or shadow value of one (market-priced) unit of the household's marginal consumption basket. If the CCF < 1, then p_e > MOC.

Another interesting case illustrates the application of equation (A3.3) to correct the economic second-best consideration arising from energy substitution possibilities. As an extreme case, suppose all expenditures diverted from energy A consumption will be used to purchase alternative energy which is subsidized by the government (e.g., kerosene for lighting, or diesel for auto-generation). In this case, b_c is the ratio of the marginal opportunity cost of alternative energy to its market price, and may be written:

$$b_c = MOC_{ae}/p_{ae}$$

Thus, from equation (A3.3)

$$p_e = MOC(p_{ae}/MOC_{ae}) \qquad (A3.4)$$

Since the alternative energy is based below its border marginal cost, i.e., b_c > 1, then p_e < MOC also. Therefore, the subsidization of substitute energy prices will result in an optimal energy A price that is below the shadow supply cost.

If it is not possible to determine the consumption patterns of specific consumer groups, b_c could be defined very broadly as the average conversion factor for all energy A users, e.g., the SCF, as discussed in the text.

Case 3: General

Equation (A3.1) is the optimal energy A price when shadow prices are used, which incorporate income distributional concerns.

Consider the case of a group of very poor consumers for whom we may assume $W_c >> b_c(n - 1)$. Therefore, equation (A3.1) may be written

$$p_s \approx n.MOC/W_c$$

An even greater simplification is possible if it is assumed that n = 1; thus

$$p_s = MOC/W_c$$

For illustration, suppose that the net income/consumption level of these poor consumers (c) is one-third the critical income/consumption level ($\overline{c}$), which is like a poverty line. Then a simple expression for the social weight is

$$W_c = \overline{c}/c = 3.$$

Therefore, $p_s = MOC/3$, which is the "lifeline" rate or subsidized tariff appropriate to this group of low-income consumers.

Appendix A3.2   The Pricing of Depletable or Nonrenewable Energy Resources

Depletable, exhaustible, or nonrenewable energy resources such as crude oil, natural gas, and coal account for most of the current commercial energy consumption in the world. In the U.S.A., for example, they supply about 94% of total and in the developing countries some 83% of commercial energy consumption[3]. Since exhaustible energy resources are subject to depletion, a critical question arises as to whether they should be used up now, or saved for future use. Thus special consideration must be given to the fact that they have a potential future value or opportunity cost.

The Hotelling Result

As mentioned earlier in Chapter 3, starting from the seminal work by Harold Hotelling, a large literature has developed on this subject[4]. Under certain simplifying assumptions (described later in this section), Hotelling's basic result, referred to as

---

[3] The World Bank, *Energy in the Developing Countries*, Washington D.C., 1980, Table 23; and *US Bureau of Mines Yearbook*, Annual. Commercial energy consumption excludes consumption of so-called traditional fuels such as firewood, dung, and crop residues.

[4] Harold Hotelling, "The Economics of Exhaustible Resources," *Journal of Political Economy*, Vol. 39, April 1931, pp. 1372-75.

the "fundamental principle of the economics of exhaustible resources", indicates that the optimal price of the resource net of extraction costs must rise over time at a rate equal to the rate of interest[5]. This conclusion is valid both in the case of a competitive resource extracting industry seeking to maximize the present discounted value of profits, as well as for an economically efficient extraction path which maximizes the present discounted value of the net benefits of resource consumption.

This general principle was graphically represented in Figure 3.3. Price at time O is equal to marginal supply costs OA plus AI. It rises at the rate of interest to J when simultaneously the deposit is exhausted and demand for it falls to zero. The usual assumption is that at that point higher-priced energy substitutes will enter into use. The necessary adjustment process, given a stationary economy, would have to come about either by a continuous decline in the output of each deposit, or by a gradual reduction in the number of producers. This postulated reduction in output is required to accommodate the usual assumption of a downward sloping demand curve. As output prices rise over time at the rate of interest, demand necessarily falls and production must decline. A less tortuous and somewhat more realistic assumption made by some analysts is that the demand curve continuously shifts outward (i.e., market demand is growing over time). This, then leads to higher demands at each given price, or unchanged demands at rising prices.

More formally, the validity of this basic proposition can be shown as follows (see mathematical section at the end of this appendix for more detailed analysis). In a competitive market:

$$r_t = P_t q_t - c q_t \qquad \qquad (A3.5)$$

where:

r_t = net profit in period t
P_t = market price in period t
q_t = output in period t
c = marginal cost of extraction (assumed constant)

The producer will attempt to maximize the present value of his discounted profits over the life expectancy of the deposit, subject to the constraint that the total quantity of the resource is fixed. Hence,

$$\sum_{t=0}^{T} q_t = \bar{q} \qquad \qquad (A3.6)$$

where:

T = time horizon of production to exhaustion

$\bar{q}$ = the total quantity of the resource in place.

[5] Solow, Robert M., "The Economics of Resources or the Resources of Economics," *American Economic Review*, vol.64, 1974, pp. 1-14. In its simplest form, Hotelling's original rule stated that the price of an exhaustible should rise at a rate equal to the interest rate, assuming a zero extraction cost.

The maximization problem becomes:

$$\text{Max} \sum_{t=0}^{T} r_t(1+i)^{-t} = \sum_{t=0}^{T} (P_t q_t - cq_t)(1+i)^{-t} \tag{A3.7}$$

where

i = appropriate market rate of interest.

Forming the Lagrangian:

$$L = \sum_{t=0}^{T} (P_t q_t - cq_t)(1+i)^{-t} - \lambda(\sum_{t=0}^{T} q_t - \bar{q}) \tag{A3.8}$$

A first order (necessary) condition for maximization of equation (A3.8) is:

$$\frac{\partial L}{\partial q_t} = (P_t - c)(1+i)^{-t} - \lambda = 0 \tag{A3.9}$$

Thus,

$$P_t = c + \lambda(1+i)^t \tag{A3.10}$$

This says that price P_t in period t must be equal to the marginal extraction cost plus an expression $\lambda(1+i)^t$ which is usually called "user cost" or "depletion premium." Let us define

$$R_t = P_t - c = \lambda(1+i)^t \tag{A3.11}$$

then

$$\frac{R_{t+1} - R_t}{R_t} = i \tag{A3.12}$$

which is the definition of the "fundamental principle". R_t is also called the resource "rent" or royalty of the depleting asset.

The fundamental principle was initially derived under a rather stringent set of assumptions, including: perfect foresight and complete certainty of future demand, the existence of a known fixed stock of homogeneous resources, an unchanging market organization, constant marginal extraction costs, and no common access effects. We summarize briefly below, subsequent work that has sought to approximate the real world more closely by relaxing some of these assumptions[6].

---

[6] For a more detailed review of the literature on the economics of exhaustible resources, see: Devarajan, Shantayanan, and Anthony C. Fisher, "Hotelling's 'Economics of Exhaustible Resources': Fifty Years Later", *Journal of Economic Literature*, vol.XIX, March 1981, pp. 65-73; and Pindyck, Robert S., "Models of Resource Markets and the Explanation of Resource Price Behavior", *Energy Economics*, vol.3, July 1981, pp. 130-9.

The first broad area of study has been market organization, in particular, the effect of monopoly on the price and depletion rate. Hotelling's original analysis suggested that a monopolist would start off with a higher initial resource price than in the competitive case, and that marginal revenue rather than price would grow at the interest rate. He also concluded that the depletion rate would be slower, because the time to resource depletion would tend to infinity for the monopolist, whereas the resource would be exhausted in a finite time under competitive conditions.

Subsequent analysis has tended to confirm the original result that monopoly slows depletion, under a wide range of conditions for the characteristics of demand. Thus, if the price elasticity of demand decreases as the output increases, or if the elasticity increases as the demand curve shifts outward over time, the monopolist would deplete more slowly[7]. Correspondingly, the monopolist would increase output relative to competitive levels in the early period and restrict production later, if the price elasticity decreased as the demand curve shifted over time. The latter case is rather unrealistic, however, because substitute resources are likely to become more available in the future, thus making demand more elastic over time, and accelerated depletion early on could imply prices growing faster than the interest rate, resulting in an unsustainable equilibrium[8].

Some recent studies have attempted to model an oligopolistic market organization consisting of a few large producers (most often based on OPEC), which is intermediate between the monopolistic and perfectly competitive cases[9]. The results here vary widely depending on the assumptions used.

The second major area of emphasis in recent studies has been the analysis of the impact of past production on the future prices and depletion rates. Supply-side effects are based on the increase in the costs of extraction as the cumulative stock of output grows. Several studies have analyzed the pattern of optimal depletion of deposits of different qualities, with the highest quality and lowest extraction cost deposits being

---

[7] Weinstein, Milton C., and Richard J. Zeckhauser, "The Optimal Consumption of Depletable Natural Resources," *Quarterly Journal of Economics*, vol.89, August 1975, pp. 371-92; Stiglitz, Joseph E., "Monopoly and the Rate of Extraction of Exhaustible Resources," *American Economic Review*, vol.66, September 1976, pp. 655-61; Lewis, Tracy R., "Monopoly Exploitation of an Exhaustible Resource," *Journal of Economics and Management*, vol.3, October 1976, pp.198-204; Dasgupta, Partha S., and Geoffrey M. Heal, *Economic Theory and Exhaustible Resources*, Cambridge University Press, London, 1979.

[8] Dasgupta, Partha S. and Geoffrey M. Heal, op.cit., 1979.

[9] Schmalensee, Richard, "Resource Exploitation Theory and the Behavior of the Oil Cartel," *European Economic Review*, vol.7, 1976, pp. 257-79; Salant, Stephen W., "Exhaustible Resources and Industrial Structure: A Nash-Cournot Approach to the World Oil Market," *Journal of Political Economy*, vol.84, October 1976, pp. 1079-93; Cramer, Jacques, and Martin L. Weitzman, "OPEC and the Monopoly Price of World Oil," *European Economic Review*, vol.8, August 1976, pp. 155-64; Pindyck, Robert S., "Gains to Producers from the Cartelization of Exhaustible Resources," *Review of Economics and Statistics*, vol.60, May 1978, pp.238-51; Hnyilicza, Esteban, and Robert S. Pindyck, "Pricing Policies for a Two-Part Exhaustible Resource Cartel: The Case of OPEC," *European Economic Review*, vol.8, August 1976, pp.139-54; Gilbert, Richard J., "Dominant Firm Pricing Policy in a Market for an Exhaustible Resource," *The Bell Journal of Economics*, vol.9, Autumn 1978, pp.385-95; Ulph, A. M., and G. M. Folie, "Exhaustible Resources and Cartels - An Intertemporal Nash-Cournot Model," *Canadian Journal of Economics*, 1980; and Newberry, David M., "Oil Prices, Cartels, and the Problem of Dynamic Inconsistency," Economic Theory Discussion Paper No. 35, Department of Applied Economics, Cambridge University, Cambridge, U.K., 1980.

exploited first[10]. More generally, if the extraction costs are expected to rise at a rate i' (for whatever reason) as cumulative production increases, while i is the interest rate, then the royalty will grow at the rate (i - i'), rather than i. In other words, the rate of increase of the depletion premium must equal the rise in the opportunity cost of future use represented by the foregone interest rate i, minus the growth of future extraction costs at the rate i'.[11]

The effects of cumulative production on demand have also been investigated lately[12]. If the stock of a durable resource like gold or silver affects the demand for it, but if this stock also depreciates over time, then Hotelling's fundamental principle still holds. However, without depreciation, the growth of the stock may tend to force the price down as time goes on. More generally, with rising extraction costs and depreciating stock, the price will follow a U-shaped path. If the existing stock is augmented by new finds, price again falls initially but rises in the future. The combined effects of cumulative production and different types of market organization such as monopoly, oligopoly, and competition, have not been studied in detail.

The impact of uncertainty on the economics of natural extraction is the third principal area of investigation. Hotelling suggested that uncertainty would cause the exploratory activity of private producers to diverge from socially optimal levels due to two opposing mechanisms. First, certain landowners could benefit from the knowledge that exploration had been successful in neighboring tracts of land. Recent work tends to confirm that exploration activity will be socially suboptimal if potential resource owners wait for others to undertake the high initial risks and costs of exploratory work, thus hoping to get a "free ride." [13]The opposite effect occurs when those who make early finds can file claims and exclude competitors. This can lead to excessive and economically wasteful exploration based on a "gold-rust" mentality, as producers vie to succeed early and block competitors.

---

[10] Herfindahl, O. C., "Depletion and Economic Theory," in: Gaffney, M. (ed.), *Extractive Resources and Taxation*, University of Wisconsin Press, Madison, 1967; Heal, Geoffrey M. "The Relationship Between Price and Extraction Cost for a Resource with a Backstop Technology," *The Bell Journal of Economics*, vol.7, Autumn 1976, pp.371-78; Solow, Robert M. and Frederick Y. Wan, "Extraction Costs in the Theory of Exhaustible Resources," *The Bell Journal of Economics*, vol.7, Autumn 1976, pp.359-70; Weitzman, Martin L., "The Optimal Development of Resource Pools," *Journal of Economic Theory*, vol.12, June 1976, pp.351-64; and Hartwick, John M., "Exploitation of Many Deposits of an Exhaustible Resource," *Econometrica*, vol.46, January 1978, pp.201-18.

[11] Cummings, Robert G., "Some Extensions of the Theory of Exhaustible Resources," *Western Economic Journal*, vol.7, September 1969, pp. 201-10; Schulze, William D., "The Optimal Use of Non-renewable Resources: The Theory of Extraction," *Journal of Environmental Economics and Renewable Resources*, vol.1, May 1974, pp.53-73; Weinstein, Milton C., and Richard J. Zeckhauser, "The Optimal Consumption of Depletable Natural Resources," *Quarterly Journal of Economics*, vol.89, August 1975, pp.371-92; Peterson, Frederick M. and Anthony C. Fisher, "The Exploitation of Extractive Resources: A Survey," *Economic Journal*, vol.87, December 1977, pp.681-721; and Levhari, David and Nissan Liviatan, "Notes on Hotelling's Economics of Exhaustible Resources," *Canadian Journal of Economics*, vol.10, May 1977, pp.177-92.

[12] Levhari, David, and Robert S. Pindyck, "The Pricing of Durable Exhaustible Resources," MIT Energy Laboratory Working Paper No. EL79-053WP, MIT Cambridge, MA, 1979; Pindyck, Robert S., "Optimal Exploration and Production of Nonrenewable Resources," *Journal of Political Economy*, vol.86, October 1978, pp.841-61; and Steward, Marion B. "Monopoly and the Intertemporal Production of a Durable Extractable Resource," *Quarterly Journal of Economics*, vol.94, February 1980, pp.99-111.

[13] Joseph E. Stiglitz, "The Efficiency of Market Prices in Long-Run Allocations in the Oil Industry," in: Gerard M. Brannon (ed.), *Studies in Energy Tax Policy*, Ballinger Publ. Co., Cambridge MA, 1975, pp. 87-94; and Frederick M. Peterson, "Two Externalities in Petroleum Exploration," in: Gerard M. Brannon (ed.).

Recent work on the uncertainty of supply seems to indicate that for deposits of uniform quality, producers who are uncertain as to the size of their deposits will extract at a slower rate than those who are certain of their resource stocks, in order to avoid running out of resources suddenly[14]. Other studies have also investigated the behavior of producers who are willing to incur additional exploration costs in order to reduce supply uncertainty, under various conditions[15].

The effects of uncertainty on the demand side have also been examined lately[16]. If the uncertainty in future prices increases with time, risk-averse producers will prefer to increase output earlier. However, if the uncertainty is constant (or decreasing), the same resource owner is likely to shift production into the future, since the volume of output at risk will be less as the resource depletes. More obviously, when there is the likelihood of the demand for the resource collapsing at some future date, extraction will be accelerated.

Unfortunately, many of the assumptions used in theoretical models are generally unrealistic in the real world of resource extraction. In fact, rarely, if ever, can we observe price patterns as those described by the fundamental principle. At the macro level, prices of depletable resources over time appear either to have fallen in real terms over extended periods of time, or apparently have remained constant[17]. In the area of oil and natural gas, for example, market prices fell steadily in real terms through the post-World War II period until the late 1960s or early 1970s. Similar price declines affected the U.S. coal mining industry. Ensuing price increases appear to have been more the result of ad hoc actions (OPEC, with regard toward oil prices, and environmental and safety regulations for U.S. coal, etc.), rather than the result of precisely calculated profit-maximizing behavior of depletable resource owners.

The reason for this discrepancy between theoretical conclusions and practical reality is that the analysis abstracts from the necessary constraints of depletable resource production. Extraction rates from any given deposit cannot be varied at will, but must be based on given geological and technological considerations. Given a newly found resource deposit, a prospective producer usually has a certain amount of freedom to choose (a) the data of start-up of production, and (b) the optimal production rate. However, once he has determined those two parameters, production

---

[14] Kemp, Murray C., "How to Eat a Cake of Unknown Size," in: *Three Topics in the Theory of International Trade*, North Holland Publ. Co., Amsterdam, 1976, pp. 297-308; Gilbert, Richard J., "Optimal Depletion of an Uncertain Stock," *Review of Economic Studies*, vol.46, January 1979, pp.47-57; Loury, Glenn C., "The Optimal Exploitation of an Unknown Reserve," *Review of Economic Studies*, vol.45, October 1978, pp.621-36.

[15] Arrow, Kenneth J. and S. Chang, "Optimal Pricing Use, and Exploration of Uncertain Natural Resource Stocks, "Technical Report No. 31, Dept. of Economics, Harvard University, Cambridge MA, 1978; Hoel, Michael, "Resource Extraction, Uncertainty, and Learning," *The Bell Journal of Economics*, vol.9, Autumn 1978, pp.642-45; Pindyck, Robert S., "Uncertainty and the Pricing of Exhaustible Resources," MIT Energy Laboratory Working Paper No. EL79-021WP, MIT, Cambridge MA, 1979; and Devarajan, Shantayanan, and Anthony C. Fisher, "Exploration and Scarcity," CRM Working Paper No. IP-290, Univ. of Calif., Berkeley, Calif., 1980.

[16] Lewis, Tracy R., "Monopoly Exploitation of an Exhaustible Resource," *Journal of Environmental Economics and Management*, vol.3, October 1976, pp.198-204; Dasgupta, Partha S., and Geoffrey M. Heal, "The Optimal Depletion of Exhaustible Resources," *Review of Economic Studies*, Symposium 1974, 1974, pp. 3-28; Long Ngo Van, "Resource Extraction Under Uncertainty About Possible Nationalization," *Journal of Economic Theory*, vol.10, February 1975, pp.42-53.

[17] See H. J. Barnett and C. H. Morse, *Scarcity and Growth*, Johns Hopkins Press, Baltimore, 1963; and V. K. Smith (ed.), *Scarcity and Growth Reconsidered*, Johns Hopkins Univ. Press, Baltimore, 1979.

economics and technological constraints usually force him to stay within relatively narrow limits for the output rate.

The Socially Optimal Price and Extraction Rate of an Exhaustible Resource

Notation:

$x(t)$ $=$ quantity of exhaustible resource that has been extracted by time t

$\dot{x}(t) = \dfrac{dx}{dt} =$ current extraction rate

z $=$ rate of use of best alternative source

$\dot{x} + z$ $=$ total consumption rate

$u(\dot{x} + z)$ $=$ utility of consumption

c $=$ cost of extraction

i $=$ interest rate

$k(t)$ $=$ unit cost of alternative supply

NB $=$ present value of benefits minus costs

a $=$ available amount of exhaustible resource; thus the constraint on exhaustion is $x \le a$

Problem

$$\text{Max} \quad \int_0^\infty [u(\dot{x}+z) - c\dot{x} - kz]e^{-it} \, dt \; ; \qquad (A3.13)$$

subject to

$$x(t) \le a .$$

The Lagrangian function for this problem is:

$$\text{Max} \quad \int_0^\infty [u(\dot{x}+z) - c\dot{x} - kz]e^{-it} + \lambda(a-x)e^{-it}]dt . \qquad (A3.14)$$

Efficiency conditions (Euler-Lagrange) for x:

$$\frac{d}{dt}\{[u'-c]e^{-it}\} = \begin{cases} -\lambda e^{-it} & t \ge T \\ 0 & t = T \end{cases} \qquad (A3.15)$$

where T is the time of exhaustion determined by

$$x(T) = a.$$

Efficiency condition for z:

$$z \begin{Bmatrix} = \\ \geq \end{Bmatrix} 0 \leftrightarrow u' - k \begin{Bmatrix} < \\ = \end{Bmatrix} 0 \qquad\qquad\text{(A3.16)}$$

from which

$$u' \begin{Bmatrix} < \\ = \end{Bmatrix} k(t) \text{ for } t \begin{Bmatrix} < \\ \geq \end{Bmatrix} 0. \qquad\qquad\text{(A3.17)}$$

Now u' = marginal utility = p = efficiency price of one unit of the exhaustible resource at time t. From (A3.15)

$$[u'-c]e^{-it} = \text{constant} = \mu \text{ for } t < T$$

or $\qquad u' = c + \mu e^{it}.$ $\qquad\qquad\qquad\qquad\text{(A3.18)}$

To determine μ observe (A3.17) for $t = T$

$$u'(T) = k(T).$$

By continuity, using (A3.18):

$$u'(T) = c + \mu e^{iT}; \qquad\qquad\qquad\text{(A3.19)}$$

yielding

$$\mu = [k(T) - c]e^{-iT}.$$

Thus

$$p = u'(t) = c + [k(T) - c]e^{i(t-T)}; \qquad\qquad\text{(A3.20)}$$

and therefore, the price of the exhaustible resource rises continuously from

$c + [k(T) - c]e^{-iT}$ at t=0, to k(T) at t=T

The premium $[k(T) - c]e^{-iT}$ must be considered a scarcity rent. Its level depends critically on the time T to exhaustion. This time may be determined by equating supply and demand. Notice that from time zero to T only the exhaustible resource is used and that at $t = T$ there is a complete switchover to the foreign resource.

$$u'(\dot{x}) = p(t)$$

determines consumption $\dot{x}$ as

$$\dot{x} = (u')^{-1}(p(t)) .$$

Then the time of exhaustion T is given by

$$a = \int_0^T \dot{x}dt = \int_0^T (u')^{-1}(p(t)dt .$$

As an illustration assume

$$u(\dot{x}) = b \log \dot{x} .$$

Thus $u'(\dot{x}) = b/\dot{x}$

$$\dot{x} = \frac{b}{p(t)} = \frac{b}{c+[k-c]e^{i(t-T)}}$$

$$a = (b/c) \int_0^T [1+(k/c - 1)e^{i(t-T)}]^{-1}.dt$$

$$= (b/c) \int_0^T h.[1+he^{it}]^{-1}.dt = (k/c - 1)e^{-iT}$$

$$= -(b/ic) \ln[h+e^{-it}] \Big|_0^T$$

$$= (b/ic) \ln[h/(h+e^{-iT})] = (b/c) \ln[he^{iT}/(1+he^{iT})]$$

$$= (b/c) \ln[1-c/k(T)]$$

Alternatively let

$$u(\dot{x}) = \beta\dot{x} - (b/2)\dot{x}^2 \text{ ; and } k(T) = k .$$

Thus $u'(\dot{x}) = \beta - b\dot{x} = p$

$$\dot{x} = (\beta/b) - (p/b)$$

$$= (\beta/b) - (1/b)[c + (k-c)e^{i(t-T)}]$$

$$a = (\beta/b)T - (1/b)\int_0^T [c + (k - c)e^{i(t-T)}].dt$$

$$a = [(\beta-c)/b]T - [(k-c)/ib][1-e^{-iT}]$$

The right-hand side is an increasing function of T so that (A3.21) has a unique root. For small values of iT, a Taylor expansion yields

$$1 - e^{-iT} = iT ;$$

$$a = [((\beta-c)/b) - ((k-c)/b)]T ;$$

and $T = ab/(\beta-k) .$

The time to exhaustion increases with the cost k of the alternative source, the available amount a and the rate b at which marginal utility decreases with consumption.

References

Baumol, W.J. and D.F. Bradford, "Optimal Departures from Marginal Cost Pricing", *American Economic Review*, June 1970, pp. 265-283.

Hotelling, H., "The Economics of Exhaustible Resources", *Journal of Political Economy*, vol. 39, April 1931, pp. 131-175.

Little, I.M.D., and J.A. Mirrlees, *Project Appraisal and Planning for Developing Countries*, Basic Books, New York, 1974.

Munasinghe, M., "Electric Power Pricing Policy", Staff Working Paper No. 340, The World Bank, Washington DC, June 1979a.

Munasinghe, M., *The Economics of Power System Reliability and Planning*, Johns Hopkins Univ. Press, Baltimore MD, 1979b.

Munasinghe, M., "The Costs Incurred by Residential Electricity Consumers Due to Power Failures", *Journal of Consumer Research*, March 1980a, pp. 361-369.

Munasinghe, M., "A New Approach to System Planning", *IEEE Transactions on Power Apparatus and Systems*, vol. PAS-79, May-June 1980b.

Munasinghe, M. and M. Gellerson, "Economic Criteria for Optimizing Power System Reliability Levels", *The Bell Journal of Economics*, vol.10, Spring 1979, pp. 353-365.

Samii, M. Vajed, "Economic Growth and Optimal Rate of Oil Extraction", *OPEC Review*, vol. 3, Autumn 1979, pp. 16-26.

Squire, L. and H. Van der Tak, *Economic Analysis of Projects*, Johns Hopkins Univ. Press, Baltimore MD, 1975.

Chapter 4

PRACTICAL APPLICATION OF INTEGRATED NATIONAL ENERGY PLANNING (INEP) USING MICROCOMPUTERS[1]

4.1 Introduction

The development of the concepts and methodology of Integrated National Energy Planning (INEP), and its subsequent application, can be traced to the energy crisis of the 1970s. Before that period energy was relatively cheap, and any imbalances between supply and demand were invariably dealt with by augmenting the supply. The emphasis was more on the engineering and technological aspects. Furthermore, planning was confined to the various energy subsectors, such as electricity, oil and coal, with little coordination between them.

From the mid-1970s onwards the rapidly increasing costs of all forms of energy, in lock-step with increasing world oil prices, stimulated the development of new analytical tools and policies with the following results. First, the need became apparent for greater coordination between energy supply and demand options, and for the more effective use of demand management and conservation (Munasinghe 1983, ERG 1985). Secondly, energy-macro-economic links began to be explored more systematically. Thirdly, disaggregate analysis of both supply and demand within the energy sector identified greater opportunities for inter-fuel substitution (especially away from oil). Fourthly, the analytical and modelling tools for energy subsector planning became more sophisticated (Munasinghe 1979). Fifthly, greater reliance was placed on economic principles, including the techniques of shadow pricing in the developing countries (Munasinghe 1980b). The INEP approach makes use of all these separate threads. Several attempts using various types of energy models were made, particularly in the second half of the 1970s, and it was soon recognized that the constraints imposed by limited data, skilled manpower, and time, posed formidable problems, especially in developing countries. Many of the early models, implemented on mainframe computers, were designed to be as all-encompassing as possible, and therefore proved to be too large and unwieldy. On the other hand, more specific models tended to overlook important energy sector or macroeconomic linkages. Finally, most models were not policy-oriented and were often treated as mere academic exercises. This initial learning process led to a more hierarchical analytical framework that recognizes at least three distinct levels of analysis, including energy-macroeconomic, energy sector, and energy subsector, as well as the interactions between these levels(Munasinghe 1980a). This approach also gives a better policy focus. More recently, the availability of microcomputers has provided analysts in

---

[1] Edited version of a paper presented at the United Nations Conference on Microcomputer Applications in Developing Countries, held in New York in September 1985; and subsequently published in *Natural Resources Forum*, vol.10, February 1986, pp.17-38. The computer modelling was carried out with the assistance of Peter Meier.

developing countries with a relatively cheap, powerful and flexible tool to develop and apply some of these ideas (Meier 1985, Munasinghe et al. 1985).

This chapter describes the development and implementation of a microcomputer-based, policy-oriented, hierarchical modelling framework for INEP in Sri Lanka. Details of the INEP methodology, and analytical models, are presented in the next section. Thereafter, a brief introduction is provided to the energy situation in Sri Lanka. Finally, the different scenarios studied, and the main policy issues and options derived from the use of the modelling framework, are summarized.

4.2 Methodology and Analytical Model for Integrated National Energy Planning (INEP)

Methodology

Because of the many interactions and non-market forces that shape and affect energy sectors of every economy, decisionmakers in an increasing number of countries have realized that energy sector investment planning, pricing, and management should be carried out on an integrated basis, e.g., within an integrated national energy planning framework which helps to analyze the whole range of energy policy options over a long period (see Chapter 2 for a more detailed description of the INEP methodology).

Coordinated energy planning and pricing require detailed analyses of the interrelationships between the various economic sectors and their potential energy requirements, on the one hand, and the capabilities and advantages and disadvantages of the various forms of energy such as electric power, petroleum, natural gas, coal, and traditional fuels (e.g. firewood, crop residues and dung) to satisfy these requirements, on the other hand. Non-conventional sources, whenever they turn out to be viable alternatives, must also be fitted into this framework. The analysis applied both to the industrial world and to developing countries like Sri Lanka. In the former, the complex and intricate relationships between the various economic sectors, and the prevalence of private market decisions on both the energy demand supply sides, make analysis and forecasting of policy consequences a difficult task. In developing countries, substantial levels of market distortions, shortages of foreign exchange as well as human and financial resources for development, large numbers of poor households whose basic needs somehow have to be met, greater reliance on traditional fuels, and relative paucity of data, add to the already complicated problems faced by energy planners everywhere.

Integrated national energy planning is motivated by the need for a flexible and continuously updated energy strategy that will promote the best use of energy resources in order to further overall socioeconomic development and improve welfare. Energy planning is, therefore, an essential part of national economic planning, and should be carried out and implemented in close coordination with the latter. In energy planning, the principal emphasis in on the detailed and disaggregated analysis of the energy sector, its interactions with the rest of the economy, and the main interactions within the various energy subsectors themselves.

The hierarchical framework depicted in Figure 2.1 (Chapter 2) clarified the scope of integrated national energy planning and supply-demand management. At the highest and most aggregate level, the energy sector is a part of the whole economy and energy planning requires analysis of the links between the energy sector and the rest of the economy. The second level of INEP treats the energy sector as a separate entity composed of subsectors such as electricity, petroleum products and so on. The third, and most disaggregate level pertains to planning within each of the energy subsectors. As indicated in Chapter 2, the three levels of INEP merge and overlap considerably in practice.

Integrated national energy planning (INEP) should result in the development of a coherent set of energy supply and energy demand management (ESM and EDM) activities which can meet the needs of many interrelated and often conflicting national objectives. Energy planning must therefore be developed to meet the overall national objectives as efficiently as possible. The specific tasks of INEP and ESM and EDM include: (a) the determination of the detailed energy needs of the economy to achieve growth and development targets, (b) the choosing of the mix energy sources to meet future energy requirements at lowest costs, (c) the minimizing of unemployment, (d) the conservation of energy resources and elimination of wasteful consumption, (e) the diversification of supply and reduction of dependence on foreign sources, (f) the meeting of national security and defence requirements, (g) the supply of basic energy needs to the poor, (h) the saving of scarce foreign exchange, (i) the contribution of specific energy demand/supply measures to possible priority development of special regions or sectors of the economy, (j) the raising of sufficient revenues from energy sales to finance energy sector development, (k) price stability, (l) the preservation of the environment, and so on.

The steps involved in the planning procedure usually include energy supply and demand analysis and forecasting, energy balancing, policy formulation and impact analysis to meet short-, medium-, and long-range goals, and the determination of a National Energy Strategy (See Figure 2.2 in Chapter 2).

In a recent review of the national energy planning experience in developing countries, Wilbanks (1987) echoes the consensus that formal national energy planning has seldom made much of a difference in important energy decisions, despite wide recognition of its importance. This clearly reflects the formidable constraints that come into play in implementing such a process.

The chief constraints that limit effective policy formulation and implementation are: (a) a poor institutional framework; (b) insufficient manpower and other resources; (c) weak analytical tools; (d) inadequate policy instruments; and (e) lack of political will.

It is important to note that all of the computerized activities may be first carried out manually, at a relatively simple level, and only later, as data and local analytical skills improve, should more-sophisticated computer modelling be pursued. Furthermore, while computer models are being developed energy policy formulation should not be neglected, key options may be examined using more-conventional techniques, and appropriate decisions taken and implemented (e.g. energy pricing, demand management and conservation, reforestation, efficient cooking stoves, choice of renewable supply technologies, etc.). Such early decisions will facilitate timely action on important issues, and they may subsequently be coherently incorporated into the longer-term national strategy when the more comprehensive computer runs are carried out. Great care must be taken to ensure that the models represent the real world as accurately as possible, and they should be designed to provide answers to the questions that senior decisionmakers might be expected to ask.

The Analytical Model

The analytical approach for integrated national energy planning is illustrated in Figure 4.1, which is the modelling analogue of the conceptual framework shown in Figure 2.1. The models have been implemented (in 1985) on a MS-DOS compatible, 16-bit micro-processor with 256 kilobytes of main memory, two floppy disk drives and a 10 megabyte hard disc (optional). The modelling begins with an analysis of the overall macroeconomy in the first of three modules of the energy macroeconomic accounting framework (ENMAC). The outputs of this step include projections of the sectoral decomposition of GDP and non-energy merchandise trade.

The RESGEN model, which represents the national energy system as a flexible network linking disaggregate energy sources with various end-uses, is run next. The demand equations in this model are driven by the GDP estimates passed from the macromodel. Other inputs are passed from the more-detailed subsector models; the refinery configuration and yield coefficients are drawn from the refinery optimization model, and the estimates of fuelwood demand are taken from the fuel model.

As part of making the energy supply-demand balance, RESGEN estimates which energy facilities must be built to meet the demand, thereby providing a year-by-year estimate of investment requirements. The basis for the electric sector investments, which account for the bulk of the total energy investment, is the generation plan of the Ceylon Electricity Board (CEB); because future electric demand scenarios result in changes in future electric load growth, the analysis includes an examination of the timing of capacity increments. An optimal dispatch model built into RESGEN also provides detailed estimates of CEB fuel consumption as a function of plant availabilities, hydro-energy limitations and the system load factor.

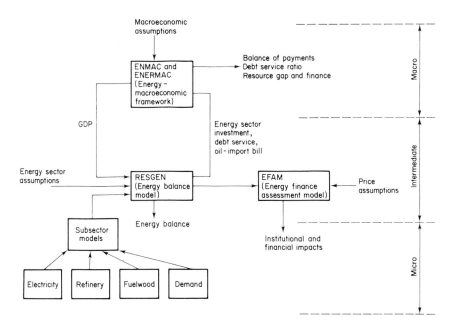

Figure 4.1: The Hierarchical Modelling Approach for Integrated National Energy Planning

The investment outlays, and their concomitant debt service obligations are passed back to the macromodel, together with the oil import bill (and the smaller earnings from bunkers and petroleum product exports). These energy sector transactions are merged with the non-energy transactions in a second module of the macroeconomic model. Finally, the third module provides overall estimates of the balance of payments, the financing necessary to cover the external resource gap, the debt service ratio and other macroeconomic impacts.

The RESGEN energy model passes the domestic energy transactions (e.g. sales from the Ceylon Petroleum Company to distributors, or Ceylon Electricity Board sales to consumers) to the Energy Finance Assessment Model (EFAM), which assembles a picture of the energy sector financial flows among the key institutions and consumers in the sector. EFAM also provides estimates of the Government revenue from the sector (from petroleum product taxes, the Business Turnover Tax on energy institutions, customs duties, etc.) The financial flows are obtained by multiplying the physical energy flows (from REGSEN) by the appropriate set of prices and taxes; EFAM can therefore be used to assess the implications of alternative energy pricing and taxation schemes.

Another more sophisticated multi-sector energy-macroeconomic model (ENERMAC) is also available, to study wage, income and price effects, factor substitution in production, structural change, etc. ENERMAC has a transactions matrix involving 10 goods/sectors, including three energy-producing sectors, crude oil imports, and six energy-consuming sectors (Munasinghe et al. 1985). The model produces a set of national accounts and balance-of-payments consistent with the corresponding outputs generated by ENMAC, as well as equilibrium wages and prices. The economy grows through sectoral investments, and appropriate sector-specific production functions are used to produce sectoral outputs, as the model simulates year-by-year into the future. ENERMAC is not fully linked to the other models, but is used in parallel, as a complement, to study specific policy impacts in a self-consistent manner.

4.3 The Economy and Energy Sector

Energy-Macroeconomic Relationships in Sri Lanka

Sri Lanka, situated in the Indian Ocean, is a small island of area 65,610 km², which includes 959 km² of inland water. The land area is compact, with a central hilly region. The rivers which spring up from this region (the most important of them is the "Mahaweli Ganga") play an important economic role in providing hydroelectric power. Another major indigenous source of energy is fuelwood. Forest cover has declined from about 44% of total land area in 1955 to about 24% in 1981, due mainly to agricultural conversion and fuelwood use.

From 1970 to 1977 Sri Lanka was essentially a closed economy, with strict exchange control regulations and import controls. This period was marked by low investments and low growth patterns; GDP grew at only 2.9% per annum on average, which was well below both the previous performance of the economy (4.4% per annum in the 1960s) and its inherent potential. One of the hardest hit sectors was the manufacturing industry -- due to the sluggish economy and the poor investment climate, investments averaged less than 16% of GDP during this period.

During the past decade international oil prices have twice risen sharply -- in 1973-4 and in 1979-80. The overall increase was from less than US$2 per barrel in the early 1970s to US$27 per barrel by 1984. During both oil shocks, the economic growth rate declined in industrial as well as in developing countries. The oil-importing developing countries continued to be highly vulnerable to events in the world economy, not only because of high oil import costs, but also due to shrinkage of export markets, official aid flows, access to international credit, etc. Each downturn in the developed countries had corresponding adverse effects on the less-developed countries. The impact of these two oil upheavals on the Sri Lanka economy is analysed below.

The impact of the first oil shock of 1973-74 was somewhat cushioned in the Sri Lanka economy by a combination of factors. The strict exchange control regulations coupled with the slow economic growth ensured that the burden of oil imports was manageable during the following few years. Though the oil import bill was a significant factor in the balance of payments, oil imports fell due to the prevailing economic climate. The turning points in the economy occurred in 1970 and 1977 with the change of governments and the very different economic policies adopted in each case.

From 1970 to 1977 the economy was highly protected from external shocks by the closed economic policies that prevailed. As a result of those policies, the first shock had no significant impact on GDP growth. Tables 4.1 and 4.2 give the keys years in which significant changes took place in the consumption trends of petroleum products and in the petroleum oil import bill. From 1973 to 1977 the average growth rate of petroleum demand fell by 3.3%. This could be interpreted as a general response to the doubling of petroleum prices in a difficult economic period. Table 4.2 shows that up to 1977 the cost of oil imports was not a source of serious concern to Sri Lanka.

Table 4.1

Consumption Trends for Major Petroleum Products[a]

Product	Consumption (1000 Tons)					Avg. Ann. Growth Rates(%)		
	1970	1977	1980	1983	1986	1970-77	1977-80	1980-86
Gasoline	148.4	111.6	107.7	117.5	130.6	-4.0	-1.2	21.3
Kerosene	272.5	213.1	188.7	159.1	154.2	-3.5	-4.0	-18.3
Autodiesel	254.5	261.4	399.5	464.3	487.3	4.0	15.2	22.0
Industrial Diesel	87.9	46.3	61.0	295.9	36.0	-8.8	9.6	--
Fuel Oil	208.8	134.7	247.2	253.1	129.0	-6.1	22.4	--
Power Sector Consumption:	133.0	7.0	58.5	--	--	-34.3	102.9	--
Fuel Oil	133.0	7.0	45.0	--	--	--	--	--
Diesel	--	--	13.5	--	--	--	--	--

a Excludes Re-export and Bunker Sales.
Source: Ceylon Petroleum Corporation

Table 4.2

Petroleum Import Bill
(US$ Millions)

	1970	1977	1980	1983	1986
A. Petroleum Imports	10.0	160.0	489.0	468.0	197.0
B. Petroleum Re-Exports	5.0	64.0	181.0	106.0	84.0
C. Net Petroleum Imports	5.0	96.0	308.0	362.0	113.0
D. Non-Petroleum Exports	337.0	667.0	864.0	953.0	1132.0
E. C as Percentage of D	1.5	14.2	35.6	38.0	10.0
US$ = Rs.	5.2	15.6	18.0	25.0	28.5

Source: Sri Lanka Customs

With the liberalization of the economy in 1977, the growth rate of GDP from 1977 to 1982 averaged more than 6%. It is creditable that this was accomplished in a period of considerable international economic turmoil -- first, international inflation accelerated (led by the doubling of oil prices), then the recession in the developed countries reduced demand for exports and constrained aid flows. However, the second oil shock of 1979- 80 had much more severe repercussions than the first, because of the open economic policy. Table 4.3 gives a clear picture of the impact of the two oil shocks. The periods are demarcated as shown because there were significant economic reactions and repercussions. The first period is 1970-73, the pre-embargo; then the 1973-77 adjustment period for the first oil shock. The years 1977-80 include the period of liberalization of the economy and the second oil shock; and 1980-86 gives the adjustment period after the second oil shock.

The rapidly improving economic growth during the post-1977 period resulted in an accelerated demand for electricity (which previously, during 1973-77, grew at an average rate of 4.7%), due to the low tariff structure and untapped potential markets. The demand was met totally by hydro-power. During 1977-80, without taking into consideration the power cuts that prevailed, electricity growth averaged 10.2%. This had a significant impact on the economy because the supply had to be supplemented by thermal generation. The marginal increase in the demand for commercial energy in Sri Lanka is directly linked to the size of petroleum imports, regardless of whether these increases take the form of higher electricity consumption or direct consumption of petroleum products.

Thus, after 1977 the combination of increased consumption and a doubling of oil prices resulted in a rapidly growing oil import bill. By 1981, the net oil import bill more than tripled and the proportion of export earnings devoted to importing oil rose from 15% to 39%. The rupee, which was pegged to the dollar (floating exchange rate), depreciated in value from Rs 15.608 in 1978 to Rs 23.529 in 1983. The manifestation of these foreign exchange difficulties along with international price increases has been a high inflation rate. Inflation, as measured on all major price indices, accelerated sharply between 1978 and 1980, before reducing significantly by about 1984, due to restrictive macroeconomic policies. The average inflation rate between 1984 and 1986 was 4.7%.

Table 4.3
Evolution of GDP,
Energy Demand and Prices for the Period 1970-1986

	Pre-Embargo 1970-73	Adj. Period for the First Oil Shock 1973-77	Intermediate Period 1977-80	Adjustment Period for the Second Oil Shock	
				1980-82	1982-86
GDP Growth Rate[1]	2.2%	3.4%	6.8%	5.4%	4.8%
Growth Rate of Total Energy Demand[2]	--	2.8%	2.3%	2.5%	--
Electricity Demand[3]	7.6%	4.7%	10.2%	10.1%	7.3%
Non-Electricity Demand[4]					
-- Demand for Petroleum Production	0.9%	-5.2%	7.2%	14.7%	-6.7%
-- Demand for Non-fuelwood Energy[5]	--	6.2%	0.4%	-0.2%	--
Changes in Energy Prices					
-- Electricity Prices[6]	-3.12%	-3.64%	32.6%	37.8%	--
-- Petroleum Product Prices[7]	11.2%	14.2%	30.0%	-3.0%	7.1%

[1] Annual average rate of change of real GDP for each specified period.
[2] Annual average rate of change of total energy demand (Commercial and non-commercial energy)
[3] Annual average growth rate of electricity demand (either in orig. unit or converted unit).
[4] Annual average growth rate of demand for each specified period.
[5] Includes all non-commercial energy sources such as firewood, crop residues, cow dung, etc., converted into a common unit (MTOE).
[6] Changes in weighted average prices (or price index of all commercial energy sources).
[7] Weighted average of petroleum product prices.

The recent decline in world prices had no effect on demand because the dollar price decrease in the price of crude was offset by the exchange rate fluctuations with the Rupee declining in value against the dollar.

Energy Supply and Demand in Sri Lanka

Principal energy sources

Sri Lanka has two major indigenous sources of energy -- hydroelectric power and fuelwood. The country's potential hydroelectric power is estimated to be in the region of 2000 MW, of which 369 MW has already been developed, with another 572 MW being harnessed when the "Mahaweli" scheme comes into operation. By the end of the decade, 50% of the potential capacity will have been realized. Hydroelectric power is used primarily to meet base load energy generation, whilst gas turbines operate in the peaking mode and also provide spinning reserve. This pattern is expected to continue for at least the next five years.

Although reliable data on fuelwood supply are difficult to obtain, the estimates clearly demonstrate the precarious and unsustainable nature of the fuelwood supply. Over the past two decades, incremental wood production -- from the natural regeneration of forests, agricultural residues and rubber replanting, etc. -- has fallen far behind consumption, and today this source accounts for less than half of the estimated annual consumption of around 5 million tons. The balance of wood supply has come mainly from the denudation of Sri Lanka's natural forest cover, which had declined from about 44% of total land area in 1956 to about 24% in 1981.

The balance of domestic demand is met by oil imports. The crude oil imported is refined into other petroleum products which are either used in the domestic market of are re-exported. Table 4.4 shows that the main types of oil imports are crude oil, kerosene and auto-diesel. Table 4.5 gives the energy consumption (petroleum and electricity) during and after the two major oil shocks.

Figure 4.2 shows the typical Sri Lanka energy supply pattern in 1983. Fuelwood (67%) dominates gross energy supply, while oil is at 24%, oil-fired electricity at 4% and hydroelectricity at 5%. Oil is the most important source in supplying useful energy or net supply (46%), with fuelwood at 38%, and 16% of electricity being supplied by both hydro- and oil (useful energy was calculated by their end-use efficiency -- see footnotes to Table 4.4 for the coefficients and conversion of hydro-power to t.o.e.)

Energy has only recently become a serious problem in Sri Lanka. The oil price increase of 1973 made petroleum, which supplies one-third of the country's primary energy requirements, a significant factor in the balance of payments. A combination of slow economic growth and a policy of stringent import controls ensured that the burden of oil imports was manageable after the first oil price increase. At the same time, the addition of new hydroelectric capacity resulted in a comfortable balance between electricity supply and demand, thus containing a demand for oil by substituting hydro-generation for thermal generation. Table 4.5 indicates that the amount of fuel and diesel oil used for thermal generation until 1979 was very low.

Table 4.4

Energy Supply (Domestic and Imported) in toe

	1970	1971	1972	1973	1974	1975	1976	1977	1978	1979	1980	1981	1982	1983
Domestic Sources														
Hydro	177	--	203	167	239	258	266	291	327	350	355	377	385	507
Fuelwood and Bagasse	--	1226	1294	1561	1561	1595	1618	2326	2234	2271	2379	2476	2380	3851
Net Imports[a]														
(i.e. imports − exports)														
Crude Oil	1819	1549	1818	1753	1526	1464	1447	1529	1443	1444	1861	1710	1940	1491
Naphtha	-115	-77	-117	-128	-100	-127	-108	-100	-74	-99	-130	-91	-75	-54
Gasoline	32	12	--	0	0	0	0	1	3	6	0	0	0	14
Av. Gas	2	0	--	1	1	1	0	0	0	0	0	0	0	0
Kerosene	98	68	23	22	9	0	9	32	25	41	0	-1	41	54
Avtur	0	-101	-81	-85	-73	-80	-68	-52	-25	-8	-134	-58	-86	-63
Auto-Diesel	56	42	17	8	8	0	8	26	82	198	42	110	183	403
Hy/M Diesel	-73	-80	-72	-72	-64	-65	-68	-74	-68	-59	-49	-36	-8	-38
Fuel-Oil	-43	-385	-443	-437	-314	-340	-408	-418	-350	-372	-489	-439	-431	316

a There are no known sources of domestic oil or petroleum products.
   Sri Lanka imports crude oil which is refined -- the negative values indicate the re-export of refined oils.

N.B. Conversion factors and coefficients based on efficiency of an average thermal base load plant:

crude oil	1 tonne	= 1.03 t.o.e.;	LPG	1 tonne	= 1.06 t.o.e.
gasoline/naptha	1 tonne	= 1.06 t.o.e.;	aviation gasoline	1 tonne	= 1.06 t.o.e.
fuel-oil	1 tonne	= 0.98 t.o.e.;	kerosene/avture	1 tonne	= 1.05 t.o.e.
diesolene	1 tonne	= 1.05 t.o.e.;	fuelwood	1 tonne	= 0.45 t.o.e.
bagasse	1 tonne	= 0.40 t.o.e.;	charcoal	1 tonne	= 0.65 t.o.e.
coal	1 tonne	= 0.70 t.o.e.;	bitumen/solvents	1 tonne	= 0.89 t.o.e.

Energy equivalent:
Hydro-electricity generation (fossil fuel replacement)
1000 kWH = 0.24 t.o.e.

Since 1978, with the rapid improvement in economic performance following the adoption of a market oriented development strategy, the amount of fuel and diesel oil used for thermal generation increased dramatically. Along with this change, there has been a substantial increase in demand for all forms of commercial energy, which rose in aggregate at a rate of 8.8% per annum in the period 1978-80. Petroleum consumption has grown even more rapidly because of the increased demand for electricity in the post-1977 period, which had to be met by increased thermal generation. Table 4.5 shows that for 1983, oil for thermal generation in the form of diesel and fuel oil has increased very rapidly.

Table 4.5

Basic Energy Consumption in Sri Lanka

		Pre-Embargo 1973	Adjustment Period 1974	Intermediate Period 1979	Adjustment Period Second Oil Shock 1983
1.	Electricity consump.	74.497	76.737	111.65	153.992
2.	Imports				
	Diesel	0.00	9.673	208.48	426.190
	Fuel-oil	0.00	0.00	0.00	0.000
	Crude Oil	1805.83	1575.518	1487.34	1536.732
3.	Fuel for thermal generation				
	Diesel	1.363	0.468	1.46	264.366
	Fuel-oil	19.078	4.186	18.11	48.989

Data from the Energy Balance Tables (in t.o.e.).

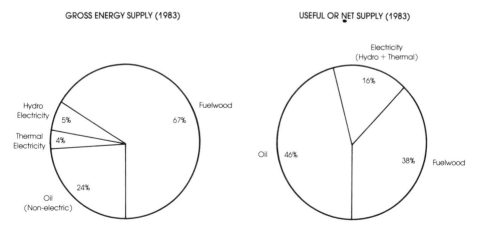

Figure 4.2: Sri Lanka Energy Supply Patterns

Sri Lanka has access to a variety of economically viable, non-conventional renewable energy resources -- solar, wind, biomass and minihydro -- which could be utilized to meet some of the country's energy demand in the medium term.

Solar energy: The location of Sri Lanka assures it of a relatively high and uniform level of insolation, which could be harnessed for both water heating and crop drying. A very few households currently use hot water; the main market for these heaters will initially lie in the commercial and tourist sectors. The use of solar energy for crop drying is an important alternative to be developed because tea and other crop processing industries consume over one million tons of fuelwood, or an estimated 20% of total consumption, per year.

Minihydro: While emphasis in Sri Lanka has been on large hydro-power schemes, about 10 MW of small schemes (5-250 kW range) have been operating in the tea estates of the central region since 1925. However, these have been abandoned because of the availability of cheap and reliable electricity from the national grid. In addition to the rehabilitation of existing plants, potential sites for minihydro schemes exist in the hilly areas and in the irrigation systems of the north central part of the island.

Other renewables: Apart from solar and minihydro, a number of renewable energy applications are promising. These include generation of biogas from animal wastes, producer gas from rice husks and coir briquettes, and wind energy for water pumping and electricity generation in isolated areas.

It is roughly estimated that all of these non-conventional sources will contribute only about 2% of total energy requirements in 1990, and less than 5% by the year 2000. Nevertheless, even this modest contribution will be useful because it will help to displace expensive imported oil and scarce domestic fuelwood at the margin.

Energy demand by source

Developing a detailed picture of sectoral energy consumption patterns in Sri Lanka has been hampered by the absence of reliable data at a sufficiently disaggregated level, even for the commercial fuels. With the inclusion of fuelwood the margin of error increases because estimates of fuelwood consumption tend to vary considerably depending on the source. However, the best estimate for 1984 for fuelwood (used in the energy balance tables) is about 9 million tons per year. A major effort has been made recently, to identify household fuelwood consumption at the disaggregate level, i.e., Urban, Suburban, Rural, Estate, by Wet Zone and Dry Zone (see Chapter 12).

Nevertheless, preliminary analysis suggests as typical the energy consumption pattern illustrated in Figure 4.3. Transport consumes 54% of Sri Lanka's commercial energy, while industry and commercial consume 26%, with domestic demand amounting to 17%, and others 3%. These percentages change dramatically when fuelwood is included in the analysis -- then domestic consumption accounts for the major share (68%), industry and commercial for 18%, transport for 13% and others for 1%.

Even though the data available are not as reliable as might be wished, some useful information about consumption patterns and trends is discernible.

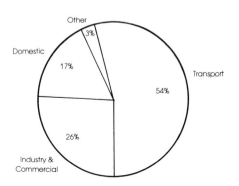

COMMERCIAL ENERGY
ELECTRICITY & OIL (1983)

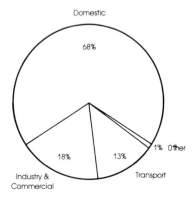

ALL ENERGY
ELECTRICITY, OIL & FUELWOOD (1983)

Figure 4.3: Sri Lanka Energy Consumption Patterns (1983)

Fuelwood: The absence of reliable data on fuelwood makes it difficult to identify the pattern in total energy demand and to correlate it with economic variables. Past estimates indicate no major shift from non-commercial to commercial energy sources over the last two decades. In fact, the data point towards an increase in the consumption of fuelwood as prices for commercial fuel (such as kerosene) increase.

Commercial energy: The consumption trends of commercial energy have closely reflected the overall performance of the economy. Between 1970 and 1977 the near stagnation of economic activity and growth in real incomes was reflected in a largely constant level of commercial energy demand, with rising electricity consumption being offset by an average 3.3% per annum fall in the demand for petroleum products. With the liberalization of the economy, demand for all forms of commercial energy has increased at an average rate of 8.8% per annum.

From 1970 to 1977 the consumption of all petroleum products fell, with the exception of LPG (used mainly for cooking) and diesel autofuel. This has been partly due to the virtual elimination of petroleum electricity generation that followed the addition of new hydroelectric capacity, and partly due to the response of demand to the doubling of prices in a difficult economic period. Since 1977 most products have shown increased growth in an improved economic climate. The oil demand in the power sector for thermal generation has shown more than average increases for diesel and fuel-oil. Only the consumption of gasoline and kerosene continued to fall after the post-1977 period. This was a reflection of the price-sensitivity of demand for both these fuels.

In contrast to petroleum consumption, electricity demand continued to grow at an average rate of 7% during the period 1970-77. This has been due to (a) the attractiveness of electricity as a source of energy (because there were no tariff increases during this period) and (b) the existence of a potential untapped market for electricity. Consequently, the demand for electricity showed less responsiveness to price and to changes in economic performance than petroleum products which rose in price by more than 50%. Since 1977 electricity demand has accelerated -- electricity sales grew at an average of 9.6% annually until 1980. This figure does not include the 3% reduction in demand due to prolonged power cuts in 1980 which was caused by the high growth rate of consumption and an unexpected and severe shortage of rainfall. The liberalised import of electrical appliances for domestic use has also contributed to the increase in sales to the household sector. The post-1977 increase in electricity consumption has had a significant impact on the economy, because this demand had to be met by increased imports of petroleum products for use in thermal generation.

Energy demand by sector

In the energy demand table that is presented below (Table 4.6), the sectors have been demarcated in the following manner: 1. industry/agro-industry; 2. transport; 3. household/agriculture; 4. government, commercial, and others.

Table 4.6

Sectoral Demand for Energy

Energy-consuming sector	1973	1974	1975	1977	1978	1979	1980	1981	1982
Industry/agro-ind.	781.78	716.52	699.31	886.09	966.25	989.01	909.25	998.20	1003.88
Transport	474.38	407.43	411.93	441.31	503.45	523.42	578.00	597.76	658.00
Household/ Agriculture	1604.51	1729.00	1804.35	1858.64	1763.63	1762.16	1914.90	1967.45	1908.75
Government, comm. and others	16.30	13.31	18.34	26.39	29.03	33.58	36.41	35.85	41.09
Total	2876.68	2869.31	2933.93	3212.43	3263.36	3308.17	3438.56	3599.26	3611.72

N.B. Units in million t.o.e.

Industry and agroindustry: The industrial sector accounts for more than 50% of electricity consumption, about 33% of petroleum consumption and about 25% of the fuelwood used in the country. Fuelwood is an important source of energy for agro-industry in the rural areas (e.g., tree crop processing). Eighteen large industrial organizations in the public sector account for 35% of total electricity sales; while 10 large companies account for over half of the sector's petroleum consumption. In Table 4.6 the sluggish growth of industry from 1973 to 1975 can be seen in the decline in energy demand during this period.

Transport: This sector depends entirely on petroleum products for energy, and transport therefore accounts for more than half of the total demand for petroleum products. Diesel is the predominant transport fuel (75% of the sales), which reflects the extensive public transport network, and also the policy of pricing diesel well below gasoline. As a result of this price differential, the proportion of diesel car registration rose from 14% in 1978 to 35% in 1980. To reverse this trend, the government raised the price of diesel to 60% the price of gasoline in 1980-81, and increased the licence fees of diesel cars to three times that of gasoline cars.

Household and agriculture: While per capita energy consumption in Sri Lanka is low by international standards, and most households use energy for only cooking and lighting, the energy requirements in the household sector account for nearly half of the country's primary energy consumption. The bulk of household energy requirements is met by fuelwood, which will continue to be the predominant source for the next decade. Only 13% of households have access to electricity, and the consumption of kerosene, which is mainly used for lighting, has been declining over the past decade in response to higher prices. The demand for energy in the household/agriculture sector will continue to grow with the increase in population and the rising standard of living.

Government, commercial and others: This sector consumes about 1% of the total demand for energy in the economy.

Energy Policy Coordinating Framework

During the period 1982-4 an effective organizational framework for overall energy coordination and integrated national energy planning and policy analysis was set up. In particular, a number of urgently needed and beneficial, specific activities have also been carried out, such as the preparation of the national energy strategy (NES), the national energy demand management and conservation programme (MEDMCP) and the national fuelwood conservation programme (NFCP).

Upto mid-1982 a major barrier to effective integrated energy planning was the large and varied number of ministries and line agencies involved in the different energy subsectors, with inadequate coordination among them (as depicted in the upper part of Figure 4.4.).

Electricity (Ministry of Power and Energy/Ceylon Electricity Board -- CEB; Mahaweli Ministry/Mahaweli Authority--MA);
Petroleum (Ministry of Industries and Scientific Affairs/Ceylon Petroleum Corporation--CPC);
Fuelwood (Ministry of Land and Land Development/Forest Department -- FD);
Overall science and energy policy and research and development (Natural Resources, Energy and Science Authority -- NARESA).

In late-1982 President Jayewardene set up an Energy Coordinating Team (ECT), under a senior energy advisor, to help to remedy this situation (see lower part of Figure 4.4). The rationale underlying the ECT concept was that the new framework, in the first instance, was not intended to be another bureaucracy that would seek to control the energy sector. The objective was to coordinate and facilitate the work of relevant ministries and existing line agencies, prevent duplication of effort and policy conflicts, supplement weak or neglected areas in the energy sector, and provide direct advisory inputs to the President. In any case, major structural changes in the organization of the energy sector could not be undertaken in the short-run. The ECT framework was the most practical method of formulating energy policy in an integrated manner and carrying out urgently needed tasks in the sector.

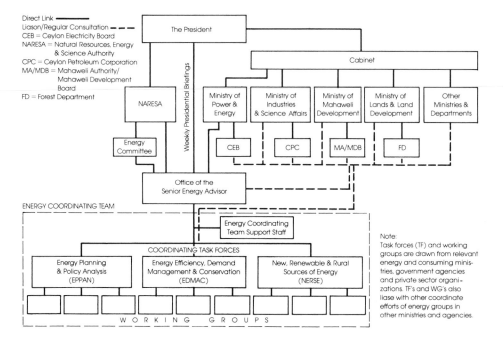

Figure 4.4: Organization of New Energy Co-ordinating Framework

ECT consists primarily of three coordinating task forces that cover the following areas:

a) Energy Planning and Policy Analysis (EPPAN);
b) Energy Efficiency, Demand Management and Conservation (EDMAC); and
c) New, Renewable and Rural Sources of Energy (NERSE).

The coordinating task force (CTF) members are senior managers from the relevant line organizations seconded to help in ECT activities, and therefore they could be relied upon to implement ECT policy. Decisions agreed at CTF meetings would normally be conveyed to the President through the senior energy advisor and, if necessary, would reach the appropriate line agency through the Cabinet, thereby increasing the effectiveness of implementation.

All of the ECT staff were drawn from the Ministry of Power and Energy (MPE) or seconded to this ministry from other bodies. The entire ECT therefore gradually fell more under the Ministry of Power and Energy, while retaining its interministerial policy coordinating role. These developments have essentially permitted MPE to take a greater responsibility for INEP and policy analysis, and to build more capability in the energy area -- an aspect that had been relatively neglected before 1983, due to the MPE's almost exclusive preoccupation with the CEB and electric power. The creation of the Lanka Electricity Company (jointly owned by the CEB and Ministry of Local

Government and Housing) in 1984, to gradually take over the local authority networks, and incorporation of the CPC within the MPE early in 1985, greatly strengthened policy coordination in the commercial fuel sector (i.e. electricity and oil products).

4.4 National Energy Strategy

Scenarios and Analytical Design

The analytical approach adopted for this study was to superimpose the policy options that lie under the control of the Sri Lanka Government onto a series of scenarios that capture the key external factors over which the decision-maker has no control. Among the most important of these external factors are the world economy, which determines Sri Lanka's external trade environment, and such factors as level of interest rates on the external debt. Because of the dependence of the electric sector on hydroelectricity, rainfall variations represent another important source of uncertainty.

Economic growth

Ideally, one would wish to project the domestic economic growth rate as a function of domestic policy, and the external environment. However, the present state of the art of macroeconomic modelling is such that great difficulties are still encountered in quantifying some of the key relationships. Indeed, the experience in Sri Lanka since the economic liberalization of 1977-78 disproves much of the common wisdom concerning the short-term impact of external shocks, (oil price increases in particular), on the rate of economic growth.

We have therefore elected to use the domestic growth rate as one of the exogenous assumptions of our analysis; three scenarios of GDP growth are postulated over the period 1985-95, ranging from a high case of 5.5% annual GDP growth to 1995, to a low case of 3.5% annual growth to 1990, falling to 2.5% in the early 1990s.

The base case assumes a 5.5% growth from 1985 to 1989, which is consistent with the projection of the Ministry of Finance and Planning in its latest annual report on Public Investment (Ministry of Finance and Planning 1985). From 1990 to 1995 we assume that the growth rate falls to 4% per annum. This scenario implies a continuation of the growth trend over the seven years since the economic reforms were introduced by the incoming administration in 1978. Even though this trend was maintained during a period of severe external shocks -- the oil price increase of 1979-80, sharp increases in the price of imported goods due to worldwide inflation, as well as falling world market shares of the international tea and rubber trades -- growth rates in the late 1980s in excess of this trend are most improbable. Nevertheless, we do examine a case in which the 5.5% rate is maintained through to the mid-1990s.

However, there are a number of reasons for the GDP growth rate to be substantially less than 5.5%. There is no guarantee that Sri Lanka's significant growth in manufactured exports will continue, which, together with the increasing external payments burden, may begin to cause dislocations in the economy. Our low case scenario therefore posits a GDP growth rate of 3.5% to 1990, falling to 2.5% thereafter.

It should, of course, be noted that these scenarios are not in the nature of forecasts or predictions; they are used in this study for the sole purpose of examining the consequences of energy policy options under different sets of conditions.

Oil price

The future condition of the world oil market is extremely difficult to foretell. Moreover, the complexity of the market, with the intricate interactions between the prices of different crudes and petroleum products, further complicates the situation for a small oil-importing country such as Sri Lanka. Even without some cataclysmic disruption in the world oil supply situation, the next five years will bring significant changes to the petroleum product market in Southeast Asia, as the new refineries in the Persian Gulf come on-stream. Therefore, although we use the landed price of crude as the index of world oil price, we shall see that the interplay of petroleum product prices around this level has implications for Sri Lanka of the order of millions of dollars per annum. The two scenarios examined are as follows. In the high world oil price (WOP) case, we assume constant real prices at US$214/tonne until 1988, followed by an annual increase of 4% thereafter (again in real terms). This brings the 1995 real price to about the levels experienced at the very peak of the oil crisis in the early 1980s. (The 1984 average c.i.f. Colombo crude price was US$214/tonne).

The low world oil price case assumes constant real prices until 1989, with a 1% per annum real price increase thereafter. Again, it should be stressed that we use these scenarios for indicative purposes only, and make no judgement as to which of these scenarios is more probable. Indeed, the entire thrust of the national energy strategy is the identification of policy initiatives that are robust (i.e. relatively unaffected) under the expected uncertainties.

By the late 1990s Sri Lanka will be importing substantial amounts of coal, especially once the Trincomalee coal units of the Ceylon Electricity Board are on-line. We have assumed that coal prices will track oil prices, and escalate current c.i.f. coal prices (about US$45 to 50/tonne) at the same rates as oil prices.

Hydrological uncertainties

A national energy strategy must be concerned with short-term as well as long-term issues, of which temporary disruptions to the supply are among the most important. As Sri Lanka becomes more dependent on hydroelectricity, the ability of the Ceylon Electricity Board to cope with drought years also becomes more important because most of the major impoundments are concentrated in a relatively small area of the hill country. The impact of a failure, delay or abnormal monsoon can be potentially quite serious, as evidenced by the situation in 1983. We therefore examine two cases: the current planning basis of the Ceylon Electricity Board that is based on firm + 25% of secondary hydro-energy, and a case based on firm hydro-energy only (corresponding roughly to a 1-in-50 year hydrological event). It should, of course, be noted that there is a one-in-five chance that this event will, in fact, occur at some time over the next ten-year period. Table 4.7 represents the energy levels from hydro plants associated with these two cases.

The analytical design

The analytical design for the model runs is shown in Figure 4.5. In constructing the overall scenarios, one obvious issue is the degree to which the world oil price and

GDP assumptions are correlated. Increases in oil price are only one of several types of external shocks that Sri Lanka has experienced (and will experience in the future); and the adjustment mechanisms to these external shocks can be quite complex (Munasinghe 1984). Thus, it is not possible to forecast a direct impact on GDP from a given oil price shock (as the experience of Sri Lanka in the years 1977-82 reflects very well). Indeed, the impact of the relative ease with which Sri Lanka was able to adjust to the shocks of the 1970s, of which additional external financing was a major part, will only now be felt as the debt service obligations become due. For the same reason, the fact that oil prices are currently falling in real terms does not necessarily imply a faster domestic growth rate.

Table 4.7

Energy from Hydroelectric Plants (GWh per year)

	Base Case Firm + 25% Secondary	Firm Hydro Only (1-in-50-Years)
Existing Hydro-Plants	1691	1531
Victoria	767	695
Samanalawewa	440	431
Kotmale	368	316
Randenigala	391	366
Broadlands	69	60
Rantembe	181	158

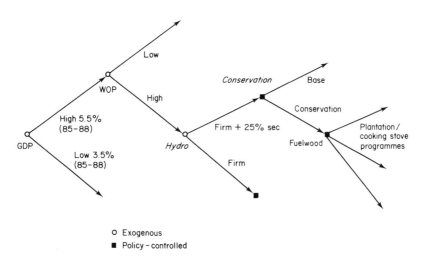

○ Exogenous

■ Policy – controlled

Figure 4.5: Model Runs

Given these circumstances, the basic modelling design is structured around the four possible combinations of oil price and GDP growth. In the case of the electric sector analysis we also include the hydro-energy uncertainties.

Onto these basic scenarios which capture the exogenously determined factors, we superimpose a series of cases which reflect the policy interventions under consideration. These include initiatives for energy conservation, electric sector demand management, pricing, fuelwood planting and cooking stove programmes, refinery management and oil import strategies, fuel substitutions, and others. The detail of these strategies are presented next.

The Basic Directions of Policy

Given Sri Lanka's precarious balance of payments position, its absence of fossil fuels, and the critical fuelwood situation, the basic directions of policy are clear. Indeed, in several areas vital and correct policy initiatives have already been launched. The basic principles can be elaborated as follows.

Increasing the efficiency of energy use

Increasing energy efficiency is not merely for short-term benefit, but must be pursued consistently over the longer term. Lacking its own fossil resources, for the next few decades the bulk of Sri Lanka's incremental energy must come from imported fossil fuels, until sometime in the 21st century when newer energy technologies may well replace fossil fuels. Without a sustained effort to maximize the efficiency of fossil fuel utilization, development objectives will inevitably be compromised.

In a similar vein, those domestic resources that are available must be utilized more effectively. The forest resource is a valuable asset upon which the bulk of the population still depend for their basic energy needs. Unless fuelwood is used more efficiently, the long-term consequences will be catastrophic. Therefore, the national energy demand and conservation programme (for commercial fuels), and the national fuelwood conservation programme (for improved domestic cooking stoves), must be expanded rapidly and pursued vigorously by the task forces which have already been established by the Government of Sri Lanka.

Efficient pricing

Recent changes in electricity and oil prices have brought average commercial fuel prices close to economically efficient levels (i.e. border price). These favourable trends must be maintained to ensure good demand management. While average prices are reasonable, the detailed structure of electricity and petroleum product prices need to be further revised -- especially the price of kerosene and diesel fuel relative to that of gasoline.

Reducing the vulnerability to external shocks

Over the past decade Sri Lanka has experienced numerous external shocks affecting both the energy sector and the economy as a whole, particularly the two oil shocks of the 1970s and the 1983-84 drought. In order to reduce this vulnerability, diversification of both the type and source of energy is key; increasing coal use for power generation and industrial energy, purchasing petroleum products and crude from a variety of sources including the spot market, would all decrease vulnerability as well as cost.

Maximizing domestic resources

Hydroelectricity and fuelwood represent the two main domestic fuels of Sri Lanka. Even if commercial oil finds are made in the next few years, and even if the efforts to commercialize other renewable energy technologies -- small hydro, producer gas, wind, solar heating, etc. -- are successful, until the year 2000, conventional hydro and fuelwood will be the main sources of domestic energy.

Rationalizing the institutional framework

Before 1983 the institutional framework was fragmented, with the various energy sector line institutions like Forest Department, Ceylon Electricity Board, Ceylon Petroleum Corporation, Natural Resources, Energy and Science Authority, Mahaweli Development Authority, etc., all reporting to different Ministries. Starting in 1982 an Energy Coordinating Team was set up to formulate and coordinate policy. This mechanism is working well with each of the three task forces: Energy Planning and Policy Analysis, Energy Demand Management and Conservation and New Renewable and Rural Sources of Energy responsible for one major programme (National Energy Strategy, National Energy Demand Management and Conservation Programme, and National Fuelwood Conservation Programme, respectively), as well as many smaller initiatives. This framework should be maintained and strengthened.

More recently the Lanka Electricity Company was created as a privately incorporated but government owned entity, to take over electricity distribution, gradually, and the Ceylon Petroleum Corporation was absorbed within the Ministry of Power and Energy -- further consolidating policy coordination and implementation in the commercial fuels sector. The National Energy Strategy should continue to be implemented using the framework of the Energy Coordinating Team for overall coordination, and the line agencies for implementation.

The specific policy initiatives necessary to implement these broad directions can be divided into three categories: (i) short-term options that provide measurable results within 1-3 years; (ii) medium-term options, whose gestation period is such that implementation measures must be undertaken now, even though results will require 5-10 years and (iii) long-term options that address issues likely to be experienced after 1995.

Short-term Options

Conservation initiatives

A comprehensive programme of conservation for commercial fuels, encompassing electricity as well as petroleum products in the transportation and industrial sectors, is of high priority. This will have long-term as well as short-term benefits. If the present goals of the National Energy Demand Management and Conservation Programme (NEDMCP) are met (see Table 4.8), the savings on the aggregate oil import bill by 1990 are estimated as shown in Figure 4.6. In addition, the electric utility has already launched a programme to reduce its own losses from about 20% of generation in 1984 to less than 15% by 1990.

The conservation programme in therefore seen to provide substantial benefits independently of both the rate of economic growth and the state of the world oil market. Moreover, as may be seen in our detailed analysis of the electric sector

(Figure 4.7), the conservation programme also serves to cushion the impact of droughts; under the current capacity expansion plan of the Ceylon Electricity Board, attainment of the electricity conservation targets reduces oil consumption to very low levels, even in drought years.

Table 4.8

**National Energy Demand Management
and Conservation Programme -- Conservation Goals**

	1990 Saving (%)	Equivalent Annual Impact on Growth Rate (%)
Electricity[a]		
Domestic	5	-1.0
Large Industry[b]	10	-2.0
Small + Medium Industry	10	-2.0
Commercial	10	-2.0
Local Authority	5	-1.0
Petroleum Products		
Auto-Diesel	10	-2.0
Gasolene	10	-2.0
Fuel-Oil	10	-2.0

a   The Ceylon Electricity Board loss reduction programme is included in the base case.
b   In addition, the conservation scenario assumes implementation of the industrial projects identified in the recent World Bank pre-feasibility studies over the period 1987-89.

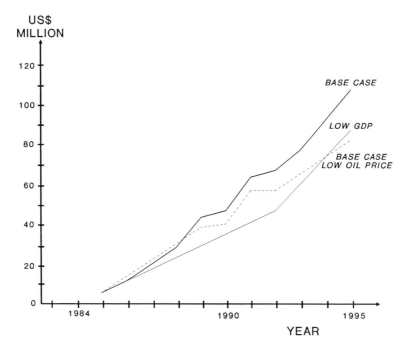

Figure 4.6: Net Foreign Exchange Saving due to Conservation Programme

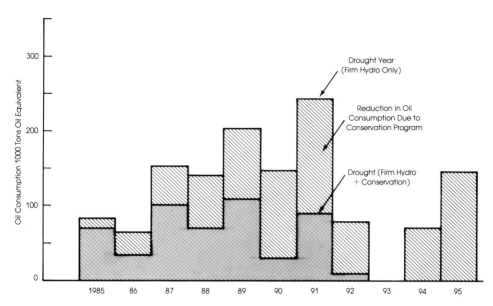

Figure 4.7: Impact of Conservation Programme on Ceylon Electricity Board (CEB) Oil Consumption in Any Given Drought Year

The National Fuelwood Conservation Programme

A detailed analysis (described in Chapter 12) shows the urgency of the problem, and the potential impact of failure to pursue the programme with the greatest urgency. Our estimates indicate that from fuelwood consumption alone (i.e., ignoring such factors as construction timber demands), the natural forest cover will decline from about 1.6 million ha (about 24% of land area) to 0.3-0.5 million ha by 2010, depending on assumptions about the sustainable yield. Obviously, at these levels of resource depletion, sharp price increases for fuelwood can be expected, leading, in turn to possible substitution by expensive, imported petroleum products. Moreover, the environmental consequences of almost complete denudation of forest cover are equally severe. The National Fuelwood Conservation Programme involving the rapid and systematic introduction of efficient cooking stoves into 2.5 million households over the next five years, must be given top priority.

Oil acquisition strategy

Given the volatility of the world oil market, the principal priority is for a more flexible acquisition strategy that can respond quickly to relative price changes. Our detailed analysis indicates that whilst the current operation of Sri Lanka's oil refinery is near optimal, small changes in relative prices have a significant impact, particularly when crude prices are in imbalance with those of refined products. A start towards more flexible operation has already been made by allowing Ceylon Petroleum Company to purchase a higher fraction of crude on spot markets, and a refinery optimization model, derived from the one developed by the Energy Coordinating Team, will be used to assist purchasing strategy. The Single-Point Mooring Buoy project will also serve to lower the total crude cost by about $6/tonne and will have the additional benefit of reducing congestion in Colombo harbour. However, there remain some areas where lack of flexibility hinders optimal management, such as the long time-lag involved in adjusting foreign bunker prices.

Continued attention to the oil acquisition strategy is especially warranted in light of the significant changes in the regional oil market anticipated as a result of the large additions of refinery capacity in the Persian Gulf countries that will come on-stream over the next few years. Whilst the precise impact is subject to uncertainty, in light of the worldwide excess refining capacity, the low crude acquisition cost for these refineries will undoubtedly allow them to increase their market share of refined products at the expense of older, smaller refineries.

Pricing policy

We have examined the importance of maintaining a domestic petroleum product pricing system based on the foreign exchange cost to the country, by simulating the energy system under alternative price elasticity assumptions. Case 1 (Table 4.9) assumes that domestic prices will stay at their current levels in real terms; the impact on oil consumption (and the oil import bill) is simulated by assuming zero price elasticity of demand. Cases 2 and 3 reflect different levels of price response to the increases in the real price of oil following the base case scenario for the world oil price.

These results indicate the serious consequences of any failure to maintain domestic retail prices consistent with border or economically efficient prices.

Table 4.9

Impact of Petroleum Product Pricing Policy

Case	Oil Imports[a] (x1000 t.o.e.)	Foreign Exchange ($ million)
No Price Adjustment	2678	625
Prices Adjusted to Border Price		
price elasticity = -0.15	2594	596
price elasticity = -0.3	2517	568

[a]Net of bunkers and petroleum product exports.

Options for the Medium-to Long-Term

A second set of options can be expected to become effective over the medium- to long-term; even if they are implemented aggressively it will be at least 1990 before they will have any measurable impact on the overall energy situation. However, just because of their long gestation period, it is important that these programmes begin to be pursued vigorously now.

Plantation programmes

While the National Fuelwood Conservation Programme is clearly essential, it must be recognized that even an aggressively promoted cooking stove programme does not address the long-term problem. Indeed, a detailed analysis (see Figure 12.7 in Chapter 12) shows that the breathing space afforded by a fuelwood conservation programme over the next few years must be used to put in place a plantation programme of at least 10,000 ha per annum, in addition to the programmes already under way (that provide for about 5000 ha per annum). The long-term foreign exchange consequences of a depleted forest resource are extremely serious, quite aside from the impact on rural families whose household budgets would then face the cost of commercial fuels. In 1985, fuelwood is estimated to have produced some 4300 tons of oil equivalent of energy; even when one takes into account the much higher efficiencies at which petroleum-utilizing devices operate, this still represents an avoided foreign exchange cost of US$200 million.

Renewables

The New, Renewable and Rural Source of Energy task force was established by the Government of Sri Lanka to coordinate the development of a variety of renewable energy sources. Whilst some of these technologies appear promising, a concerted effort will be necessary to establish coherent implementation. To examine the scope of the impact of such efforts, we have postulated an optimistic scenario for the penetration of these technologies into the economy, as shown in Table 4.10.

Table 4.10

Maximum Possible Renewable Case

	Basis	1995 GWh
Small Hydro	15 MW by 1995	39
Wind	5 MW by 1995	26
Producer Gas	One 150 kW unit/year	5
Solar water heaters	30000 panels in place, at 6 kWh equiv./day	21
Photovoltaics	10000 panels in place	8
Biogas	5000 systems, at 1.8 kWh/day	11

Even under these rather optimistic assumptions, our analysis indicates that these technologies would displace only 2% of the Ceylon Electricity Board's 1995 generation. The corresponding reduction in the oil import bill amounts to only 1% by 1995.

Finally, we turn to a discussion of a long-run option, which will not affect the energy system until well after 2000, but which merits continued attention.

Nuclear energy

Until the electric system load reaches at least several thousand megawatts, nuclear power plants are not viable on the basis of present data, from a technical, systems and economic standpoint. Because a 2000 MW demand can be expected at the earliest, in the next century, nuclear power would be an option only beyond the year 2000. However, it should be noted that unlike other South Asian countries, whose longer-term power generation prospects are expected to rely heavily on domestic resources (lignite, coal and natural gas), the long-term prospects for power generation in Sri Lanka are unclear. Even if all the remaining hydropower is exploited, (including small hydro), at some point substantial thermal generation for baseload is inevitable. Therefore, whilst nuclear energy is not an option of any immediacy, the situation needs periodic review, especially if technical innovations make smaller units in the 300-500 MW size range, economically viable. Training of manpower and monitoring of nuclear technological developments abroad should be pursued, to maintain readiness.

4.5 Conclusion

The basic rationale for developing the concepts and methodology of integrated national energy planning (INEP) may be traced to the oil price increases and energy crises of the 1970s. The need for more coordinated, systematic and effective energy policy formulation and implementation resulted in the development of a hierarchical framework for INEP and policy analysis. This approach includes analysis at three interrelated levels: the energy-macroeconomic, energy sector and energy subsector levels.

The INEP methodology and models may be implemented quite straightforwardly and inexpensively using the 16-bit micro-processors available in 1984-5. All computerized activities should be first verified through manual calculations, at a relatively simple level, and only later, as local analytical skills and understanding improve, should more-sophisticated computer models be developed. The models must reflect the real-world constraints as closely as possible, and have a policy focus that will facilitate quick responses to the kinds of questions that senior decisionmakers might normally pose.

The application of this approach in Sri Lanka, during the past three years, indicates that it has great promise for other developing countries as well. It should be noted that in Sri Lanka the success achieved in the energy sector arose not only from the systematic application of the hierarchical microcomputer-based INEP modelling methodology, but also because of a number of related improvements, such as the clear identification of national policy goals, selective and coordinated use of policy instruments, restructuring of the organization framework to strengthen policy formulation, coordination and implementation, and the training of local staff and institution building.

References

Energy Research Group (ERG), *Priorities and Directions for Energy Research and Policy in Developing Countries*, IDRC-UNU, Ottawa, 1985.

Meier, Peter, "Energy Planning in Developing Countries: The Role of Microcomputers", *Natural Resources Forum*, vol.1, January 1985, pp. 41-52.

Ministry of Finance and Planning, *Public Investment Programme 1984-1988*, Government of Sri Lanka, Colombo, Sri Lanka, 1985.

Munasinghe, M., *The Economics of Power System Reliability and Planning*, Johns Hopkins University Press, Baltimore MD, 1979.

Munasinghe, M., "Integrated National Energy Planning (INEP) in Developing Countries", *Natural Resources Forum*, vol. 4, 1980a, pp. 359-74.

Munasinghe, M., "An Integrated Framework for Energy Pricing in Developing Countries", *The Energy Journal*, vol. 1, July 1980b, pp. 1-30.

Munasinghe, M., *Energy in Sri Lanka*, SLAAS, Colombo, Sri Lanka, 1980c.

Munasinghe, M., "Third World Energy Policies: Demand Management and Conservation", *Energy Policy*, vol. 4, March 1983, pp. 4-18.

Munasinghe, M., "Energy Strategies for Oil Importing Developing Countries", *Natural Resources Journal*, vol. 24, April 1984, pp. 351-68.

Munasinghe, M., Dow, M. and Fritz, J. (eds), *Microcomputers for Development*, National Academy of Sciences, Washington DC, 1985.

Wilbanks, Thomas, J., "Lessons from the National Energy Planning Experience in Developing Countries", *The Energy Journal*, Special LDC issue, vol.8, July 1987, pp. 169-182.

Chapter 5

ENERGY STRATEGIES FOR OIL IMPORTING DEVELOPING COUNTRIES[1]

5.1 Introduction

The two rapid oil price increases during 1973-74 and 1979-80 have left a lasting impact on the entire world. While the economies of all countries, except the oil exporters, have suffered, the most adverse consequences were felt by a group of oil importing developing countries (OIDCs) (see Appendix A5.1 for a complete list of both low and middle income OIDCs).

This chapter seeks to identify possible adjustment strategies that the OIDCs might adopt in the mid-1980's and beyond. Before attempting to do so, two salient points should be recognized. First, the economic adjustments that OIDCs had to make in the past were, to a large extent, governed by the global environment because of tight international linkages via trade, borrowing, investment, and aid. Therefore, any analysis of the OIDC's future prospects and policy options must begin with a general understanding of how the world economy coped with the two oil-price shocks, and how external conditions specifically affected the oil importers. Second, energy related problems cannot be meaningfully separated from development issues, especially in the context of the developing countries. Accordingly, potentially useful strategies for energy management and planning are closely linked with successful development policies for management and adjustment of national economies.

The remainder of this paper is structured as follows: the upcoming section seeks to analyze the impact of the past oil crises on the world economy in general, and on the oil importers in particular. Energy and economic development issues in the OIDCs are described in the next section. In the final section, future energy options and adjustment strategies that are likely to be successful in the OIDCs are discussed.

5.2 The Effects of Past Oil Price Increases

World Economy

During the past decade, international oil prices have risen sharply twice, in 1973-74 and 1979-80 (see Figure 5.1). Overall real crude oil prices have risen by a factor of six over a ten year period since 1972. The responses of the world economy to the two energy shocks have exhibited similarities as well as differences (World Bank 1983b). In both cases, the economic growth rates of the industrialized and developing countries declined, but the second recession was less precipitous and longer lasting, as shown in Figure 5.2.

---

[1] Edited version of a paper published in *Natural Resources Journal*, vol.24, April 1984, pp.351-68.

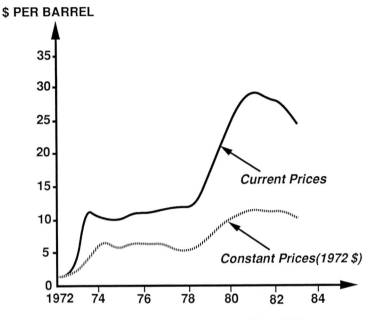

Figure 5.1: Petroleum Prices, 1972-1983

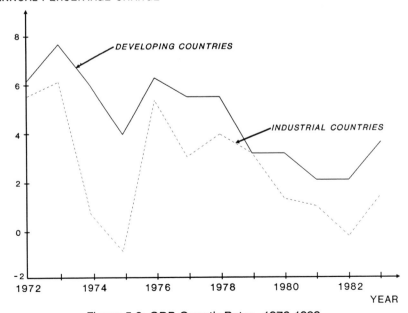

Figure 5.2: GDP Growth Rates, 1972-1983

The differences in response may be attributed to the macroeconomic policies adopted by the major industrial powers in each case. During the first crisis, conventional monetary and fiscal expansion policies were adopted to counteract the recessionary effects of high oil import bills. The oil crisis, however, helped to highlight structural rigidities and defects in the western economies which required structural adjustment rather than traditional macroeconomic stabilization policies. Protection of high cost industries and wage rigidities in the struggle to maintain the high levels of money income led to wage-price spirals. The resulting persistent inflation eroded real growth, and high interest rates and investment uncertainty deepened the recession. The first oil price increase did, however, result in a move towards energy conservation and substitution away from petroleum, which began to pay off handsomely by the end of the 1970s.

Most of the industrialized countries adopted somewhat different policies after 1979-80, which were based on their experiences during the previous decade. Tight monetary policies controlled inflation, but large fiscal deficits and high short term interest rates discouraged or delayed investment, increased unemployment, and prolonged the recession. Only towards late 1983 was there some promise of a world-wide economic upturn in 1984.

The OIDCs continue to be highly vulnerable to developments in the world economy, not only because of high oil import costs, but also due to shrinkage of export markets, official aid flows, access to international credit, and private foreign investments in domestic economies. Each downturn in the industrialized nations had corresponding adverse impacts on the developing countries, although some (especially the newly industrialized far eastern group) were able to cope better than others. Specific mechanisms by which the oil price shocks have affected petroleum importers are analyzed next.

Balance of Payment Effects

The drastic changes in the price of oil in the 1970s had major financial and balance-of-payments repercussions on the oil importing countries. Total energy imports as a percent of total merchandise exports in 1960 had amounted to less than 11 percent worldwide. In 1977, energy import costs had increased to between 16 and 40 percent of exports for the low-income, non-oil producing countries; to 24 percent for the middle-income countries; and to 20 percent for the industrialized countries. However, these average percentages hide rates of dependency that are much higher for a number of individual countries. Some of them, such as Jordan, Pakistan, Panama, Syria, and Turkey, spent between 40 to 90 percent of export earnings on oil imports, and the United States and Japan spent about 31 percent and 32 percent, respectively. Given the more than 100 percent oil price increases in 1979-80, these percentages have increased substantially since then, in most cases. Projections made for 1990 for member countries of the Asian Development Bank indicate that energy imports may account for between 55 and 120 percent of export earnings in low-income countries, and between 17 and 50 percent for the middle-income group, in spite of the fact that the projections also foresee a significant substitution of other energy resources for oil (Sankar and Schramm 1982).

These increased foreign exchange requirements for oil imports were a major contributor to a significant deterioration in the balance of payments of many of the oil importing countries. As a result, their external debt load increased sharply. This is particularly true for developing countries. Since much of their oil expenditure has to be financed through foreign exchange borrowings, rather than increased exports, the accumulation of debt and declining international credit-worthiness of many oil importing developing countries are major unresolved issues. The special problems of the third world are discussed in greater detail later.

Direct Macroeconomic Effects

One of the most important direct effects of the energy price increases in the 1970s was the resulting fall in real incomes of oil importing countries. World oil prices rose by some 350 percent in 1973-74, and by about 140 percent in 1979-80. These increases occurred in response to relatively small reductions in available world supplies, proving that the short-run demand elasticity for oil is low. In both periods, panic buying reinforced the upward pressures on prices, with the result that spot market prices (which account for between 5 to 15 percent of world trade) rose even faster than the announced contractual prices. Given the uneven distribution of oil producing and importing countries, these drastic price rises resulted in major real income transfers from importing to producing countries. The consequence was, of course, that real income in the importing countries had to fall.

Assume the share or fraction of energy costs in GNP is ES. Then, in the worst case, where the price-elasticity of energy demand is zero and no energy substitution is possible, a simple and essentially static analysis shows that an increase in energy process of p percent will reduce real national income at most by [p x ES/(1 - ES)] percent. Assuming a typical value of 0.1 for ES, real income will fall by a maximum of 1.1 percent following a ten percent rise in energy costs, neglecting the dynamic effects of the energy price shock to be discussed later. Thus, if the energy cost share (ES) is small, it will reduce the adverse impact on national income, basically because the economy is less dependent on energy and therefore less vulnerable to the price increase. However, for a given value of ES, the greater the possibilities of substituting other relatively cheaper inputs for energy in various productive activities (i.e., a higher value for price elasticity), the smaller the decline in real national income.

The direct effects will be the same whether the price of imported energy rises or domestic energy sources become more expensive to exploit. Only countries with significant amounts of cheap (and preferably exportable) energy resources will not be adversely affected. It is important is realize the distinction between national income and national output. Thus, if there is little substitution of other inputs such as capital and labor for energy, real output or GNP will be relatively unaffected. But, since more of this product is used to pay for expensive energy, less will be available as wages and profits, i.e., real incomes and the standard of living will decline. Paradoxically, the greater the substitution of other inputs for energy in production, the larger the fall in real GNP, but the smaller the reduction in real national income.

Dynamic Effects

The dynamic effects of an energy price increase occur as the economy seeks to adjust to this sudden shock, encumbered by wage and price rigidities and constraints. The sharper and more unexpected the increase, the more severe the shock. As discussed in the previous section, the increased share of output claimed by energy costs implied reduced incomes for other factors of production such as capital and labor. However, in the post-1973 period various economic agents in the oil importing countries sought to maintain their real incomes by raising wages and prices of other goods. These actions simply boosted money incomes (with little effect on real income) and triggered a spiral of wage-price inflation.

In addition to the inflationary effects mentioned above, the adjustment of the economy will also cause real output to fall. All the well-known adverse effects such as increased unemployment, decreased GNP growth rate, and general recession, were felt in oil importing countries after the 1973 and 1979-80 oil price increases. In many cases, the tendency of workers to resist decreases in real wage levels and increases in other input costs, resulted in reduced profits. This led to layoffs and decreases in output. At the same time, uncertainty regarding prices, interest rates, and profits resulted in reduced investment. Consumer demand also reacted negatively to reduced future real incomes. Thus the world economy went into recession during the period 1973-75, with the uniformity and synchronization of country responses being enhanced by the tight linkage due to large trade and capital flows among them.

Future Trends

These immediate, macroeconomic effects of the income transfers from oil importers to oil exporters are diminishing, however, as price-induced substitutions of other energy resources and conservation measures take hold. In the long-run, the higher oil prices lead to a decline in the use of oil, even though it is not clear at this point in time if world consumption rates will fall in absolute terms or only relative to rates that would have prevailed at lower prices. In the industrialized world, oil consumption in 1980 had actually declined relative to 1978, the year of peak consumption. In the developing countries, however, oil consumption is likely to rise further in order to support the essential process of economic development and growth, and to switch over from traditional to commercial, energy-dependent, modern methods of production.

Oil-substitution, itself, generally requires higher initial investment to provide the same level of service that would have been obtained with the use of oil. This substitution process is costly. Although the average costs of electric energy will be lower for atomic or coal-fired alternatives than for oil, over the life expectancies of the respective plants, the problem is that higher initial capital investments are needed per unit of output. To bring about such substitution requires a significant increase in the amount of investment relative to the amount of useful output produced. Higher savings and lower consumption rates are needed to finance these shifts in the capital/output ratios of energy-producing and energy-consuming equipment and facilities. But these increases in capital requirements put a major strain on world capital markets and are a contributing factor to the higher real costs of capital in recent years. These increased capital costs have placed a heavy burden on the already capital-short, oil-importing, developing countries. They also have reduced the economic advantage of oil-substitution.

Because there is less time for dynamic adjustment, sudden increases in the world oil price are more detrimental to the economies of oil importers than a gradual price rise. While there is general agreement that oil prices will continue to rise (because oil is a depleting resource), the rate of increase is less certain. Recent estimates range between zero and three percent per year, on average, over the next two decades. Greater conservation efforts by oil importers will help to limit world oil price increases, whereas unforeseen supply disruptions in oil producing areas could lead to sharp prices rises.

There will also have to be considerable adjustment in the oil refining sectors of many countries. As more refining capacity comes on-stream in the OPEC countries during the 1980s, many less efficient refineries in other countries will have to be phased out. Also, as heavier crudes that yield relatively more of the heavier refinery fractions predominate over lighter crudes in the future, and demand for fuel oil drops relative to the lighter products, refineries will have to adapt, e.g., by installing cracking facilities. This renders obsolete most of the existing distillation-only refining capacity, and puts a premium on high-cost, cracking facilities that are in short supply.

5.3 Oil Importing Developing Country (OIDC) Issues

The problems encountered by the oil importing developing countries require special analysis because these nations are the least well-equipped to deal with the increases in petroleum prices. Most of the oil importing developing countries, such as Brazil and Korea, financed their increased energy import bills by external borrowings following the 1973 oil price increase. This was necessary because they were unable to boost exports sufficiently to balance their foreign trade. A few, like Taiwan, sought to cut back sharply on their domestic demand for oil. On the whole, the OIDCs succeeded in cushioning their economies from the oil price shock, and posted a 4.5 percent growth rate of real GNP, while the Organization for Economic Cooperation and Development (OECD) countries were deep in recession. However, the increasing debt service burden of the OIDCs makes it unlikely that continued foreign financing of energy needs can be sustained indefinitely into the future. Between 1970 and 1979, their debt service as a percentage of GNP increased from 1.2 to 2.7 percent for low-income countries, and from 1.5 to 2.2 percent for middle-income countries. The future looks even bleaker for a number of them. For 12 major energy importing Asian countries, the Asian Development Bank predicts that energy imports as a percent of GNP will amount to almost 15 percent by 1990, as against a range of 3 to 7 1/2 percent in 1978.

The more detailed pattern of foreign exchange borrowings by OIDCs shows that there was a sharp increase in borrowing after the 1973 oil price increase, which gradually decreased up to 1978, only to rise again following the volatility of international oil markets during 1979-80. Many of these loans were obtained from private commercial banks, and therefore not under concessionary terms usually provided by international aid agencies. These rapid increases in short-term borrowings have elevated the debt service burden of several countries to dangerous levels. For example, by 1985, the more industrialized, middle income OIDCs are projected to spend about 29 percent of their export earnings to meet interest and amortization payments on their foreign debt.

Increased borrowing immediately after a sudden oil price increase is generally in the interest of the OIDCs. An economy is usually most rigid in the short run, with few possibilities for energy substitution in production and consumption. Therefore it makes sense to borrow more heavily in the initial period following the oil price increase, assuming that energy substitution and conservation programs will provide greater flexibility in later years. However, it is clear that the ability to withstand repeated energy shocks will be diminished if the magnitude and frequency of these price increases is too great to permit economies to adjust to new equilibria and to allow debt service ratios to fall to acceptable levels. While the demand for foreign loans may not be very sensitive to the cost of borrowing (i.e., interest rates and terms of repayment), the supply of funds, especially from the commercial banks, will depend critically on credit worthiness. Already, preliminary results indicate that the OIDCs were not able to cushion their economies from the effects of the most recent oil price shocks as well as they did in the post-1973 period.

Both the direct and dynamic effects of higher energy costs discussed earlier will continue to reduce already low real incomes and living standards, decrease output and employment levels, and fuel inflation in the OIDCs. Fortunately, in the next decade or so, energy substitution and conservation policies will help to alleviate these problems. However, the third world will still need increasing amounts of energy to sustain its drive for economic growth and industrialization. Thus, according to the World Bank, total commercial energy consumption in oil importing developing countries will increase from 12.4 million barrels a day of oil equivalent in 1980 to 22.8 million barrels by 1990 (World Bank 1983a). Not all of this increase, of course, will be in the form of oil consumption. For example, for 19 Asian countries, oil dependence is projected to decrease from some 78 percent in 1978 to 65 percent by 1990, even though in absolute terms oil consumption in these countries is expected to double (UNESCAP 1981). As oil dependence declines relative to total GNP, the negative effects of high and rising oil prices will become less significant for income and employment.

As mentioned earlier, energy related investments in developing countries for developing new energy sources and for conservation programs will also be substantial. According to estimates by the World Bank, for example, the energy-related investment needs of the developing countries as a whole are projected to rise from some 34.4 billion U.S. dollars in 1980 to approximately 82.2 billion dollars per year by 1990 (in 1980 U.S. dollars). This represents an average annual increase of 12.3 percent over the decade.

In summary, solving the energy problems of the third world will be a formidable challenge. In the past, commercial banks have been willing to act as intermediaries by holding loans from OIDCs, and issuing their own internationally recognized instruments to finance oil payments and energy related investments. Since this cannot continue indefinitely, greater direct flows of petro-dollars from the oil-surplus countries to the OIDCs in the form of concessionary loans for investments, etc. may be required. More aid from both multilateral and bilateral sources. as well as higher levels of private foreign investment, will be required. The developed countries should also be willing to run greater trade deficits than OIDCs.

We note that any evolution of international economic relationships will depend on many difficult and unknown political factors. Energy will be only one issue, albeit an important one, to be thrashed out within some broader framework such as North-South dialogue and the new inter-national economic order (NIEO) discussions. It is very clear, however, that whatever the outcome of international developments, the more efficient use of energy, and demand management and conservation policies pursued within individual countries, as well as more effective exploitation of indigenous energy resources and supply management, will play an important role in reducing the adverse effects of the energy crisis in those countries willing to adopt appropriate policies.

5.4 Role of Energy Planning and Management

Because of the intimate link between energy and development issues, we will examine the energy planning and management framework as well as the policy instruments available to tackle the OIDC's energy problems, before setting out the strategies to be adopted (see Chapter 2 for a more detailed discussion).

It is generally accepted that the broad rationale underlying modern energy management and planning is to make the best use of available energy resources for promoting economic development, and improving social welfare and the quality of life. Therefore, energy planning is an essential part of the overall management of the national economy, and should be carried out in close coordination with the latter. However, in energy management and planning, the principal emphasis is on the comprehensive and disaggregate analysis of the energy sector with due regard to the main interactions with the rest of the economy, and among the different energy subsectors themselves. The efficient management of government energy-related corporations and, where necessary, the provision of correct investment and price signals to the private sector, are an integral part of successfully implementing national energy policies.

In a strictly technical sense, the best strategy might be to seek the least costly method of meeting future energy requirements. However, energy planning also includes a variety of other and often conflicting objectives, such as reducing dependence on foreign sources, supplying basic energy needs of the poor, reducing the trade and foreign exchange deficits, priority development of special regions or sectors of the economy, raising sufficient revenue to finance energy sector development (at least partially), ensuring continuity of supply, maintaining price stability, preserving the environment, and so on.

In general, energy planning requires analysis at the following three hierarchical levels in relation to fundamental national objectives: (1) links between the energy sector and the rest of the economy; (2) interactions between different subsectors within the energy sector; and (3) activities in each individual energy subsector. The steps involved in the planning procedure usually include energy supply and demand analyses and forecasting, energy balancing, policy formation, and impact analysis, to meet short-, mid-, and long-range goals. Implementation of the results of this analysis could be considered within the framework of a formal national energy master plan (EMP), or a more decentralized policy package that relies on voluntary responses of private energy producers and consumers to market prices. This will generally require the coordinated use of a number of interrelated policy tools such as: (1) physical controls and legislation; (2) technical methods (including research and development); (3) direct investments or investment inducing policies; (4) education and propaganda; and (5) pricing.

Energy planning may be carried out initially at a relatively simple level, but, as data and analytical capabilities improve, more sophisticated techniques, including computer modeling, may be used. The institutional structure could also be rationalized by setting up a central energy authority or ministry of energy, whose principal focus should be on energy planning and policy-making. Some central guidance and coordination of the many policy tools, energy supplying institutions, and consuming sectors, is necessary even in countries in which energy supply activities are dominated by the private sector. The influence of government actions in the various energy subsectors is quite pervasive in all countries. Regardless of the degree of centralization of planning functions, the execution of policy and day-to-day operations would remain the responsibility of government institutions or private firms, such as electric utilities or petroleum corporations, that already exist.

Policy Instruments

The policy tools available for energy planning and management include pricing, physical controls, technical methods (including research and development), and education and promotion. Since these tools are interrelated, their use should be well coordinated (see Chapters 2 and 3 for details). Price is most effective in the medium- and long-term. In terms of economic efficiency, price indicates the consumer's willingness-to-pay and use-value of energy to the supplier, while to the consumers, it signals the present and future opportunity costs of supply based on various energy sources.

Physical controls are most effective in the short-run when there are unforeseen shortages of energy. All methods of physically limiting consumption are included in this category (for example, load shedding and rotating power cuts in the electricity subsector, and reducing the supply of petrol or banning the use of cars during some periods). Technical means include, on the supply side, the cheapest means of producing a given form of energy, the best fuel mix, research and development of substitute energy sources such as solar or windpower, and on the demand side, introducing higher efficiency energy conversion devices such a better wood burning stoves, etc. Education and promotion include, on the supply side, efforts to make people aware of external diseconomies such as pollution, and supportive of reforestation schemes to preserve the environment; and on the demand side, education for energy conservation.

Pricing and investment decisions should be closely related. Energy supply systems (for example, electricity generation, transmission and distribution, oil and gas wells and pipelines, coal mines and forests), usually require large capital investments with long lead and life times. Once the investment decision is made (usually on the basis of the conventional least cost method of meeting demand by subsector, with due regard for interfuel substitution possibilities), there is a lock-in effect with respect to supply. Therefore, prices should be related to the long-term planning horizon. On the demand side, energy conversion devices (e.g., cars, gas cookers, electric appliances, machines, etc.) are expensive relative to average income and have relatively long lifetimes, thus limiting the ability of consumers to respond to changes in relative fuel prices in the short run.

5.5   Future Energy Options and Adjustment Strategies

Global Scenario

The energy prospects of the developing countries, and the OIDCs in particular, depend on supply-demand projections based on likely evolution of the world economy. For the period 1985-95, the expected average growth rate of real gross domestic product (GDP) of the developing countries and the industrialized countries would be 5.5 and 3.7 percent, respectively (World Bank 1983a). In the former group, the middle income countries are estimated to grow most rapidly at 5.7 percent, while the low income Asian countries, with an average growth rate of 4.9 percent, are expected to do better than their African counterparts having growth rates averaging only 3.3 percent. Global oil consumption is predicted to increase by only about one percent per year, up to 1995, while the real oil price is projected to grow at 1.6 percent. Although short-term fluctuations in energy markets (especially oil) will remain unpredictable, the above assumptions are reasonable long-run trends, given that oil prices must eventually approach the costs of potential replacements such as synthetic fuels. In particular, short-run declines in world petroleum prices should not lull the OIDCs into a false sense of security.

Table 5.1 shows the expected consumption and imports of various forms of commercial energy in the OIDCs. Although overall annual energy consumption will grow at five percent, the increase in oil use will be limited to about half this value. A combination of conservation and indigenous energy resource development policies will permit the OIDCs to reduce their petroleum imports from 44 to 28 percent of total commercial energy use between 1980 and 1995. Despite these hoped for successes, their net oil imports will increase from 295 million tons of oil equivalent (toe) in 1980 to about 386 million by 1995, when oil will still be supplying 39 percent of total commercial energy needs. Total commercial energy imports will rise at an average rate of three percent, from 288 million toe to 449 million toe, over the same period.

Table 5.1

**Expected Commercial Energy Consumption and Imports
in the Oil Importing Developing Countries**

	Consumption			Imports		
	1980 Million toe	1995 Million toe	1980-95 % growth per year	1980 Million toe	1985 Million toe	1980-95 % growth per year
Oil	360	531	2.6	296	386	1.8
Coal	186	442	5.9	-6	58	—
Natural Gas	26	120	10.7	-1	5	
Primary Electricity	98	306	7.9	0	0	0
Total	670	1399	5.0	288	449	3.0

Source: *The Energy Transition in Developing Countries*, The World Bank, Washington DC, August 1983, Chapter 1.

Meanwhile, biomass accounts for as much of the gross energy requirements of OIDCs as commercial fuels. In many countries it is used not only for fuel but also for construction timber, a total use which is several fold greater than the safe sustainable yield from already depleted forest cover. The future consumption of fuelwood will be determined mainly by the availability of supply. Unless significant afforestation efforts are undertaken, accessible forest cover will disappear within the next two or three decades, especially in the low-income Asian and African OIDCs. In addition to the hardships imposed on the predominately rural poor in these countries due to the inability to meet basic energy needs, other undesirable effects, including topsoil erosion, declining agricultural productivity, desertification, reservoir siltation, and reduced retention of water in catchment areas, will also manifest themselves.

Broad Energy Options

The principal energy options available to OIDCs are: (a) improving the efficiency of both energy supply and consumption for short- and medium-run gains, and (b) increasing the pace of development of indigenous energy resources, and restructuring their economies for longer-run payoffs.

Energy Efficiency

In most countries, the highest return on investments in the energy sector today may be realized from projects directed at increasing energy efficiency (see Chapter 6 for a more detailed discussion). On the demand side, energy efficiency improvements or conservation and demand management measures should be vigorously pursued by providing energy consumers with the latest technical knowledge, financial incentives through appropriate price signals and taxes or subsidies, and educational and promotional information. While the concept of energy conservation is intuitively appealing in a period of increased costs and scarcity of energy, the desirability of particular energy conservation policies must be verified by applying specific tests that compare their costs and benefits.

Two purely technical measures of the efficiency of energy use may be derived from the first and second laws of thermodynamics. The principal weakness these measures have is that they focus almost exclusively on the amount of energy used in a particular process and do not take into consideration the necessary inputs of other scarce resources such as capital, labor, and land. Also, the first and second law criteria may not always be consistent.

By contrast, a comprehensive and unambiguous test of specific energy conservation policies is based on the concept of economic efficiency and cost-benefit analysis. Generally, a conservation measure gives rise to cost savings benefits, B, due to a reduced consumption or substitution of energy, and to additional costs, C_1, of implementing the conservation policy (including hardware costs), and to costs C_2, representing benefits foregone due to reduced energy consumption. If B exceeds the sum of C_1 and C_2, the conservation measure is desirable. However, in some cases, increased energy consumption may improve overall economic benefits, e.g., if the actual price of an energy product is well above its marginal opportunity cost (MOC), this price should be lowered toward MOC, with a consequent increase in demand.

In terms of present discounted values, these economic costs and benefits should be evaluated and compared on a life cycle basis. Appropriate shadow prices or measures of the opportunity costs of goods and services must be used to verify whether the given policy will increase economic welfare from a national viewpoint. If so, the same calculation must be repeated using market prices to check whether private individuals will actually find it profitable to adopt these measures. Often, since market prices diverge from opportunity costs, it may be necessary to change taxes, prices, and legislation to promote a desirable conservation policy.

Conservation options in transport, buildings, industry, and electricity supply will now be summarized. The principal purpose of a transportation system is to physically convey people or goods from one location to another. Therefore, any measure that increases the payload in terms of energy used per passenger-mile or ton-mile would help the conservation effort. Important methods of achieving this result include: changing from more to less energy intensive transport models or to cheaper fuels; increasing the technical efficiency of energy use of given modes of transportation; and changes in behaviour and overall systems effects.

In the case of lighting, space heating, and cooling of buildings, three factors affecting the consumption of energy are: behavioural characteristics and attitudes of occupants; the type of energy-using equipment installed; and architectural design practices and materials used. Keeping living and working space lighted and cool are the chief concerns in the tropics, where most of the developing countries lie. In these areas, the use of air-conditioning is growing rapidly for commercial buildings such as businesses, hotels, etc., and to a lesser extent for residences of upper income urban and expatriate groups whose numbers, fortunately, are small.

Contrary to widespread belief, many industries are unaware of potential decreases in energy use that can be realized quite simply and are extremely cost effective. Because of the concentrated nature of such energy users, governments as well as energy suppliers and utility companies can be particularly effective in legislating improvements, counselling, providing energy audits, and helping consumers carry out technical improvements. Four broad areas for industrial energy conservation are: (a) waste heat recovery and cogeneration, (b) other retrofits and improvements in operation, (c) major changes in manufacturing processes and production methods, and (d) recycling and recovery of waste materials.

Efficiency improvements may also be realized in energy production and distribution. Loss reduction in petroleum refinery operations as well as distribution and retailing activity are areas in which significant gains could be made. In electric power supply, the three principal opportunities for conservation arise in (a) generation, (b) transmission, and (c) distribution. Furthermore, conservation at the end-use stage may also be achieved by two principal methods: improving the technical efficiency of energy-using devices and appliances, or changing the shape and characteristics of the load through demand management and load control techniques.

Energy Resource Development

OIDCs can reduce their oil import bills and overall energy costs substantially by exploiting and developing their indigenous resources more vigorously. The greatest potential for increasing domestic commercial energy production lies in the petroleum, natural gas, coal, hydroelectric, and nuclear energy subsectors.

The development of these resources requires: (a) better national energy planning, policy analysis, and formulation of strategies, (b) accelerated identification, evaluation, exploitation, and marketing of specific energy resources, and (c) improved capability of energy sector institutions to manage and operate such projects. In view of the massive and non-marginal nature of many of these schemes, more pre-investment activity is required to avoid serious misallocations of investments and waste. At the same time, the mobilization of both domestic and foreign financial resources to support the projects themselves requires a major effort by the OIDCs.

For the OIDCs as a whole, the World Bank estimates that almost $900 billion (in constant 1982 dollars) will be required over the next decade. About one third of these investment requirements will be in foreign exchange. To finance these needs, the low-income OIDCs require greater flows of official assistance on concessional terms. Middle-income OIDCs will need better access to international capital markets to increase commercial borrowing on the best possible terms, if excessive debt service burdens are to be avoided. At the same time, the remaining two thirds of investment must come from domestic sources. Energy sector institutions, like petroleum companies, coal mining firms, and electric utilities, have to play a vital role in contributing adequately to their own investment needs. In particular, realistic pricing policies for commercial energy must be pursued to preserve and strengthen the financial viability of these energy sector institutions.

Strategies for Specific Energy Subsectors

Oil: Exploration and development of petroleum must be rapidly increased by identifying and promoting acreage suitable for drilling, and on terms sufficiently attractive to international oil companies. At the same time, domestic expertise and the capabilities of national oil companies (where appropriate) must be strengthened, not only to monitor the efforts of multinational and protect national interests, but also to engage directly in exploration, development, and refining.

Natural Gas: Although the availability of this resource is far more widespread than realized earlier, the lack of an integrated gas development strategy, unavailability of infrastructure, and uncertainty as to future markets, have hindered more rapid development. Because of the very project-specific nature of gas costs and the high costs of transport to markets, greater efforts must be devoted to promotion and market development, pricing, and contractual arrangements for gas use. Domestic institutional capability must be strengthened and more systematic exploration has to be carried out.

Coal: Although coal is a much more abundant resource than oil or gas worldwide, OIDCs are not making adequate use of their indigenous deposits or inputs of this resource. Coherent strategies for coal use, better coordination among different coal suppliers (both local producers and importers), between coal suppliers and users, improved infrastructure and management, and more rational pricing policies are required.

Electricity: This subsector will absorb about two thirds of total investments in commercial energy over the next decade due to its highly capital-intensive nature and relatively high growth rates of demand. Better optimization, especially of distribution networks, and improved demand management and pricing policies are crucial as power systems increase is size and complexity. Particular attention must be paid to identifying and developing hydroelectric resources, based on post-oil crisis relative fuel price changes.

Geothermal: This resource is quite widespread, but lack of data and clear national policy has hindered development. Reconnaissance work, field surveys, and exploratory drilling, as well as market surveys and studies of contractual arrangements between the potential producers and users of geothermal steam, must be given early attention if this situation is to be remedied.

Biomass Fuels: This energy source supplies at least half the gross energy needs of OIDCs, mainly in rural areas where over 80 percent of the population lives. Serious efforts have to made in order to avoid severe fuelwood shortages, deforestation, and attendant ills in many of these nations within the next two decades. On the supply side, massive reforestation schemes must be launched. These initiatives need to be supported by the strengthening of local institutions and grass roots infrastructures, the use of low-cost tree planting methods (suited to projects ranging from small community woodlots to large commercial fuelwood plantations), and better integration of fuelwood programs with other rural and agricultural activities. On the demand management side, the promotion of higher efficiency wood stoves, fuel-switching to charcoal, and other policies, should be vigorously pursued. Most importantly, preoccupation with commercial fuels should not be permitted to dominate the biomass subsector and starve it of resources and attention.

New Energy Sources: Systematic efforts are needed to research, adapt, fieldtest, commercialize, and disseminate the new technologies (such as small hydro, solar, and wind energy). However, because of site-specific resource endowments, the economics of these schemes must be proven on a case by case basis. While the viabilities of these technologies have already been demonstrated, their contribution to total national energy needs will be only a few percent, at most. To analyze the usefulness of these technologies in specific areas, local institutional capability must be developed to deal with the monitoring and adapting of new discoveries and technological improvements from abroad, rather than to unnecessarily duplicate or rediscover such advances. In any case, the commercialization and widespread popularization of new energy sources will remain a difficult problem for many years to come.

5.6   Conclusion

We conclude by noting that the broad energy policy options and specific subsector strategies described above will remain relevant over a reasonable range of future oil prices. Most OIDCs have not yet fully adjusted to the sharp increases in energy prices of the 1970s, and unless there is a dramatic reversal of these prices relative to other goods and services (e.g., back to pre-1973 levels), the policy options and conclusions described in this paper are unlikely to be significantly altered.

Appendix A5.1   List of Oil Importing Developing Countries

Low Income

Afghanistan, Bangladesh, Benin, Bhutan, Burma, Burundi, Cape Verde, Central African Republic, Chad, Equatorial Guinea, Ethiopia, Fiji, Ghana, Guinea, Guinea-Bissau, Haiti, India, Kampuchea, Democratic Lao PDR, Madagascar, Malawi, Mali, Mozambique, Nepal, Niger, Pakistan, Rwanda, Sao Tome and Principe, Sierra Leone, Somalia, Sri Lanka, Sudan, Tanzania, Togo, Uganda, Upper Volta, Viet Nam, Zaire.

Middle Income

Argentina, Barbados, Bolivia, Botswana, Brazil, Cameroon, Chile, Colombia, Cost Rica, Cuba, Dominican Republic, El Salvador, Greece, Guatemala, Guyana, Honduras, Hong Kong, Israel, Ivory Coast, Jamaica, Jordan, Kenya, Korea (PDR), Korea (Republic of), Lebanon, Lesotho, Liberia, Mauritania, Mongolia, Morocco, Nicaragua, Panama, Papua New Guinea, Paraguay, Philippines, Portugal, Senegal, Singapore, Thailand, Turkey, Uruguay, Yemen Arab Rep., Yemen PDR, Yugoslavia, Zambia, Zimbabwe.

References

Sankar, T.L., and G. Schramm, *Asian Energy Problems*, Asian Development Bank, Manila, Philippines, 1982.

UNESCAP, *32 Economic Bulletin for Asia and Pacific*, Bangkok, Thailand, 1981, pp. 46-62.

World Bank, *The Energy Transition in Developing Countries*, Washington DC, August 1983a.

World Bank, *World Development Report*, Washington DC, August 1983b.

Chapter 6

ENERGY DEMAND MANAGEMENT AND CONSERVATION[1]

6.1　Energy Conservation

Basic Issues

Using both price and non-price tools, energy supply and demand management (ESDM) techniques help establish economically efficient or optimal patterns and levels of energy consumption (see Chapters 2 and 3 for details of coordinated application of policy instruments for ESDM). This may involve reducing the consumption of some forms of energy and increasing the use of others that are cheaper or more suitable. Energy conservation is an important element of ESDM and involves measures that specifically seek a deliberate reduction in the use of energy below some level that would otherwise prevail. Such reduction involves elimination of outright waste, reduction of energy-using activity, substitution of one form of energy for another, or substitution of other productive factors like capital and labour for energy.

A recent estimate (World Bank, 1983) indicates that by 1990, developing countries can save over 4 million bbl/day oil equivalent or about 15 percent of total commercial energy consumption if effective conservation policies are adopted, although this will not be easy. Thus, inappropriate pricing of energy resources is not the only reason for inefficient energy conservation decisions. In many developing countries, the lack of foreign exchange resources forces governments to maintain strict import controls. Therefore, it is often impossible for large energy users to import new, more energy-efficient equipment to replace existing plant, even though they are usually able to secure their share of high-cost imported fuel supplies to keep their existing fuel-inefficient equipment operating. In countries in which fuel prices are subsidised at the same time, there is little incentive for such equipment owners to press for appropriate changes in import policies.

Conservation issues unique to developing countries arise in the case of households that depend on traditional fuel resources such as firewood, charcoal and dung. These often employ primitive cooking techniques like open fires that are highly inefficient, using only about 5 percent of the inherent heat energy of the fuel. Heavy population pressures, dwindling firewood resources resulting in sharply increased costs of fuelwood-gathering, as well as increased soil erosion, reduced availability of crop residues from new short-term, high yield crop varieties, all combine to make this one of the foremost and serious energy problems in the majority of developing countries. One promising solution is the use of simple cooking stoves, constructed of locally available materials at out-of-pocket costs barely exceeding a few dollars, which improve energy efficiency by a factor of two to three in laboratory tests and perhaps

---

[1] Edited version of a guest lecture presented at the USAID sponsored Energy Management Training Program for senior officials from developing countries, held at the Institute of Technology Policy in Development, State University of New York, Stonybrook, NY, in October 1978.

by 50 percent or more in actual day-to-day household use (see Chapter 12). It must be noted that socio- cultural factors affecting the acceptability of such new devices should be considered to successfully disseminate these.

Conservation Economics

Some conservation is achieved simply by reducing or eliminating certain energy-using activities. Foregoing Sunday pleasure driving, using a lower thermostat setting and shutting off appliances and lighting fixtures when not directly needed, are typical examples. Other conservation measures may require the substitution of energy by either capital or labour. Examples are: reusing heat in industrial processing, the energy-saving reductions in the weight of vehicles by better engineering or lighter materials, or the use of improved insulation.

The substitution of some form of costly, or scarce, energy resource by some other that is more readily available is an important conservation measure. Examples of this are the use of coal instead of fuel oil in heat processes, the use of natural gas instead of petroleum products for power plants where gas is plentiful compared to oil, or the use of gasohol instead of petrol for transport. In a physical sense (as measured by Btu consumed), such substitution may not 'save' energy. In an economic sense, however, such substitution may be quite sensible, given the economic scarcity values of the alternative fuels.

The pursuit of energy conservation as a goal raises the issue of up to what point the reduction of energy consumption is socially beneficial or desirable (see also Chapter 1 for a related discussion of economic efficiency, energy efficiency and energy conservation). Common sense indicates that 'wasteful' energy use should be discouraged, but there is a limit beyond which conservation becomes too costly in terms of foregoing other resources or useful outputs, thereby causing more harm than good. The principal objective of a given policy should be the maximisation of the welfare of a society over time. If aggregate consumption or production (e.g. gross domestic product or GDP) is taken as a proxy for aggregate welfare, then welfare maximisation implies the use of scarce resources such as energy, capital, labour and land in such a way that output is maximised. Reductions in the use of energy will contribute to this goal, provided that the added costs of such conservation measures or process changes do not outweigh the value of the energy savings achieved.

In simple terms, the adoption of a given conservation measure is economically justified, if $\delta B > \delta C_1 + \delta C_2$; where δB, δC_1 and δC_2 are the economic values of marginal benefits (mainly energy-savings), marginal additional input costs and marginal reductions in consumption benefits, respectively.

This condition should be achieved over the life expectancy of the activity, implying one of expected lifetime costs, not just presently prevailing cost relationships. For example, if energy costs are expected to increase relative to other input costs or the value of output over time, greater substitution by non-energy inputs (i.e. higher levels of energy conservation) is called for. If the time element is introduced, the conservation criterion becomes:

$$\sum_{t=0}^{n} B_t/(1+r)^t \quad > \quad \sum_{t=0}^{n} (C_{1t}+C_{2t})/(1+r)^t \tag{6.1}$$

where B_t, C_{1t}, and C_{2t} are the respective annual energy savings, additional input costs and losses in consumption benefits in year t and r is the discount rate, all defined in terms of appropriate shadow prices.

Technical Efficiency of Energy Use

The technical efficiency of energy use is usually defined in terms of the First and Second Laws of Thermodynamics. The First Law efficiency measures the relationship between total energy inputs and useful energy outputs. The Second Law efficiency relates to a more subtle concept, one that defines the optimal efficiency as the minimum amount of thermodynamic (heat) differential needed to complete a given task.

The *First Law of Thermodynamics* in its simplest form, states that energy (i.e. chemical, electrical, gravitational, heat, mechanical, nuclear, etc.) can only be transformed from one form to another, but cannot be created or destroyed. The corresponding efficiency of an energy using process may be defined as:

e_1 = useful energy output/energy actually input

Application of this efficiency measure requires definition of the boundaries of the system within which the process occurs, and the determination of energy flows across these boundaries. This can be demonstrated by a simple example, the act of heating water in a home by a wood-burning stove as shown in Figure 6.1. Let E_1 be the energy input representing the calorific value of the firewood burned, E_0 the useful energy output absorbed by the water, and E_L the conductive, convective and radiant heat losses. Then the First Law of Thermodynamics defines the energy balance as $E_1 = E_0 + E_L$, and

$$e_1 = E_0/E_1 = 1 - (E_L/E_1) \tag{6.2}$$

Thus, the First Law efficiency of any process may be determined by correctly identifying all the appropriate energy flows and losses. However, this type of energy 'book-keeping' may be quite complicated for a complex system such as a thermal electric power station, involving flows of many forms of energy, including heat, electrical, mechanical and chemical energy (Ahern 1980).

Energy balance analysis provides a convenient framework for determining the First Law efficiencies from primary energy source to final end use, and therefore may be used as one criterion to analyse the efficiencies of different energy delivery systems. For example, in the case of domestic water heating by either natural gas or electricity, the respective First Law efficiencies of the end-use processes are about 0.5 and 0.95. This seems to show that the use of electricity is superior. However, what must also be considered are the efficiencies of the energy production and delivery systems. The First Law efficiency for generating electricity from natural gas at the power station is about 35 percent, and electricity losses in the transmission and distribution networks may be about 10 percent, while the losses in the gas delivery system are approximately 30 percent.

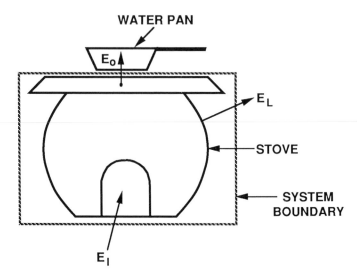

Figure 6.1: First Law Efficiency Analysis of Heating Water

Hence, the First Law efficiency of the total chain from gas to hot water via the electric option is given by:

$$e_{IE} = 0.35 \times 0.9 \times 0.95 = 0.30$$

The corresponding efficiency for direct heating of water using piped gas is:

$$e_{IG} = 0.7 \times 0.5 = 0.35$$

Overall, therefore, the direct gas option appears to be superior.

What must be noted, however, is that this simple analysis neglects many other relevant factors such as the convenience of using electricity versus gas, the substitutability of the two energy sources with respect to other non-cooking energy uses, the relative costs of the delivered energy, etc. These other considerations may well be dominant, and often-times economically more attractive to the user.

The *Second Law of Thermodynamics* seeks to distinguish between energy that is available and unavailable for doing useful work. It states that the entropy (or unavailable energy) of a closed system must remain constant or increase over time. The entropy of a system is closely linked to its state of order. For example, if there are two glasses of water, one at 100 degrees C and the other at 0 degrees C, then by virtue of the temperature difference heat can flow from the hotter to the colder glass. This flow may be used to perform useful work (e.g. using a thermocouple).

If the two glasses of water are mixed together and then separated again, each full glass will be at a temperature of 50 degrees C (assuming there are no heat losses). This has eliminated the temperature differential. At the same time it has also eliminated the possibility of any heat flow between the two glasses, and the capability of extracting useful work from the system. The system entropy has increased while its state of order has decreased since there is now only one category of lukewarm water available. However, the total heat content of the system is unchanged since there was no heat loss. The lower entropy of the original system can be regained by the use of external energy to heat one glass and/or cool the other. But if this occurs, the system is no longer closed to the outside world as required by the Second Law definition. Furthermore, the Second Law also ensures that the available energy used externally to restore the two-glass system to its original state will always be greater than the available energy which can be re-extracted from the system. Thus, even if the original hot-cold system is restored, the total available energy in the system and its external environment would have decreased further, i.e., total entropy has increased.

The Second Law efficiency relates the minimum input required to perform a given task, to the maximum useful work that could have been extracted from the fuel used. It can be defined as:

$$e_2 = \frac{\text{Theoretical minimum energy required}}{\text{Maximum useful work available from actual energy input}}$$

In the simple case of a heat transfer from a hot source to a cold reservoir which is to be heated, the theoretical minimum energy required E_M is defined with respect to the ideal Carnot energy cycle between two temperatures, by (Ahern 1980):

$$E_M = E_0(T_T - T_A)/T_T \tag{6.3}$$

Where E_0 is the quantity of thermal energy transferred, T_T is the absolute temperature (in degrees Kelvin) at which the heat is transferred, and T_A is the absolute (ambient) temperature of the environment. But $E_0 = e_1.$(maximum useful work available), and therefore using equation (6.2), one may write:

$$e_2 = e_1(T_T - T_A)/T_T = e_1(1 - T_A/T_T) \tag{6.4}$$

In this simple example, an increase in First Law efficiency e_1 implies an increase in Second Law efficiency, and vice-versa, provided the other parameters remain unchanged. If T_T is high, i.e., $T_T >> T_A$, then e_1 and e_2 are approximately equal, but if the temperature differential is small, e_2 may be much lower than e_1.

Equation (6.4) is not generally applicable and is used here to simply illustrate the relationship between First and Second Law efficiencies in this special case. e_1 and e_2 are usually linearly independent. Examples have even been quoted where an increase in e_1 is accompanied by a decrease in e_2 (Hertzmark 1981). For a discussion of the various formulae that apply when different forms of energy (such as mechanical, heat, etc.) are involved, see American Physical Society (1975).

As a numerical illustration of equation (6.4), consider a process such as fluidised bed coal combustion to produce electricity where heat is transferred at a very high temperature. The corresponding First and Second Law efficiencies are approximately the same, usually lying between 0.4 and 0.45. In contrast, the First Law efficiency of a gas furnace used for space heating would fall approximately between 0.75 and 0.8, while the corresponding Second Law efficiency would be only about 0.05 to 0.1. This large difference is caused by the fact that natural gas, which is a high quality fuel with a very high flame temperature (1,500-2,000 degrees C), is being used to supply low quality heat, i.e., the burning gas heats air or water to an intermediate temperature which, in turn, transfers thermal energy to the living space. The Second Law efficiency is low because heat is ultimately transferred at a relatively low temperature difference of a few hundred degrees K.

The exclusive consideration of First Law efficiency only may conceal the fact that high quality (or high temperature) energy sources such as fossil fuels are being used for relatively low temperature processes like water and space heating or cooling, industrial process steam production, and so on. Consideration of Second Law efficiency may permit a better matching of energy sources and uses, so that high quality energy, which may be scarce, is not used for performing low quality work. Some approximate First and Second Law efficiencies for typical energy uses or processes are given in Table 6.1.

It should be noted that both First and Second Law efficiencies can be increased by cascading energy use. Thus, a working fluid such as steam may be successively utilised in several processes. As the steam cools along the chain of processes, the quality of heat desired is matched with the steam temperature at each stage to provide the best overall efficiency.

Table 6.1

First and Second Law Efficiencies for Some Typical Energy Uses

Use	First Law Efficiency	Second Law Efficiency
1. Electricity generation or traction (large scale)	0.9-0.95	0.3
2. Industrial steam production	0.85	0.25
3. Fluidised bed electricity generation	0.4-0.45	0.4-0.45
4. Transportation (diesel powered)	0.4	0.1
5. Transportation (gasoline powered)	0.25	0.1
6. Space heating or cooling	0.5-0.8	0.05
7. Domestic water heating	0.5-0.7	0.05
8. Incandescent lightbulb	0.05	0.05

Energy Accounting Frameworks

Increased concerns about the finiteness of the world's depletable energy resources, together with the shock of the petroleum price rises in the 1970s, have led a number of analysts to conclude that energy should be made the unit of account for all production and consumption processes and activities. Such an energy theory of value would seek to establish the relative values of all other goods and services in relation to a numeraire, or yardstick, based on the energy embodied in them. This would elevate energy to the principal scarce resource, but would neglect the value of all other scarce factors needed in production, mainly land, labour and capital. In a market economy, price levels are determined by the interaction of supply and demand forces, but in such a single factor theory of value they would be determined by supply only, namely, the supply or use of one single factor -- in this case, energy. Such single-factor theories of value are not new, of which the best known is the labour theory of value developed by Adam Smith and Karl Marx. Attempts at using energy as the principal unit of account have also been made prior to the 1970s as well.

The major flaw in any attempt to make energy input the major criterion for determining the value of any output or activity is that other resources, as well as time, are needed to produce such output. These resources, as well as those of time are not costless. They have scarcity values and their costs cannot be neglected. If this happens, misallocation of one or all of these other resources is bound to occur. The simple analysis given below illustrates this point, as well as the differences between optimal energy use as defined by Second Law efficiency and the economic viewpoint.

Consider an industrial activity (Figure 6.1) in which some final output (Q) is produced by employing energy (E), and other non-energy inputs (I). For simplicity, both E and I are considered homogeneous aggregates although, in practice, each is likely to consist of many different sub-categories. The activity may be described by the production function:

$$Q = Q(E, I)$$

Production is said to be economically efficient if the output is produced at minimum cost. This may be represented mathematically by the requirement:

Minimise: $p_e.E + p_i.I$, subject to $Q = \overline{Q}$

where p_e and p_i are the prices of energy and other inputs respectively, and $\overline{Q}$ is the constant (target) level of output.

The economics of the industrial process is analysed geometrically in Figure 6.2, where $Q = Q$ is the isoquant or constant level of final output that can be produced by using various combinations of E and I as specified by the production function. The economically efficient or optimal, cost-minimising combination of inputs is (E_e, I_e) at the point of tangency B, between the isoquant and the isocost line AC (which represents different combinations of E and I that have the same total cost to the producer). The isocost line satisfies the equation: $p_e.E + p_i.I$ = constant, and has the slope $-(p_e/p_i)$. It should be noted that AC will become steeper as the price of energy rises relative to other inputs, thus pushing the point of tangency B further up along the isoquant and thereby reducing the economically optimal level of energy input below E_e.

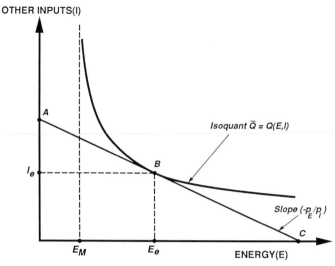

Figure 6.2: Production Isoquant for an Energy Using Activity

According to the Second Law viewpoint, the optimal or minimum energy that should be used for production is E, represented by the vertical asymptote to the isoquant. This represents the case in which energy is effectively considered to be the only scarce resource. In other words, the costs of all other inputs may be neglected, so that the line AC tends towards the vertical, with an infinite slope. Clearly, in this case, the thermodynamically minimum amount of energy (i.e. Second Law efficiency = 1) is less than the economically efficient level E, but an infinite quantity of (costless) other inputs would also be required. Thus, using the economically optimal energy input will generally lead to a Second Law or technical efficiency considerably less than unity.

A subsidiary problem arising out of attempts to elevate relative energy consumption to the sole criteria for ranking is that First and Second Law efficiencies may not coincide and, hence, may not always be consistent with each other.

Another problem that arises with various energy accounting frameworks that have been developed in recent years is that energy itself is not a homogeneous and freely interchangeable commodity. For example, there is a vast difference in the convenience of, say, a million kcals., available in the form of electricity, gasoline, lignite or peat, for different energy uses. Given the often unique matching of specific energy sources and uses, it is also not possible to draw up a hierarchical, qualitative ranking order that would define energy resources in terms of consistently declining usefulness. Electricity, for example, is extremely useful for lighting lamps or providing stationary mechanical energy through the use of electric motors, but it is an awkward and costly energy source for independent vehicle propulsion.

Similarly, energy accounting frameworks that claim inefficiency for various types of energy production processes, because the net output of usable energy of a given process is less than the total input of energy needed in its production, can be rather misleading. For example, the energy inputs of high fertiliser-cum-pesticides-cum-mechanical energy agricultural production processes may be substantially higher than the outputs of the resulting agricultural production, but the latter, in the form of digestible food, may be far more valuable and useful for the intended purpose than the original energy inputs required for its production (Chapman 1975 and Herendeen 1972). As another example, a given quantity of energy inputs for electric power production provided by coal is far less valuable (has lower economic opportunity costs) than a similar quantity of energy supplied in the form of fuel oil or diesel fuel (at least in North America).

For all of these reasons, energy audits, energy book-keeping, technical energy efficiency and energy Btu balance information should be used only as a supplement to the economic assessment of conservation measures, but never as the sole criterion for deciding the appropriate level of energy use for a given activity. (See Hannon et al. 1979, pp. 227-241 and Webb and Pearce 1975, pp. 318-331, for illustrations and critiques, respectively, of energy accounting frameworks.)

6.2 Scope for Applications of Energy Conservation

The practical application of energy conservation policies requires the disaggregate analysis of technical, economic and behavioural relationships underlying various types of energy conservation and end use. This section attempts to summarise the principal practical possibilities for energy conservation in the near term in several selected energy producing and consuming sectors of the economy, based on recent experiences of both industrialised and developing countries. Since the emphasis here is on conservation, mention of improvements in efficiency generally refer to increases in the First Law efficiency of energy use that will yield actual reductions in energy inputs required to perform a particular task. It is also understood that the desirability of adopting any conservation measures must depend on the economic criteria discussed in the previous section, and on the social, political, overall physical and other constraints peculiar to the developing country concerned.

Transportation

The principal purpose of a transportation system is to physically convey people or goods from one location to another. Therefore, any measure which increases the payload in terms of energy used per passenger-mile or ton-mile would help the conservation effort. Important methods of achieving this result include: (a) changing from more to less energy-intensive transport modes; (b) increasing the technical efficiency of energy use of given modes of transportation; and (c) changes in behaviour and overall systems effects. Each of these three aspects are examined below.

Less energy-intensive modes

Table 6.2 summarises some typical characteristics of the chiefly used transport needs. The energy intensity figures for a given mode will vary widely depending on the geographic characteristics, goods transported, behavioural characteristics, and so on. However, even on a rough basis, it may be seen that switching modes could provide substantial savings. For example, a change from passenger car travel to mass transit modes such as bus or rail, or a transition from freight trucks to freight trains, would reduce fuel consumption. In a period of rapidly rising petroleum prices, conservation in the principally liquid fuel using road transport mode should have a high priority. In particular, savings in traffic congestion costs in urban areas and also reductions in air pollution may be significant. However, behavioural, physical and other impediments such as the unwillingness of motor car owners to use public transport, or the inaccessibility of railway stations for freight hauling will make it difficult to effect these changes.

Table 6.2

Typical Energy Use Characteristics of
Principal Transport Modes (1975-80)

	Energy Intensity		Share of Energy Consumption[a]	
	Btu/Passenger Mile	Btu/Ton Mile	Industrialized Country[c]	Developing Country[d]
Walking/bicycle/animal[b]	300-500	-	<.01	.05
Pipeline	-	300-600	.05-.1	<.05
Water	-	400-700	<.05	.05-.1
Railway	2,000-3,000	500-900	<.05	<.05
Bus	1,000-1,500	-	.01-.1	.05-.1
Truck	-	1,500-2,000	.1-.2	.35-.45
Car	2,000-4,000	-	.4-.5	.25-.35
Air	5,000-9,000	15,000-25,000	.05	.05

[a] As a fraction of total commercial energy consumption.
[b] Non-commercial energy use given as a fraction of commercial energy total.
[c] Estimates based on OECD, IEA and USDOE data.
[d] Estimates based on World Bank (1980).

Improved technical efficiency

The technical efficiency of energy use may be increased by introducing more fuel-efficient engines, improving the quality of roads, electrifying railways, and so on. A combination of price, legislation and government investments or other initiatives can be used effectively.

Behavioural changes

Behavioural changes include car pooling, getting people to live closer to their place of work, using alternative methods of communication like telephones where possible, and so on. In many cases, people may be very resistant to adopt these changes in lifestyles, many of which affect the whole socio-economic system rather than the transportation system alone (e.g. urban living patterns, travel and migration patterns, etc.). In developing countries, some of the developmental changes themselves may encourage shifts to move towards energy-intensive and modern modes, e.g., use of motor vehicles instead of walking, bicycles or animal-drawn carts. Therefore, the desirability of any conservation policy must be assessed against the overall economic criterion discussed earlier. Co-ordinated use of price and non-price tools are again important. For example, public exhortations alone are unlikely to be effective.

Households

Three factors affect the consumption of energy in households: (a) behavioural characteristics and attitudes of occupants; (b) energy-using equipment installed; and (c) architectural design practices and material used. Keeping living and working space lit and cool are the chief concerns in the tropics where most of the developing countries lie. In these areas, the use of air-conditioning is growing rapidly for commercial buildings such as businesses, tourist hotels, etc., and, to a lesser extent, for residences of upper income urban and expatriate groups whose numbers are fortunately small in this respect. In countries which are located more in the temperate and colder zones, lighting and both space heating and cooling are required.

The principles that govern the application of energy conservation practices remain the same. Thus, the full range of policy tools, including increases in energy prices, legislation, tax incentives, and so on, will help to implement conservation measures. However, these policies and their consequences must be simple and easily comprehensible. Educating occupants of buildings (especially domestic residents) concerning simple conservation practices, making them aware of new but readily available energy-saving devices, and explaining the consequences of new pricing structures and taxes should have a high priority. The so-called 'information gap' is particularly critical in this area of conservation.

Behavioural changes

Changes in behaviour and attitudes often take time to occur. For example, admonitions to switch off unused lights or set back thermostats may take years to sink into public consciousness, especially if these requests run up against false but commonly held beliefs. For instance, in Indonesia, where a fixed charge lifeline electricity tariff was in effect, low income households were found to be using their lightbulbs for as many as sixteen hours a day. This occurred despite an energy conservation campaign, because it was widely believed that switching lights on and off would reduce bulb lifetime more than if they were kept continuously lit, while the electricity bills were fixed and unrelated to kilowatt-hour consumption.

In other cases, people are unwilling to give up comforts they have grown accustomed to, unless some costs are involved. Thus, requests to set back thermostats in many countries have not been effective except when accompanied by increased energy prices, and only after the effect of increased energy bills were felt. Public resistance may also occur in developing countries where people who are just beginning to enjoy the benefits of economic growth resent being asked to cut back on consumption of electricity for lighting, air-conditioning, and so on. Pricing of energy at economic opportunity cost is very useful in all these cases, because consumers can get the correct price signal and then choose how much energy to use on the basis of willingness-to-pay. Even then, responses to price changes could be slow because these adjustments in energy use patterns may imply major expenditures for purchasing new energy-using equipment as discussed below. In brief, behaviour changes that facilitate conservation may be realised only slowly, and policy makers should fully investigate local attitudes and idiosyncrasies with respect to energy use patterns.

Improved energy use equipment

Improvements in energy-using equipment and appliances in buildings are an obvious target for conservation programmes. Occupants must be made aware of the many opportunities for replacing inefficient equipment, such as furnaces and air-conditioners, retrofits or improvements to existing equipment, or simply improved operation and maintenance procedures. Technical advice, energy audits and guidance could be provided by the government, especially in the case of large buildings (e.g. some of the modern heating and cooling systems are very effective), using an array of techniques ranging from heat pumps to computerised control of equipment in different parts of the building. Legislation on minimum energy efficiency standards for equipment and appliances is also helpful.

As mentioned earlier, the high cost of replacing old equipment may delay consumer response to higher energy price signals. For example, the lump sum cost of a new refrigerator may be a significant fraction of income, thus causing the consumer to wait until his old inefficient refrigerator is worn out before replacing it. Replacing incandescent lightbulbs with fluorescent fittings is another energy-saving measure whose costs may deter a poor consumer. This phenomenon is particularly significant in developing countries where incomes are low and the fuel may be relatively cheap or subsidised (relative to its shadow price). For example, several programmes are under way to replace open hearth fires (whose First Law efficiency is only about 5 percent) with simple stoves that are three or four times as efficient. These have had limited success, and only when government officials provided the improved stoves free or at a subsidised price, coupled with a strong promotion campaign. In all these cases, financial incentives or subsidies on new equipment could be most effective. Hence, energy-saving improvements in equipment will be realised quicker, in general, with the combined use of higher prices, legislation, public education and equipment subsidies.

Architectural improvements

Architectural design, building practices and construction materials used is the third area in which energy conservation gains may be made (Dallaire 1974). Policymakers may make a significant impact by altering building codes and implementing legislation relating to minimum efficiency standards. The orientation of buildings, location of windows, type of glass used, and other architectural features can improve heat losses. Use of improved insulating materials and high standards of construction to avoid flaws or gaps in insulation are also helpful. If buildings are not completely enclosed as in some developing countries, proper design will promote natural air-conditioning. The use of simple local materials by a well-informed and imaginative architect, may become an effective tool for conservation -- for example, brick tiles (instead of asbestos), higher ceilings and installation of fans, are often substitutes for air-conditioning.

There are practical limits to conservation gains that may be achieved in this respect. Improving construction practices or using better building materials will become increasingly costly and, beyond a certain point, these would not justify the increased energy savings, according to the economic criterion described earlier. Again, a perfectly airtight and insulated building may be ideal from the viewpoint of energy efficiency, but would be stifling and uncomfortable to occupants, impose health hazards due to stale or polluted air being constantly recirculated, and so on. In brief, savings due to energy conservation must be weighed against both the quantifiable and sometimes non-quantifiable costs incurred.

Industry

Improvements in the efficiency of industrial energy use cover such a broad range of techniques that only the general principles can be touched on here. Contrary to widespread belief, many industries are unaware of efficiency increases that can be realised quite simply and are extremely cost-effective. Because of the concentrated nature of industrial energy users, both governments as well as energy suppliers and utility companies can be particularly effective in legislating improvements, counselling, providing energy audits and helping consumers carry out technical improvements. Four broad areas for conservation here are: (a) waste heat recovery and co-generation; (b) other retrofits and improvements in operation; (c) major changes in manufacturing processes and production methods; and (d) recycling and recovery of waste materials. These will be briefly examined in turn.

Waste heat recovery and co-generation

Most large industries use energy for heating and a significant fraction of this thermal energy is expelled into the external environment at temperatures well above ambient conditions, usually in the form of hot gases, steam, or water. This waste heat can be harnessed in a number of ways, thus improving the overall efficiency of energy use in the plant by as much as 30 percent. In completely integrated or total energy systems (also called co-generation systems), fuel would be used to generate electricity, yield process heat for industrial use, heat buildings in the area (i.e. district heating), provide hot water, process solid and liquid waste, and so on. A central concept in this type of system is that the overall efficiency of energy use for the total plant be maximised rather than the efficiency of any single component or sub-system such as electricity generation (Bos et al. 1977). In fact, the energy efficiency of certain components may have to be reduced below what it would have been if these were operating on their own. The gains in other parts of the system more than compensate for this loss, and thus overall efficiency improves. For example, the exhaust heat from an electric power generator in a co-generation scheme would be extracted at a somewhat higher temperature than a stand-alone unit, with consequent loss of power output. However, the waste heat could be used much more efficiently in another task because it is available at a higher temperature.

Potential for development of co-generation or total energy systems can be best realised when new industrial plants are being set up. Many examples of co-generation already exist in developed countries and there is also considerable scope for such schemes in large industrial estates being set up in many developing countries. In many cases, legal and institutional barriers to agreements that facilitate the exchange of energy between different entities such as utility companies, industries and municipalities, appear to pose greater difficulties than technical constraints. Energy policy makers should take action to smooth out these problems. In the case of existing industries, where major changes in plant layout are not possible, there is still scope for more limited use of waste heat. For example, an industrial plant using steam for heating could also run an auxiliary generator to produce electricity, or hot exhaust gases could be used for drying industrial materials, pre-heating incoming air, and so on.

The effectiveness with which waste can be put to use depends on several factors, including the temperature of the exhaust and the degree of compatibility with the quality of heat required in the particular application, the availability of sufficient quantities of waste heat to achieve economies of scale, and the distance between the source of the waste heat and its final use. In general, the higher the temperature of the exhaust fluids, the more efficiently it can be used based on the thermodynamic concept of cascading. Some industrial activities that produce waste heat at different temperatures are presented in Table 6.3.

Retrofitting and operating efficiency improvement

The second broad area for encouraging conservation is in the improved operation of existing plant and by appropriate retrofits. Adapting old equipment for co-generation is, of course, also a form of retrofitting, but this has been discussed earlier. There are many other ways in which the energy efficiency of industrial processes may be improved. For example, thermal insulation or lagging of boilers and pipes carrying heating or cooling fluids may be increased, mixing of fuel and air could be improved to provide better combustion, heat transfer can be enhanced, and so on. More sophisticated techniques, such as computerised control of industrial processes, can also increase conservation. In many cases, detailed energy audits by external experts can pinpoint these improvements, identify new energy-efficient devices that are readily available, and demonstrate the cost effectiveness of such conservation practices to the industrialists concerned.

Process changes

The third aspect of conservation involves major changes in industrial activity. Shifts in technology and production processes most often occur in response to changes in the relative prices of energy and other inputs such as capital and labour. Thus, an increase in the real cost of energy would favour a shift towards a less energy-intensive technology. It is noted that autonomous technological improvements can also occur quite independently and sometimes contrary to price changes, due to inventions that improve the efficiency of industrial processes. For example, in the case of aluminium smelting which is one of the most energy-intensive industrial processes, the electricity requirements for smelting a kilogram of aluminium for bauxite ore decreased from about 20 kilowatt-hours in 1940 to about 17 kilowatt-hours by 1975 despite an overall decrease in the real price of electricity. With the added impetus of higher energy costs, a new chlorine process now being introduced will decrease energy consumption to about 10 kilowatt-hours per kilogram of aluminium (Charpie and McAvoy 1978). More generally, the energy inputs per dollar of industrial value added in the US decreased from about 110,000 Btu to 80,000 between 1943 and 1975, reflecting both improvements in the energy efficiency of specific industrial activities and changes in the composition of total output. Appropriate price signals regarding higher energy costs and incentives to encourage research and development to increase the energy efficiency of major industrial production processes are important tools in the conservation specialists' arsenal.

Waste material recovery and recycling

While the bulk of manufactured products are derived from the processing of raw input materials, the recycling of previously manufactured but discarded materials may be less energy-intensive. The difficulties of collecting and sorting waste materials prior to recycling could significantly increase processing costs especially where labour inputs are required to do this. Some typical figures for energy saving through recycling are given in Table 6.4.

Table 6.3

Sources of Waste Heat by Temperature Range

High Temperature		Medium Temperature		Low Temperature	
Source	Temperature (F)	Source	Temperature (F)	Source	Temperature (F)
Nickel refining furnace	2500–3000	Steam boiler exhausts	450–900	Process steam condensate	130–190
Aluminum refining furnace	1200–1400	Gas turbine exhausts	700–1000	Cooling water from	
Zinc refining furnace	1400–2000	Reciprocating engine	600–1100	• Furnace doors	90–130
Copper refining furnace	1400–1500	exhausts		• Bearings	90–130
Steel heating furnaces	1700–1900	Reciprocating engine	450–700	• Welding machines	90–190
Copper reverberatory	1650–2000	exhausts (turbo charged)		• Injection molding	90–190
furnaces		Heat treating furnaces	800–1200	machines	
Open hearth furnace	1200–1300	Drying and baking ovens	450–1100	• Annealing furnaces	150–450
Cement kiln (dry process)	1150–1350	Catalytic crackers	800–1200	• Forming dies	80–190
Glass melting furnace	1800–2800	Annealing furnace cooling	800–1200	• Air compressors	80–120
Hydrogen plants	1200–1800	systems		• Pumps	80–190
Solid waste incinerators	1200–1800			• Internal combustion	150–250
Fume incinerators	1200–2600			engines	
				Air-conditioning and	90–110
				refrigeration condensers	
				Liquid still condensers	90–190
				Drying, baking and curing	200–450
				ovens	
				Hot processed liquids	90–450
				Hot processed solids	200–450

Source: Rohrer and Kreider (1977, p 5)

Table 6.4

Energy Savings From Recycling (1978)

Material	Share of Energy Costs in Value of Output	Energy Use for Processing (kWh/kg)		Saving (%)	Chief Constraints
		from Raw Material	from Waste Material		
Glass	0.35	2.3	2.3	None	Collection
Paper	0.35	1.9	0.95	50	Separation
Steel	0.35	13.4	6.6	50	Impurities, separation & collection
Plastics	0.05	13.0	0.58	95	Technology Commercially Unavailable

Electric Power

Electric power is a relatively mature energy sub-sector where conservation techniques are well developed. This permits clear illustrations of the links between energy conservation, demand management and pricing. The three principal opportunities for improving energy efficiency and conservation in this case arise in respect of: (a) generation; (b) transmission and distribution; and (c) end use of electricity. Emerging technological options are described in OTA (1985) and Johansson et al. (1988).

Generation efficiency

Conservation gains in production of electricity may be achieved through efficiency improvements in individual generating plants or with respect to the whole power system. Switching some generation, where possible, from fossil fuels to renewable and new sources (such as solar, wind and wave power) can also conserve depletable energy resources. The possibilities are extremely country-specific and depend on resource endowments. Efficiency improvements in generation technology have occurred steadily over the last fifty years or more. Many of these advances have stemmed from economies of scale as unit sizes of generators have increased. For example, the largest steam units of about 200 MW available in 1930 had First Law efficiencies of less than 20 percent, while the largest unit size for a current thermal plant is about 1,500 MW which operates at much higher steam pressure and temperatures to achieve First Law efficiencies of about 35-40 percent. New technologies, such as fluidised bed combustion and magneto-hydrodynamic generation, could improve this figure substantially in the future, but thermodynamic laws will limit ultimate efficiencies to around 55 percent.

In the case of large, modern hydro-electric generating units, the hydrostatic or potential energy of stored water is already converted into electrical energy at efficiencies exceeding 90 percent and the scope for improvement is somewhat limited. Retrofitting of existing thermal and hydro plant, and improving operating and maintenance procedures to at least bring them up to original design standards is another area for conservation. The co-generation type arrangements discussed earlier under industrial conservation will also improve efficiency. While being introduced, a new plant is likely to be highly capital-intensive. The alternative of upgrading existing units is so case-specific that high inputs of skilled manpower will be required. The cost effectiveness and desirability of these various options will have to be established case by case according to the overall economic criterion for energy conservation schemes.

System-wide improvements in the efficiency of producing electricity can also be achieved by correctly matching the available technology to the pattern of demand. Meeting a certain shape of load duration curve at the least possible cost requires optimal long-range planning and operation of the power system. For example, least-cost generation planning of an all-thermal system implies that steam or nuclear plants should be built for base load duty (i.e. operating at least 6,000 out of 8,760 hours per year) because their fuel costs are low, although their investment costs are high. The same logic dictates that gas turbine units, which have low capital costs but high fuel costs, should be used for peak period operation, usually about 2,500 hours per year. Similarly, in optimal system operation and load despatch, the available generating plant is used sequentially, starting with the newer base load units that are cheapest to run and ending with old or peaking units that have the biggest fuel costs. Generally, electric utilities offer scope for improvements in system efficiency, especially in many developing countries where engineering-economic optimisation of system planning and operation is neglected or poorly done.

Transmission and distribution efficiency

Conservation in the delivery of electric power is achieved by reducing technical losses in the transmission and distribution (T&D) networks (Munasinghe and Scott, 1982). These losses may be as high as 30 percent of gross generation in some developing countries, although norms in industrial countries are about 10 percent. The determination of optimal or desirable loss levels are based essentially on the trade-off between increased capital costs of augmenting T&D capacity, and corresponding savings in both kilowatt and kilowatt-hour losses. The rapid increases in the costs of electricity supply in the 1970s indicate that the levels of losses previously considered desirable are likely to be unacceptably high today. As shown in Figure 6.3, the optimal trade-off occurs when total costs defined as system costs plus the cost of losses (all in present discounted value terms over a long period of about 10-20 years) are minimised. The desirable loss level shifts from L_L to L_H as energy costs rise. Losses due to theft can also be significant, reaching levels of 10-15 percent in some developing countries. US and European norms are about 2-3 percent. Such losses may be reduced by appropriate improvements in legislation and management of the power utility.

It may be noted that, as system losses decrease, the quality of electricity supplied may also improve (e.g., better voltage and fewer supply interruptions or outages). Therefore, some adjustment to total costs, defined above, may be required to account for the accompanying change in consumption benefits due to improved quality. The magnitude of consumption does not change due to loss reduction because these losses were not consumed originally, in any case.

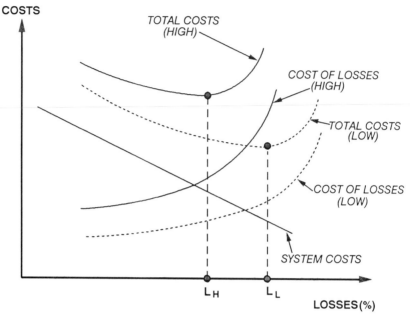

Figure 6.3: Optimal Trade-off Between Losses and System Costs for Electricity Transmission and Distribution Systems (total costs = costs of losses + system costs)

End use efficiency

Energy conservation at the end use stage may be achieved by two principal methods: improving the technical efficiency of energy-using devices and appliances, or changing the shape or characteristics of the load through demand management techniques. The first aspect, increasing the energy efficiency of devices and appliances, has already been discussed in the sections on energy conservation in households and industry. The second aspect uses demand management as a tool to conserve energy and increase the economic efficiency of energy use. In the electricity sector, the term load management is used synonymously with demand management. Because of the relative sophistication and maturity of this sector, load management techniques are well developed and fall into two basic categories: soft load management, which relies on prices, financial incentives and public education to achieve voluntary changes in consumer electricity user patterns; and hard load management, which seeks to realise the same result by actual physical control of consumer loads.

It is more costly to supply electricity during certain seasons or hours of the day known as peak periods than during other off-peak periods. Therefore, changing the shape of the power utility's load curve by shifting electricity consumption from peak to off-peak periods will reduce the costs of supply and conserve energy. Charging higher prices (equal to long-run marginal costs) during peak time-of-day or seasonal periods signals to the consumer that an attempt should be made to switch at least some of the load to off-peak periods (Munasinghe 1981). Separate capacity and energy charges may also be used. Shifts from peak to off-peak consumption result in an increase in the load factor. However, from an economic efficiency point of view, the objective of load management is not to achieve a load factor of 1.0, but to see as far as possible that the price or consumers' willingness-to-pay (i.e. benefit) equals the marginal cost of supply, at all times. Providing financial incentives to retrofit old equipment, improve power factor (by adding a capacitor bank), and so on, are also soft demand management techniques.

The clearest example of hard load management is the case of interruptible loads, where certain industrial consumers receive cheap power but may be cut off or shed at short notice when the total system load approaches the available capacity (during peak periods). Domestic loads, such as water heaters, can also be controlled through ripple control or radio by the utility. Within the next decade, advances in solid state hardware and metering will allow greater control in switching of individual loads through use of micro-processors, and so on.

Traditional Fuels and Environmental Effects

While shortages of traditional fuels are widespread, use efficiencies of these fuels are also generally appallingly low. A substantial percentage of users worldwide simply place a cooking pot on stones over an open fire (which costs them little). However, this process will utilise only about 5-8 percent of the heat energy of the woodfuel. Even quite primitive stoves will increase fuel-use efficiencies to about 15 percent, or by a factor of 2 to 3, while modern, efficient woodstoves may utilise as much as 50-60 percent of the available heat energy of the fuel.

Laboratory and field tests have shown that improved cookstoves, constructed out of local materials for between $2-$20, may save one-half or more of the original fuel needed. Stoves may be made of metal by local artisans and sold in local markets. Alternatively, these may be made of clay and sand by local masons, who could be taught initially by government extension services or private voluntary organisations. Researchers in at least thirty less developed countries are currently developing cookstoves adapted to local cooking and are attempting to spread their use.

In terms of material costs and resulting savings in energy use, the widespread introduction of improved cookstoves is one of the most cost-effective ways to reduce mounting pressures on traditional energy resources (see Chapter 12). It can yield quicker results, if properly implemented, than efforts at re-afforestation which require a minimum of 6-8 years from planting to harvesting. The major problem involved in their widespread introduction and adaptation is that of social acceptability and appropriate organisation. Therefore, at least initially, costs to the promoting organisations are likely to be high.

In regions with high densities of animal population (e.g. cattle or pigs), biodigesters may provide a useful and cost-efficient source of energy. The low-Btu gas produced by such biogas units can be used for cooking, lighting, or the operation of spark-ignition engines. Major problems affecting the widespread introduction and utilisation of these digesters are: (a) the high initial costs (between $400 and $600) for a family-size installation under South and South-East Asian conditions; (b) the need for continuous operation and continuous maintenance and supervision of the system to keep it operating; and (c) the costs of collecting the dung to feed the digester. Therefore, digesters have had their most notable success in areas in which animal density per family is high (6-10 animals per family), and where animals are stabled, which drastically reduces collection costs. Pig manure is more suitable than cow manure. This may help explain the notable success of digesters in China, where pigs are common, as against Pakistan and India, where only cattle manure is available and animals usually are not stabled. An added advantage of the use of digesters, compared to the direct burning of dried manure as fuel, is the fact that the fertilising properties of residual material from biogas digesters are retained and even enhanced.

The need for understanding the impact of energy activities on the environment is becoming increasingly important. It should be noted that the economic criterion for conservation described earlier seeks to include environmental gains and losses, wherever these can be identified, in the cost-benefit analysis, so that the desirability of a conservation measure is judged in relation to its environmental impact. This is important because different energy conservation practices can either improve or worsen the environment.

For example, in the case of automobile exhaust emission, pollution-limiting devices will generally decrease fuel efficiency. Therefore, there is a conflict between the conservation and environment objectives, requiring the trading-off of various gains and losses. On the other hand, reducing the use of woodfuel in certain developing countries may prevent severe deforestation problems that may lead to soil erosion, loss of vegetation, reduced watershed potential, downstream siltation and flooding. Thus, conservation of fuelwood is consistent with the ecological goal, but may involve other costs such as substitution of a more expensive commercial fuel for firewood. Once again, an economic analysis that takes these various external factors into account provides the basis for rational decision making. Where quantification of environmental costs and benefits is difficult, judgement must be used -- based on social, economic, political and other factors.

While many energy supply activities as well as energy uses produce important negative environmental effects, some supply activities also create significant external benefits. Well-known examples are those related to multiple outputs from hydro-power projects such as irrigation and/or potable water supplies, flood protection and navigational or recreational benefits. The value of these joint outputs have long been recognised because of their clearly identifiable and measurable outputs.

However, there exists another group of joint benefits from a different type of energy supply project -- woodfuel plantations -- that takes on increasing importance in those parts of the world where most of the population depends on indigenous biomass resources to satisfy basic cooking and heating fuel requirements. Few systematic attempts have been made to evaluate these external benefits, even though available evidence suggests that these may be larger even than the on-site benefits of the plantations themselves. While the latter may often be marginal, measured in terms of conventional benefit-cost analysis, inclusion of these extended benefits may well prove that such projects have a far higher rate of return than initially estimated.

As an example, the likely on-site effects of a reforestation project may be considered. The direct outputs are likely to be firewood and/or charcoal, timber, animal feed and, perhaps, wildlife and recreation. A second, and most important, consequence of the reforestation of denuded land is the reduction in soil losses. As many studies have shown, tree growth on previously unprotected sloping land will dramatically reduce water run-off rates. For example, a study on reforestation showed that peak flow rates of run-off from storm water decreased by 75 percent over a 6 to 8 year period (Harrold 1971). As a consequence, soil losses from erosion are reduced. This has one important on-site effect; soil productivity is maintained over much longer periods of time and the output of the land (in the form of usable biomass) is enhanced. Such benefits from avoided losses of land productivity may, in some cases, be large enough to justify reforestation as a soil erosion control measure alone.

In addition, however, there are usually important off-site benefits. Eroded material from an unprotected site would usually enter some water course. This could lead to increased turbidity and decreased fish production. More importantly, it would lead to sediment build-up in stream-beds, reservoirs, shipping channels and harbours. Such sediment deposits lead to increased flooding, decreased reservoir life and high costs of dredging. Increased sediment inflows at the Tarbela Dam, Pakistan's largest hydro project, are estimated to have reduced total reservoir life by more than twenty years, as compared to original estimates. Dredging costs due to increased sedimentation in the harbour of Buenos Aires exceeded five million dollars a year in the mid-1970s (Cano 1978). Taken together, the reduction in these losses as a result of a reforestation project designed primarily for firewood production may well outweigh the direct, on-site benefits.

Unfortunately, few studies are available that provide estimates of the actual magnitude of these on and off-site interrelationships. The reason for this dearth of evidence can be found in the difficulties of linking the consequences of reduced run-off and sediment production from a given site with downstream effects that are often hundreds or even thousands of miles away. While it is possible to detect the aggregate relationships -- for example, the drastic reduction of tree cover in the Himalayan Mountain chains are undoubtedly the major cause of huge flood losses in the Gangetic plains in India -- it is difficult to tie individual sites to specific downstream effects. Much more effort will be needed to establish these linkages so that the resulting benefits can be taken appropriately into account.

Other problems are endemic to reforestation projects. First, the issue of common property resource ownership -- most of the original forest stands were denuded because the fuel source was owned by everyone in common. Second, the benefits from avoided off-site losses must be counted in the benefit-cost evaluation of reforestation efforts; this would allow for higher investments per unit of land; but no revenues could be collected to actually pay for these investments. The public sector would have to assume the burden, thus producing future benefits to downstream users. However, such investments would pay little dividends downstream because of the very nature of the benefits, i.e. 'avoided' damages that would remain invisible to the recipients. Third, the gestation period for such projects is long, usually at least 6-8 years, even for fast growing species. If local fuel availability is already strained, newly planted trees may not survive to maturity because of illicit cutting that usually cannot be prevented by policing or fines. In the Upper Mangla Dam watershed protection area in Pakistan, for example, over 60 percent of the indigenous population had outstanding fines for illicit cutting (WPWPA 1961). Needless to say, such fines are rarely paid.

Some Recent Developments

Experience with Policy Applications

In a recent review of over thirty country energy studies (mainly developing countries), the following constraints to effective energy conservation were identified (Gaskin and Gamba, 1983):

(i) *poor awareness* - due to lack of understanding of the problem and inadequate information;

(ii) *incorrect attitude* - arising from the misconception that energy conservation implies deprivation or sacrifice, and the low priority accorded to energy efficiency;

(iii)*weak institutions* - inadequacy of government as well as private sector organisations in formulating and implementing energy management and conservation policies;

(iv)*insufficient technical 'know-how'* - inability to diagnose, design and implement technical solutions to energy efficiency related problems;

(v) *economic and market distortions* - irrational response to conservation measures because of price and other market distortions, or socio-economic factors; and

(vi)*capital shortages* - inability to finance technically and economically viable energy conservation projects.

The same review paper also identified the following corrective measures:

(a) Educational and promotional activities
(b) Improved legislation
(c) Reorganisation of the institutional framework
(d) Technical assistance and energy audit training
(e) Rational pricing policies
(f) Economic, fiscal and trade policies
(g) Financial assistance and allocation of funds.

The specific constraints and the energy management and conservation strategies that would be most appropriate to address each problem are summarised in Table 6.5.

Table 6.5

Constraints and Resolving Measures in Energy Management

Constraints	Conservation Measures
Awareness and attitude	Educational and promotional activities
Institutions	Improved legislation and institutional framework
Technical	Technical assistance and energy audit training
Economic and market	Rational pricing, economic, fiscal and trade policies
Capital	Financial assistance and allocation of funds

An earlier study analysed the relative effectiveness of various conservation methods, taking into account factors such as technical and economic viability (Beijdorff and Stuerzinger 1980). Their ranking is summarised below under three categories:

Very effective conservation measures

industry:
- improved maintenance of equipment
- recycling of waste material
- energy management
- integrated design of processes

transport:
- training of drivers
- weight reduction of passenger cars

buildings:
- training of heat managers
- improved control of air-conditioning
- improved boilers

Moderately effective conservation measures

industry:
- correct choice of energy and combustion technology
- improved insulation

transport:
- reduced vehicle air resistance
- transmission improvements
- engine improvements

buildings:
- improved efficiency of lighting
- draught reduction
- room thermostats
- improved electric cooking appliances
- waste heat recovery
- integrated design with insulation

Not always effective or technically and economically uncertain measures

industry:
- increased performance of electric motors
- co-generation of heat and power

transport:
- reduced losses from friction
- newly designed engines

buildings:
- increased performance of electric motors
- individual heat metering in houses
- heat pumps
- double/triple window glazing
- insulation in houses
- district heating

Energy Efficient Technologies for the Future

In view of worldwide concerns about potential future shortages of energy and serious environmental consequences of energy related activities, considerable efforts have been made towards developing more energy efficient technologies for both the supply and use of energy. The relationships between economic efficiency, energy needs and environmental costs have been discussed already in Chapter 1 and this chapter. One future option that has emerged as a particularly attractive one to improve energy management and reduce environmental damage, involves a faster transition from the technology of today to the more energy efficient world of the future (see Section 1.3 and Appendix A1.1 in Chapter 1) -- this will have implications for energy research and development policy and funding in both the industrialized and developing countries (see Chapter 14). Tables 6.6 and 6.7 summarize the results of a recent survey of the most promising energy technology options and generic technologies that cut across the energy sector (Fulkerson et al. 1988). Efficiency improving options for the electric power sector were described earlier in this section.

Table 6.6

Promising Energy Technology Options

Transportation efficiency

- *Advanced automotive engine technologies*: efficient gas turbines and low-heat-rejection (LHR) reciprocating engines are promising technologies which require improvements in high-temperature materials and lubrication, and attention to the adequacy of combustion and emission control as well. Continued improvement in smart fuel injection systems and, more broadly, combustion enhancing technologies will benefit conventional engines and permit the use of unthrottled engines in spark-ignition versions, perhaps with LHR, for light-duty, light-fuel (gasoline, methanol) applications with notably improved efficiency and low emissions.
- *Continuously variable transmission*: permits optimum operation of engines
- *Automated dynamic traffic control*: smart systems can optimize traffic flow and reduce fuel use
- *Improved aircraft efficiency*: composites, plastics and light alloys may simplify manufacture while saving weight; more efficient by-pass engines should be economical without sacrificing performance; improvements in design and materials should reduce drag; and better operations control should offset increased congestion.

Building efficiency

- *Heat pumps*: major potential gains from more efficient electric and gas-fired equipment
- *Lighting*: more efficient lamps as well as optimum control to meet lighting needs have significant potential
- *Smart control systems - sensors and controls*: precise determination of energy needs and control to reduce waste
- *Envelopes*: heat losses can be sharply reduced with advanced materials and system design
- *Manufactured buildings and components*: economic method of construction that promises significant energy benefits if innovative concepts are included
- *Computer-assisted design for efficiency and cost control*: very economic energy reduction in new buildings; immediate payoff that will continue to grow
- *Existing building retrofits*: improving predictions of energy savings and how building occupants affect energy use will promote cost-effective retrofits

Industrial energy efficiency

- *Catalysts*: improved catalysts can reduce energy requirements of many chemical processes
- *Sensors and controls*: improve process efficiency by precise delivery of exact energy needs using intelligent sensors
- *Separations*: developments include membranes, supercritical fluid extraction, and improvements to distillation with much lower energy requirements
- *Advanced heat management*: optimization of heat flows by improving monitoring and control, high temperature heat pumps, recuperators, and storage can reduce losses substantially
- *Cogeneration*: steam-injected aeroderivative turbines, fuel cells, and other innovations make continuing progress likely for both industry and large building applications.

Table 6.6 (contd.)

Industrial energy efficiency (contd.)

- *Pulp and paper processes*: integration of fermentation into the conventional pulping process promises significant energy savings
- *Steel processes*: advanced steelmaking processes can reduce energy use by 50% as well as increase productivity
- *Agricultural techniques*: new plants and new techniques for cultivation and harvesting promise to reduce requirements for energy as well as for water and fertilizer

Electricity applications

- *Superconductor applications*: great improvement in the efficiency of motors, transmission lines, etc., if the new materials prove feasible
- *Power electronics*: efficient control of motors and other electrical devices

Advanced conversion to electricity

- *Aeroderivative gas turbines* (intercooled steam-injected gas turbine, etc.): low cost, very efficient; may be technology of choice for electric generation if gas is available or when coupled to coal or biomass gasification
- *Brayton cycle*: high-temperature gas turbine combined-cycle utilizing MHTGR should yield 45-50% efficiency in electricity production
- *Kalina cycle*: possible 50% efficient conversion for combined gas turbine and kalina steam/ammonia turbine cycles if capital costs can be reduced
- *Fuel cells*: very efficient electric generators with low NO_x emissions if gas is available, but cost and longevity are uncertain
- *Hot gas cleanup*: key to high-efficiency gasification of coal and biomass

Petroleum

- *Enhanced oil recovery*: major opportunity for increasing oil availability as oil prices increase
- *Field characterization techniques*: extend use of enhanced oil recovery and optimize infill drilling

Natural gas

- *Exploration and drilling techniques*: new gas fields (e.g., deep gas) at moderate cost
- *Unconventional gas techniques*: extend use of enhanced oil recovery and optimize infill drilling

Coal

- *Oil substitutes*: coal-water mixtures and micronized coal can provide a relatively easy replacement for industrial use of oil; advantages for fluidized bed combustion
- *Fluidized bed combustion*: economic and environmental advantages for both utility and industrial coal combustion
- *Bioprocessing*: economically desulphurized coal and potential breakthroughs in gasification and liquefaction
- *Gasification*: key to greatly expanded use of coal as a replacement for natural gas and perhaps oil
- *Liquefaction*: most likely way to replace large quantities of oil

Nuclear fission

- *Improving light water reactor (LWR) technology*: substantial energy contribution from increased availability of existing plants and improved public acceptance from incident-free, high-productivity operation; advanced LWR technology could reduce cost and incorporate passive safety features

Table 6.6 (contd.)

Nuclear fission (contd.)

- *Modular high temperature gas reactor*: advanced concept featuring passive safety should enhance public acceptance; standardized modular design; potential for very high efficiency and process heat applications; could be crucial for CO_2 reduction
- *Liquid metal fast breeder reactor*: important option for ensuring long-term fuel supply; urgency of need will increase if concern about greenhouse effect leads to large-scale nuclear deployment; passive safety features need to be proven
- *Waste management techniques*: implementing a waste management plan based on public participation and consensus is necessary for public health and a prerequisite for nuclear revival

Fusion

- *Fusion power*: inexhaustible, CO_2-free energy source (with potential for relatively small environmental impacts); long term development program but should provide valuable spinoffs; magnetic fusion R&D international in character
- *Fissile fuel breeder*: uses fusion technology to produce fuel for fission reactors

Biomass

- *Feedstock development*: increased plant productivity can make biomass a significant liquid energy source; new sources of energy (e.g., hydrogen and oil from algae)
- *Conversion technology*: fermentation, other direct liquefaction techniques, and gasification (indirect liquefaction) tailored to feedstock species are keys to biomass derived transportation fuels to replace fossil fuels
- *Municipal solid waste processing*: produce energy from recycled materials while reducing landfill problems

Solar electric

- *Photovoltaic energy conversion*: cost breakthroughs possible; already economic for some applications; small packages with appropriate storage could be future technology of choice, especially if CO_2 is a problem
- *Solar thermal*: may be cheaper than photovoltaics but is more complex and lacks market niches to grow in
- *Hydroelectric*: methods to realize 50 GW(e) additional capacity focus on analysis and minimization of environmental effects to fish and other aquatic life
- *Wind turbines*: power electronics, better materials, and improved aerodynamics should lead to significant cost reductions

Storage

- *Advanced batteries*: key to electric vehicles and photovoltaics
- *Thermal storage*: new materials, some using chemical processes or phase changes, could improve solar thermal economics and intermittent processes

Source: W. Fulkerson et al. (1988)

Table 6.7

Generic Technologies that Cut Across the Energy Sector

Microelectronics and sensors

- Smart systems for control of industrial processes, combustion efficiency, building heating/cooling/lighting, etc.
- Sensors for determining conditions in harsh environments

Advanced materials

- Ceramics for high-temperature engines
- Surface treatments, including low-friction materials
- Superconductors for motors, power electronics, and transmission lines
- Materials by design
- Lightweight structural materials
- High-temperature, erosion- and corrosion-resistant materials for hot gas cleanup, turbines, heat exchangers, etc. in harsh environments

Biotechnology

- Improved plants for high biomass productivity
- Microbes for coal cleaning, oil recovery, and hydrogen production
- Genetic engineering of improved enzymes

Separations

- Improved distillation
- Membranes
- Supercritical fluid extraction
- Low-grade ore recovery (including recovery from seawater)

Combustion science

- Efficiency improvement and environmental control of internal combustion engines and boilers
- Enhanced fuel switching capability
- Municipal waste incineration

Geosciences

- Improved understanding of reservoirs for enhanced oil recovery
- Gas exploration techniques
- Unconventional gas recovery
- Categorizing and evaluating geothermal energy resources
- Waste immobilization and isolation

Effluent Management

- Waste reduction and recycling
- Pollution control techniques for improving the efficiency of transforming and scavenging harmful effluents
- More manageable waste forms (stable and degradable)

Table 6.7 (contd.)

Decision making and management

- Planning for technologies involving social risk (e.g., more effective mechanisms for public participation in decision making)
- Managing the reduction in the emissions of CO_2
- Implementing high energy efficiency strategies
- Utility least-cost planning
- Planning for uncertainties

Source: W. Fulkerson et al. (1988)

6.3 Case Study in Energy Conservation

As an example of the trade-off between capital and operating costs, consider a particular end use for energy such as home lighting, and assume there is a choice of two distinct types of lightbulbs, incandescent and fluorescent. For simplicity, begin by assuming that both have the same economic cost, same lifetime and provide light output of the same quality. If the fluorescent bulb uses less electrical energy than the incandescent one, then replacing the latter by the former is a conservation measure that results in an unambiguous improvement in economic as well as technical efficiency. In this case, using fluorescent bulbs instead of incandescent lamps reduces the economic resources expended to provide the desired output, i.e., lighting. Electrical energy has been conserved, with no change in other economic costs and benefits.

Next, assume that the fluorescent bulb is more costly to install. There is a trade-off between the higher capital cost of the fluorescent lamp and the greater consumption of kWh by the incandescent bulb. The relevant data to determine whether substitution of incandescent by fluorescent bulbs is economically justified are summarised in Table 6.8. At this stage, a distinction is made between the economic value (or opportunity cost or shadow price, as discussed earlier) of a good or service, and its market price. The former is relevant to decision-making from a national perspective and the latter is more appropriate from a consumer's viewpoint.

The notional cost (based on economic values) of using the incandescent and fluorescent bulbs over their two-year lifetimes are, respectively:

$$EC_I = 10.5 + 16 + 16/(1 + r)$$
$$EC_F = 32 + 4.4 + 4.4/(1 + r)$$

Assuming an economic discount rate of $r = 0.1$, it is found that $EC_I = 41.0 > EC_F = 40.4$.

The energy cost saving of $(16 - 4.4) = 11.6$ dineros per year for two years has been compared against the increase in capital costs $(32 - 10.5) = 21.5$ dineros. It is found that $(16 - 4.4) + (16 - 4.4)/(1 + r) > (32 - 10.5)$. Therefore, using fluorescent lightbulbs, with their associated reduction in energy consumption, will improve economic as well as technical efficiency.

Table 6.8

**Physical and Economic Data to Assess Economic Efficiency
of Energy Conservation for Lighting**

		Incandescent Bulb	Fluorescent Bulb
Installation cost (dineros)	Economic value (opportunity cost)	10.5	32
	Market price	18	36
Physical energy consumption (kWh per year during two-year lifetime)		40	36
Value of energy consumption (dineros per year during two-year lifetime)	Economic value (marginal opportunity cost)[a]	16	4.4
	Market price[b]	12	3.3

[a] Dineros 0.4 per kWh.
[b] Dineros 0.3 per kWh.

Note, however, that if r = 0.2 is used, EC_I = 39.8 < EC_F = 40.1, and the conservation measure is no longer beneficial. This reduction in the relative value of conservation will always occur with increases in the discount rate, because increases in initial investment costs are traded off against the future cost savings realised by conservation. This finding has important policy implications. Energy users who confront high opportunity costs of capital (e.g. those in many developing countries) will find costly capital-intensive energy conservation measures relatively less attractive than users who have access to low-cost sources of capital. This means that economically 'optimal' conservation measures may differ significantly among different countries.

Market imperfections and private consumers

So far, the analysis has been based on the national viewpoint, using values for all inputs and outputs (including those for energy) reflecting economic opportunity or shadow costs. However, market prices may differ from shadow values because market imperfections, particularly in the pricing and availability of energy, abound in most countries.

To illustrate the effects of these divergencies, the simple lightbulb example may be used again. The private costs (based on market prices) of using incandescent or fluorescent lighting, respectively are as follows:

$$PC_I = 18 + 12 + 12/(1 + R) \text{ ; and } PC_F = 36 + 3.3 + 3.3/(1 + R)$$

At a discount rate of R = 0.1 (e.g. the market interest rate based on private bank rates): PC_F = 40.9 < PC_I = 42.3. This means that a rational consumer would prefer to use incandescent light bulbs, because this is the cheaper option. At any higher discount rate, the advantages of the incandescent system over the fluorescent one increases further. Thus, since market prices diverge from real economic costs, consumers would make economically inefficient energy use decisions.

Price and non-price policy interactions

In addition to appropriate pricing, there is a wide variety of direct and indirect policy measures that can be taken to bring about desirable levels of energy conservation. Among these are direct regulation of energy uses, regulation of the use of energy-consuming equipment and appliances, mandatory standards, mandatory information requirements about energy consumption rates, taxes and subsidies, appropriate infrastructure investments for energy-saving facilities (e.g. better roads, railroads, marine shipping facilities), education and propaganda, and others.

To analyse some of the effects of such conservation-oriented policies, the lightbulb example can be taken up once again. As has been found, existing market prices have made it more attractive for users to opt for the incandescent lightbulb system. To resolve this difference between optimal economic and private market choices, the first option policy makers might consider could be to raise the market price of electricity from 0.3 dineros per kWh to its economic value of 0.4 dineros per kWh. This yields the result: $PC_I = 40.5 > PC_F = 44.4$ and rational electricity consumers will make the correct decision in favour of fluorescent lighting. In addition, setting the electricity price equal to its marginal opportunity costs will help to establish electricity consumption for non-lighting purposes also at optimal levels.

Suppose that public resistance or other social pressures make it impossible to raise electricity prices. Let the economic value of an incandescent bulb be its cost of production or producer price, while the imposition of a government tax of 7.5 dineros determines the market price. Similarly, assume that an import duty of 4.0 dineros represents the difference in the c.i.f. import cost (32 dineros) and the market price of fluorescent bulbs. Instead of raising electricity prices, an alternative policy option might be to raise the tax on incandescent lightbulbs to 9.5 dineros, making the market price 20 dineros. In this case, $PC_I = 42.9 > PC_F = 42.3$, which encourages the desirable consumer decision. Reducing the duty on fluorescent bulbs to 2 dineros, and thereby lowering the retail price to 34 dineros, would also yield a favourable result, since now: $PC_I = 40.9 > PC_F = 40.3$.

Some combination of the tax increase and lowering of duty could also be used. From a strictly economic viewpoint, and ignoring effects outside the lightbulb market, reducing the import duty would be preferable to raising the producer tax -- because the former action reduces the divergence between market price and economic opportunity cost of fluorescent bulbs, whereas the latter has the opposite effect and increases the market distortion in the price of incandescent lightbulbs.

Next, assume that the tax on incandescent lightbulbs cannot be increased because the legislation affects a much larger class of related products. Similarly, suppose that the import duty on fluorescent bulbs cannot be reduced because it would undercut the price of a high-cost local producer and drive the producer out of business. In this instance, some final options left to the energy policy maker might be to legislate that all incandescent lightbulbs be replaced by fluorescent ones, or to give a direct cash subsidy to consumers who adopt the measure, or to mount a major public education and propaganda campaign to bring about the required change.

Legal barriers, capital rationing or lack of credit facilities, inappropriate foreign exchange rates, price controls, externalities and many other factors interfere in the normal functioning of the energy market. Other complications arise from a lack of knowledge of available alternatives as well as other costs and prices, and the lock-in effects of long-lived facilities and equipment. All of these factors tend to distort rational choice patterns, with the result that private energy use and conservation patterns diverge substantially from those found to be optimal from a rational viewpoint (i.e. based on economic efficiency criteria).

Complications

If the useful lifetimes of technological alternatives are different, then economic comparisons become somewhat more complicated. This would be the case in the earlier example if the lifetime of incandescent bulbs were to be only one year while that of fluorescent lamps was three years. Two alternative approaches could be used to overcome this difficulty. In the first, the investment costs of each alternative would have to be annuitised over its lifetime at the appropriate discount rate, and the associated energy consumption and other recurrent costs for one year would be added on. Then the total costs for each option would be compared. The second method would compare the full costs of each alternative over a much longer period, say 20 years, including the costs of periodic replacement of worn-out equipment and taking into consideration the scrap value of left-over equipment. The two methods should give consistent results, assuming the same values are used for parameters such as the discount rate.

Another difficulty associated with changes in the benefits of consumption arises if the quality of the end product of energy use is different for the two alternatives. Consider a comparison of electric versus kerosene lamps for lighting. In addition to the differences in equipment and fuel costs, the cost-benefit assessment of the two options should also include a term to recognise that electricity is likely to provide lighting of a superior quality. While the quantification, in monetary terms, of this qualitative superiority will be difficult, one measure might be the willingness-to-pay of the consumers for the different forms of lighting, usually represented by the area under the relevant demand curve. The ease and convenience of using a fuel, the danger from its use, its social acceptability, and so on, are all factors that may affect the consumer choice.

Specific conservation measures such as rationing have a quality effect that must be taken into account. For example, with the physical rationing of petrol, the cost or welfare loss to the consumer due to the reduction in the miles the consumer can travel in a car must be added to the cost of implementing the rationing scheme, and then compared with the benefits of reduced petrol supply. Once again, the willingness-to-pay of petrol users would be the appropriate measure of the foregone consumption benefit. However, in the long run, petrol consumption could also be reduced by the introduction of a more fuel-efficient car engine without (perhaps) requiring a reduction in the miles travelled. This shows that a reduction in energy consumption does not always imply a reduction in consumption benefits; a major focus of the appropriateness of conservation policies should be the service derived from the energy use.

Finally, the costs and benefits associated with externalities should be included in the economic cost-benefit comparison of alternatives. For example, improvements in technical efficiency or fuel substitution measures may give rise to pollution, as in the case of conversions from oil-burning to coal-fired electric power plants. These additional 'external' costs should be explicitly evaluated in the analysis. The effects of sunk costs must also be recognised. Thus, if an oil-burning generating plant already exists, the initial comparison must allow for the fact that the system costs of the oil option has no associated capital costs until the plant is physically fully depreciated.

References

Ahern John E., *The Energy Method of Energy Systems Analysis*, John Wiley & Sons, New York, 1980, pp.24-30.

Alessio, Frank J., "Energy Analysis and the Energy Theory of Value", *The Energy Journal*, vol. 2, no. 1, Jan. 1981.

American Physical Society, "The Efficient Use of Energy", US Government Printing Office, Washington DC, 1975.

Baum, Warren C., "The World Bank Project Cycle", *Finance and Development*, The World Bank, Washington DC, December 1970.

Baumol, W.J. and D.F. Bradford, "Optimal Departure from Marginal Cost Pricing", *American Economic Review*, June 1970.

Beijdorff, A.F. and P. Stuerzinger, "Improved Energy Efficiency: The Invisible Resource", presented at 11th World Energy Conference, Munich, West Germany, September 1980.

Bos et al., "The Potential for Co-generation Development in Six Major Industries by 1985", FEA Report, Resource Planning Associates, Cambridge, MA, 1977.

Cano, R., "Argentina, Brazil and the La Plata River" in A. Utton and L. Teclaff (eds.), *Water in a Developing World*, Westview Publishing Company, Boulder CO, 1978.

Charpie, Richard A. and Paul McAvoy, "Conserving Energy in the Production of Aluminium" *Resources and Energy*, vol.1, September 1978.

Dallaire, G., "Designing Energy Conserving Buildings", *Civil Engineering*, April 1974.

Davidson, R., "Optimal Depletion of an Exhaustible Resource with Research and Development towards an Alternative Technology", *Review of Economic Studies*, March 1978.

Fulkerson, W. et al., *Energy Technology R&D*, Oak Ridge National Lab., Tenn., USA, 1988.

Garfield, P.J. and W.F. Lovejoy, *Public Utility Economics*, Prentice-Hall, Englewood Cliffs NJ, 1964.

Gaskin, Gary and Julio Gamba, "Factors which Influence the Rational Use of Energy", presented at OLADE International Seminar on Rational Use of Energy in Industry, Lima, Peru, July 1983.

Hannon, Bruce M. et al., "The Dollar, Energy and Employment Costs of Protein Consumption", *Energy Systems and Policy*, vol.3, No.3, 1979.

Harrold, Lloyd L., "Effect of Vegetation on Storm Hydrographs", Biological Effects on the Hydrological Cycle, Proceedings of 3rd International Seminar for Hydrology Professors, Lafayette, Ind., 1971.

Hartwick, J.M., "Substitution Among Exhaustible Resources and Intergenerational Equity", *Review of Economic Studies*, March 1978.

Heal, G., "The Relationship between Price and Extraction Cost for a Resource with a Backstop Technology", *The Bell Journal of Economics*, vol.7, Autumn 1976.

Hertzmark, Donald, "Joint Energy and Economic Optimization: A Proposition", *The Energy Journal*, vol.2, no.1, Jan. 1981.

International Energy Agency (IEA), *Energy Conservation*, Organisation for Economic Cooperation and Development, Paris, 1981.

Johansson, Thomas B., B. Bodlund and R.H. Williams, *Electricity*, Lund University Press, Sweden, 1989.

Munasinghe, Mohan, "The Costs Incurred by Residential Electricity Consumers due to Power Failures", *Journal of Consumer Research*, vol.7, March 1980.

Munasinghe, Mohan, "Principles of Modern Electricity Pricing", *IEEE Proceedings*, vol. 69, March 1981.

Munasinghe, Mohan and Walter G. Scott, "Energy Efficiency: Optimisation of Electric Power Distribution System Losses", Energy Department, The World Bank, Washington DC, 1982.

Munasinghe, Mohan and Jeremy J. Warford, *Electricity Pricing*, Johns Hopkins University Press, Baltimore and London, 1982.

Office of Technology Assessment (OTA), *New Electric Power Technologies*, U.S. Congress, Washington DC, July 1985.

Peck, A.E. and O.C. Doehring, "Voluntarism and Price Response: Consumer Response to the Energy Shortage", *The Bell Journal of Economics*, vol.7, Spring 1976.

Pinto, Frank J.P., "The Economics of and Potential for Energy Conservation and Substitution", presented at 5th Annual International Meeting of IAEE, New Delhi, India, January 1984.

Rohrer, W.M. and K. Krieder, "Sources and Uses of Waste Heat", *Waste Heat Management Guidebook*, NBS Handbook 121, US Government Printing Office, Washington DC, January 1977.

Samii, M.V., "Economic Growth and Optimal Rate of Oil Extraction", *OPEC Review*, vol.3, 1979.

Seneca, Joseph J. and Michael K. Taussig, *Environmental Economics*, second edition, Prentice-Hall, Englewood Cliffs NJ, 1979.

Walker, James M., "Voluntary Responses to Energy Conservation Appeals", *Journal of Consumer Research*, vol.7, June 1980.

Webb, Michael and David Pearce, "The Economics of Energy Analysis" *Energy Policy*, December 1975.

West Pakistan Water and Power Authority (WPWPA), Mangla Watershed Management Study, Lahore, Pakistan, 1961.

World Bank, *Energy in the Developing Countries*, Washington DC, 1980

World Bank, *The Energy Transition in Developing Countries*, Washington DC, 1983.

Chapter 7

NATIONAL ENERGY POLICY IMPLEMENTATION: ENERGY CONSERVATION IN SRI LANKA[1]

7.1 Introduction

This chapter seeks to describe how a national energy demand management and conservation programme (NEDMCP) was successfully formulated and implemented in Sri Lanka during the period 1982 to 1986, as part of the national energy strategy (see Chapter 4 for further details on the latter). It provides some flavour of the many background activities that are essential to support practical implementation of an energy conservation strategy. The first section of the paper is based on the introductory speech made by the author, at the Senior Executive Seminar on Demand Management and Conservation for high level ministry officials and heads of government corporations, that helped launch a major effort in this area, in mid 1983. The presence of President Jayawardene at this gathering underscored the importance attached to sound energy management, by the government. The second part of this chapter describes some of the follow-up to the seminar, where the EDMAC Task Force of the Ministry of Power and Energy vigorously pursued the NEDMCP, in collaboration with other concerned government institutions (Munasinghe 1985).

The NEDMCP, which also received assistance from foreign donors, consists of the Industrial Energy Conservation Programme (IECP) dealing with industrial and commercial energy users, as well as conservation programmes in the transport, household, and agricultural sectors, and among energy supply institutions. As indicated in Figure 7.1, the IECP was implemented in 4 phases involving (1) sensitization; (2) training and technology transfer; (3) project analysis, financing and implementation; and (4) transition to self-sustaining activity. The Senior Executive Seminar was a critical activity in phase 1.

The NEDMCP also includes the Transport Energy Conservation Programme (TECP), since this is the other sector in which there is significant oil use. The first phase of TECP consisted of a comprehensive study by a team of foreign and local consultants, which helped to identify areas for immediate action that can yield short-term benefits, as well as medium- and long-term programmes that may require significant investments and effort. Conservation activities aimed at household energy users were pursued also under the NEDMCP, mainly through public education and media campaigns. Energy use in agriculture and rural areas was studied to identify where conservation efforts could be most effective. The introduction of new efficient fuelwood cooking stoves in about 2.5 million Sri Lanka houses was the high priority

---

[1] The first part of this chapter is an edited version of the plenary opening address delivered at the Senior Executive Seminar on Demand Management and Conservation, Colombo, Sri Lanka, July 1983 and subsequently published in M. Munasinghe (ed.), *Energy Conservation in Sri Lanka*, Government Press, Colombo, Sri Lanka, 1983; while the second part is adapted from M. Munasinghe, *National Energy Demand Management and Conservation Program*, Ministry of Power and Energy, Colombo, Sri Lanka, 1985.

objective of the National Fuelwood Conservation Programme (NFCP), launched by the NERSE Task Force (see Chapters 4 and 12). Finally energy efficiency improvements in the Ceylon Electricity Board (CEB) and Ceylon Petroleum Corporation (CPC), will continue to yield significant savings.

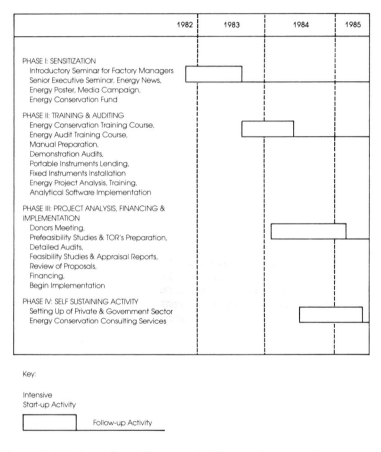

Figure 7.1: Industrial and Commercial Energy Conservation Program

While energy demand management and conservation is an attractive activity with significant payoffs in the short to medium run, the long-run options include development of new energy resources including hydro, biomass and (imported) coal, as well as oil and gas exploration, and peat development. These alternatives are being studied within the framework of a National Energy Strategy (NES), using sophisticated energy modelling techniques (see Chapter 4).

7.2   The Senior Executive Seminar and Energy Outlook in Early 1983

The purpose of this section is to provide a brief introduction to the Senior Executive Seminar on Energy Demand Management and Conservation and explain its basic objectives and relevance to the participants -- high level managers from the public and private sectors in Sri Lanka. The subject is developed through a set of rhetorical questions.

Let us first ask the fundamental question: "What is Energy Demand Management and Conservation?"

Through demand management and conservation we seek to guide and limit the patterns of energy consumption and make them conform to levels that are desirable or optimal from the viewpoint of the whole national economy. In the process, we avoid wastage and improve the efficiency of energy use. Energy conservation does not mean that we deprive ourselves of precious energy. We all know that Sri Lanka needs more energy to grow in the future. Therefore we should use our limited energy resources as efficiently as possible. This is the goal of demand management and conservation.

The second question is "Why is Energy Demand Management and Conservation so important?"

One crucial reason is that since the energy crisis in 1973, the cost of the oil as well as all other forms of energy have risen sharply, and are unlikely to decrease significantly. For a developing country like Sri Lanka which is short of foreign exchange, the high price of imported oil, as well as the costs of building new energy producing facilities (such as hydroelectric dams), provide strong justification for treating energy conservation as a high priority task.

There is also another very important rationale for energy conservation. As you well know, under the leadership of President Jayawardene, Sri Lanka adopted a new liberalized economic policy in 1977. As a result of this bold initiative, we have recorded an unprecedented average annual economic growth rate of 6.2% over the last 5 years, at a time when the world economy was generally in recession. However, this rapid growth has resulted in an enormous burden being placed on all aspects of our national infrastructure, including energy. Today, Sri Lanka is like a young child which has rapidly outgrown its clothes. While a new suit of clothes is being prepared, we have to make do with our old garments. In other words since our energy facilities are severely strained, we have to build new ones. However, new facilities like hydroelectric dams need many years to complete. Therefore while new long-run energy resource development is taking place, we have to rely on demand management and conservation techniques in the short run, to help us balance the available supply of energy against the increasing demand.

In short, a well implemented national conservation programme can yield, within 2 to 3 years, energy savings of up to Rs. 500 million per annum, with very high benefit to cost ratios, because such conservation projects are most profitable.

Third, let us examine why we are having this Seminar.

The bulk of commercial energy consumption, that is electricity and petroleum products, occur within the large industrial and commercial establishments represented in this room.

Without exaggeration, those present at the Seminar are the cream of senior management decision-making talent in Sri Lanka. Through decisive action, they can have an immediate impact on energy conservation in their own institutions. Further, through their leadership and demonstration, there can be multiplier effects throughout the rest of the economy, particularly with respect to conservation practices among the multitude of smaller consumers. While many of the participants are already well aware of energy conservation and have launched some of their own initiatives, we hope this seminar will help to heighten consciousness on this subject. It is designed to provide the participants with the necessary background information and orientation to assist them in making critical policy and executive decisions on various energy options, identifying demand management and conservation opportunities and evaluating energy efficiency project proposals. The seminar will also provide a forum for exchanging views on the subject.

Fourth, I will summarize the programme of energy activities we are launching.

In late 1982, President Jayawardene approved the setting up of an Energy Coordinating Team (ECT) in the Ministry of Power and Energy, supervised by the Senior Energy Advisor.The ECT's objective is to coordinate and facilitate the work of relevant Ministries and existing line agencies working in the energy area, prevent duplication of effort, and supplement weak or neglected areas.

The ECT consists of the following three Task Forces and their support staff (see Figure 4.4 in Chapter 4):

1. Energy Planning and policy Analysis (EPPAN);
2. New, Rural and Renewable Sources of Energy (NERSE);
3. Energy Efficiency, Demand Management and conservation (EDMAC).

The EDMAC Task Force is examining energy pricing policy options as well as loss reduction efforts in the Ceylon Electricity Board and Ceylon Petroleum Corporation, and conservation programmes in sectors such as industries, transportation, agriculture and households. However, as evidenced by this seminar, our principal emphasis recently has been on the largest energy using industrial and commercial establishments in both the public and private sectors of this country.

We have already had an introductory seminar on this subject for senior factory managers from these institutions. We also hope to have a more detailed and practical energy demand management and conservation course for about 50 senior factory managers starting in September, 1983. This will be followed by detailed energy audits of selected energy consuming institutions, the preparation of comprehensive conservation projects, and the submission of these project proposals to suitable financing agencies within and outside the country. EDMAC will also prepare a manual for carrying out energy audits and then extend this training programme so that there will be an ever expanding group of governments and private sector specialists skilled in energy demand management and conservation techniques. Within two or three years, the whole energy conservation programme should become self-sustaining. To summarize, we will strongly promote, assist and catalyse energy conservation efforts, but ultimately, the energy consumers themselves must take the initiative.

Fifth and finally, the Seminar participants may well ask "What can I do to make this national demand management and conservation effort a success?"

Much of what we hope to achieve will depend on the support of senior managers. The government will do its best to provide technical know-how and a climate that promotes conservation. But it is the managerial skills of high level executives that will make or break these programmes, especially at the implementation stage.

We note that energy conservation generally comes in three phases. First there are good house-keeping measures like switching off lights, keeping furnaces well tuned, improving the insulation, and so on, which are fairly obvious and are relatively costless to implement. Second, there are the so-called "retrofits" which involve substantial investments, for example the replacement of a boiler. A feature of most of these energy conservation measures is that they are extremely cost effective. Third, firms may decide to make significant changes in their production processes. All these arguments suggest that energy conservation is presently the cheapest way of buying additional energy resources to meet future consumption needs.

Therefore, the Seminar attendees are urged to:

(1) follow-up vigorously on the good house-keeping measures that will be recommended to you by your technical staff.
(2) initiate new energy conservation projects in their own corporations, and also support the ones that are brought up by their technical staff.
(3) keep in close touch with the ECT through a designated officer, preferably a factory manager or a senior manager who can participate actively in our training and energy audit programme.

In conclusion, I would like to summarize the overall, future energy prospects for Sri Lanka as we perceive it in mid-1983. Although the picture is grim (especially if no policy changes are adopted), it may be viewed as a challenge which could be overcome. Electricity consumption will continue to grow at about 7 or 8 per cent per annum for the next 10 years. In other words, the electricity facilities will have to roughly double every eight or nine years, requiring enormous investments of about Rs. 30,000 million and commensurate operating costs. In the area of oil, consumption will continue to grow at about 6 percent. This means that the net oil import bill which amounted to about 40 per cent of Sri Lanka's total imports in 1983, will hover around the 45 per cent mark for the rest of this decade. We have to conserve oil, and substitute other sources of energy as much as possible. In the area of fuelwood, the percentage of forest cover in Sri Lanka has declined from 40 per cent in 1960 to around 25 per cent in 1980. To prevent further deforestation. massive replanting efforts exceeding 500,000 acres will be required for fuel-wood alone, leaving aside the further requirements for construction timber. Unfortunately the new and renewable sources of energy such as small hydro, wind and solar energy are expected to contribute only a few per cent of the total energy requirement up to the year 2000.

Sri Lanka's policy options are therefore very limited. In the short run, by reducing losses in the Ceylon Electricity Board and Ceylon Petroleum Corporation, we hope (within about 3 or 4 years) to save up to 400 million rupees a year. Similarly through conservation programmes aimed at industrial, commercial transport and household consumers, another 400 or 500 million per year can be saved. Also, through the introduction of an improved domestic cooking stove, we can reduce fuelwood use.

In the medium to long-run we have to continue our conservation efforts while developing new energy sources. Oil exploration will continue but with limited prospects; Sri Lanka really cannot depend on it. In the field of electricity, hydro development will dominate until about 1990 when imported coal will become an important added source of energy. Re-afforestation will be the major priority for fuelwood. In the very long run, of course, one can look to economic structural adjustment. That is, we have to find a much less energy intensive growth path that the one taken by the industrialised countries. For example, the Government can try to avoid some of the less desirable aspects of the heavy industrial and manufacturing phase of economic development, including high energy use, pollution and urban slums. The farsighted programme initiated and promoted by President Jayawardene, which involves the use and application of computers in Sri Lanka, is in fact one of the principal means by which we can move directly from an agricultural economy to a knowledge-intensive, services-oriented economy (Munasinghe et al. 1985).

In conclusion, energy demand management and conservation is one area where Sri Lankans can do much for themselves with only a modest input from foreign sources. I have every confidence that through the good example and leadership demonstrated by our senior executives and managers, Sri Lanka can achieve her energy goals more quickly.

7.3   Implementation of Energy Management Policies (1982–86)

The NEDMCP seeks to achieve greater energy efficiency in the use of commercial fuels (electricity and oil) in the following sectors: (a) Industrial and Commercial; (b) Transport; (c) Household and Others; (d) Energy Supply -- Ceylon Electricity Board (CEB), Lanka Electricity Company (LEC), Ceylon Petroleum Corporation (CPC); and (e) Agriculture (see Table 4.8 and Figures 4.7 and 4.8, in Chapter 4 for details of the quantitative goals and impact of the NEDMCP). In the short-run (up to 5 years), the energy policy options that provided the best pay-off involve demand management and conservation. The NEDMCP and national fuelwood conservation programme (NFCP) have been designed for this purpose. In the medium-run (5-10 years), further development of energy resources will yield results, including hydro and coal for electricity, fuelwood plantations and oil exploration. The long-run (10-15 years) policy objective was to plan and implement macro-economic and sector specific structural adjustment measures leading to an economically optimal, less energy intensive growth path.

Energy Pricing Policy

Until about 1981, energy policy in Sri Lanka was based mainly on sociopolitical considerations and financial or accounting criteria such as earning sufficient sales revenues to meet operating and investment costs of energy supplying firms. Since 1982 however, there has been increasing emphasis on the use of economic principles in order to encourage more efficient consumption and production of energy. More specifically, economic efficiency has been recognized as a useful starting point for price setting, based on the need to optimize resource allocation and output growth. At the same time, several other pricing policy objectives including the financial requirements of energy supplying institutions, social equity and basic energy needs of the poor, comprehensibility and stability of energy prices, metering and billing constraints, and special considerations such as regional development, also influence energy prices.

Since these criteria are often in conflict with one another, the Sri Lanka integrated energy pricing policy uses the flexible methodology described in Chapter 3, to accommodate tradeoffs among them. Thus in the first stage, a set of prices based on the marginal opportunity costs (MOC) of supply is sought, to meet the strict economic efficiency objective. In practice, it has proved easier to begin the optimal pricing procedure from MOC, because supply costs are generally well defined (using techno-economic considerations). In the second stage of price setting, the MOC-based efficient prices are adjusted to meet the other goals of pricing policy (indicated earlier).

Although the scope of this chapter does not make it possible to provide a detailed analysis of the evolution of actual energy prices in Sri Lanka, some general points are well worth noting. Petroleum prices were raised in July 1983 to reflect higher costs, and the virtual elimination of the general subsidy on kerosene in the process was particularly significant. This revision brought about an important rationalization of the price structure, since it made possible the increase of industrial diesel prices without fear of substitution by cheap kerosene. Gasoline prices are significantly above border prices and provide an important source of revenue. In the case of electricity, tariffs were rationalized starting in 1982, bringing them more in conformity with long-run marginal costs. Thus, commercial energy prices generally reflect efficiency prices and are supportive of demand management efforts.

Industrial and Commercial Energy Conservation Program (IECP)

As mentioned above, the industrial and commercial sector has been a major consumer of Sri Lanka's oil and electricity. Thus IECP has a potential for realizing energy savings upto about five hundred million rupees per year, within a 2 to 3 year period. This programme, which consists of four phases, was launched by EDMAC in collaboration with the Ministry of Industries and Scientific Affairs and other government energy institutions, to promote demand management and conservation (DMC) among large industrial and commercial consumers (see Figure 7.1).

The four phases were designed as follows:
Phase I: sensitization and an information campaign to promote energy conservation among decisionmakers, senior company executives and plant managers.
Phase II: training of plant engineers in the technoeconomic and financial evaluation of conservation possibilities.
Phase III: identification, analysis, financing and implementation of specific conservation projects among large industrial and commercial energy consumers.
Phase IV: dissemination of energy conservation expertise, by promoting energy conservation among middle and small size industrial and commercial enterprises, and the establishment of energy conservation as a self-sustaining activity in industry and commerce.

Under Phase I, a two-week introductory course for senior energy managers in large private and public sector establishments was held. In this course there was unanimous support for the present and continuing work of the NEDMCP. A proposal to set up an Energy Conservation Fund to finance energy conservation and substitution projects was developed and submitted to the Cabinet of Ministers. The fund was set up in 1983 with an initial contribution of Rs. 5 million from the Ministry of Finance and Planning, and with further contributions coming from both government and private organizations as well as foreign sources. As described earlier, a short Senior Executive Seminar, inaugurated by the President of Sri Lanka, was also held in July 1983 for over 150 heads of large enterprises and senior ministry officials. Once again, very strong support was expressed for the present and future activities in DMC.

Phase II began with the intensive training course on DMC for key plant managers and engineers held in December 1983, followed by in-depth energy audits at selected factories scheduled from February to April 1984. The 50 participants in the training course were chosen from among the largest energy consuming public and private sector industrial and commercial institutions. These firms accounted for over 70% of oil and electricity consumption by the industrial and commercial sector in Sri Lanka, and 22% of total oil and electricity used in Sri Lanka, in 1983. Both foreign and local specialists delivered lectures to participants. A comprehensive energy conservation and audit manual which fully describes the latest energy conservation techniques, was distributed to all participants. This knowledge was used to carry out more comprehensive energy audits at two selected large energy consuming firms, analyze this data and also prepare energy conservation feasibility studies for financing. The latest instrumentation for the audits was obtained from abroad, with the assistance of USAID. Information and reports arising from these energy audits were used as input to Phase III.

With the completion of Phases I and II, Phase III began with a donors/financiers meeting arranged in January 1984 to inform potential foreign and local sources of funding about NEDMCP. The results of Phase II (plus other work along the same lines), was used in the formulation and appraisal of major conservation projects in the industrial and commercial sector. Assistance was also given by the Energy Coordinating Team (ECT) supported by expert consultants, to prepare pre-feasibility studies and detailed terms of reference (TOR's), to carry out feasibility studies, and to obtain funding for projects. Provisions were also made to monitor and supervise projects during implementation with general advisory and support functions being carried out by the ECT during this period.

With many large state owned energy consuming industries coming under its purview, the Ministry of Industries and Scientific Affairs has played an active role within IECP. In 1982 the Ministry set up a Working Committee of chairmen of corporations to examine the energy consumption patterns in the manufacturing corporations under the Ministry and to recommend suggestions for energy conservation. This Committee made several recommendations. In the same year, the Minister of Industries and Scientific Affairs directed that all manufacturing industrial corporations appoint an Energy Manager in their corporation so that there would be a high level officer who could monitor the energy consumption and devise energy saving measures.

As part of Phase III, several foreign donors in collaboration with the ECT, began participating in programs of assistance to the Corporations coming under the Ministry of Industries and Scientific Affairs, and other public and private sector industries. The UNIDO provided assistance to four public corporations under the Industries Ministry: Sri Lanka Cement Corporation, Sri Lanka Ceramics Corporation, Sri Lanka Steel Corporation and Paranthan Chemicals Corporation. The UNIDO also agreed to finance an Energy Consultancy Service for the National Engineering Research and Development (NERD) Centre and to provide an "Energy Bus" to conduct mobile energy audits. The Swedish Development Agency (SIDA) financed the supply of equipment and energy audits in four other public sector institutions: the National Paper Corporation, Ceylon Plywoods Corporation, State Hardware Corporation and British Ceylon Corporation. An energy audit of the Ceylon Oxygen Co. led to the recommendation for an investment in retrofits. Implementation of this proposal has resulted in a significant annual saving of electricity.

In May-June 1984, a World Bank team assisted by ECT staff carried out pre-feasibility studies of energy conservation projects in 18 large industrial and commercial institutions in Sri Lanka. This study, which was part of the joint UNDP/World Bank Energy Sector Management Assessment Program (ESMAP) was the most comprehensive of the studies carried out thus far in the industrial/commercial sector. Sixteen industrial plants, one hotel and the Colombo General Hospital were the targets of this study. The industrial plants included public sector corporations manufacturing products such as steel, plywood, paper, ceramics and chemicals; one state owned tea factory; and several private industries. These studies identified possible energy conservation projects which involved work ranging from low-cost measures such as changes in operational procedures, to more expensive investments, such as waste heat recovery systems. Total energy cost reductions of almost 25% were identified, yielding annual savings of about US$ 4.2 million for a one-time total investment of US$ 9.1 million.

Some of the institutions surveyed already had ongoing conservation programs and required no further technical or financial assistance. In most cases, however, the need for specific assistance was identified by the study. In such cases, the next step was to evaluate the identified projects at the feasibility level. In anticipation of donor support for such feasibility studies, the government started to put into place the institutional framework to implement the ensuing conservation projects. In particular, attention was paid to a financing program. EDMAC initiated a dialogue on energy conservation with two of the largest local development banks -- National Development Bank and the Development Finance Corporation of Ceylon -- who indicated an interest in setting up the administrative procedures required for expediting the financing of these projects.

In the fourth and final phase which has been under way since late 1984, the core team of specialists trained during Phase II and III began helping to train and assist a much wider group of Government and private sector specialists in DMC. They also encouraged other institutions to offer energy audit and conservation services, based on the manuals and case studies produced in Phases II and III. Energy audit and conservation services have become routinely available to middle and small size enterprises, and such activities are also being actively promoted through bodies such as the Chamber of Industries and Chamber of Commerce. Another encouraging development was that several public and private sector organizations began to offer energy audit and conservation services to industry, thus building towards Phase IV, where conservation would become a self-sustaining activity. A non-governmental professional body called the Sri Lanka Energy Managers Association (SLEMA) was also set up in 1984. It continues to expand and encourage DMC activities in Sri Lanka through seminars, training programmes, advisory and consulting services, and a wide range of other professional activities.

Transportation Energy Conservation Programme (TECP)

A Special Working Group (SWG) on Energy in Transport was set up which included senior managers from concerned government Ministries, Departments and Corporations. It was assisted by both local and foreign experts. The SWG concentrated initially on drawing up a list of energy saving recommendations that will have an immediate impact. These proposals were put up to the government for implementation.

As a longer-term objective, the SWG also identified areas for further study in the context of overall transport sector policy, including optimal inter-modal choice, urban and rural locational and demographic patterns, etc.

Energy Supplying Institutions

The National Energy Demand Management and Conservation Programme also incorporates and promotes loss reduction programmes in the CEB, LEC and CPC. In the case of the CEB and LEC, distribution loss reduction programmes have been started which look at:

(a) Reconductoring of existing lines where necessary;

(b) Correction of power factor on transmission lines; and
(c) Distribution transformer load management.

Annual savings of up to Rs. 500 million would be possible after this programme is completed, during the period 1985-90.

The CPC also has implemented a programme of loss reduction in their refining operations and are monitoring the losses which occur in the distribution of petroleum products.

Household and other

The ECT supported and encouraged the efforts of the CEB and CPC in disseminating electricity and oil saving measures through the media, leaflets and other means.

In Oct-Nov 1985, representatives of the Dutch Government together with the ECT carried out a study to identify potential areas for assistance in energy efficiency, demand management and conservation, and in new, renewable and rural sources of energy. The broad objective of identified projects was the decrease in annual consumption of firewood in the short term, and the establishment of infrastructure for a balanced production/consumption system for fuelwood to support the existing NFCP for dissemination of fuelwood efficient stoves in urban and rural areas in Sri Lanka (see Chapters 4 and 12). On the supply side, the proposal also covered rural electrification outside the CEB grid, as well as the installation of solar PV cells in isolated rural areas.

Agriculture

Work on the potential for energy saving and substitution in agriculture was initiated in collaboration with other conerned government agencies, including the Agricultural Research and Training Institute (ARTI). Here again, the Dutch financed study identified many energy consumption possibilities, including:

1. Installation of efficient fuelwood fired furnaces in the tea industry.
2. Installation of efficient fuelwood fired furnaces in the rubber industry.
3. Energy efficiency survey in the tea industry (with possible follow-up in the rubber and coconut industries).

In 1983, the share of exports from tea, rubber and coconut amounted to over 50% of Sri Lanka's total. These industries are also major consumers of firewood. Thus, it is appropriate that they became the focus of attention for energy conservation in agro-industry.

As a result, the following areas were identified for potential savings in the tea manufacturing process:

1. Reducing fuelwood consumption by proper storage of fuelwood, installation of high efficient heaters, and the more efficient use of energy.
2. Changing over from industrial diesel to cheaper furnace oil.
3. Installation of power factor correction equipment.

Besides the use of direct conservation measures to reduce the annual fuelwood consumption, the Dutch study also identified two other areas for increased energy efficiency on tea estates. The first of these is producer gasification of fuelwood for electricity generation. In this case, clean flue gases become available for the drying of the tea, thus avoiding high stack losses and increasing efficiency by about 40%. The other area is fuelwood plantations, in which old and less suitable tea growing fields may be used for establishing fuelwood plantations.

Firewood is consumed in the rubber industry for sheet and crepe rubber, the two final products at the estate level. Uprooted rubber trees are the main source of firewood at present, but this source is fast dwindling as the current replantation programme comes to an end. The following measures were proposed for energy conservation in the rubber industry:

1. Installation of covered firewood storage in order to dry the wood before firing;
2. Installation of efficient furnaces;
3. Installation of an economizer (water/flue gas heat exchanger) in the stack, which would reduce present stack temperatures of about 250°C to about 100°C; and
4. Use of modern processes such as vacuum drying.

References

Munasinghe, M., *National Energy Demand Management and Conservation Programme (NEDMCP)*, Ministry of Power and Energy, Colombo, Sri Lanka, 1985.

Chapter 8

ENERGY DEMAND ANALYSIS AND FORECASTING[1]

8.1 Introduction

Energy planning is impossible without a reasonable knowledge of past and present energy consumption and likely future demands. These consumption patterns are significantly affected by energy prices. Any demand analysis and demand forecast, therefore, must take explicit account of relative and absolute energy prices, because prices not only affect choices among alternative energy sources, but also choices between the use of energy versus other alternative inputs such as capital and labor, or choices between energy and nonenergy consuming activities.

However, prices of specific energy resources are only one set of parameters that affect use. Others, such as availability, reliability of supply, uniformity of quality, convenience in use, technical and economic characteristics of energy-using equipment and appliances, population growth, income, rate of urbanization, as well as social habits, acceptability, and knowledge by potential users, are as important or even more important than price in determining demand. Hence any analyses of past and present consumption patterns and forecasts of future demands have to take these other factors explicitly into consideration.

Nevertheless, prices may substantially affect energy consumption patterns, at least in the long run, since substitutes, in the form of alternative energy resources, or capital, or labor, can be found, or consumption habits may be changed. For sector planning purposes, therefore, estimates are needed of the short- and long-run price elasticities of demand for every specific energy resource. Such estimates are usually based on some form of econometric analysis. However, for a number of reasons which are discussed in greater detail below, such aggregate statistical measures are usually unsuitable for demand forecasts in developing nations. Even in industrialized nations they are subject to wide margins of error. Hence direct sector and activity-specific estimates are likely to provide more reliable results.

Demand forecasts could be made either on the basis of statistical evaluations and projections of past consumption trends, or on the basis of specific micro-studies. The former approach is appropriate in industrialized nations in which data coverage is excellent and energy-consuming activities are ubiquitous, complex, as well as mature, so that changes from observed trends are slow. In most developing nations, although trend-line extrapolation is common, a micro-survey-research type approach will usually be more useful because it will yield more reliable results. This is so because statistical data are often lacking, or of poor quality. Furthermore, sectoral demand changes resulting from specific policies, such as rural electrification programs or the establishment of new industrial plants, for example, can be very substantial relative to existing demand. Such program- or project-specific effects on future demand usually

---

[1] Edited extract from M. Munasinghe and G. Schramm, *Energy Economics, Demand Management and Conservation Policy*, Van Nostrand Reinhold, 1983, Chapter 7.

cannot be forecast on the basis of observed past or present consumption data. However, such case-by-case investigations must necessarily be limited to surveys of the larger energy consumers or energy-related development programs. Both for reason of costs and time, forecasts for sectors such as urban or rural households, commercial activities, or transportation, for example, must normally be based on statistical data analysis, although specific factors such as changes in relative prices, disposable income, rate of urbanization, or sectoral production, must be specifically considered as determinants of future sectoral energy demands.

8.2   The Importance of Energy Demand Forecasts

There are three interrelated reasons for the importance of accurate energy demand forecasts. The first is that the timely and reasonably reliable availability of energy supplies is vital for the functioning of a modern economy. The second is that the expansion of energy supply systems usually requires many years. And the third is that investments in such systems generally are highly capital intensive, on average, accounting for some 30% of gross investments in most countries. If forecasts are too low, energy shortages may develop whose costs are usually a large multiple of the volume of energy not supplied; but if forecasts are too high, large amounts of capital with high opportunity costs might be uselessly tied up for long periods of time. Either of these consequences is costly to an economy; far more costly than the resources that may have to be marshaled to undertake detailed and reliable demand studies that could help to avoid such errors.

A number of recent studies have shown how costly such errors can be. If supply shortages develop as a consequence, more expensive foreign energy supplies may have to be imported, emergency equipment may have to be installed, rationing may have to be introduced, and forced outages may occur. In Thailand, for example, the net value of refined petroleum product imports rose from 15 percent of unrefined crude oil imports in 1972 to 21 percent in 1977 because local refinery capacity was not expanded in time to meet rapidly growing demands (see Chapter 13). In the late 1970s in both Sri Lanka and Columbia, delays in expanding low-cost hydropower plants forced the installation of small size thermal generation with high fuel costs to bridge the gap. Also in Columbia, restrictions had to be imposed on gasoline sales in 1979 because of rapidly rising high-cost imports, even though the country had been a net exporter of crude oil until 1975/76, and its prospects for additional domestic oil discoveries are rated high.

Rationing or forced interruptions of energy supplies usually lead to substantial losses in output and consumer welfare. This is so because the cost of energy is low, relative to the value of output or services received from energy use. This is apparent from Table 12.10 which shows that in the USA, for example, electricity costs to industry averaged only 1.2 percent of the value of output in 1979. These percentage ratios are reasonably typical for developed as well as developing countries, although the recent petroleum product price increases will have increased them for some of the latter. Hence, while the cost of energy is quite low relative to the value of output, without energy no output could be produced.

In a detailed case study of the costs of outages of electricity supply in Brazil, Munasinghe found that in 1976 the net loss in the value of industrial output from forced outages amounted to about $1-6 per kWh lost, while for residential consumers the estimated outage cost per hour during the evening period was approximately equal to the income wage rate of the household affected (Munasinghe & Gellerson 1979).

Overestimates of future demand may be equally costly, if expansion plans are based upon them. For example, the electric generating plant expansion program for a government-owned South American utility system was originally based on a demand growth forecast of some 6.5% per year throughout the 1980s. This called for the addition of several hundred MW of hydroelectric capacity by about 1987, which in turn was used to justify a large, integrated water development scheme that included important irrigation components as well. The overall development, costing in excess of 1.5 billion dollars, could not be justified on the basis of the irrigation component alone. A midway review of expected power demand showed that the original estimates were far too high. As a consequence, the first stage of the hydroplant component of the scheme (now well under way) will probably not be needed for at least another four years beyond the originally forecast date. Evaluated at an opportunity cost of capital of at least twelve percent, this results in an approximate net loss to the national economy of some 350 million dollars (net of agricultural net benefits), which expressed in present value terms, is a sum equivalent to some 90% of the country's annual public investment budget. This is a staggering loss indeed.

These examples clearly show the importance of accurate demand forecasts. The need for forecast accuracy is greater, the larger the time horizon for new energy supply installations. Thermal power plants may need 4 to 6 years to complete, although high-cost gas turbines or diesel power plants can usually be commissioned on an emergency basis within 1 to 2 years, with the result that many utility systems use them excessively because of initial forecasting errors. Nuclear power plants need 8 to 12 years to build, and hydropower plants about 5 to 8 years. Oil and gas fields from initial seismic surveys through exploratory drilling to first production may need 5 to 15 years, refineries 3 to 6 years, and forest plantations for firewood some 5-30 years.

We may conclude that the need for forecast accuracy is directly related to the size, cost, complexity, and irreversibility of projected supply components. In relatively small and simple economies, in which marginal additions to demand are either satisfied from readily available local resources or through incremental imports of widely available finished or semifinished energy products (gasoline, diesel, fuel-oil, coal, or diesel power plants) elaborate, long-term demand forecasts are not so important. This does not negate the need in such cases for predictions of import requirements, balance of payments effects, etc., but for these purposes general trend analysis based on economic aggregate data may suffice. On the other hand, in countries where decisions have to be made with respect to large additions to existing energy systems that will require many years to complete, or where new energy sources are to be introduced (e.g., natural gas), accurate demand forecasts are of crucial importance, and substantial planning resources should be allocated for their preparation and continued updating.

8.3   Forecast Methodologies

Various methodologies can be used make energy demand forecasts. The most important ones are:

1. Trend analysis.
2. Sector-specific econometric multiple-correlation forecasts.

3. Macroeconomic or input-output based forecasting models.
4. Surveys.

Trend Analysis

Trend analysis is the most commonly used approach. It consists of the extrapolation of past growth trends assuming that there will be little change in the growth of the determinants of demand such as incomes, prices, consumer tastes, etc. These trends are usually estimated by a least squares fit of past consumption data or by some similar statistical methodology. Depending on the availability of data, they may be estimated either on a national basis for a given energy source (e.g., gasoline), or they may be broken down by region, by consuming sector (e.g., households, commercial enterprises, industry, transportation, etc.), or by both. Frequently, ad hoc adjustments are made to account for substantial changes in expected future demands due to specific reasons. For example, this may take the form of projecting on a case-by-case basis the expected demands of new industrial plants or other economic activities. This combination of overall trend projection together with survey-research type specific adjustments is used for power planning in many developing countries.

The main advantage of this approach is its simplicity. Forecasts can be based on whatever data are available. The major disadvantage is that no attempt is made to explain why certain consumption trends were established in the past. The underlying, and usually unstated, assumption that whatever factors brought about consumption changes in the past will continue unchanged in the future as well is, of course, a rather limiting one in a world in which relative energy prices are changing at rapid rates, and in a direction opposite to that observed until just a few years ago.

Econometric Multiple Correlation Forecasting

Econometric forecasting techniques are usually somewhat more sophisticated, and, in theory, hold out the promise of greater forecast accuracy. Past energy demand is first correlated with other variables such as prices and incomes, and then future energy demands are related to the predicted growth of these other variables. However, these methods are frequently nothing more than a special form trend analysis if the projections of the selected determinants themselves are based on historical trends in turn. The other problem that they encounter is that of data availability. Usually it is difficult, if not possible, to obtain the required time series that are needed to produce statistically acceptable (i.e., statistically significant) results. Not only are data series often incomplete, they are also subject to changes in definitions over time and, even more frequently, subject to substantial errors. Furthermore, the need for "proving" statistically "significant" results is such that long periods of time have to be covered, periods long enough to have experienced significant changes in the underlying structure of the economy. Hence, the confidence in the results must be low, even if they pass the test of statistical significance. However, the advantages of econometric studies are that they can take a number of important, demand-determining variables, such as price, income, number of vehicles, etc., explicitly into account.

The formulation of a typical residential energy demand model would be based on consumer theory in economics (Nicholson 1978). The direct utility function of a consumer which indicates the intrinsic value derived from the consumption of various goods, may be written:

$$U = U(Q_1, Q_2, ... Q_n; \underline{Z})$$

where Q_i represents the level of consumption of good i in a given time period (e.g., one year) and $\underline{Z}$ is a set of parameters representing consumer tastes and other factors.

The set of prices $P_1, P_2, \dots P_n$, for these n consumer goods, and the consumer's income I, define the budget constraint:

$$I \geq \Sigma\, P_i Q_i$$

Maximization of the consumer's utility U subject to the budget constraint yields the set of Marshallian demand functions for each of the goods consumed by the household:

$$Q_i = Q_i(P_1, P_2, \dots P_n; I; \underline{Z}) \text{ for } i = 1 \text{ to } n. \tag{8.1}$$

Consider the demand function for a particular fuel (e.g., gas). Then equation (8.1) may be written in the simplified form:

$$Q_g = Q_g(P_g, P_e, P_o, P; I; \underline{Z})$$

where the subscript g denotes gas, while subscripts e and o indicate the substitute forms of energy, electricity and oil (e.g., for cooking), and P is an average price index representing all other goods.

Next, assuming that demand is homogenous of degree one in the money variables (i.e., prices and income) we may write:

$$Q_g = Q_g(P_g/P, P_e/P, P_o/P; I/P; \underline{Z}) \tag{8.2}$$

Thus, starting from consumer preference theory, we may arrive at a demand function for a given fuel which depends on its own price, the prices of substitutes and income, all in real terms. The effects of other factors $\underline{Z}$, such as quality of supply, shifts in tastes, and so on can also be explicitly considered[2].

The final specification of an equation such as (8.2) could vary widely (Taylor 1977, Pindyck 1979). Q_g could be household consumption or per capita consumption; the demand function could be linear or linear in the logarithms of the variables or in the transcendental logarithmic form and could include lagged variables; and $\underline{Z}$ could include supply side constraints such as access to supply, and so on.

Analogously, the industrial demand for energy may be derived from production function theory in economics. For example, consider the output of a particular firm of industry over a given time period:

$$X = F(K, L, M, Q_1, \dots Q_n; \underline{S})$$

where K, L, and M represent the inputs of capital, labor and other nonenergy materials respectively; Q_i is the input of the ith form of energy, and $\underline{S}$ is a set of

---

[2] More specific examples of the effects of supply quality on energy demand are discussed in the companion volume: *Electric Power Economics*.

parameters that represents other factors such as shifts in technology, industrial policy, and so on[3].

The problem posed in production theory is the minimization of the costs of producing a given quantity of output X, given exogenous prices of inputs (Shepard 1953). In principle, the solution yields, as in the household case, a set of energy demand functions:

$$Q_i = Q_i(P_K, P_L, P_M; P_1, ..., P_n; X; \underline{S})$$

As before, we may use one of the nonenergy input prices as numeraire, (e.g., P_K) and rewrite Q_i in normalized form:

$$Q_i = Q_i(P_L/P_K, P_M/P_K, P_1/P_K..., P_n/P_K; X/P_K; \underline{S})$$

The demand for energy at time t is therefore a function of its own price, the prices of energy substitutes, the prices of nonenergy inputs, and other factors $\underline{S}$. Many different choices of variables and specifications of demand function may be used.

In this way demand functions for various fuels could be developed for other end-use sectors such as transport, agriculture, and so on. The demand function may be estimated by standard econometric techniques. The estimated equations then could form the basis for future demand forecasts.

The main difficulties with this approach are:

1. The mechanistic nature of the econometric equations and their extrapolation into the future, which often fails to capture structural shifts in demand growth. Such structural shifts are particularly important in developing countries as a result of the introduction of new technology (e.g., tractors instead of draft animals, auto manufacturing instead of assembly operations, or rural electricity instead of kerosene lamps).
2. The difficulties of separating out short-run and long-run effects in the analysis of changes in the structure and level of prices (Pindyck 1979).
3. The lack of an adequate data base to make accurate regression estimates. In developing countries this problem is particularly severe, because energy price and consumption data by consuming sector are usually lacking, income data are unreliable or nonexistent and do not account for changes in income distribution, and statistical data of output and sales of specific industries are often unobtainable because of their confidentiality if the number of producers is small. Even in industrialized countries with far better data coverage, demand studies should be based on specific processes, rather than broad classifications such as "iron and steel production," or "household use."
4. The inherent limitation of estimating procedures that concentrate on energy prices as demand determinants, but do not account for the prices, availability, life expectancies and replaceability of the energy-using appliances and equipment that

---

[3]   To avoid the problem of different types of capital, labor etc., it is necessary to assume weak separability of the inputs K, L, M and $E_i = (Q_1, Q_2, ...Q_n)$, so that each may be represented as an aggregate, with a distinct, composite price index, i.e., P_K, P_L, and P_M. Furthermore, in order to be able to determine the minimum cost mix of capital, labor, materials and energy, it is assumed that the individual energy inputs, i.e., oil, gas, electricity, coal, etc., are subject to homotheticity. This makes it possible to use a two-step process. First the mix of fuels that make up the energy input are optimized and in the second step, the optimum growths of capital, labor, other material inputs and energy are chosen. This, for example, was the approach used by Pindyck (1979).

must be utilized with alternative energy sources (the case study of the Thai tobacco industry in Chapter 13 indicates the importance of these factors). This problem is particularly acute under the assumption of homotheticity for all alternative energy sources, since energy users will base their decisions on total systems cost rather than on energy cost only.

5. The problem that for almost the whole post-World War II period until the early 1970s real costs of commercial energy sources are falling, while they have been rising steeply, albeit irregularly, since. Econometric data series, unless they rely on cross-sectional data only (not a practical procedure in developing countries), necessarily utilize the data of these past periods of falling prices. These are unlikely to yield reasonable estimates of future energy demands because of the sharp reversal in relative prices trends.

6. The fact that specific energy resources are often allocated by governmental fiat, or determined by such factors as availability or reliability of supply, rather than observable market price. Another important factor, particularly in developed countries, may be fuel quality, such as the sulphur content of coal.

7. The problem that demand elasticities, even if they were estimated accurately, are likely to change significantly themselves, rather than remain constant, if price changes of energy are large. This is so because for most activities the ability to substitute other resources for energy (including alternative energy resources) is limited.

Because of these problems, it is not surprising that the results of various empirical studies of energy demand functions vary by substantial margins even in the industrialized nations. For example, some of them found that in industry, capital and energy are substitutes for each other, while other studies concluded that they are complementary to each other (Pindyck 1979). Estimates of the own price elasticity of aggregate energy use range from - 0.3 to -0.8, while for specific energy sources the range is much larger. For example, for the U.S., long-run price elasticity estimates for electricity range from -0.5 to -1.2, and for oil they range from -0.22 to as much as -2.82.

One cross-country study of energy demand in the industrialized market economies indicated that during the period 1950-70, the elasticities of total and commercial energy demand with respect to gross domestic product (GDP) were 1.78 and 1.55 respectively, while the corresponding price elasticities were -0.055 and -0.026 (Beenstock & Willcocks 1981). Another paper gave total energy demand elasticities with respect to GDP in the range 1.3 to 1.4 for a group of developing countries during 1970-76 (Zilbfarb & Adams 1981). Other estimates made for developing countries are likely to be less reliable (Pindyck 1979). A more recent study by Siddayao (1986) clearly illustrates many of the problems of energy demand estimation in developing countries.

What we must conclude, then, is that most of these econometric studies of energy demand aggregates are probably of limited value in industrialized countries and practically useless for developing nations. More specific studies, of clearly defined subsectors such as urban residential energy demand by city size and income, for example, may be more promising and useful, even if the required disaggregation reduces the more mechanical aspects of statistical significance.

Macroeconomic and Supply-Demand Based Models

In the United States, Canada, and Europe a number of large, multisector energy planning models have been developed in recent years. These models are either additions to already existing general purpose macroeconomic models, or they were specifically constructed to analyze energy supply and demand relationships.

Basically, an energy model connects a number of energy variables with various driving variables. A simple model, for example, would relate how total energy use and prices result from a driving force on the demand side (say, consumer income) and a constraint on the supply side (say, the cost of production of energy). More detailed models would distinguish between the various end uses of energy (heating, processing, transportation, etc.) and several energy sources such as petroleum fuels, natural gas, hydro, coal, wood, etc., each with its own production constraint. The relations must be estimated on the basis of empirical information. The major sources for these empirical estimates are technological information relating to past and future production and utilization possibilities, and econometric estimates of past demand, supply, and other economic behavior relations (production by activity sector, income, number of vehicles, rate of electrification, etc.). Much of the technical information consists of physical quantities of inputs and outputs with input quantities sometimes aggregated into cost estimates.

If the models are to yield determinate answers, the number of independent relations and of binding constraints must at any time equal the number of energy variables projected.

Figure 2.4 (Chapter 2) provides a compressed view of the characteristics of a number of energy models that were developed for the United States. Three groups of "driving" variables are identified in these models: (a) policy variables, (b) realization variables, and (c) blends of the two. Variations of the policy variables chosen allow estimates to be made of policy impacts, and variations of realization variables permit sensitivity analyses that trace the differences in policy variables when alternative facts of nature pertain. Blend variables represent a mixture between policy and realization variables. Typically, these models consist of a large number of variables that are related to each other through sets of behavioral equations and/or constraints. Figure 8.1 presents the flow diagram of one such model that was developed by Data Resources, Inc.

It contains about 200 econometric equations estimated on annual data for 15 years, and projects final demands for, and consumption of energy in four fuel sectors: coal, electricity, petroleum, and natural gas. A submodel of the utility sector, in turn, allocates the generation of electricity between hydroelectric, nuclear, and fossil-fuel generated electricity. Demands are forecast for 13 geographic regions of the United States, in each of four final consuming sectors: commercial, industrial, residential, and transportation. Projection of energy prices were taken from other sources, i.e., the Federal Energy Administrative model, judgements about Federal Power Commission regulatory rulings on natural gas prices, and projections of OPEC oil prices.

The major advantages of such comprehensive modeling efforts are that they yield internally consistent estimates of future demand and supply relationships, and they make it possible to test the effects of various assumptions about policy and realization variables.

However, the construction of such models requires not only a very substantial amount of intellectual resources, but also quite detailed and reliable sets of statistical data. The latter are usually unavailable in a consistent and comprehensive form in developing countries. Hence what has been said about the data problems of econometric demand forecasts in the previous section applies even more forcefully to the construction of comprehensive energy models.

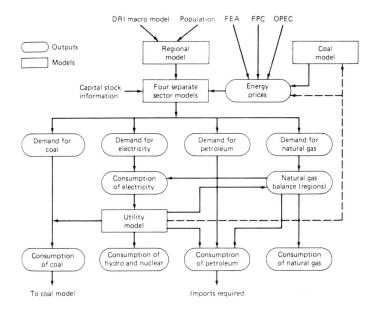

Figure 8.1: Schematic Diagram of the Data Resources Inc. Energy Model

Models, for all their intricacies and sophistication, have another drawback. By trying to model and optimize a whole economy with all its complex interrelationships, specific details may still be insufficient for reasonably accurate forecasting purposes. This becomes apparent from a comparison of the results of the six U.S. energy models analyzed in a National Academy of Sciences (1978) study. With all of the models normalized in terms of basic assumptions, projected production and consumption rates for the year 1990 vary significantly among the various models. This can be seen from the data in Table 8.1, which show for example, differences in projected total energy consumption of between 96.2 and 114.5 quads of energy, and for electricity generation between 2.8 and 4.3 quads (where a quad is equivalent to about 500,000 barrels of oil equivalent or 10^{15} Btu). These ranges are quite large and of little help for sector-specific planning purposes.

Over time, as data coverage improves and a better understanding is gained about the interrelationship of the various policy and realization variables and energy use, energy models may become useful as tools for energy planning. For the time being, however, even if they can be constructed at all, their role as forecasting and planning tools will be quite limited.

Table 8.1

**Comparison of Selected Outputs of Primary Energy
and Electric Energy for 1990 From Six U.S. Energy Models**

	Intermediate Run Models		Long Run Models			
	FEA	DRI	DESOM	ETA	NORD-HAUS	SRI
Domestic Energy Production	93.4	--	93.6	81.5	81.1	94.7
Coal Production	25.3	25.2	20.5		28.1	29.8
Natural Gas	22.2	--	31.6	46.6	21.1	19.3
Oil and Natural Gas Liquids	29.4	11.6	24.9		5.2	24.0
Nuclear Energy	12.3	--	11.3	10.1	26.7	16.7
Solar Heating and Cooling	0.0	--	0.1	0.0	0.0	0.8
Other	4.2	4.7	4.9	4.6	0.0	4.2
Oil and Gas Imports	21.1	--	18.9	23.3	15.1	14.2
Total Energy Consumption	114.5	107.9	112.5	104.8	96.2	108.9
Electricity Generation (10^{12} kWh)	4.3	4.1	3.1	3.3	2.8	4.1

Source: National Academy of Science, *Energy Planning for an Uncertain Future*, Washington DC, 1978, p 47.

Surveys

Given the limitations of the other forecasting methodologies, surveys potentially provide a direct and reliable tool of demand analysis and forecasting. In essence, surveys consist of a list of more or less sophisticated questions that are put to energy users in order to measure and record their present consumption and future consumption plans. The basic types of questions that might be asked are the following:

1. How much energy (of each type) do you use per month/year?
2. What do you use it for?
3. How much do you pay per unit of energy used (by energy type)?
4. What do you produce or sell and what is the value added of each major product line?
5. Can you identify specific energy uses with specific outputs?
6. What is your net income (for households)?
7. What are your future expansion plans, and their timing, and what additional energy requirements do they imply?
8. What additional energy-using appliances or equipment are you planning to acquire in the foreseeable future (identify)?

The major problems afflicting surveys are the following:

1. They require substantial amounts of time.
2. They can be costly.
3. They require skilled interviewers.

4. Energy users may be unable to provide the information asked because they themselves do not know.
5. Energy users may be unwilling to provide the information for competitive reasons or because of fear of the consequences of revealing the information, etc.
6. Energy users may wittingly or unknowingly give inaccurate answers.
7. Future energy user plans may be vague, or too optimistic/pessimistic.

The major drawbacks are costs on the one hand, and ignorance, or unwillingness to provide the information, on the other. Because of costs, surveys must generally be limited to major energy consumers such as medium- to large-size industrial plants, mines and smelters, large transportation companies, utility companies, important governmental energy users (e.g., armed forces), etc. Fortunately, these enterprises and activities usually account for a large percentage of total energy consumption in developing countries.

In the industrial sector, energy consumption per unit of output is substantial for only a few activities. In the USA, for example, in 1967, six industrial groups[4] used some 128 btu per dollar of output, while the rest of all other industries combined used only 21 btu. Overall, these six industrial groups accounted for some 80% of total U.S. industrial energy consumption, but for only 36% of total value added. Similar, although usually somewhat less concentrated industrial consumption patterns exist in developing countries. Industrial surveys of energy utilities, therefore, should first of all concentrate on those activities that are known to be high users of energy per unit of output, and second on those industrial plants and activities that are large relative to the country's industrial sector as a whole. Second, surveys should attempt to evaluate the energy-use implications of new economic development programs, such as irrigation, industrial settlements, mining and hydrocarbon developments and rural or urban electrification programs, etc. However, care must taken (and seasoned judgement employed) to assess the realism of these specific projected development programs. Not infrequently, these represent more the dreams of somewhat overoptimistic development planners or politicians than the cold reality of realizable objectives.

The use of surveys will be less practicable for analyzing the consumption of ubiquitous sectors such as households, farms, and small-scale commercial and industrial enterprises. For these sectors, survey costs are generally high as well as time consuming. They also require the hiring and training of a large number of enumerators -- not an easy task in most developing countries.

However, energy consumption surveys could be usefully combined with others, such as general population censuses or income studies, etc.. On occasion, useful information may be available from already existing surveys (for example, see De Backer and Openshaw 1972). However, because of their costs such surveys will usually be undertaken only as one-time efforts. Because results usually do not become available until quite some time after the actual data collection phase, the information may already be outdated. However, this is problematic only if substantial changes in some consumption-related factors have taken place in the meantime, such as drastic changes in prices, or availabilities of competing energy resources (see Chapter 13).

Another limitation is that such surveys usually cannot elicit any useful information from respondents about future energy consumption intentions. Demand projections,

---

[4] food and kindred products (6%); paper and allied products (7%); chemicals and allied products (18%); petroleum and coal products (15%); stone, clay and glass products (7%); and primary metals (27%).

therefore, must be developed on the basis of estimated trends using more or less sophisticated methods that take account of the various identifiable energy demand determinants such as disposable income, household formation, etc.

In general, the need for surveys of these ubiquitous demand sectors and the required degree of accuracy of the results will depend on the importance of the information thus acquired. If significant and potentially costly decisions must be based on it, requirements for accuracy will be high; but if the information is needed only for statistical record keeping, relatively crude estimates may suffice.

8.4 Verification

Whatever methods are used to estimate sector energy consumption, verification, at least in aggregate terms, is usually possible if reliable data exist either about total supply or total consumption or both. The latter will usually be the case for electricity and natural gas, because supply and consumption form closed systems with metering at both ends. The only troublesome aspects are autogeneration by nonpublic enterprises, leakage, transmission-distribution losses, and outright theft. The latter is a serious problem for electric utilities in many countries. For petroleum products and coal, reasonably accurate supply data can usually be obtained from production, refinery, and import and export statistics. Data will usually be poor or nonexistent for both supply and consumption of indigenous energy resources such as wood, charcoal, dung, crop residues, etc.

Verification starts from the necessary equality between supply and consumption per time period. Total production, plus imports minus exports, minus net additions to storage, minus autoconsumption minus processing and transportation losses have to be equal to total consumption. This flow from the supply to the demand side has been shown in Figure 8.2 which depicts the basic supply-demand relationships of the petroleum products sector. In most countries reliable supply data are available for the supply side, except perhaps for net changes in storage, autoconsumption, and conversion and transportation losses. However, since the number of entities involved in these activities usually is small, these data could probably be obtained and assembled with relatively little effort. On the demand side, reliable consumption data will usually be available only for a few enumerated sectors or activities, although these may account for a substantial percentage of total consumption. After these have been accounted for, estimates must be made for the remaining sectors. These should be checked for reasonableness against sample surveys, and statistics such as numbers of cars, buses, and trucks times average miles times miles per gallon, number of households times average consumption, etc. Consumption, plus losses, plus net additions to inventories, added over all consuming sectors has to be equal to the total available supply.

Verification problems and estimation errors may arise from illegal diversions of specific energy sources to alternative uses. This, for example, is common in countries in which kerosene is heavily subsidized because of its importance as a cooking and lighting fuel for the poor. As a consequence, kerosene is often illegally diverted to other uses such as additives to motor fuels or for use in privately-owned diesel generators. Furthermore, little, if any, information (except, perhaps, installed capacity) is usually available about privately owned generating plants or other stationary power sources such as diesel-driven irrigation pumps. Another problem is that in some regions consumption data are biased because of smuggling to neighboring countries, or because of substantial sales to temporary visitors.

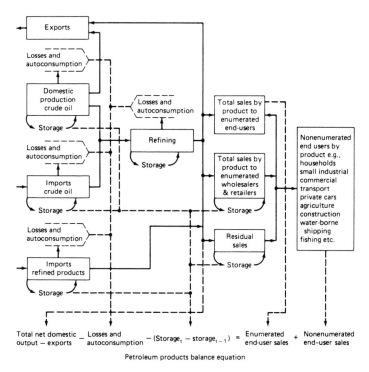

Petroleum products balance equation

Figure 8.2: Supply/Demand Accounting Framework for Petroleum Products

Another means to check estimated consumption data for their reasonableness is to compare them with published consumption data for similar activities in other countries. Detailed data have become available in recent years in most industrialized nations. Institutions such as OECD, the U.S. Department of Energy, and others regularly publish detailed consumption data for specific activities and production processes.

Verification is not limited to the analysis of past consumption data. Projections for the future can also be checked, at least for internal consistency with other projections. For example, projected consumption of gasoline (which may have been estimated on the basis of trend analysis of past consumption only) could be checked against the projected number of vehicles in circulation, their likely annual mileage and their expected consumption per mile or kilometer. If the technical characteristics of the vehicles are expected to change, this may imply significant changes in future gasoline consumption -- a development that would not be apparent from either simple trend analysis or econometric projections that use as determinants only the estimated number of vehicles in circulation. Similar internal consistency checks are possible taking into account new developments such as rural electrification, or irrigation developments based on power-driven pumps, or new industrial development projects.

8.5   Electric Power

The electric power sector is one of the most important elements within the broader energy framework. Fortunately, demand analyses and load forecasts for this sector have a better foundation than those of other energy sources because of the availability of accurate consumption data from individually metered customers, although such data may not always be available in a convenient format, for analytical purposes. These provide a more detailed and reliable base for future projections than the other types of data that usually provide the main source of information for non-electric energy sources. However, electricity demand forecast errors are usually more serious because of the long lead times for new equipment installations, their high initial capital costs and the difficulty of replacing electricity by other energy sources, except for cooking, heating, and domestic lighting purposes; but even for these uses, different appliances are needed. Forecasts that turn out to be too low may lead to costly, short-term solutions for alleviating capacity shortages, such as the installation of high-cost generating plants (diesels or gas turbines), or to rationing or forced supply interruptions. In some areas, lack of sufficient capacity has effectively shifted industrial expansion and economic growth. Overestimates, on the other hand, will lead to the tying-up of scarce investment capital and other resources. Figure 8.3 indicates schematically the various types of losses that can result from forecast errors. Load forecasting, therefore, plays a critical part in the electric systems planning process.

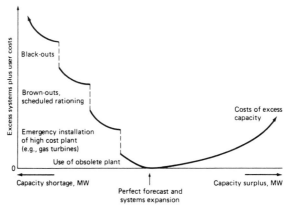

Figure 8.3: Effects of Forecast Errors on System & User Costs

The main elements of load forecasting which are relevant to the system planning process are reviewed in this section, and further details regarding these aspects may be found in the cited references (FPC 1970, IAEA 1984, IEEE 1980 & 1981, Sullivan 1977). Unlike in the traditional engineering context where demand is synonymous with capacity or power, we use the terms demand and load forecast interchangeably to indicate the magnitude as well as the structure of the requirements of both electrical power and energy (i.e., kW and kWh respectively), except in instances where it is necessary to make appropriate distinctions. The structure of demand includes disaggregation by geographic area, by consumer category, and over time, as well as characteristics such as load factor, diversity factor and system losses.

A knowledge of loads at the disaggregate level is required because the demand characteristics vary by type of consumer, by geographic area, and over time, and therefore the properties of the aggregate demand (e.g., at the system level) may be quite different from the characteristics of the individual loads. Since demands by individual consumer groups and/or by region may grow at different rates, aggregate demand will also change. Disaggregate loads are very important in the system planning process. Whereas for generation planning purposes the system may be modeled as a point source feeding a single lumped load, in the design of transmission networks, the characteristics of demand by region and by major load center (e.g., a city) become important. Ultimately, for distribution grid planning, a detailed knowledge of demand at each load center is required. Furthermore, the sum of many disaggregate demand forecasts for different local areas within a region, estimated by using a variety of techniques, can often serve as a useful check on an independently made global forecast for the same region.

Before we discuss the other characteristics of demand, it would be helpful to examine the basic relationship between power and energy. The commonly used unit of energy in heavy current electricity applications is the kilowatt-hour (kWh). The rate of energy per unit time is called power (or sometimes, capacity), which is measured in kilowatts (kW). Therefore, it follows that energy in kWh is the product of power in kW and time in hours. The distinction between power and energy is important because the same amount of energy may be delivered within a small interval of time at a relatively high rate of power flow, or over a longer period at a lower power level. This point is best exemplified in nuclear fission, by the contrast between the practically instantaneous explosion of an atomic bomb, and the controlled release of power from a nuclear reactor.

The load factor (LF), which is the ratio of average to maximum (or peak) kW over a given interval of time, may be calculated at various levels of aggregation, e.g., for a single customer or the whole system, on a daily or annual basis, and so on. It is important, because the size or capacity (and therefore cost) of power system components are determined to a great extent by their capability to handle peak power flows. Since the majority of customers require their maximum kW only during a short peak period during the day, the LF is also a measure of the intensity of capacity use. A load forecast may be made either in terms of the peak power, or the total energy consumed, during a given period (e.g., one year), with the conversion from one unit to the other being made by the use of the LF. In general, the kW peaks of different customers will not occur simultaneously. The diversity factor for a group of consumers is a measure of the divergence of spreading over time of the individual peak loads, and permits the computation of the combined peak load for the group in terms of the disaggregate peak values.

The total amount of both kW and kWh generated at the source will be greater than the corresponding values consumed because of losses in the system. Generation losses are mainly of the station use type, i.e., for driving various auxiliary equipment at the power plant itself. Transmission and distribution network losses are basically resistive losses, including transformer losses. Another type of loss which is important in some countries in theft, and allowances must be made for it in the demand forecast. Since it is also a type of electricity consumption, ideally, the corresponding user benefits and outage costs should also be considered in the optimizing process; in practice this would be extremely difficult to do, because little is likely to be known about the consumers and ethical considerations may make it difficult for the planning authority to give special consideration to such illegally appropriated benefits.

Load forecasts are made for time periods of varying duration. Very short-term demand projections are made on an hourly, daily or weekly basis for purposes such as optimizing system operation, and scheduling of hydro units, while short-run forecasts ranging between one and three years are used in hydro reservoir management, distribution system planning and so on (Gross and Galiana 1987). The time horizon for medium-term demand projections is about four to eight years, which corresponds to the lead times required for major transmission and generation projects. Such forecasts, therefore, are especially useful to determine the next steps in building these facilities. Long-range demand projections, usually of a duration of 10 to 35 years, are extremely important in long-run system expansion planning. The type of most relevant to the topic addressed in this study is the long-range forecasts. All the methods discussed earlier, trend analysis, econometric-multiple correlation techniques, macroforecasts, and surveys are used for this purpose.

All the methodologies discussed so far have dealt with deterministic load projections, where uncertainty is usually accounted for by parametric shifts in the forecasts to test for sensitivity. Recently, more sophisticated techniques involving the use of matrix methods (e.g., input-output matrices, to capture the interrelationships between productive sectors), as well as stochastic processes (e.g., representing sectoral growth of probabilities in terms of a Markov model), have permitted explicit consideration of probabilistic effects (IAEA 1976, Prasad et.al 1973, 1974). However, the resulting long-range demand forecasts are still deterministic. Once again, for sensitivity testing purposes, the basic assumptions may be varied to provide low-, medium- and high-demand forecasts, covering a range of relevant values of load growth.

Special care must be taken in cases in which substantial tariff changes are expected. While, for reasons discussed earlier in this chapter, existing estimates of price-demand elasticities for both the short- and long-run are suspect, prices changes, particularly if they are substantial in real terms, are likely to have a significant effect on consumption. How significant will depend on many local factors such as the ability of users to pass on cost increases to customers, the price and availability of substitute energy sources (and their total costs including needed changes in equipment), the effect of these tariff changes on real income, etc. No generalization is possible. Table 8.2 lists some of the major factors that are likely to determine the demand for electricity. Estimates of future changes in these determinants are needed to project demand.

We conclude this section with the following summary. There is no single, universally superior approach to load forecasting. The more sophisticated techniques tend to obscure the basic methodological assumptions as well as weaknesses in the data, and therefore the simpler techniques may be more appropriate in situations where the available information is known to be unreliable. Whenever possible, survey approaches should be used to forecast the demand of large users. This may account for a substantial percentage of the total load. Frequent updating of this information, to account for unexpected changes is an important additional requirement. The determinants of demand for the remaining, ubiquitous sectors have to be carefully selected, because they vary from case to case, and the level of disaggregation chosen will depend on the data, as well as on the ultimate purpose of the projection. Demand forecasting is a dynamic process in the sense that the procedure must be repeated often, in light of improved information and techniques of analysis. This building up of a reliable data bank is an invaluable tool in this process of constant revision.

Table 8.2

Major Demand Determinants of Electricity

A. **Residential Sector**
1. Number of households (or population)
2. Real family income weighted by income distribution
3. Price of electricity
4. Connection charges
5. Availability of service (urban, rural)
6. Reliability of service
7. Cost and availability of electricity-using fixtures and appliances
8. Availability and cost of consumer credit
9. Costs of alternative energy source (kerosene, LPG, natural gas, charcoal, firewood, coal)
10. Degree days below or above reasonable comfort range[1]

B. **Commercial Sector**
1. Sales or value-added of nonsubsistence commercial sector
2. Price of electricity
3. Connection charges
4. Costs of electricity-using appliance relative to those using alternative fuels for space conditioning
5. Costs of alternative fuels for space conditioning including costs of appliances
6. Reliability of service
7. Working hours of various types of commercial establishments

C. **Industrial Sector**
1. Price of electricity (demand and energy charges by type of service)
2. Type of industry and its electric intensity[2]
3. Degree of market power of individual industry
4. Relative price of alternative energy sources[3]
5. Reliability of supply
6. Comparative total costs of autogeneration
7. Availability

D. **Agricultural Sector**
1. Price of electricity
2. Availability
3. Reliability of service
4. Supply costs of alternative energy systems, e.g., diesel-driven irrigation pumps and milling and processing equipment, kerosene for lighting, etc.
5. Comparative total costs of autogeneration

E. **Public Sector**
1. Price of electricity
2. Per capita revenue of municipal governments
3. Number and size of public schools
4. Expenditures on armed forces and police (i.e., size of forces)
5. Types of public water supply (e.g., deep-well pumps)

---

[1] These types of load (heating and cooking) are generally limited to middle and high income earners.
[2] Electric energy intensity can be checked against consumption data of similar production processes in other countries.
[3] Only for industrial activities for which alternative fuels or energy sources represent technologically feasible sources of supply; the implied substitution would likely require complete equipment substitution for already existing plants.

Finally, it should be noted that in some cases institutionally imposed constraints which suppress demand, such as peak lopping or nonconnection of customers, and the presence of captive generation, may lead to a substantial gap between the potential (or underlying) and the achievable (or realistic) demand.

8.6 Natural Gas

The analysis and forecasting of natural gas demand raise some special issues. While the measurement of existing or past consumption is relatively simple because supply networks are closed systems with metering at both ends, forecasting future demand is not because of the relative ease of substitution by other energy sources. Most larger industrial utility and institutional gas users are equipped to switch to alternative fuels, such as fuel oil or coal, if this proves to be more advantageous. This applies to the major uses of gas as a source of process heat or boiler fuel, although not to its use as chemical feedstock. However, in most countries use of gas for these purposes is minor. It also does not apply to residential or small-scale commercial users because these usually do not own multiple-fuel appliances.

A second problem for the demand analysis of gas is that its supply requires heavy front-end investments, and that these investments are subject to substantial economies of scale. Once installed, such supply networks have a rather long life expectancy. Hence, secure, long-term markets are needed to write off these investments over periods that approximate their useful life in order to reduce unit capital costs, and large throughputs for customers are required for the same reason. Competing fuels, such as fuel oil or coal do not face the same difficulties because they can be supplied in discrete quantities if needed, providing more flexibility and reducing fixed costs.

Residential markets, which represent a major component of gas consumption in northern latitudes, are almost nonexistent in the developing world. This is so because most of the latter are located in subtropical or tropical zones, eliminating the need for residential heating, which is the major domestic source of consumption in the former. Low income levels in developing countries prevent the use of air conditioning units in all but a few households, and gas demands for other appliances, except cooking, are low as well. As a consequence, the fixed costs of house connections are usually prohibitive because potential consumption levels per connection are too low.

Another problem that increases fixed costs results from the fluctuating nature of demand. In countries with substantial space conditioning needs for heating and/or cooling, peaks are seasonal, although gas field production preferably should be kept constant the year around. As a consequence, storage facilities and larger distribution pipeline diameters are needed. All of these factors work against the supply of natural gas to small-scale users.

Presently prevailing thinking about the real value of gas reinforces this problem. Since the beginning of the so-called energy crisis in 1973/74, general agreement has been reached among energy pricing analysts as well as governments that cost-of-supply gas pricing schedules are no longer justified. Instead it is argued that gas prices should be raised to the going prices for petroleum fuels on a btu-equivalent basis. While this appears to be eminently reasonable from the point of view of opportunity-cost accounting, it also eliminates any incentive to smaller-scale users to switch to gas from alternatives such as fuel oils, LPG, or others. This is so because the initial connecting costs of natural gas are much higher than those for other fuels so that total cost of supply are necessarily higher, if btu-equivalent prices are charges for the gas. In countries in which natural gas supplies are relatively ample and petroleum products must be imported (such as Pakistan, Thailand, and Colombia, for example) it could be argued that gas prices should be set so that the total cost to the consumer (including initial fixed costs) are somewhat lower, or at least not higher, than the total supply costs of other substitutable energy sources (see Chapter 3).

Particular problems in demand forecasting are encountered if natural gas is to be introduced into new regions and markets. On the one hand, a large and costly supply network has to be constructed, but on the other, no preexisting market exists. In earlier times, when natural gas was not considered as a valuable, exhaustible fuel with high alternative use values now or in the future, gas was priced at low promotional rates that often only reflected its marginal supply costs, excluding the costs of exploration which usually were written off against the costs of higher-value crude oil exploration (MacAvoy 1983). As a result, gas prices on btu-equivalent basis, were frequently so much lower than prices of competing fuels that development of markets through displacement of alternative fuels was highly successful. Now, with prices set close to or equal to fuel oil prices, market development can be a major problem unless captive markets can be tapped. Such captive markets may be developed by government fiat, if for example, electric utilities are ordered to switch from alternative fuels to natural gas. This, for example, is the case in Thailand, where the government-owned natural gas pipeline will initially sell most of its available through-put to the government-owned utility company (see Chapter 13).

Where such government-enforced consumption of natural gas is impractical, long-term contracts with large-scale users are usually required to assure the financial viability of new gas supply network. In order to arrange such contracts, sufficient demand must exist or must be created. This is a serious problem in gas-rich regions and countries such as Algeria, most of the Persian Gulf oil producing states, Trinidad and Tobago, Bolivia, Indonesia, the northern Australian shelf, and the North slope of Alaska, as well as Mexico. While natural gas may be plentiful, local markets are too small or nonexistent to absorb potential output.

If deposits consist of gas only, this creates no overwhelming problem since the gas can be left in the ground until markets are developed. However, if the gas is associated gas that must be produced together with oil and cannot be reinjected, then often flaring becomes the only alternative. To find markets elsewhere, either expensive, long distance pipelines have to be built, liquefaction plants installed to supply overseas markets, or chemical feedstock plants developed which in turn have to sell much of their output in world markets, because domestic markets usually are too limited to absorb the output capacity of large-scale, economically efficient plants. However, given the very substantial supplies of natural gas existing in many inconvenient, remote places throughout the world, the temptation to convert them into chemical feedstock is large, and a potential, large oversupply of such chemicals becomes a constant threat. Future market demands for their output at stable prices therefore are quite uncertain, at least in the intermediate and long-run.

Demand forecasts for natural gas can be conveniently divided into four groups: The first is domestic captive demand that is secured through long-term contracts at predetermined prices. If such contracts are backed by the coercive power of government, few risks or uncertainties remain, except for potential variations in consumption (below some agreed-upon maximum ceiling) resulting from changes in demand for gas customer's outputs.

The second consists of projected future, domestic demand by industrial, commercial and residential sectors that are free to make choices between natural gas and alternative fuels within a market in which prices of alternative fuels are subject to market forces. Under these circumstances the demand for gas may vary significantly as a result of price changes of alternative fuels, and these changes can be quite abrupt for industrial users that are equipped to switch readily to alternative fuels. The effects of such relative price changes on domestic, small-scale industrial and commercial users will be less, because of the need for the installation of alternative appliances. However, longer-term trends in new equipment markets may be strongly influenced by such relative prices changes.

The third consists of offshore or long-distance markets that must be reached through long pipelines or liquefaction installations. Because of the high capital costs of such systems, demand is usually guaranteed through long-term sales contracts that assure to the financing institutions, repayment of the costs of development and a reasonable rate of return. In these cases, demand uncertainties are minimized once the supply contracts have been signed. However, the question whether such markets can be developed is usually highly uncertain, as indicated by the unsuccessful attempts to bring more Algerian gas into the United States, the unsettled future of the proposed Alaska gas pipeline, and the long drawn-out negotiations about Mexican gas sales to the U.S..

The fourth, consists of projected markets for gas-derived chemicals and fertilizer products. These are probably the most uncertain markets of all, given the large, potential competition from similar producers around the world and the relatively low freight costs for the chemical feedstocks and finished outputs produced. Before such ventures are started, detailed market studies are needed, and long-term sales contracts with reliable customers may be a necessity. However, such long- term sales contracts almost always are subject to some adjustment clauses that relate to prevailing world market prices, with the result that quantities sold may be assured, but not the prices. Some of the major demand determinants for natural gas are listed in Table 8.3.

8.7 Coal

Coal until the early twentieth century, was the major industrial and domestic fuel in the industrialized world. However, since then it has been rapidly displaced by the far cleaner, easier-to-handle petroleum fuels and natural gas. In recent years, the use of coal was largely limited to the production of steam for thermal powerplants or industrial boilers, or, in the form of coking coal, for the smelting of iron ores. A few developing countries maintain some railroad systems with coal-fired steam-engines as well (India and the Peoples Republic of China, for example).

The price increases in of hydrocarbon fuels in recent years has made coal once more an attractive alternative source of energy. At US$25 per barrel of fuel oil, a ton of lowly lignite could cost as must as $60 on a btu-equivalent basis, and a ton of high-quality steam coal as much as $115. However, such a simple comparison is misleading because of the much higher handling and equipment costs involved in the utilization of coal. Nevertheless, with mining costs of coal running anywhere between US$5 to US$40 per ton in major coal producing areas, the cost differential with oil may permit a resurgence of coal utilization in some countries in the future, despite potential environmental handicaps.

Table 8.3

Major Demand Determinants of Natural Gas

A. **Residential and Commercial Sector**
   1. Price of delivered gas
   2. Price of alternative fuels
   3. Connection charges for natural gas (together with (1))
   4. Availability
   5. Real family income weighted by income distribution[1]
   6. Degree-days below reasonable comfort levels
   7. Degree-days (and humidity) above reasonable comfort level
   8. System costs of alternative (electric) air conditioning units
   9. Cost of gas-using appliances relative to those utilizing other energy sources

B. **Industrial and Electric Utility Sector**

   I. **Process and Space Heating Requirements**
      1. Price of delivered gas
      2. Price of alternative fuels
      3. Availability
      4. Long-term price stability and supply reliability
      5. Laws and regulations affecting gas utilization
      6. Demands for industrial and electric utility outputs

   II. **As Chemical Feedstocks and Fertilizers**
      1. Domestic demands for outputs of conversion plants
      2. Relative costs of competing domestic or imported products
      3. World market prices for excess output that must be exported
      4. Price of gas to processing plant
      5. Costs of industrial conversion

C. **Export Sector**

   1. Potential delivered costs of gas in importer's country relative to alternative source of supply (gas or competing fuels)
   2. (Political) Security of supply to importing country

---

1   Equally important will be the local distribution of high and medium income residential areas as well as their rate of development. New natural gas connections may be quite feasible economically if they are systematically built into new middle to upper class housing developments, so that high density of connections can be achieved.

To analyze and forecast the demand for coal it is useful to divide this fuel into several subgroups. As can be seen from Table 8.4, carboniferous, or coal, resources occur with a wide variety of physical characteristics and quantities. The table presents a rather simplified division in terms of caloric values only. From a consumption point of view, a more useful division might be one that divides existing deposits into coking coal, steam coal and lignite. The line of division between these three major grouping is quite fuzzy, with many deposits, for example, more or less suitable for use as coking coal.

Table 8.4

**Approximate Calorific Values of
Various Grades of Coal**

	GJ/Ton[1]	btu/lb[1]
Anthracite	33	14,300
Bituminous Coal (average)	29	12,500
Coke	28	12,000
Subbituminous Coal	25	10,600
Brown Coal and Lignite	15	6,300
Peat	8	3,400

[1]   GJ (Gigajoule is approximately equal to 0.95 million btu; 1 ton = 1,000 kg = 2,208 lbs.

Source: David Crabbe and Richard McBride (eds.), The World Energy Book, MIT Press, Cambridge MA, 1979.

Coking coal commands premium prices substantially in excess of prices for steam coal. F.O.B. export prices from Western Canada and Australia, for example, range from US$35 to 60 per ton for shipment to Japan. As another example, Poland finds its economically worthwhile to export its coking coal from the Silesian mines to Cuba, Argentina, and Japan, while Australian coal is sold both in Japan and Great Britain.

Exports of steam coal are all but nonexistent at the present time. However, Australia, Western Canada, the U.S., Poland, and Colombia, to name only a few major producers or potential producers, are hoping for significant steam coal exports provided that the prices of liquid hydrocarbons are high enough. If the present high prices of hydrocarbon fuels persist, their large-scale replacement by coal as the principal boiler fuel in the future appears to be only a question of time.

Major problems confronting the wider utilization of coal include adverse environmental impacts and transportation costs. Table 8.5 shows rates typical for the United States for various shipping modes. What they indicate, for example, is that transportation in ordinary railroad hopper cars will double the price of coal (costing only $20 per ton at the mine pits), if the shipping distance is about 750 miles. Because of these high transport costs, it is usually prohibitive to ship low-btu coal, such as lignite, over any great distance. Mine-mouth utilization, usually in electric powerplants, is the only economically feasible form of use in such cases.

Demand forecasts for coking coal are usually relatively simple. There are a few, but rather large customers, and the negotiating of long-term sales contracts with them usually precedes mine development. Markets, therefore, are generally assured before development.

The major sources of demand for steam coal are electric powerplants, industrial plants that need heat, and, in some countries or regions, the small-scale commercial, industrial, and household sectors. While some of these uses may already be well established so that projections of future use can be made from an existing base, potential future markets may be substantially larger and broader given the rapid increase in costs of previously favoured hydrocarbon fuels.

Table 8.5

Representative U.S. Transport Costs for Coal

	Distance Assumed (Miles)	Cost Per Ton-Mile[1] (US cents/Ton-Mile)
Unit Train	300	1.46
Conventional Train	300	2.70
River Barge	300	0.62
Slurry Pipeline	273	1.25
Ship	n.a.	1.04

Source: Great Lakes Basin Commission, Energy Facility Siting in the Great Lakes Coastal Zone: Analysis and Policy Options, Ann Arbor, MI, Jan. 14, 1977, Table 33.

The potential, future demand will depend on the projected industrial and utility needs for process heat, and high pressure steam; the cost of delivered coal relative to fuel oil, natural gas, and LPG; the rate at which new plants capable of using coal will be built or existing ones can be converted; and the additional costs in equipment, operation, and maintenance of using coal instead of alternative fuels.

The major users in most countries are likely to be electric utilities. The demand of these utilities will depend on the underlying demand for electricity and the total delivered cost of electricity from coal-fired powerplants relative to the cost of electricity from other potential sources such as hydro. However, it may also depend on governmental policy which may enforce the use of coal in new power generating plants. On occasion, time pressure to bring new capacity on-line may lead to the construction of coal-fired plants, even though other alternatives that have longer construction time horizons promise to have lower generating costs. In some countries, the potential demand for steam coal may be met from imports, if domestic energy resources at reasonable costs are not available. Such potential imports may come from coal-rich, low-cost producing areas such as South Africa, Australia, Western Canada, Alaska, the Guajir Peninsula of Colombia, and other regions with large, low-cost coal deposits close to tidewater locations.

Domestic and small-scale commercial/industrial demands for coal may already exist or develop in regions in which alternative fuel sources are scarce and expensive. Coal may become a substitute for more traditional fuels such as charcoal and firewood, if the latter supplies become scarce.

Export demands for coal will generally be developed under long-term sales contracts. Scale economies, the need for special handling and dock loading equipment, unit trains or slurry pipelines, etc. usually require that the quantities sold in export markets be large, typically amounting to several million tons per year. Hence, future demand generally depends on the successful conclusion of such (long-term) sales contracts.

The market for lignite is more restricted than that for steam coal because of the much lower heat value of lignite coals. Lignite is mostly used for the production of electricity in thermal powerplants specially equipped to handle the particular type of lignite available. Because of the low btu/ton ratio, lignite-fired powerplants usually are built close to the mine site. The economics of such plants is affected by the higher equipment, operating and material handling costs of lignite versus other fuels, and the distance of such mine-mouth powerplants to load centers (i.e., transmission costs). As in the case of steam coal plants, the demand for lignite is determined by the underlying demand for electricity and the costs of obtaining the latter from alternative sources.

A secondary market for lignite may develop for industrial, commercial, and domestic purposes if other fuels are scarce are expensive. Because of the generally low quality of raw lignite, such markets are often served through the intermediates of lignite briquetting plants (See Chapter 13 for an example from the Thai tobacco industry). Such plants usually produce some by-products as well, such as tar oil. Table 8.6 summarizes major demand determinants for coal.

8.8   Petroleum Products

Petroleum products and their uses have been at the heart of the so-called energy crisis of the 1970's. Their convenience in use, relative cleanliness, and easy transportability have made them the preferred, and at least until recently, lowest-cost energy source for a wide variety of uses. In this century, most of our transportation systems and equipment, and much of our industrial as well as commercial and domestic energy uses have become strongly dependent on the use of liquid hydrocarbons. For the majority of them, suitable substitutes are simple not available at present or are only available at system utilization costs that exceed those of petroleum-based-ones by substantial margins. Even the most strenuous efforts and policy measures designed to develop substitute energy sources and energy-using systems will require decades to make a decisive impact. In the meantime, many of our most vital activities will remain quite dependent on the availability and use of petroleum products, regardless of their price.

However, the demand for liquid fuels is not entirely inelastic. Within limits, substitutes are available, but the options for utilizing them instead of petroleum varies widely among different uses. Some of these substitutes may be far more expensive in terms of total energy systems costs; others may require substantial time periods until conversion to their use could be accomplished. In any case, wholesale conversions from crude-oil based petroleum product uses to such substitutes may require many years of persistent and costly efforts.

There are five major types of petroleum substitutes available. The first is simply the possibility to do without them or to do with less. Curtailing pleasure driving in private automobiles or changing thermostat settings are typical examples. The second consists of the substitution by other energy sources. Examples are the use of coal, natural gas, or wood in the production of process heat or steam, the use of ethylene instead of gasoline, or the substitution of hydro for fuel oil based thermal power plants. The third consists of the substitution of capital for energy. Better insulation, recovery of waste heat, or replacement by more energy-efficient equipment fall into this category. Closely related to the substitution by capital is the fourth source, namely technological change. Systematic reductions in vehicle weights, use of cogeneration equipment instead of straight gas or steam turbines in power and steam production, or the use of electronic ignition instead of pilot lights come to mind. Fifth, labor can be used as a substitute for petroleum-based energy. Animal-drawn plows instead of tractors, hand loading instead of fork-lift trucks, hand shovels and pickaxes instead of bulldozers or tractors in construction, are some examples.

Table 8.6

Major Demand Determinants of Coal

A. Coking Coal
1. Mining costs
2. Shipping costs to potential customers
3. Export taxes or other levies, if any
4. Physical characteristics of coal
5. Demand for raw iron from blast furnaces
6. Costs of delivered cooking coal from alternative suppliers
7. Considerations of security of supply to customer
8. Costs of alternative reducing fuels (e.g., natural gas in Mexico)

B. Steam Coal

I. Electric Utilities and Industrial Steam Plants
1. Mining costs
2. Quality (physical characteristics and heat rate)
3. Transportation costs to user's plant
4. Costs of alternative fuels
5. Additional equipment operating and handling costs to user compared to other fuels
6. Governmental regulations affecting fuel choices by users
7. Total costs of electricity from steam-power plant delivered to load centers
8. Costs of electricity from potential alternative sources delivered to load centers
9. Growth in demand for   (a) Electricity
                                  (b) Industrial output of plants using coal

II. Residential and Small-Scale Industrial and Commercial Sectors
1. Delivered costs at retail
2. Costs and availability of alternative fuels (charcoal, wood, LPG, fuel oil, kerosene, natural gas etc.)
3. Number of households
4. Household income
5. Degree days below reasonable comfort level
6. Consumer habits

Because of the potential availability of substitutes, the demand for petroleum-based energy resources can never be completely price inelastic, provided price changes are large (as they certainly have been in recent years). Furthermore, since time is often needed to switch-over, the price elasticity is usually greater in the long-run than in the short-run. This is confirmed by most of the demand studies that have been undertaken in recent years. Unfortunately, as has already been pointed out, few, if any of these analyses (at least those that relied mainly on econometric estimates) have been able to determine with any degree of confidence how long the so-called long-run really might be, and what the likely short- or long-run price estimations are over varying potential ranges of price changes. Given the drastically changed environment with respect to petroleum product prices, availability, and security of supply, observations of past consumption trends can provide only a limited and generally unreliable guide for estimating future consumption trends.

A more appropriate approach appears to be to take explicit account of the specific variables that are likely to affect future demand. Among these variables are specific government policies that affect energy use and prices, petroleum product and alternative energy resource prices, potential investments in alternative energy supply systems, potential technological change, the cost and feasibility of energy conservation measures, etc. In other words, demand projections should be based on estimates of the technological, socioeconomic, and managerial feasibility of utilizing either petroleum-based or alternative energy sources, the potential for reducing petroleum energy inputs per unit of output or unit of consumption, and the likely effects of governmental policies related to energy using activities. Such estimates are likely to yield more reliable projections than those that are anchored in past relationships of economic activities, relative prices, and petroleum product consumption patterns.

The rapid changes in the cost of petroleum products by about an order of magnitude within a decade or so, has been a major factor in economic dislocation and inflationary pressures in many countries, as well as in the rapid and dangerous increase in the external indebtedness of most petroleum importing developing countries. For these countries, accurate demand forecasting for petroleum product uses, given a range of potential prices and availabilities, is obviously of major importance for their economic well-being and growth. However, accurate demand forecasts are equally needed for countries that are more or less self-sufficient in petroleum products as well as those that are modest exporters with limited crude oil reserves at the present time. For them, some of the important policy questions are how much oil should be exported now to earn needed foreign exchange given perceived domestic needs tomorrow, what domestic prices should be charged given world market prices, how domestic demands may change if domestic prices are changed, and what the negative effects of domestic price changes -- increases in particular -- may be in economic or political terms (for example riots and civil unrest).

While there is basically only one source of petroleum products at present -- i.e., crude oil -- the products derived from crude oil serve a wide variety of different markets and different needs. Hence demand analysis must be subdivided into the various, use-determined subsectors such as transportation, power production, industrial process heat, chemical feedstocks, construction, agricultural uses, armed forces, etc. Within these broad groupings, further subdividing may be necessary to reflect distinct and independent uses (e.g., fuels for tractors, irrigation pumps, and processing machinery in agriculture).

The demands for petroleum products are demands that are derived from other primary activities or human wants and needs. Therefore, the driving demand determinants for petroleum products are the demands for these primary outputs, such as the transportation of goods or people, the provision of heat for processing or cooking, etc. Hence demand forecasts have to be based on forecasts of the levels of these petroleum using activities, subject to the possible use of substitutes now and in the future. Given the rapid changes in the technology of energy using systems and appliances that have been stimulated by the drastic changes in petroleum prices, special attention must be placed on the potential feasibility and time-path of introducing such new or improved technologies. As existing equipment wears out or becomes inefficient because of high energy costs (e.g., gas turbines or airplanes) it will be replaced by others, subject to constraints such as investment capital availability, technological know-how, etc. New plants and new or expanding activities, unfettered by the deadweight of sunk investments, will tend to utilize substantially more energy installations and equipment. Because much of this new equipment as well as the lay-out and design of new plants is imported from industrialized nations, which have felt the brunt of high petroleum prices for some time, the transfer of such energy-saving technologies should be rapid. Unfortunately, such rapid transfers are unlikely to affect existing plants and equipment which have a tendency to be kept in operation far longer than in industrialized nations, because of chronic investment capital shortages in most developing nations. Such existing tendencies and constraints have to be taken explicitly into account in the projection of future demands.

As pointed out above, demand forecasts have to be made for each separate use. For some of them, mainly industrial users, a survey-research approach could yield the best results. Cement plants, pulp and paper mills, steel mills, fuel-oil-based powerplants, chemical producers that use petroleum as feedstocks, refineries, etc. are likely to be in a better position to forecast their own future demand than anyone else. However, cross-checks should be made to compare their projected consumption patterns per unit of output with those elsewhere, particularly in comparable plants in other nations. If substantial differences are discovered, further investigations may be warranted to find out why, and if changes and improvements could be brought about.

Unfortunately, the majority of petroleum product uses originate in ubiquitous, widely-spread activities such as transportation, agriculture, construction, and so on. For these sectors, forecasts have to be based on use categories, like private cars, taxis, commercial transport, railroads, water-borne shipping, aviation, armed forces, heating and cooking, lighting (i.e., kerosene), etc. Within these sectors, specific and basically independent subsectors must be distinguished, such as the use of diesel fuels in agriculture for deepwell pumps for irrigation and/or water supply, agricultural tractors, produce trucks, drying sheds, or individual generator sets. Diesel will also be used in commercial transport, for industrial or isolated power plants, for construction equipment, and for boats and ships. Total projected diesel fuel demand then is the sum of all of these individual demands, but in most cases the demand determinants for each individual subsector may be quite independent of each other.

Table 8.7 indicates some of the likely demand determinants for various types of petroleum product uses. It also indicates (in a separate column) the most likely substitutes that may affect demand in the specific sector. Obviously, these substitutes, and their availabilities and costs, are themselves determinants of demand for the given fuel in question. The importance of the various determinants will vary from country to country and often from region to region or place to place. Country, region and time-specific studies are needed to isolate the more important determinants and to estimate their likely effect on future demand.

8.9 Traditional Fuels

Traditional fuels comprise a wide variety of materials -- all of them of organic origin -- that serve as the primary energy source for over one half of the world's population. They include firewood, charcoal, dung and crop residues. The demand for them is entirely regional or local because of high transportation costs relative to their value, with the possible exception of charcoal. While most of the traditional fuels are used in households or small-scale commercial enterprises (e.g., restaurants), some of these

Table 8.7

**Major Demand Determinants and
Potential Substitutes for Petroleum Products**

DETERMINANTS	MAJOR POTENTIAL SUBSTITUTES

I.   GASOLINE

A.   Passenger Vehicles (automobiles)

1. Number of vehicles in circulation	1. Cost and convenience of public transport
2. Number of families with Incomes above specified minimum (for car ownership)	2. Cost of taxi fares
3. Growth of modern sector GDP	3. Cost of diesel-fueled vehicles and cost of diesel fuel
4. Costs of new cars	4. Cost of LPG conversion and cost and availability of LPG
5. Automobile license fees or taxes	5. Cost of kerosene (for gasoline dilution)
6. Price of gasoline	
7. Average annual mileage per vehicle	
8. Import restrictions on new automobiles or assembly plants	
9. Cost and availability of spare parts	
10. Road conditions	
11. Degree of traffic congestion	
12. Technical characteristics of existing and future automobile stock (e.g., gas mileage)	
13. Tax rules re deductibility of automobile expenses	
14. Number of taxis in circulation	
15. Technical characteristics of taxis (i.e., gas mileage)	
16. Average annual mileage of taxis	
17. Public policies toward government ownership and use of passenger automobiles	
18. Armed forces demands	
19. Number of motorcycles in circulation	
20. Number of persons or families with income above specified minimum for motorcycle ownership	

B.   Buses

1. Number of gasoline-driven buses in circulation	1. Diesel buses
2. Technical characteristics of buses (e.g., gas mileage) including age	2. Trucks used for passenger transport
3. Average annual mileage per vehicle	3. Bicycles
4. Public subsidies, if any	4. Number and costs of taxis, private cars, or motorcycles
5. Costs and availability of new buses	5. Increase in local employment opportunities
6. Costs and availability of spare parts	6. Existence of alternative passenger transportation modes (railroads, boats)

Table 8.7
(continued)

DETERMINANTS	MAJOR POTENTIAL SUBSTITUTES

B.   Buses (continued)
7.   Fares per passenger or passenger mile
8.   Cost of gasoline
9.   Degree of traffic congestion
10. Urban layouts (i.e., distance between residential, industrial, and commercial areas)
11. Miles of nonurban road network
13. Population growth
14. Per capita income
15. Privately owned buses including school buses, armed forces, company-owned, etc.)
16. Public ownership of bus systems and available budgets for their maintenance and expansion

C.   Gasoline-Driven Trucks

1. Number of trucks in circulation	1. Diesel-operated trucks
2. Technical characteristics of vehicles (e.g., gas mileage) including age	2. LPG-operated trucks
3. Average carrying capacity per vehicle	3. Rail transport, convenience, costs
4. Costs and availability of new trucks driven vehicles, etc.)	4. Other transport modes (boats, animal-
5. Cost and availability of spare parts	
6. License fees and vehicle taxes	
7. Level and characteristics of regulated tariffs, if any	
8. Real gross domestic product (GDP) by sector (i.e., mining, agriculture, industrial output, etc.)	
9. Public sector-owned vehicles (post office, municipal services, armed services)	

D.   Other Gasoline Using Equipment

1. Construction machinery	1. Cost and availability of electricity and electric-driven equipment
2. Stationary machinery (pumps, processing equipment, construction equipment, generator sets, etc.)	2. Cost of alternative diesel-or LPG-operated equipment
3. Boats	
4. Gasoline-using aircraft	
5. Gasoline-driven agricultural machinery	
6. Real GDP by sectors which tend to use gasoline-operated equipment	

Table 8.7
(continued)

DETERMINANTS	MAJOR POTENTIAL SUBSTITUTES

II. DIESEL FUELS

A. Automobiles and Taxis
1. Overall cost and availability of diesel-driven vehicles relative to gasoline-driven ones
2. All other determinants as for gasoline-driven vehicles. (See I, A)

1. Total costs and availability of gasoline- and LPG-driven vehicles
2. Public Transport
3. Cost of kerosene (as fuel admixture)

B. Buses and Trucks
1. Availability and cost of diesel-driven buses and trucks
2. All other determinants as for gasoline-driven buses and trucks (See I, B and C)

1. Total costs and availability of gasoline-driven vehicles

C. Construction Machinery
1. Level of heavy construction activity in private and public sectors
2. Cost of equipment
3. Equipment availability (possible import restrictions)

1. Gasoline-driven equipment
2. Cost of unskilled construction labor

D. Agriculture
1. Number of farm tractors
2. Technical characteristics of tractors (size, hp, fuel consumption per hour)
3. Cost of tractors

4. Government or bank supported farm mechanization programs
5. Tractor availability
6. Farm size

7. Average farm income
8. Cost of diesel fuel

9. Diesel-driven water pumps

10. Other stationary farm machinery
11. Diesel-driven generator sets
12. Diesel-oil fired drying kilns and sheds
13. Harvesting machinery

1. Animal-driven farm implements
2. Cost of unskilled farm labor

3. Total cost of gasoline-operated tractors
4. Cost of kerosene (as fuel substitute)
5. Light fuel oil (as fuel substitute)
6. Gasoline- or electricity driven water pumps
7. Biogas driven pumps
8. Wood, charcoal, straw, etc. for drying operations
9. Gasoline-driven harvesting machinery

E. Misc. Diesel-driven Machinery
1. Cost of diesel generator sets

2. Cost of diesel fuel

3. Public support programs for noncentral power station supplied rural electrification

1. Cost of electricity supplies from alternative sources
2. Costs of alternative gasoline-driven machinery and equipment
3. Steam- or electricity-driven locomotives

Table 8.7
(continued)

DETERMINANTS	MAJOR POTENTIAL SUBSTITUTES

4. Industrial and mining developments
   in isolated areas without electric power supply
5. Mining machinery and equipment
6. Diesel use by armed forces
7. Diesel-operated boats and ships
8. Diesel-locomotives
9. Public sector demands for diesel-driven
   equipment (e.g., road maintenance)

III. LPG

A. Residential Sector and Commercial Sectors

1. Price per kg	1. Wood (price, availability)
2. Cost of supply bottles	2. Charcoal (price, availability)
3. Cost of cooking-heating equipment	3. Kerosene (price, availability)
4. LPG distribution networks	4. Coal (price, availability)
5. Per family income	
6. Population growth in LPG supply areas	
7. Social acceptability as homecooking fuel	

B. Transportation

1. Cost per kg	1. Cost of gasoline-driven cars
2. Cost of vehicle conversion	2. Cost of diesel-driven vehicles

C. Industry

1. Price and availability	1. Price and availability of alternative fuels and feedstocks
2. Fuel and feedstock demands	

IV. KEROSENE AND JET FUELS

A. Residential and Commercial Sectors

1. Price	1. Cost and availability of other cooking/heating fuels (LPG, wood, charcoal, coal, etc.)
2. Cost of kerosene lamps and/or cooking/heating equipment	2. Availability and cost of electricity (mainly for lighting)
3. Per family income	
4. Population growth	
5. Social acceptability as a cooking fuel	

Table 8.7
(continued)

DETERMINANTS	MAJOR POTENTIAL SUBSTITUTES

B. Transportation
   1. Aviation demands
   2. Price relative to diesel and gasoline
       for possible dilution of these primary fuels

C. Chemical Feedstocks
   1. Demand for chemical intermediates
       (plastic, fertilizers, ethylene, etc.)

                1. Cost and availability of alternative
                    feedstocks (e.g., natural gas, LPG)
                2. Price and availability of imported
                    chemical intermediates.

V. FUEL OIL

A. Electric Power Generation
   1. Price

   2. Demand for electricity

   3. Generating systems-expansion plans
       (if based on fuel oil)

                1. Natural gas (price, availability,
                    systems costs)
                2. Coal (price, availability,
                    systems cost)
                3. Hydro (availability, systems
                    cost)

B. Industrial Uses
   1. Price

   2. Energy input requirements for various
       industrial processes
   3. Levels of industrial outputs by industry
       or process
   4. Needs for self-owned generating plants
       (permanent or backup service)

                1. Natural gas, coal, LPG, wood,
                    charcoal, straw, other biomass
                    fuels (price, availability,
                    systems costs)
                 2. Potential for energy
                    conservation

C. Commercial and Domestic (for heating purposes)
   1. Price

   2. Degree days below reasonable comfort range

                1. Total system costs of using
                    alternative fuels
                2. Potential for energy conservation

biomass fuels are also used for industrial purposes (e.g., bagasse in sugar factories, wood residues in sawmills and pulp and paper mills, and charcoal in steel mills).

Perhaps the most important characteristic of these traditional fuels is that in most regions only a small percentage enters commercial channels, i.e, are bought and sold. Most users gather them personally. For them, costs are represented by the time required to collect and transport the fuel to the family's residence.

Shortages of these traditional fuels are developing in many countries of the world (see Chapters 11, 12 and 13). These shortages are particularly severe in regions in which alternative, commercial fuels are not available, or only at costs that are beyond the reach of most of the people living there. Continuing population growth and ever-diminishing availability of fuel resources such as wood or crop residues then force increased use of animal dung, which in turn reduces its availability as a natural fertilizer. This, in turn, decreases crop yields and increases erosion. Ultimately, such increased shortages force out-migration, because long-term human survival without access to a minimum of cooking fuel is not possible.

In spite of the wide recognition of the pervasiveness of this problem, few reliable statistics of existing demand/supply relationships are available. The major source of information has been the FAO, which publishes annual statistics of forest products as well as crop and livestock production (FAO Annual). The latter makes it possible to estimate the approximate available quantities of crop residues and animal dung. The FAO bases its data on published government statistics which often are quite unreliable. In some cases, for example, they include only production data from managed forests. Furthermore, the FAO data do not disaggregate industrial and domestic fuelwood and charcoal use.

Studies of traditional fuels have to be not only country- but also region-specific. Transportation costs severely restrict the utilization of firewood beyond a narrow radius. According to a 1975 Indian survey by R. Mather, 70 to 100% of fuel requirements will be obtained from forests that are no more than 10 km from a village; beyond a distance of 15 km, fuelwood use virtually stops and is replaced by crop residues, dung, or charcoal. Of course, in regions where the latter substitutes are in equally short supply, distances traveled to gather fuel may be somewhat longer. However, for physical reasons they rarely exceed one or two days on foot or animal. In a number of countries, gathering the necessary fuel for cooking consumes as much as one-quarter of the total available working hours of a family, while in some regions in Upper Volta and Niger fuel purchases require 20-40% of the average working family income. Because of the high cost of transportation, demand and cost studies have to be undertaken on a regional or subregional basis. Ecological conditions often vary drastically from one region to the next. In the Andes countries, for example, average biomass (i.e., wood) production on a per capita basis is more than ample. However, most of it is concentrated in the unpopulated tropical flatlands of the interior while in the populated highlands and the desertlike coast, severe shortages are the rule.

While local availability will be a major factor in the consumption of firewood, another factor that will affect demand is climate. The use of properly designed cooking stoves instead of open fires may reduce fuel needs significantly (see Chapter 12). Higher local income levels will result in the substitution by other fuels, such as kerosene, LPG or even electricity. Coal may be used in some regions where it is abundant, as in the central regions of Colombia where many small, family-owned coal mines are operating. A list of the likely demand determinants is shown in Table 8.8. Detailed studies on a regional basis are needed to evaluate their validity and quantitative effects.

Table 8.8

Major Demand Determinants for Traditional Fuels
(Wood, Charcoal, Crop Residues, Dung)

A. Residential and Commercial Sectors
1. Local/regional population
2. Availability as a common property resource
3. Market price
4. Family income and income distribution
5. Degree-days below reasonable comfort range
6. Availability and price of other fuels including appliance costs (coal, LPG, kerosene, etc.)
7. Knowledge, availability, and costs of efficient stoves
8. Social customs (will largely affect alternative fuel choices)

B. Industrial and Agroindustrial Sectors
1. Needs for crop drying and kiln fuels (e.g., tobacco, bricks, ceramics, etc.)
2. Needs for process steam and in-plant electricity (e.g., bagasse for sugar mills, kiln-drying of lumber, process heat of pulp and paper mills, etc.)
3. Availability as a residual of production (e.g., bagasse, wood chips and shavings, coconut husks)
4. Market prices
5. Costs and availability of alternative fuels

8.10 Summary

We may conclude that it is important to avoid errors in demand projections because they often lead to shortages of energy which may have serious repercussions on economic growth and development. The methodologies for demand forecasting include, historical trend analysis, sector-specific econometric multiple correlation methods, macroeconomic or input-output methods, and empirical surveys. In general, the relatively sophisticated econometric and input-output approaches are easier to apply in the developed countries, while data and manpower constraints indicate that the simpler techniques will be more effective in the developing countries. There is no universally superior method of demand forecasting, and the use of several different methods is recommended to cross-check the final result.

In this chapter, we have discussed the problems of verifying patterns of energy consumption. Price subsidies and anomalies in the availability of energy products lead to leakages and use of fuels in unexpected and undesirable activities. The energy use patterns for traditional fuels are difficult to determine and project, because well-established markets do not exist for these products. This chapter also contains a detailed description of the determinants of demand in the various energy subsectors including: electric power, natural gas, coal, petroleum products, and traditional fuels and nonconventional sources.

References

Beenstock, M. and P. Willcocks, "Energy Consumption and Economic Activity in Industrialized Countries", *Energy Economics*, vol.3, October 1981, pp. 225-32.

Ben-Zion, Zilbfarb and F. Gerard Adams, "The Energy-GDP Relationship in Developing Countries", ibid., pp. 244-48.

De Backer, A. and K. Openshaw, "Timber Trends Study, Thailand: Detailed Description of Surveys and Results", FAO, Report No. TA 3156, Rome, Italy, 1972.

Federal Power Commission (FPC), *The Methodology of Forecasting*, 1970 National Power Survey, Washington DC, 1970.

Food & Agriculture Organization (FAO), *Yearbook of Forest Products*, Rome, annual.

Food & Agricultural Organization (FAO), *Production Yearbook*, Rome, annual.

Gross, G. and F. Galiana, "Short Term Load Forecasting", *Proc. IEEE*, vol. 75, Dec. 1987, pp. 1558-73.

IEEE, "Load Forecast Bibliography, Phase I", *IEEE Trans. in Power App. Syst.*, vol. PAS 99, 1980, pp.53-8.

IEEE, "Load Forecast Bibliography, Phase II", *IEEE Trans. in Power App. Syst.*, vol. PAS 100, 1981, pp. 3217-20.

International Atomic Energy Agency (IAEA), *Nuclear Power Planning for Indonesia*, Vienna, 1976

International Atomic Energy Agency (IAEA), *Expansion Planning for Electrical Generating Systems*, Vienna, 1984.

MacAvoy, Paul, *Energy Policy*, Norton, New York, 1983.

Munasinghe, M. and M. Gellerson, "Economic Criteria for Optimizing Power System Reliability Levels", *The Bell Journal of Economics*, vol.10, Spring 1979, pp. 353-365.

Nicholson, W., *Microeconomic Theory*, Second Edition, Dryden Press, Hinsdale, Ill., 1978, Chap.4.

Pindyck, Robert S., *The Structure of World Energy Demand*, MIT Press, Cambridge MA, 1979.

Prasad, N.R., J.M. Perkins and G. Nesgos, "A Markov Process Applied to Forecasting, Part II - The Demand for Electricity", IEEE Power Engineering Society Winter Meeting, New York, January 1974.

Prasad, N.R., J.M. Perkins and G. Nesgos, "A Markov Process Applied to Forecasting. Part I - Economic Development", IEEE Power Engineering Society Summer Meeting, Vancouver, July 1973

Schipper, L., S. Meyers and J. Sathaye, "Energy Demand in the Developing Countries", Report No. LBL-16260, Lawrence Berkeley Lab. Berkeley, California, June 1983.

Shepard, R.W., *Cost and Production Functions*, Princeton Univ. Press, Princeton, N.J., 1953.

Siddayao, C.M., *Energy Demand and Economic Growth*, Westview Press, Boulder CO, 1986.

Sullivan, R.L., *Power System Planning*, McGraw Hill International Book Co., New York, 1977, Chap.2.

Taylor, Lester D., "The Demand for Energy: A Survey of Price and Income Elasticities", in: *International Studies of the Demand for Energy*, W.D. Nordhaus (ed.), North Holland, Amsterdam, 1977.

Chapter 9

ENERGY PROJECT EVALUATION AND PLANNING[1]

9.1   Introduction

The successful processing of a development project usually involves several well defined steps. In order to place energy project decisions and economic cost-benefit analysis in its proper perspective, we summarize below the systematic approach used by the World Bank in a typical project cycle that includes: identification, preparation, appraisal, negotiations and financing, implementation and supervision, and evaluation (Baum 1978).

The Project Cycle

Project identification involves preliminary selection (by the borrowing country and the Bank) of potential projects that appear to be feasible and conform to national and sectoral development goals. In the preparation phase which may last one year or more, the borrower (often assisted by consultants) studies the engineering-technical, environmental, institutional, economic and financial aspects of a proposed project. At this stage, the Bank may provide staff guidance and financial assistance or help borrowers obtain other assistance to carry out the studies. Project appraisal consists of a comprehensive and systematic review of all aspects of the project, by Bank staff, including typically a four week field visit. They prepare an appraisal report that discusses comprehensively, the national and sectoral strategies, as well as the engineering-technical, environmental, institutional, economic and financial issues.

The appraisal report is used as the basis for negotiations at which the borrower and financier (i.e., the Bank) discuss the measures required to ensure the success of the project, and the conditions for funding. The resulting agreements are included in loan agreements which together with the appraisal report are considered and accepted by the Bank's Board of Executive Directors and the borrowing government. The borrower is responsible for implementing the project according to conditions mutually agreed on with the Bank, especially with respect to procurement of goods and services for the project in conformity with Bank guidelines that seek to ensure efficiency and economy in these procedures. Supervision of the implementation process is carried out by the Bank through periodic field visits and progress reports from the borrower. The Bank has its own annual reviews of supervision reports to continually update and improve implementation. Evaluation is the final stage of the project cycle, following disbursement of the loan. Project performance audits are carried out by an independent Bank department involving review of previous project documents and field visits, where appropriate. This analysis yields valuable experience that helps improve the work at all stages of the project cycle, for future projects.

---

[1] Edited version of a guest lecture presented at the European Economic Community (EEC) Training Seminar on National Energy Planning and Management for senior officials from developing countries, held in Ispra, Italy, in May 1982.

Economic Justification and Cost-Benefit Criteria

The procedure for the economic justification of an energy project begins with the preparation of a demand (or market) forecast (see Chapter 8). The next step involves the least cost alternative, benefit measurement and cost-benefit analysis, which are all interlinked and depend on the economic criteria described below.

Two related criteria are useful in the economic evaluation of investment projects: maximization of net benefits or minimization of costs. Maximization of net benefits is the more general approach, used in the cost-benefit analysis stage, to justify the use of scarce resources in an energy project, rather than elsewhere in the economy. To make optimal inter-sectoral allocation decisions in such situations requires the explicit determination of all benefits and costs over the lifetime of the investment. By contrast, a cost minimization approach, used in the least-cost solution stage, eliminates the need to measure the value of the benefits provided. This approach assumes that a given level of energy demand must be provided in similar quantities and qualities, whatever the supply source. The question then becomes simply one of selecting the lowest-cost method of supplying energy consumers. Both these criteria are helpful and used in a complementary way to evaluate projects.

Following usual cost-benefit practices, the basic objective function to be maximized here is developed in terms of net benefits or income. This leads to maximum economic efficiency in resource allocation. Under certain restricting assumptions mentioned earlier, net benefit maximization is equivalent to minimization of economic costs., Making efficiency, at least initially, the sole criterion for the choice among alternatives has obvious technical advantages. We find that the choice of efficiency as the goal provides us with an unambiguous ranking order among alternative energy schemes. Any project that yields more net income will be preferable to one that yields less, provided that we ignore the problems that are common to all objective functions, including the evaluation of uncertainty and risk, of unpredictable changes in technology and relative price levels, of the valuation of intangibles and nonmarketed outputs, of positive or negative externalities or spillovers, and the troublesome issue of individual and collective time preferences.

However, from the consumers' viewpoint, it is not really income that we ought to maximize but welfare, or total utility. The result is that an analysis which tells us how to maximize income does not necessarily tell us whether or not we are also maximizing welfare. Nevertheless, the choice of income maximization could be defended if the government would be willing to approach more equitable distribution patterns by redistributing income from the original beneficiaries to those whom the authorities feel to be more deserving. Another alternative is to use appropriate shadow prices as a weighting device. The issue is discussed below.

Given the prevalence of non-efficiency considerations like low-incomes and a large non-monetized sector in many areas, does it still make sense to begin by analyzing the efficiency solution? The answer is: Yes, it does. First of all, it is useful to know by itself, which of the various alternatives will result in the largest increase in total net income to the national economy. Second, only if we do know how much income is obtainable can we make an assessment of the "costs" that various distributional or nonquantifiable objectives may have. The efficiency measure provides us with something of a yardstick that can be used to measure the consequences of the latter even if it cannot tell us what their real value is. In some cases we might find that these costs are unacceptable high. In others it might turn out that the proposed beneficiaries of a specific distributional objective may voluntarily opt for compensatory payments instead, if they find that such payments could make them better off. Knowing the economic losses associated with the realization of non-efficiency goals would greatly facilitate evaluations of potential trade-offs between the multidimensional objectives that usually form part and parcel of any comprehensive national development program, and associated energy strategy.

What we can conclude is that despite its shortcomings, an income maximization function serves a useful purpose for the evaluation of alternative development policies and energy investment decisions. What must be remembered, however, is that finding the most efficient solution by itself does not answer the question: which of the various policies are preferable in terms of overall community welfare? It only provides us with a tool that can be used to calculate the necessary sacrifices in terms of total income that are needed in order to include other and possibly broader social objectives.

Ideally, the unweighted income maximization function should tell us which of the various alternative energy schemes will result in the greatest net increase in real per capita (or perhaps per family) income for the relevant population as a whole. The relevant population consists of the present and future population living within the decisionmaker's jurisdiction. If the latter is represented by a national government, then the analysis should provide an estimate of the net increase in real national income. If it is a regional government, the relevant population is the regional one, and the income to be maximized should be the regional rather than the national one.

The objective function has been formulated in terms of total net benefits, whereby net benefits represents the present-value excess of all economic benefits over all economic costs, and all required inputs have been treated as costs without an attempt at further disaggregation. A crucial aspect of such an objective function (which has as its goal the maximization of net economic benefits resulting from a series of interdependent public and private activities), is that it has to account for the opportunity costs of foregone alternative outputs elsewhere in the economy. In addition, it has to account for the fact that energy users will try to maximize net income (or well-being) from energy-derived outputs. This requires explicit evaluation of the joint costs and benefits of the energy-using systems, rather than of supply options alone.

As indicated earlier, economic cost-benefit analysis of projects, is typically one of the important analyses carried out in the critical appraisal stage -- the point at which a final decision is made regarding the acceptance or rejection of an energy project. In addition to this economic test, it was mentioned that a number of other aspects including technical, environmental, institutional, and financial criteria also need to be considered in project appraisal. We summarize next some criteria commonly used in the cost-benefit test of a project, with the emphasis on economic rather than financial evaluation.

The most basic rule for accepting a project is that the net present value (NPV) of benefits is positive:

$$NPV = \sum_{t=0}^{T} (B_t - C_t)/(1+r)^t$$

where B_t and C_t are the benefits and costs in year t, r is the discount rate, and T is the time horizon.

Both benefits and costs are defined as the difference between what would occur *with and without* the project being implemented. As described later, for the economic testing, B, C, and r are defined in economic terms and appropriately shadow priced using efficiency border prices. In particular, the shadow price of r is the accounting rate of interest (ARI). However, for the financial analysis of projects, B, C and r may be defined in financial terms.

If projects are to be compared or ranked, the one with the highest (and positive) NPV would be the preferred one, i.e., if $NPV_I > NPV_{II}$ (where NPV_i = net present value for project i), then project I is preferred to project II, provided also that the scale of the alternatives is roughly the same. More accurately, the scale and scope of each of the projects under review must be altered so that, at the margin, the last increment of investment yields net benefits that are equal (and greater than zero) for all the projects. Complexities may arise in the analysis of interdependent projects.

The internal rate of return (IRR) is also used as a project criterion. It may be defined by:

$$\sum_{t=0}^{T} (B_t - C_t)/(1 + IRR)^t = 0 .$$

Thus, the IRR is the discount rate which reduces the NPV to zero. The project is acceptable if IRR > ARI, which in most normal cases implies NPV > 0 (i.e., ignoring cases in which multiple roots could occur -- this may happen if the annual net benefit stream changes sign several times). Problems of interpretation occur if alternative projects have widely differing lifetimes, so that the discount rate plays a critical role.

Another frequently used criterion is the benefit-cost ratio (BCR):

$$BCR = \left[\sum_{t=0}^{T} B_t/(1+r)^t \right] / \left[\sum_{t=0}^{T} C_t/(1+r)^t \right] .$$

If BCR > 1, then NPV > 0 and the project is acceptable.

Each of these criteria has its strengths and weaknesses, but NPV is probably the most useful. The NPV test may be used to derive the least-cost rule. In the case of energy projects, the benefits of two alternative technologies are often equal (i.e., they both serve the same need or demand). Then the comparison of alternatives is simplified. Thus:

$$NPV_I - NPV_{II} = \sum_{t=0}^{T} (C_{II,t} - C_{I,t})/(1+r)^t ;$$

since the benefit streams cancel out. Therefore, if

$$\sum_{t=0}^{T} C_{II,t}/(1+r)^t > \sum_{t=0}^{T} C_{I,t}/(1+r)^t ;$$

this implies that $NPV_I > NPV_{II}$.

In other words the project which has the lower present value of costs is preferred. This is called the least-cost alternative (when benefits are equal). However, even after selecting the least-cost technology, it would still be necessary to ensure that the project would provide a positive NPV.

9.2   Shadow Pricing

In this section, the reader will be provided an overview of the chief concepts and applications of shadow pricing. The material presented seeks to provide an introduction to this complex subject. Further details are available in various publications on shadow pricing (Munasinghe and Warford 1977, Ray 1984, Squire and Van der Tak 1975).

In the idealized world of perfect competition, the interaction of atomistic profit-maximizing producers and utility-maximizing consumers gives rise to a situation that is called pareto-optimal. In this state, prices reflect the true marginal social costs, scarce resources are efficiently allocated and, for a given income distribution, no one person can be made better off without making someone else worse off (Bator 1957).

However, conditions are likely to be far from ideal in the real world. Distortions due to monopoly practices, external economies and diseconomies (which are not internalized in the private market), interventions in the market process through taxes, import duties and subsidies, all result in market (or financial) prices for goods and services which may diverge substantially from their shadow prices or true economic values. Furthermore, the reliance on strict efficiency criteria for determining economic welfare implies the passive acceptance of the existing (skewed) income distribution -- this may be socially and politically unacceptable, especially if there are large income disparities. Such consideration necessitate the use of appropriate shadow prices (instead of market prices) of inputs to the energy sector, to determine the optimal investment program as well as energy prices, especially in the developing countries where market distortions are more prevalent than in the industrialized countries.

Consider a general equilibrium model of the economy in which the national goal is embodied in an acceptable objective function such as aggregate consumption. This consumption is to be maximized subject to constraints that might include limits on resource availabilities, distortions in the economy, and so on. Then, the shadow price of a given scarce economic resource represents the change in value of the objective function, caused by a marginal change in the availability of that resource. In the more specific context of a mathematical programming macro-economic model, the optimal values of the dual variables (that correspond to the binding resource availability constraints in the primal problem) have dimensions of price, and could be interpreted as shadow prices (Luenberger 1973, Sassone 1977). While the general equilibrium approach is conceptually important, it is too cumbersome and data-intensive to use in most cases. Therefore in practice, partial equilibrium techniques may be used that evaluate the impact of the change in the availability of a given resource on a few key areas, rather than throughout the economy (see Figure 3.1 in Chapter 3).

Two basic types of shadow prices exist. These involve whether or not society is indifferent to income distributional considerations. To illustrate this point, consider the simple national goal of maximizing the present value of aggregate consumption over a given time horizon. If the consumption of different individuals is added directly regardless of their income levels, then the shadow prices derived from such a model are termed efficiency prices because they reflect the pure efficiency of resource allocation. When increasing the consumption of the lower income groups becomes an important objective, this consideration is given a greater weight in evaluating aggregate consumption. Then, the resultant shadow prices are called social prices.

The goal of shadow pricing is therefore, either efficiency- or socially-oriented. In brief, efficiency shadow prices try to establish the actual economic values of inputs and outputs, while socially-oriented shadow prices take account of the fact that the income distribution between different societal groups or regions may be distorted in terms of overall national objectives. This may call for special adjustments, usually by giving greater weight to benefits and costs accruing to the poor relative to the rich. In our analysis, we will place primary emphasis on efficiency shadow pricing, but will also make use of social shadow prices and social weights, mainly for determining subsidized energy prices and lifeline rates (see Chapter 4 on pricing policy).

Nonpriced inputs and outputs must be shadow-priced to reflect their economic opportunity costs. Major categories of such nonpriced inputs and outputs are public goods and externalities. Public goods are defined as those goods and services that are free to all without payments once they have been made available, such as transportation and navigation facilities, and police protection. Externalities are defined as beneficial or adverse effects imposed on others, for which the originator of these effects cannot charge or be charged (as the case may be).

Unfortunately, many externalities are not only difficult to measure in physical terms, but even more difficult to convert into monetary equivalents (i.e., to measure the "willingness to pay" of the parties affected by the externalities). Quite often therefore, the approach taken is to impose regulations and standards, expressed in physical measurements only, that try to eliminate the perceived external damages. However, this approach may not be effective, because no attempt is made to compare the costs of compliance with the real benefits provided (i.e., damages avoided).

Numeraire

To derive a consistent set of economic shadow prices for goods and services, a common yardstick or numeraire to measure value is necessary, as illustrated by a simple example. If one wishes to compare bananas with grapefruit, the equivalent units might be either one banana for one grapefruit, or one kilo of bananas for one kilo of grapefruit. In the first instance, the common yardstick is one fruit; in the second, it is the unit of weight. Clearly, if the weights of the two types of fruits are different, the result of the comparison will depend on the numeraire used.

With a numeraire of economic value the situation is more complicated, because the same nominal unit of currency may have a different value depending on the economic circumstances in which it is used. For example, a rupee-worth of a certain good purchased in a duty free shop is likely to be more than the physical quantity of the same good obtained for one rupee from a retail store, after import duties and taxes have been levied. Therefore, it is possible to distinguish intuitively between the border priced rupee, which is used in international markets free of import tariffs, and a domestic-priced rupee, which is used in the domestic market subject to various distortions. A more sophisticated example of the value differences of a currency unit in various uses arises in countries where investment for future economic growth is considered inadequate. In these instances, a rupee-worth of savings that could be invested to increase the level of future consumption, may be considered more valuable than a rupee devoted to current consumption.

The choice of the numeraire, like the choice of a currency unit, should not influence the economic criteria for decisionmaking, provided the same consistent framework and assumptions are used in the analysis. For example, only one difference exists between a study using centavos as units and one using pesos (where the peso is defined as one hundred centavos). In the study using centavos all monetary quantities will be numerically one hundred times as large as in the one using pesos. Therefore, the numeraire may be selected purely on the basis of convenience of application.

A most appropriate numeraire in many instances is a unit of uncommitted public income at border shadow prices (Little and Mirrlees 1974). Essentially, this unit is the same as freely disposable foreign exchange available to the government, but expressed in terms of units of local currency converted at the official exchange rate. The discussion in the next section is developed in relation to this particular yardstick of value. The border-priced numeraire is particularly relevant for the foreign exchange scarce developing countries. It represents the set of opportunities available to a country to purchase goods and services on the international market.

The basic rationale underlying the system of efficiency prices, using border prices as the numeraire, may be understood at a more intuitive level, if we make use of the following simplified physical analogy.

In Figure 9.1, the sea level, which is a universal reference level, may be compared to the undistorted baseline for efficiency pricing. Thus all heights in metres measured with respect to the sea level, denoted by the abbreviation mS, are like border prices. By contrast, heights of objects measured from the local ground level and represented by the symbol mL, are like domestic market prices evaluated relative to the distorted local economy. It is interesting to compare the strengths and weaknesses of the two sets of prices, by pursuing the physical analogy further.

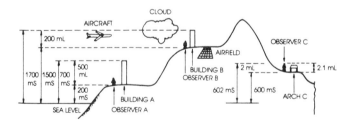

Figure 9.1: A Physical Analogy to Border Pricing

With the respective heights as indicated in the figure, consider an aircraft approaching the landing field, located on a high plateau. As he approaches land, the aircraft pilot has the following conversation (by radio), with observer A on the ground:

Pilot: It's fine and clear up here, except for some clouds coming up ahead. How is it down there?

Observer A: It's sunny down here too, but unfortunately I am standing in the shade of a 500 metre tall building.

Pilot: I see the tower well below me. It is a nice looking building. Thanks for the information.

The pilot now continues on and enters the cloud. He then records the following exchange with observer B, standing on the plateau.

Observer B: How is it up there? You are covered by clouds, but you might want to know that the tallest building in town is only 200 metres high.

Pilot: Fine thanks. I just overflew a 500 metre high tower with a lot of room to spare, so I should clear your town quite easily, although I can't see a thing.

It is not difficult to imagine the unfortunate consequences if the pilot fails to gain altitude, to clear building B.

Fortunately, professional pilots are rarely so naive, and use a much more scientific basis for exchanging information on altitude. Thus if both observers A and B indicated the respective heights of their buildings as 1500 and 1700 metres, with respect to sea level, the pilot would be able to avert the potential tragedy. In a similar vein, the use of border prices provides a measure of economic value relative to a standard reference that is independent of the local observer. On the other hand, domestic market prices are distorted by local constraints (such as import duties and taxes), and these usually vary quite arbitrarily depending on the good or service under consideration. Therefore, the latter set of prices may be a rather misleading basis on which to make rational economic decisions.

However, market prices are the prices that the average consumer perceives and deals with every day. To him, the border pricing framework that the national planner uses for his investment decisionmaking is a theoretical construct which is very "shadowy" indeed. Therefore, when it comes to implementing practical pricing policies, domestic market prices play a key role. The physical analogy will clarify this point further.

Consider individual C (a blind man) who lives on the other side of the mountain, and has never seen the ocean. Suppose a well-meaning but impractical friend is advising him about potential obstacles in his path. The following conversation ensues:

Individual C: Is there anything ahead of me?

Friend: Yes, you have to walk under an arch. The top of the arch is 602 metres above sea level.

Individual C does not understand the concept of sea level, but knows that he is only 2.1 metres high. If he proceeds on this basis, he is likely to bump his head. What is relevant for his decisionmaking is the height of the arch above the local ground level. If his friend advised him correctly that this height was only 2 metres, he could duck his head and pass safely under the arch.

The parallel with energy price setting is the following. For example, as explained in Chapter 3, the strict long-run marginal cost (LRMC) of electricity supply is first calculated in border prices. However prior to implementation, it must be converted into an equivalent market price -- by dividing the LRMC by an appropriate consumer-specific conversion factor (Munasinghe and Warford 1977). It is this reconverted market price that the rational consumer will understand, because his willingness-to-pay depends on the distorted local prices of other competing goods and services. In other words, the reconversion automatically adjusts for distortions relative to local market conditions (like the local ground level).

Using Shadow Prices

The estimation and use of shadow prices is facilitated by dividing economic resources into tradeable and nontradeable items. Tradeables and nontradeables are treated differently. The values of directly imported or exported goods and services are already known in border prices, that is, their foreign exchange costs converted at the official exchange rate. However, locally purchased items whose values are known only in terms of domestic market prices, must be converted to border prices, by multiplying the former prices by appropriate conversion factors (CF).

$$\text{Border(Shadow) Price} = \text{Conversion Factor x Domestic(Market) Price}$$

$$BP = CF \times DP$$

For those tradeables with infinite elasticities -- of world supply for imports and of world demand for exports -- the cost, insurance, and freight (C.I.F.) border price for imports and the free-on-board (F.O.B.) border price for exports may be used (with a suitable adjustment for the marketing margin). If the relevant elasticities are finite, then the change in import costs or export revenues, as well as any shifts in other domestic consumption or production levels or in income transfers, should be considered. The free trade assumption is not required to justify the use of border prices since domestic price distortions are adjusted by netting out all taxes, duties, and subsidies.

To clarify this point, consider the household shown in Figure 9.2, where a child is given an allowance of twenty pesos a month as pocket money. The youngster may purchase a bag of sweets from the grocery store at a price of two pesos. Since the parents want to discourage consumption of sweets, however, they impose a fine of one peso on each bag. The fine is exactly like an import duty, and the child must surrender three pesos for every bag of candy (valued at its domestic price, inside the household). From the family's perspective however, the total external payment for the item is only two pesos, because the one peso fine is a net transfer within the household. Therefore, the true economic cost (or shadow price) of the bag of lollipops to the household is two pesos (i.e., its border price), when the impact of the fine on the distribution of income between parent and child is ignored.

A nontradeable is conventionally defined as a commodity whose domestic supply price lies between the F.O.B. export price and C.I.F. import price. Items that are not traded at the margin because of prohibitive trade barriers, such as bans or rigid quotas, are also included within this category. If the increased demand for a given nontradeable good or service is met by the expansion of domestic supply or imports, the associated border-priced marginal social cost (MSC) of this increased supply is the relevant resource cost. If decreased consumption of other domestic or foreign users results, the border-priced marginal social benefit (MSB) of this foregone domestic consumption or of reduced export earnings, would be a more appropriate measure of social costs.

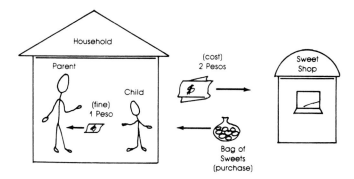

Figure 9.2: Household Analogy to Shadow Pricing of a Traded Good

The socially optimal level of total consumption for the given input (Q_{opt}) would lie at the point where the curves of MSC and MSB intersect. Price and non-price distortions lead to nonoptimal levels of consumption $Q \neq Q_{opt}$, characterized by differences between MSB and MSC. More generally, if both effects are present, a weighted average of MSC and MSB should be used. The MSB would tend to dominate in a short-run, supply constrained situation; the MSC would be more important in the longer run, when expansion of output is possible.

The MSC of nontradeable goods and services from many sectors can be determined through appropriate decomposition. For example, suppose one peso-worth, of the output of the construction sector (valued in domestic prices), may be broken down successively into components. This would include capital, labor, materials, and so on, which are valued at pesos C_1, C_2,... C_n in border prices. Since the conversion factor of any good is defined as the ratio of the border price to the domestic price, the construction conversion factor equals:

$$CCF = \sum_{i=1}^{n} C_i$$

The standard conversion factor (SCF) may be used with nontradeables that are not important enough to merit individual attention, or lack sufficient data. The SCF is equal to the official exchange rate (OER) divided by the more familiar shadow exchange rate (SER), appropriately defined. Using the SCF to convert domestic priced values into border price equivalents, is conceptually the inverse of the traditional practice of multiplying foreign currency costs by the SER (instead of the OER), to convert foreign exchange to the domestic price equivalent. The standard conversion factor may be approximated by the ratio of the official exchange rate to the free trade exchange rate (FTER), when the country is moving toward a freer trade regime:

$$SCF = \frac{OER}{FTER} = \frac{eX + nM}{eX(1-t_x) + nM(1+t_m)}$$

where X = F.O.B. value of exports, M = C.I.F. value of imports, e = elasticity of domestic supply of exports, n = elasticity of domestic demand for imports, t_x = average tax rate on exports (negative for subsidy), and t_m = average tax rate on imports.

The most important tradeable inputs used in energy projects are capital goods and petroleum-based fuels. Some countries may have other fuels available, such as natural gas or coal deposits. If no clear-cut export market exists for these indigenous energy resources, then they cannot be treated like tradeables. As described in Chapter 3, if there is no alternative use for the fuels, an appropriate economic value is the MSC of production or of extracting gas or coal, plus a markup for the discounted value of future consumption foregone (or "user cost"). If another high value use exists for such a fuel, the opportunity cost of not using the resource in the alternative use should be considered the economic value of the fuel. The most important nontradeable primary factor inputs are labor and land, the next subjects for discussion.

The foregone output of workers used in the energy sector is the dominant component of the shadow wage rate (SWR). Consider a typical case of unskilled labor in a labor surplus country -- for example, rural workers employed for dam construction. Complications arise in estimating the opportunity cost of labor, because the original rural income earned may not reflect the marginal product of agricultural labor. Furthermore, for every new job created, more than one rural worker may give up former employment. Allowance must also be made for seasonal activities such as harvesting, and overhead costs like transport expenses. Based on the foregoing, the efficiency shadow wage rate (ESWR) is given by:

$$ESWR = a.m + c.u,$$

where m and u are the foregone marginal output and overhead costs of labor in domestic prices, and a and c are corresponding conversion factors to convert these values into border prices.

If we are interested only in efficiency pricing, then we may stop here. However, if social pricing is important, consider the effect of these changes on consumption patterns. Suppose a worker receives a wage W_n in a new job, and that the income foregone is W_o, both in domestic prices; note that W_n may not necessarily be equal to the marginal product foregone m. It could be assumed, quite plausibly, that low-income workers consume the entire increase in income $(W_n - W_o)$. Then this increase in consumption will result in a resource cost to the economy of $b(W_n - W_o)$. The increased consumption also provides a benefit given by $w(W_n - W_o)$, where w represents the MSB, in border prices, of increasing domestic-priced private sector consumption by one unit. Therefore,

$$SWR = a.m + c.u + (b - w)(W_n - W_o)$$

The letter b represents the MSC to the economy, resulting from the use of the increased income. For example, if all the new income is consumed, then b is the relevant consumption conversion factor or resource cost (in units of the numeraire) of making available to consumers one unit worth (in domestic prices) of the marginal basket of n goods that they would purchase. In this case

$$b = \sum_{i=1}^{n} g_i.CF_i$$

where g_i is the proportion or share of the i th good in the marginal consumption basket, and CF_i is the corresponding conversion factor.

The corresponding MSB of increased consumption may be decomposed further; $w = d/v$, where $1/v$ is the value (in units of the numeraire) of a one-unit increase in domestic-priced consumption accruing to someone at the average level of consumption (c_a). Therefore, v may be roughly thought of as the premium attached to public savings, compared to "average" private consumption. Under certain simplifying assumptions, $b = 1/v$. If $MU(c)$ denotes the marginal utility of consumption at some level c, then $d = MU(c)/MU(c_a)$. Assuming that the marginal utility of consumption is diminishing, d would be greater than unity for "poor" consumers with $c < c_a$, and vice versa.

A simple form of marginal utility function could be: $MU(c) = c^{-n}$. Thus,

$$d = MU(c)/MU(c_a) = (c_a/c)n .$$

Making the further assumption that the distribution parameter $n = 1$, gives:

$$d = c_a/c = i_a/i$$

where i_a/i is the ratio of net incomes, which may be used as a proxy for the corresponding consumption ratio.

The consumption term (b-w) in the expression for SWR disappears if, at the margin: (a) society is indifferent as to the distribution of income (or consumption), so that everyone's consumption has equivalent value $(d=1)$; and (b) private consumption is considered to be as socially valuable as the uncommitted public savings $(b=1/v)$.

The appropriate shadow value placed on land depends on its location. Usually, the market price of urban land is a good indicator of its economic value in domestic prices, and the application of an appropriate conversion factor (such as the SCF) to this domestic price, will yield the border-priced cost of urban land inputs. Rural land that can be used in agriculture may be valued at its opportunity costs -- the net benefit of foregone agricultural output. The marginal social cost of other rural land is usually assumed to be negligible, unless there is a specific reason to the contrary. Examples might be the flooding of virgin jungle because of a hydroelectric dam that would involve the loss of valuable timber, or spoilage of a recreational area that has commercial potential.

The shadow price of capital is usually reflected in the discount rate or accounting rate of interest (ARI), which is defined as the rate of decline in the value of the numeraire over time. Although there has been much discussion concerning the choice of an appropriate discount rate, in practice the opportunity cost of capital (OCC) may be used as a proxy for the ARI, in the pure efficiency price regime. The OCC is defined as the expected value of the annual stream of consumption, in border prices net of replacement, which is yielded by the investment of one unit of public income at the margin.

A simple formula for the social-priced ARI, which also includes consumption effects, is given by:

$$ARI = OCC [s + (1 - s)w/b],$$

where s is the fraction of the yield from the original investment that will be saved and reinvested.

Usually, the rigorous estimation of shadow prices is a long and complex task. Therefore, the energy sector analyst is best advised to use whatever shadow prices have already been calculated. Alternatively, the analyst would estimate a few important items such as the standard conversion factor, opportunity cost of capital, and shadow wage rate. When the data are not precise enough, sensitivity studies may be made over a range of values of such key national parameters.

9.3 Case Study: Electric Power

The economic evaluation of an electric power project consists of three basic steps: (a) demand forecast; (b) least cost investment program; and (c) cost-benefit analysis. Before discussing these steps in more detail, it is useful to examine the iterative interaction between the investment decision and output pricing policy.

Investment-Pricing Interaction

Consider the basic steps in this analysis, as summarized in Fig. 9.3. The load-demand forecast is made by systematically taking into account all factors that might have quantitative relationships with future electricity consumption, such as price, income, economic growth, population growth, energy substitution, etc., as well as judgmental factors including effects of energy conservation programs. The assumptions made regarding the future evolution of electricity price is especially critical. Several alternative long-run investment programs (or system expansion plans) are then identified to meet the demand growth, subject to various constraints including minimum acceptable reliability of supply, environmental and safety criteria, and so on. The least cost or cheapest alternative (in present discounted value terms and using shadow prices) is selected as the optimal program.

However, economic theory indicates that the benefits (to society) of electricity consumption will be maximized if the output prices are set equal to the marginal costs of supply based on the least cost plan. In practice, prices will be adjusted to reflect not only long-run marginal costs (LRMC) of supply, but also other financial, social and political criteria. Whatever future prices result, they must be compared to the prices assumed in making the original demand forecast. If there is inconsistency then the demand forecast may have to be adjusted and the investment plan reviewed again.

The above considerations indicate that the investment and pricing decisions are closely interrelated. The simplified case study presented below illustrates this point, and also indicates how shadow prices are used in practice. The project is a hydroelectric plant with a 950 million m^3 of storage capacity providing about 7,500 GWh of energy in an average year, and about 5,350 GWh in a dry year. The cost of the associated transmission spur line and substation to link up with the interconnected national power grid, are included in the project.

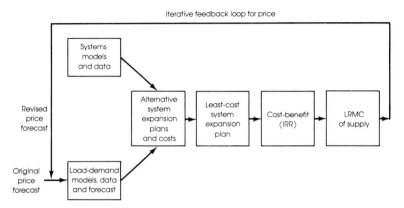

Figure 9.3: Interaction of Investment Decision, Price and Demand Forecast

Demand Forecast

The demand forecast for the customers to be served by the power utility over the period 1981-1990 was prepared on the basis of historical trends and recorded indices for each consumer category for each of the years from 1973 to 1980 (see Table 9.1). Trend curves were derived to project monthly and annual requirements which were subsequently adjusted to reflect population growth trends, sector economic conditions and market saturation effects. Residential consumption grew at an average annual rate of 11.5% in the period 1974-1980, and is expected to grow at an average annual rate of 12% in the period 1981-1990. Also, residential consumption augmented its share of the market from 36% in 1973 to 42% in 1980, as a result of increased urbanization and access to service, as well as expansion of services to semi-rural areas. This trend is expected to continue over the next few years, and by 1990 residential consumption would represent about 47% of total sales.

Commercial consumption grew at an average annual rate of 9% in the period 1974-1980, and is expected to grow at an average annual rate of 9.8% in the period 1981-1990. Commercial consumption, which represented 17% of sales in the period 1973-1980, is expected to decrease slightly to 16% in the period 1981-1990. Industrial consumption grew at an average rate of 7.9% in the period 1974-1980, and is expected to grow at an annual average rate of 9.9% in the period 1981-1990. The industrial consumption share of the market which decreased from 34% in 1973 to 32% in 1980, is expected to decrease slightly to 29% by 1990. Government and Public Lighting grew at an average growth rate of 4.6% in the period 1974-1980, and is expected to grow at an average growth rate of 8.4% in the period 1981-1990, as a result of future distribution system expansion. Government and Public Lighting consumption has shown a slightly decreasing share of total consumption, and is expected to represent about 8% of total sales by 1990.

Table 9.1

Actual and Forecast Sales and
Gross Generation for System
(GWh)

	Residential	%	Commercial	%	Industrial	%	Government & Pub.lighting	%	Total Sales	%	Losses and¹ Station Use %	Total Requirements
Actual												
1973	782		367		742		292		2183		433	2616
1974	923		411		809		305		2448		426	2874
1975	1042	39	450	17	855	32	316	12	2663	100	695 21	3358
1976	1175		513		945		347		2980		625	3605
1977	1237		589		995		353		3174		836	4010
1978	1392		628		1104		351		3475		787	4262
1979	1549		622		1168		374		3713		968	4681
1980	1672	42	673	17	1263	32	401	10	4009	100	1139 22	5226
Average Growth rate (1974–1980) %	11.5		9.0		7.9		4.6		9.1		14.8	10.4
Forecast												
1981	1808		741		1420		441		4410		1341	5751
1982	2029		813		1556		477		4875		1489	6364
1983	2278		893		1706		516		5393		1628	7021
1984	2558		981		1869		559		5967		1741	7708
1985	2875	44	1077	16	2049	31	604	9	6605	100	1897 22	8502
1986	3233		1182		2246		654		7315		2107	9422
1987	3637		1298		2461		708		8104		2171	10275
1988	4094		1425		2697		766		8982		2285	11267
1989	4610		1565		2956		829		9960		2466	12426
1990	5193	47	1719	16	3240	29	896	8	11048	100	2670 19	13718
Average Growth rate (1981–1990) %	12.0		9.8		9.9		8.4		10.7		8.9	10.1

¹ As a percentage of total requirements.

Other consumption, which includes station use (mainly pumping for storage) and losses, grew at an average annual growth rate of 14.8% in the period 1974-1980, and is expected to grow at about 8.9% in the period 1981- 1990. Actual losses represented about 22% of total gross generation requirements in the period 1974-1980. Historical losses are relatively large and may include a substantial amount of theft. This problem is presently being studied for the entire sector, and remedial action would be implemented as a result of the study. The utility expects to reduce such losses gradually to about 15% by 1987, as a result of the measures to be implemented.

Least Cost Solution

Because of systems effects, the hydro project cannot be analyzed by itself. Instead, it must be clearly demonstrated (using shadow prices) that this hydro scheme is the next project which appears in the optimal or least-cost generation expansion program. We outline next how this least-cost sequence was selected from among the various other alternative expansion programs.

The utility has prepared a first report to establish the least cost expansion for the sector for the period 1984-1988, on the basis of the economic comparison of incremental costs for several alternative expansion programs, including thermal plants (both fuel-oil and coal-fired steam units), gas turbines and hydroelectric projects. The alternative expansion programs were designed to meet the sector energy and peak demand requirements through 1990, at acceptable reliability levels.

The studies are carried out using a model with stochastic variables for both hydrology and demand, and with the restriction that under adverse hydrological conditions occurring less than once in 20 years, energy requirements would not have to be met. The operation of the system is then simulated through computer models to estimate the operational costs of each alternative program and to compute the probability for the program of not meeting the system requirements. Adjustments are introduced to ensure that capacity deficits would have a probability of occurrence of less than 5% in any one year of the period. The investment program which has the least cost is then selected as the system expansion program. It has the lowest net present value of all associated costs, discounted at 13% (which is the estimated opportunity cost of capital).

Sensitivity analysis of the program costs to variations in the discount rate (10% and 15%) and to fuel prices (plus or minus 20%), do not show any substantial changes in the merit order of the best and next-best alternatives. The analysis also shows that the results are insensitive to a reasonable range in variation of the standard conversion factor (corresponding to the shadow-priced exchange rate). Also, the results are insensitive to the use of other shadow prices, since neither the timing of individual plants within a proposed expansion program, nor the ranking of the several alternative programs are affected, whether conversion factors are used or not. The utility annually reviews and revises (if necessary) the least-cost expansion program for the sector.

Cost-Benefit Analysis

In the cost-benefit calculation, it is once again impossible to isolate the effects of the hydro project from the rest of the system. Therefore costs and benefits associated with the utilities total investment program from 1981-91 are compared (see Table 9.2).

Table 9.2

Costs and Benefits for Expansion Program[2]

Year	Year No.	Invest-ment Costs	O&M and Fuel Costs	Total Costs	Total Benefits from Incremental Sales Revenues[1]
1981	1	17.6	-	17.6	-
1982	2	90.9	-	90.9	-
1983	3	73.2	-	73.2	-
1984	4	117.5	-	117.5	-
1985	5	133.6	-	133.6	-
1986	6	214.0	-	214.0	-
1987	7	173.2	12.7	185.9	89.7
1988	8	175.8	80.7	206.5	161.0
1989	9	109.5	57.7	167.2	231.1
1990	10	145.3	98.9	244.2	309.4
1991	11	196.5	98.9	295.4	309.4
1992	12	0.0	98.9	98.9	309.4
:	:	:	:	:	:
:	:	:	:	:	:
2036	56	0.0	98.9	98.9	309.4

Present Values (Market Prices)

Discount Rate					Net Present Value	
8	862	659	1521	2137	616	
10	768	464	1232	1516	284	
12	687	339	1026	1114	88	
14	617	255	872	842	-30	IRR = 13%
16	558	194	752	650	-102	
18	505	152	657	510	-147	
20	460	120	580	407	-173	

Present Values (Border Prices)

Conv. Factor =	0.86	0.91		0.92	

Discount Rate					
8	741	600	1341	1966	625	
10	660	422	1082	1395	313	
12	591	308	899	1025	126	
14	531	232	763	775	12	IRR = 14%
16	480	177	657	598	-59	
18	434	138	572	469	-103	
20	396	109	505	374	-131	

[1] Assumes 1981 average tariff level will continue unchanged in real terms.
[2] All costs and benefits in millions of Pesos (P 1 = US$1 at the official exchange rate).

The investment costs are based on the least-cost generation program and the associated transmission and distribution expansion programs required to deliver power to consumers. Annual recurrent costs based on operation and maintenance (O&M) expenditures and fuel purchases are also included in the table. All market priced costs are converted to border (shadow) prices by applying conversion factors as indicated.

Ideally, benefits should be measured on the basis of the total willingness-to-pay of consumers for electricity supplied. In economic theory, this is represented by the area under the demand curve OBCD in Figure 9.4, where the price is p_o and consumption is Q_o.

Unfortunately the position of the demand curve is not easily determined. Therefore, we use the revenues represented by area OACD (or $p_o.Q_o$) as a minimum (proxy) measure of benefits, since this is readily available from billing information. With this approach, the consumer surplus benefits ABC are neglected. The total benefits shown in Table 9.2 are actually the incremental sales revenues derived from the increased production of electricity, made possible by the 1981-90 investment program. The market priced benefits are converted to border prices using the standard conversion factor (SCF = 0.92).

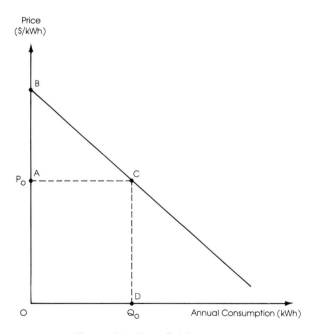

Figure 9.4: Benefit Measurement

On this basis, the internal rate of return (IRR) using shadow prices is about 14% (see Table 9.2), which compares favorably with the opportunity cost of capital (OCC) of 13%. Even with this minimum measure of benefits, IRR > OCC, and therefore NPV > 0. When the neglected consumer surplus benefits are included, NPV will be even larger and the project and investment program are acceptable. The IRR in market prices is also calculated in the table, for comparison -- it is quite similar.

A sensitivity analysis was carried out to estimate the impact on the IRR, of possible changes in cost and revenues. These are summarized in Table 9.3 below:

Table 9.3

Internal Rate of Return on Investment Program (%)

	Benefits		
	85%	100%	115%
Costs			
100%	11	15	17
115%	10	12	15

If the cost of the program increases by 15%, the rate of return would be about 12%. If the program costs do not increase but benefits are 15% lower than estimated, the return would be about 11%. If the program costs increased by 15% and the benefits decreased by 15%, the return on the investment program would be about 10%.

Next, we discuss another important conclusion that can be drawn regarding pricing policy, using the above analysis. An approximate measure of the *average* LRMC is provided by the following ratio:

$$LRMC = PVC(r)/PVE(r)$$

$$\text{where} \quad PVC = \sum_{t=0}^{T} C_t/(1+r)^t$$

= present value of total costs (as shown in the table)

$$PVE = \sum_{t=0}^{T} kWh_t/(1+r)^t$$

= present value of stream of incremental output associated with the above costs.

Assume that both PVC and PVE are evaluated using the opportunity cost of capital (r = OCC) as the discount rate (based on efficiency prices).

Suppose that the average electricity price level (p) used for estimating revenues is equal to LRMC, i.e., p = LRMC.

Therefore, $p = PVC(r)/PVE(r)$; or equivalently, $p.PVE(r) = PVC(r)$.

Furthermore, since $(p.kWh_t)$ represents revenues, $p.PVE(r) = PVB(r)$;

where PVB is the present value of benefits using incremental revenues as a proxy.

Clearly when p = LRMC, then from the above PVB(r) = PVC(r); and therefore, r = OCC = IRR, by definition. Thus, since we have used incremental revenues as benefits in the case study, and the IRR is close to the OCC, then we may conclude that the average price also approximates the LRMC (which is economically optimal). It is easy to see that if IRR < OCC, then p < LRMC and vice versa. Therefore, the value of IRR in this calculation serves a very useful purpose (although it understates the full benefits). The comparison of IRR with OCC is not so much an accept/reject criterion for the investment decision but rather, indicates whether the average tariff level is above or below the (optimal) average LRMC level.

In summary, correct interpretation of the IRR value allows us to make a first round judgement regarding the adequacy of average price relative to LRMC, although more definitive conclusions on pricing would require a comprehensive comparison of the structure of existing tariffs and LRMC (see Chapter 3) .

Appendix A9.1 Conversion Factors (CF)

For a given commodity, the conversion factor may be defined as the ratio of its border price (in terms of the chosen foreign exchange numeraire) to its domestic market price. As an example, we analyze below the general case of an input into the energy sector that is also consumed by nonenergy sector users. The input is supplied through imports as well as domestic production.

TS is the total supply curve consisting of the sum of WS and DS which are the world and domestic supply curves (see Figure A9.1). DD is the domestic demand curve of nonenergy sector users, while TD is the total domestic demand when the requirements of the energy sector PD are included. The domestic market price of the input is driven up from P to (P+dP) due to the effect of the increased demand PD. The corresponding world market C.I.F. (import) prices are smaller by a factor $1/(1 + t_m)$ where t_m is the rate of import duty on the input. The level of consumption due to nonenergy sector users only (i.e., without the power sector demand), would be Q = D, of which M would be supplied through imports and S from domestic production. The total domestic consumption with PD included is (Q+dQ), which is composed of nonenergy sector demand D-dD and energy sector demand (dQ+dD). In this situation, the respective quantities (M+dM) and (S+dS) are imported and domestically supplied.

Let us consider the marginal social cost (MSC) of meeting the energy sector demand. First, there is the increased expenditure of foreign exchange (i.e., already in border prices) for extra imports:

$$d(FX) = M.dP(1 + e_w)/(1+t_m)$$

where $e_w = P.dM/M.dP$ is the price elasticity of world supply. Second, we consider the increased resource cost of additional domestic supply:

$$d(RC) = f.(S.dP.e_d)$$

where $e_d = P.dS/S.dP$ is the price elasticity of domestic supply, and f is the conversion factor which transforms the cost of supply from domestic to border prices. Next, the decrease in the benefit of consumption of nonenergy sector consumers should be considered as a cost:

$$d(BD) = w_c.(D.dP.n_d)$$

where $n_d = P.(dP/D).dP$ is the relevant price elasticity of domestic demand (absolute value), and w_c is the social weight attached to domestic consumption at the relevant consumption level. Fourth, there is the effect due to the increase in income of nonenergy sector consumers:

$$dI_c = (b_c-w_c).[D.dP.(n_d-1)]$$

where b_c is the border priced resource cost of increasing domestic consumption (of other goods) by one unit. Finally, the effect of increased income accruing to domestic producers is:

$$dI_p = (b_p-w_p).(S.dP)$$

where b_p and w_p represent the shadow priced resource cost and marginal social benefit (MSB) respectively, of a one-unit increase in the income of the producers.

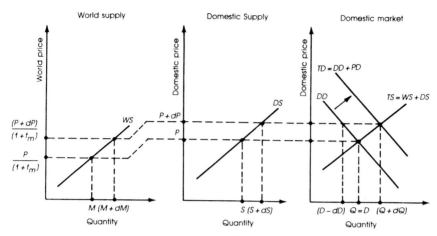

Figure A9.1: Conversion Factor for an Importable

The total cost of the input to the energy sector in shadow prices is

$$d(BP) = d(FX) + d(RC) + d(BD) + dI_c + dI_p$$

The corresponding cost of the input in domestic prices is:

$$d(DP) = P.(dD+dQ) = dP(D.n_d+S.e_d+M.e_w)$$

Therefore, the expression for the conversion factor may be written:

$$CF_m = d(BP)/d(DP)$$

$$= \frac{M[(1+e_w)/(1+t_m)] + S(fe_d+b_p-w_p) + D(b_c n_d+w_c-b_c)}{Me_w + Se_d + Dn_d}$$

Often, this expression may be considerably simplified:

Tradeable Input

Case I: Small country assumption (e_w very large):

Therefore, $CF = 1/(1+t_m)$

Nontradeable Input

Case IIa: No imports ($M=0$) and perfectly elastic supply, (e_d very large); or
Case IIb: No imports ($M=0$), perfectly inelastic demand (n_d very large) and no income effects ($w_p = b_p$ and $w_c = b_c$):

Therefore, $CF_2 = f$

Case IIIa: No imports ($M=0$) and perfectly elastic demand ($n_d = 0$); or
Case IIIb: No imports. perfectly inelastic supply ($e_d = 0$), and no income effects ($w_p = b_p$ and $w_c = b_c$).

Therefore, $CF_3 = b_c$

We note that the corresponding conversion factor for an energy sector input which is domestically produced for export as well as nonenergy sector domestic consumption, may be derived analogously:

$$CF_x = \frac{X[(n_w-1)/(1-t_x)] + S(fe_d+b_p-w_p) + D(b_c n_d+w_c-b_c)}{Xn_w + Se_d + Dn_d}$$

where X represents exports, t_x is the tax rate on exports, n_w is the price elasticity of world demand, and the other symbols are as defined earlier.

References

Bator, F.J., "General Equilibrium, Welfare and Allocation", *American Economic Review*, March 1957, pp. 22-59.

Baum, W.C., "The World Bank Project Cycle", *Finance and Development*, Dec. 1978, pp. 2-9.

Little, I.M.D. and J.A. Mirlees, *Project Appraisal and Planning for Developing Countries*, Basic Books, New York, 1974.

Luenberger, D., *Introduction to Linear and Non-linear Programming*, Addison-Wesley, Reading MA, 1973.

Munasinghe, M., *The Economics of Power System Reliability and Planning*, Johns Hopkins University Press, Baltimore MD, 1979.

Munasinghe, M. and J.J. Warford, "Shadow Pricing and Evaluation of Public Utility Projects", Report No. GAS 14, Energy Department, World Bank, Washington DC, 1977.

Ray, A., *Cost Benefit Analysis*, Johns Hopkins University Press, Baltimore MD, 1984.

Sassone, P.G., "Shadow Pricing in CBA: Mathematical Programming and Economic Theory", *The Engineering Economist*, vol.22, Spring 1977, pp. 219-33.

Squire, L. and H. Van der Tak, *Economic Analysis of Projects*, Johns Hopkins University Press, Baltimore MD, 1975.

Chapter 10

NON-CONVENTIONAL ENERGY PROJECT ANALYSIS AND NATIONAL ENERGY POLICY[1]

10.1 Introduction

Modern societies require increasing amounts of energy for domestic, industrial, commercial, agricultural and transport uses. Arrayed against these energy needs are short-term, depletable fossil fuel supplies -- petroleum, coal and natural gas -- as well as the longer run, renewable energy sources. The latter include hydro, solar, geothermal, wind, tidal, OTEC and biomass. Traditional or non-commercial fuels such as firewood and animal waste are particularly important in developing countries, amounting to about 40 percent of their total energy consumption in 1975 (Munasinghe and Warren 1979). Because of the high costs of energy in recent years, a systematic approach to energy policy making is particularly important. Making the economically important decisions and adopting rational pricing policies in the energy sector should have a high priority especially in the capital and foreign exchange scarce developing countries.

Much attention has been focused on investment planning and pricing of commercial forms of energy like electricity, oil, coal and gas, which dominates the world energy scene. However, the energy crisis has increased the attractiveness of biomass fuels as well as other renewable energy technologies such as solar, wind etc. and re-emphasized their role as significant sources of energy. Thus for example, the total world use of energy in 1980 was only about one tenth of the annual photosynthetic conversion of sunlight via biomass (Hall 1980).

A consistent methodology for economic and financial evaluation of small or decentralized energy projects is developed in this paper. The principles underlying this framework are generally applicable also to other large scale public investment projects in the energy sector, but in this paper the analysis has been adapted to meet the special difficulties that arise in the evaluation and implementation of the new and renewable technologies such as those described in Chapter 11.

The next section of this paper reviews the concepts of integrated national energy planning (introduced in Chapter 2) in the context of renewable energy projects. The reader is referred to Chapter 9 also, for a detailed discussion of project analysis which is relevant here. An outline of the methodology is presented thereafter, including the economic criteria for the acceptance of a new technology (based on shadow prices and the national viewpoint), the financial requirements for successful implementation (based on market prices and the private viewpoint), and the policy implications of this analysis. Finally, a case study involving solar photovoltaic water pumping (for irrigation) is analyzed, to illustrate the economic and financial calculations and their interaction within the context of national energy and economic policy.

---

[1] Edited version of a paper published in the *International Journal of Ambient Energy*, vol.4, April 1983, pp. 79-88.

10.2 National Energy Planning and Project Analysis Framework

From a national perspective, three basic policy decisions are required for successful energy management. First, the appropriate level of demand for energy that must be served to achieve social goals such as economic development and meeting basic human needs should be determined. Second, the optimal mix of energy sources must be established that will meet the desired demand based on several national objectives such as minimum cost, independence from foreign sources and continuity of supply, conservation of resources and elimination of wasteful energy consumption, environmental considerations and price stability. The analysis is complicated by uncertainties regarding the future evolution of demand and supply, relative costs and prices, and incompatibility of the different energy sources with the various energy uses. Third, closely associated with and following the investment decision is the pricing policy which will be based on criteria such as economic efficiency in resource allocation, economic second-best considerations, sector financial requirements, social-equity considerations and other political constraints (Munasinghe 1980a). Energy pricing decisions may also have feedback effects on investment decisions through demand.

Chapter 2 described the integrated framework within which the investment and pricing policies in the whole energy sector must be determined. This framework is conceptually important even though lack of data, time and manpower resources, particularly in the LDC context, will generally preclude the analysis of a full economy-wide model when energy-related decisions are made.

In practice, a partial equilibrium framework (of the type illustrated in Figure 3.1 of Chapter 3) may be used. First, a hierarchical decomposition is made, recognizing that the different energy subsectors such as oil and fuelwood are parts of the overall energy sector, which in turn is only a portion of the entire macroeconomy (Munasinghe 1980b). Next, key linkages and resource flows between the energy sector and the rest of the economy, as well as interactions among the different subsectors, are selectively identified and analysed. In particular, scarce economic resources are valued using appropriate shadow prices such as the opportunity cost of capital, shadow wage rate, and marginal opportunity costs of different fuels (see below). In practice, surprisingly useful results may be obtained from relatively simple models and assumptions. What is important is that policy makers use a systematic framework, instead of an ad hoc approach to decisionmaking in the energy sector.

10.3 Economic and Financial Methodology

The basic steps in the methodology for making and implementing an investment decision involving rural energy sources, as well as the underlying economic and financial criteria, are depicted in Figure 10.1. Let us identify the decentralized rural energy technology under consideration by the label R. At the outset, it is important to establish the existence of a demand or market for energy services of the type to be provided by the technology R. For example, the use of kerosene for lighting in rural areas indicates that there is a potential market for an alternative energy source such as local small-scale hydro plants or diesel generators, to provide the same service.

The next step involves choice of the least-cost technology based on the national viewpoint. Shadow prices (or economic opportunity costs) are used to determine whether technology R is cheaper than any other alternative means of providing the same energy service (see Chapter 9). If technology R is not least-cost, it is rejected and we need not proceed further with the analysis.

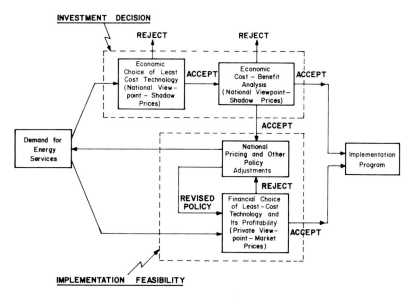

Figure 10.1:   Principal Steps in Economic and Financial Analysis for the Investment Decision and Implementation

If technology R is accepted on a least-cost basis, an economic cost-benefit analysis (CBA) is required to confirm the investment decision. The benefits derived by using technology R are compared with the project costs, once again using shadow prices. If the costs exceed the benefits, the project is rejected and goes no further. If the net benefits (i.e., benefits minus costs) are positive, then technology R is acceptable from the national viewpoint, and the decision to invest is economically justified. It is recognized that there are non-economic objectives that could influence the project decision. For example, an oil importing country may wish to develop small-scale hydro sites, even though they are not least-cost relative to oil imports, simply because independence from foreign energy sources is considered an important strategic goal. Since the economic value of such an objective is virtually impossible to quantify, it is important to rely on economic costs and benefits in carrying out the least-cost and CBA calculations. This information can then be provided to national policymakers to decide whether the strategic goals outweigh any additional costs to the economy resulting from satisfying them.

The next step in the analysis tests the feasibility of project implementation. If the project is to be financed and built by the government, e.g., small-scale hydro plant to provide rural electricity, then the principal issue is the pricing of the output. Basically, it should be verified that the demand for the energy service would still exist at the market or financial price to be charged to the consumer. As described in Chapter 3, this price should generally reflect the marginal economic opportunity cost (or long-run marginal cost) of supply, to meet the economic efficiency objective of pricing. The pricing policy for an energy output would also need to be modified by sector financial viability considerations, social-subsidized or lifeline pricing requirements for poor consumers, and other constraints and national goals.

The analysis of financial feasibility is much more critical and complicated in the case of a project involving a decentralized technology such as solar photovoltaic (PV) powered electric pumps for farm use, which is essentially purchased or paid for by private individuals who are the ultimate beneficiaries. As shown in Figure 10.1, the financial calculations seek to verify from a private individuals viewpoint using market prices, whether technology R is: (i) cheaper than any alternative method of meeting the same need; and (ii) profitable, i.e., the benefits derived from using technology R outweigh the costs. In an ideal distortion-free economy, market prices and shadow prices are identical, and the economic and financial tests of the project would yield the same answer. In practice, market prices diverge significantly from shadow prices, and therefore both economic and financial calculations have to be carried out separately.

If technology R is financially least-cost and profitable, it is clear that rational private individuals would adopt the technology. Thus the government and private investment decisions coincide, and the project implementation program can begin. If an economically justifiable project fails on one or both the financial tests, then the government must seek to adjust market prices or other policies, to make the new technology more financially attractive to private individuals. For example, a competing technology may be financially cheaper because the market price of fuel is subsidised. The required policy change then might be to remove the fuel subsidy, thus making the alternative techology more expensive, or to ban the latter altogether through legislation. The rationale underlying the policy changes is that the government should manipulate the market environment to make technology R financially attractive. Thus market prices would be brought more in line with shadow prices by eliminating taxes and subsidies, and legislative and physical controls also brought into play, where appropriate. These policy changes would not affect the shadow prices significantly, so that the economic acceptability of the project from the national perspective would be unchanged. As before, when the project is accepted according to both the economic and financial criteria, the implementation program may begin.

10.4   Case Study: Solar Photovoltaic (PV) Energy for Agricultural Pumping

The economic evaluation of a decentralized new energy technology such as the photovoltaic (PV) irrigation pumping system discussed below, and the decision to implement this technology, illustrates the close interaction of the economic and financial analyses in policy making. The example and numbers selected are purely illustrative, and should not be interpreted as advocating the superiority of one technology over the other. The economic analysis is based on the cost-benefit criteria and efficiency shadow pricing approach described in Chapter 9.

We assume that the agricultural area under consideration is so remote that electrification via the main power grid would be prohibitively expensive. The principal competitor of the PV system in this case is the diesel pump. Since the comparison is between two discrete alternatives, we need to look only at a single representative farm. But as discussed below, both economic and financial calculations need to be carried out, separately.

Consider a typical 1 hectare farm that requires about 20 m^3 per day of water, with a head of 5 m. Since the benefits are identical in both cases, we first seek to find the least-cost alternative by comparing diesel and PV system costs. The basic data for a simplified hypothetical example are summarised in Table 10.1. This example only serves to illustrate the principles involved. In actual practice, a range of parameters (e.g., different farm sizes, insolation rates, cropping patterns, system costs, etc.) may have to be considered.

Table 10.1

**Basic Data for Solar PV and
Diesel Pumping Systems**

	Solar PV		Diesel	
	Market Prices (Dom. Rs.)	**Shadow Prices (Bord. Rs.)**[a]	**Market Prices (Dom. Rs.)**	**Shadow Prices (Bord.Rs.)**[a]
Initial Cost	66,000	60,000	28,800	36,000[c]
Annual Maintenance Costs	1,100	1,000[b]	1,500	1,050[d]
Annual Fuel Costs	-	-	840[e]	1,200
Lifetime[h] (years)	10	10	5	5
Discount Rate (%)	15[f]	10[g]	15[f]	10[g]
Annual Inflation Rate (%)	10	-	10	-

[a] All foreign costs converted into border rupees (Rs.) at official exchange rate (OER) of US$1 = Rs.20.
[b] All foreign exchange costs with 10% import duty.
[c] Import subsidy of 20% on diesel pumps provided to farmers.
[d] Conversion factor = 0.7 based on spare parts and labour.
[e] Subsidy of 33% provided on diesel fuel imported at US$0.3/l. International fuel price assumed to rise at 3% per annum in real terms.
[f] Bank borrowing rate for farm loans.
[g] Opportunity cost of capital used as proxy for ARI.
[h] Solar PV is assumed to be inherently more longer-lived.

Investment Decision

Let us compare the present value of costs (PVC) of the two alternatives over a 10 year period, in economic efficiency based shadow prices (border rupees - BRs.).

Solar: $\quad \text{PVC}_{SE} = 60,000 + \sum_{t=0}^{9} 1000/(1.1)^t$

$\qquad\qquad\quad = \text{BRs. } 66,760$

Diesel: $\quad \text{PVC}_{DE} = 36,000 + 36,000/(1.1)^5 + \sum_{t=0}^{9} [1,050/(1.1)^t + 1,200\text{x}(1.03/1.1)^t]$

$\qquad\qquad\quad = \text{BRs. } 74,540$

For diesel, the compounding effect of the real increase in fuel prices of 3% per annum will partially offset the effect of discounting at the opportunity cost of capital of 10%.

On the basis of the above results, the solar PV system is the least cost alternative for irrigation pumping in this area.

Next, assume that due to the increased irrigation, the shadow priced value of the farmer's annual output of grain increases from BRs. 10,000 to BRs. 20,500 per hectare, based on the export price of grain. This increase in output value is net of any changes in costs of other inputs such as fertilizer and labor. Therefore, the present value of benefits for the 10 year period is given by:

$$\text{PVB}_E = \sum_{t=0}^{9} (20,500 - 10,000)/(1.1)^t$$

$$= \text{BRs. } 70,970$$

Since NPV = PVB_E - PVC_{SE} = BRs. 4,210, there is a positive net benefit to the country by installing solar PV pumps in farms. These results are summarised in column A of Table 10.2. Therefore, from a national viewpoint, the government is justified in taking a policy decision to encourage the use of solar PV systems by farmers, i.e., to encourage and stimulate the demand for this form of energy consumption.

Implementing the Investment Policy

Farmers will make their decisions on irrigation pumping on the basis of private financial costs and benefits. Therefore, let us analyse the present value of costs of the solar and diesel alternatives in financial terms, using market prices (Domestic rupees, DRs.):

Solar: $\quad \text{PVC}_{SF} = 66,000 + \sum_{t=0}^{9} 1,100\text{x}(1.10/1.15)^t = \text{DRs. } 75,080$

Diesel: $\quad \text{PVC}_{DF} = 28,800 + 28,800\text{x}(1.10/1.15)^5 + \sum_{t=0}^{9} [1500\text{x}(1.10/1.15)^t$

$\qquad\qquad\qquad + 840 \text{ x}(1.03\text{x}1.10/1.15)^t]$

$\qquad\qquad\quad = \text{DRs. } 72,110$

Table 10.2

Economic and Financial Tests for Investment Decision
(All amounts are in present value terms)

Item	A National Viewpoint Shadow Prices (Border Rs.)	B Private Viewpoint (Initial) Market Prices before Policy Changes (Domestic Rs.)	C Private Viewpoint (Interim) Market Prices after First Policy Change (Domestic Rs.)	D Private Viewpoint (Final) Market Prices After Second Policy Change (Domestic Rs.)
Solar PV Costs	$PVC_{SE} = 66{,}760$	$PVC_{SF} = 75{,}080$	$PVC_{SF} = 75{,}080$	$PVC_{SF} = 75{,}080$
Diesel Costs	$PVC_{DE} = 74{,}540$	$PVC_{DF} = 71{,}110$	$PVC_{DF} = 85{,}070$	$PVC_{DE} = 86{,}070$
Irrigation Benefits	$PVC_{E} = 70{,}970$	$PVB_{F} = 73{,}670$	$PVB_{F} = 73{,}670$	$PVB_{=} = 78{,}000$

CONCLUSIONS

Condition		Consequence

A. Shadow Priced Values:

$PVC_{SE} < PVC_{DE}$ — Solar PV is the economically preferred least-cost technology.
$PVB_{E} > PVC_{SE}$ — Investment in solar PV is economically justified.

B. Market Priced Values Before Policy Changes:

$PVC_{SF} > PVC_{DF}$ — Farmers will prefer diesel to solar PV pumps, financially.

C. Market Priced Values After First Policy Change:

$PVC_{SF} < PVC_{DF}$ — Farmers will prefer solar PV to diesel pumps, financially.
$PVB_{F} < PVC_{SF}$ — Farmers will find solar PV pumps financially unprofitable to install.

D. Market Priced Values After Second Policy Change:

$PVC_{SF} < PVC_{DF}$ — Farmers will prefer solar PV to diesel pumps, financially.
$PVB_{F} > PVC_{SF}$ — Farmers will find solar PV pumps financially profitable to install.

Clearly, since $PVC_{SF} > PVC_{DF}$, the average farmer who wished to acquire a pumping system, would prefer to purchase a diesel pump rather than a solar PV system. Because the market price signals are distorted, the private individual's decision does not coincide with the national policy decision based on shadow prices (as summarised in column B of Table 10.2). Therefore, the government must adjust the market prices, or adopt other policies that will make the solar PV option attractive to farmers.

First, the authorities could remove the 10 percent import duty on solar PV systems and spare parts. Then PVC_{SF} = DRs.68,250, and the solar PV pump is the least cost alternative in both financial and economic terms. However, suppose that this measure would also require the reduction of import duties on many similar photovoltaic and electric components, which the government is unwilling to consider.

A second policy alternative is to raise the price of diesel fuel until PVC_{DF} exceeds PVC_{SF} -- but let us assume that there is a strong anti-inflation lobby that can block increases in the diesel fuel price, on the grounds that this would raise transport costs too much.

A third approach might be for the government to legislate that farmers could no longer buy diesel pumps. This nonprice policy option is cumbersome and has its own host of implementation difficulties. A fourth possibility is for the government to provide low interest agricultural loans or credits to buy solar pumps.

Finally, the government could remove the import subsidy on diesel motors. This increases PVC_{DF} to DRs. 85,070, and since this is greater than PVC_{SF}, the farmers will voluntarily prefer solar PV pumps to diesel pumps. Let us assume that this policy alternative is selected for implementation (see column C of Table 10.2).

It is still necessary to consider the financial benefits aspect. The irrigation program increases the market value of farm output from DRs. 8,500 to DRs. 17,425, based on the guaranteed government purchase price for grain (which is 85 percent of the export or world market price). The present value of financial benefits for 10 years of output is:

$$PVB_F = \sum_{t=0}^{9}(17,425 - 8,500) \times (1.10/1.05)^t$$

$$= DRs. \ 73,670$$

Since PVB_F is less than the value PVC_{SF} = DRs. 75,080, the average farmer will be financially worse off if he adopts the (least cost) solar PV technology. The government must therefore make a futher change in policy. For example, it could raise the domestic grain price to 90 percent of the world market. This policy change raises the value of financial benefits, and since PVB_F = DRs. 78,000 > PVC_{SF}, the farmer will find solar PV powered pump sets financially profitable to install (see column D of Table 10.2).

Thus, this case study shows that demand management via implementation of a given investment decision (based on shadow prices) may require a related series of wide-ranging policy decisions by the government.

References

Hall, D.O., "Bio-Energy Research -- A World Perspective", in *Bio-Energy '80 Proceedings*, The Bio-Energy Council, Washington DC, 1980, pp. 501-8.

Munasinghe, M. and C. Warren, "Rural Electrification, Energy Economics and National Policy in the Developing Countries", in *Future Energy Concepts*, Institution of Electrical Engineers, London, 1979.

Munasinghe, M., "An Integrated Framework for Energy Pricing in Developing Countries", *The Energy Journal*, vol.1, July 1980a, pp. 1-30; also available as Reprint No. 148, World Bank, Washington DC.

Munasinghe, M., "Integrated National Energy Planning in Developing Countries", *Natural Resources Forum*, vol. 4, October 1980b, pp. 359-73; also available as Reprint No. 165, The World Bank, Washington DC.

Chapter 11

RURAL ENERGY ISSUES AND SUPPLY OPTIONS[1]

11.1 Rural Energy Issues

The importance of rural energy, not only for growth and development, but also to ensure minimum conditions for existence in large parts of the globe, has been increasingly recognized in the last few decades. The relevant issues are best analyzed within a wide rural energy framework, and policies derived have to be consistent with the goals of rural development and the overall national macroeconomic strategy. To set the stage for a more specific discussion of rural energy sources and options, it is useful to briefly review some of the more important and relevant background information on the status of rural energy.

In 1983, the world's population numbered about 4.6 billion, of which roughly 3.5 billion lived in the developing countries. Given that over 70 percent of the latter live in rural areas, usually under difficult conditions, the magnitude of the rural energy and development problem is very great. As discussed below, while electricity will usually provide a small fraction of total rural energy needs, its impact and ability to stimulate change may be disproportionately large.

The diversity of energy sources that may be used in the rural setting, and an indication of their range of application are shown in Table 11.1. The energy applications included in this list are confined to those related to domestic activities such as cooking, heating and lighting and to agricultural production, like ploughing, irrigation and transport. The table indicates that the bulk of urban energy demands are satisfied typically by consumption of grid electricity, gas, petroleum fuels, batteries and even wood and charcoal. Rural needs are met not only by these sources, but also by a range of other sources that have many alternative uses. The latter include human and animal muscle power, biomass (wood, vegetable residue etc.) and animal waste. Surveys of energy use in rural areas of developing countries show that it is these non-commercial sources that typically comprise the largest proportion of energy supply.

However, fossil fuels have obvious advantages in terms of their range of applications, particularly for agricultural operations and transport. Certain agricultural energy requirements, such as pumping or threshing, do not require a mobile power source and are hence candidates for the application of wind, water and solar energy conversion. However, most field operations require mobile motive power, and must depend on human and animal labor, and fossil fuels. Steam driven tractors fired by wood and coal are used in China (Dawson 1970), but this technology has almost disappeared in other countries with the availability of cheaper substitutes.

---

[1] The first part of this chapter is an edited version of a paper published in *Future Energy Concepts*, Institute of Electrical Engineers, London, UK, 1979 (co-author: Colin Warren); while the second part is an extract from M. Munasinghe, *Rural Electrification for Development*, Westview Press, Boulder, CO, 1987.

Table 11.1

Primary Energy Sources and Their Most Common Applications in Rural Areas

	Human	Animal	Biomass	Animal Waste[2]	Kerosene	Other Petroleum Fuels	Coal	Liquid Gas Biogas	Wind	Water Power	Solar	Generated Electric Power	Batteries
DOMESTIC													
Cooking Heat			x	x	x	x	x	x			x[4]	x	
Heating			x	x	x		x	x			x	x	
Refrigeration					x			x			x[5]	x	
Lighting					x			x				x	
Radio												x	x
Ironing			x				x					x	
Potable water pumping or distillation	x	x				x			x	x	x[6]		
AGRICULTURAL PRODUCTION													
Ploughing	x	x				x							
Fertilizing, sowing	x	x				x[3]							
Irrigation	x	x				x	x		x		x[7]	x	
Harvesting	x	x				x							
Threshing	x		x			x				x			
Drying			x			x	x				x[8]	x	
Grinding, Pressing	x	x	x			x	x		x	x		x	
Transport	x	x				x						x	
Storage				x[1]									
Input to energy conversion process					x		x	x		x	x	x	

[1] Anaerobic production of methane gas, pyrolytic generation of producer gas, and generation of steam or electric power.
[2] Excluding use as a fertilizer.
[3] This includes the use of petroleum fuels as feedstocks for the manufacture of fertilizer.
[4] Solar cookers are often not socially acceptable.
[5] Present high cost is a deterrent to individual household use. More applicable to community scale systems.
[6] Solar distillation has high capital costs, but for large quantities can be cheaper than fuel based methods, depending on the climate.
[7] Applications of solar energy to irrigation have not been very successful as yet. Photovoltaic cell driven pumps are expensive.
[8] The traditional method is to dry the crop by spreading it on the ground. This can lead to high crop losses. Improved methods of using solar energy to dry the crops while in the storage bins are being developed.

Source: Munasinghe and Warren (1979).

A survey of energy requirements in five villages in Uttar Pradesh, India, showed that mobile operations (tilling, sowing, fertilization, harvesting and transportation) consumed between 50% and 60% of the total energy input (including human animal power) for agricultural operations, while irrigation and threshing accounted for the rest. Of the mobile operations, tilling was by far the most energy intensive, consuming from 38% to 52% of the total energy input, depending on whether bullocks or tractors were the main source of power (Singh & Singh 1976). In areas with less irrigation than Uttar Pradesh, where high yielding grains are planted, the concentration of energy use in mobile operations and hence the importance of petroleum fuels, is likely to be greater.

Because of their non-commercial nature and concentration of use in rural areas, traditional fuels have received scant attention in the energy planning and policy-making of most countries. This is an unfortunate situation in view of two main factors. The first is that their relative abundance or scarcity affects the lives of the majority of people living in the developing countries. The second is that non-commercial fuels and both human and animal muscle power have alternative uses such as fertilization, construction and prevention of soil erosion, which create special difficulties in the pricing of fuels. Ideally, the various forms of energy should be priced so as to maximize the sum total of their benefits in all uses, and this will occur when the opportunity costs of these fuels in all uses are equalized, e.g., the use of another unit of wood in cooking results in benefits equal in value to those foregone by not using the wood for construction, or leaving the tree intact for soil conservation purposes.

In general, if the prices of commercial fuels are set so as to reflect their marginal costs, this is conducive to the efficient allocation of resources in the energy sector. However, such a policy is difficult to follow in the case of non-commercial fuels in their non-fuel uses, because some of the costs or benefits may not be perceived, or could lie in the public domain, not accruing wholly to the user of the fuel. Examples of such external diseconomies would be the cost of an increase in the local albedo and consequent adverse climatic changes, or increased soil erosion and lowering of the water table, due to the elimination of ground cover -- used as fuelwood. Another example of this kind of effect is the reduced odor, insect breeding problems and probability of spread of infection, that arise from using the sludge residue from methane gas generated in an anaerobic digester, compared to the direct use of human and animal wastages as fertilizers. Consideration of such "external" effects in the comparison of different energy sources requires detailed analysis. Thus, the implementation of rural energy projects will require a coordinated set of actions in both energy and non-energy energy related areas, with special attention to pricing aspects, if external costs and benefits are to be accounted for and internalized wherever possible. In particular, the substitution possibilities between commercial and non-commercial energy sources (e.g., between electricity, kerosene and fuelwood), and the impact of relative prices and subsidies, on the demand for these fuels, should be carefully investigated.

Table 11.2 shows estimates of the average per capita useful energy output per day, by source, for rural villages in six different countries. The figures for the useful energy output of human and animal labor, and of commercial fuels, are necessarily based on certain assumptions as to the efficiency with which the gross energy input is used. Unfortunately, one of the characteristics of non-commercial fuels is their relatively low efficiency of use (Revelle 1969, Makhijani 1976).

Table 11.2

Energy Sources in Rural Villages of Six Countries[1]

	Bihar, India	Hunan, South Central China,	Tanzania	Nigeria	Northern Mexico	Bolivia
Human labor	60	70	55	50	80	60
Animal labor	260	175	-	25	245	345
Firewood	35	690	760	520	490	1150
Crop Residues (used as fuel)	35	-	-	-	-	-
Dung	70	-	-	-	-	-
Subtotal noncommercial energy	460	935	815	595	815	1555
Fossil fuels	small	-	-	5	1560	-
Electricity	-	415	-	-	2680	-
Fertilizers	105	345	-	50	5425	-
Subtotal commercial energy	105	760	-	55	9965	-
Total useful energy available	565	1695	815	650	10480	1555
Number of persons in village	1000	1000	100	1400	420	not specified
Average cultivated hectares/person	.3	.2	.6	.4	2.6	.2
Percentage of irrigated farmland	10%	70%	-	-	35%	5%
Use of high-yielding crop varieties	little use	not specified	none	none	widespread	none

[1] The data are taken from Makhijani and Poole (1975). All figures given in kilocalories of useful energy output per day. The assumed ratio of useful energy output of total input is 2.5% for human labor, 5% for animal labor, and 5% for firewood, crop residues, and dung.

Thus, the overall efficiency of conversion of wood, vegetable residue, dung and so on, typically used by the poorest and most energy starved sections of the rural population (e.g., in open hearths), is usually about 5%. This is in sharp contrast to the average efficiency of use of commercial fuels, which is about 20%.

However, from the above table it is clear that non-commercial fuels are the major sources of energy in most rural areas. This is particularly true where subsistence agriculture is practiced, as in Bolivia, Nigeria and Tanzania, where wood and crop residues provide from 74% to 93% of the total useful energy, mainly in the form of cooking fuel, and where there is little or no use of commercial energy sources. At the other end of the scale is northern Mexico where the use of high yielding seeds is widespread, with consequent relatively high energy requirements for irrigation and chemical fertilizers. Due to the higher farm incomes in this area, there is greater use of gas, kerosene and electricity for domestic purposes. Intermediate cases occur in Bihar, India and south central China where 25% and 40% respectively, of useful energy is derived from non-commercial sources.

Such patterns of energy use reflect the energy requirement of differing agricultural systems. Subsistence agriculture, as pictured by the Nigerian, Tanzanian and Bolivian cases, implies a high dependence on human labor for field operations, the only exception being the use of small amounts of animal labor. Vegetable fuels provide the energy required for food processing (e.g., meat curing, production of raw sugar, cooking, etc.), and candles or kerosene provide lighting. The gathering of firewood and other vegetables fuels consumes large amounts of human energy in many of the more densely populated rural areas where these fuels have become scarce. This expenditure of labor, the value of which then becomes embodied in the collected fuel, combined with the scarcity value of the fuel, and the small proportion of its energy content that is appropriated as useful energy, indicates that major savings in both human labor and fuel could be attained through use of more efficient conversion devices, particularly stoves.

An important characteristic of rural energy demand is its highly seasonal nature, resulting from dependence on cropping patterns. This seasonality is one of the major factors contributing to the low rates of return of many rural electrification schemes, where low system load factors imply that large amounts of capital stock are unused during much of the year. Although domestic energy used for cooking, which forms a major fraction of total rural energy demand, is non-seasonal in nature, the additional energy requirements of the cropping season still give rise to a seasonal peak. In the same way that labor may have a relatively high opportunity cost during harvesting (in an area characterized by open or disguised unemployment during other seasons), energy would also have a greater than average value during this peak period. Non-availibility of needed energy during a harvest can, for example, lead to irreversible crop spoilage, or to late planting and hence reduced plant growth. Farmers may not be willing to purchase electricity from a grid unless their peak demand is assured (as has been experienced in the rice growing district of Suriname), or they may invest in both diesel and electric motors to ensure levels of reliability above those provided by the electric power network (as has occurred in certain regions of India and Costa Rica)[2].

The annual, per capita subsistence energy requirement currently prevalent in most rural areas of the third world, is estimated at approximately 4000 kilograms of coal equivalent (kgce), or 5×10^{-3} (BPDOE), i.e., only about 3% of the U.S. average. It has also been estimated that a tripling of this level would be required to meet basic

---

[2] See the companion volume: *Electric Power Economics*

human needs (Howe et al. 1976). The achievement of such a target is particularly important, given that at these low rates of energy consumption, the quality of life improves rapidly with increased per capita energy use.

Most of the rural energy needs during the next few decades will continue to be met from traditional sources. Rural households currently use about 1 ton of firewood per capita per year. Although estimates vary, the rate of total world consumption of wood may be rapidly approaching the rate of natural replenishment of about 10-15 billion m^3 per annum (Earl 1975, Openshaw 1977). Furthermore, the supply of wood is often not located near areas of high demand. Therefore, unless appropriate and farsighted measures are adopted, conditions will continue to deteriorate in many rural areas, as villagers spend larger amounts of time gathering fuel, remove the ground cover in ever increasing quantities with consequent environmental effects ranging from flooding and landslides to erosion and desertification, and divert other resources such as dung to fuel-use, from their alternative uses as fertilizers.

Firewood alone comprises more than a quarter of total energy consumption in the developing countries (Makhijani & Poole 1975). As the share is far higher in rural areas (see Table 11.2), the development of a rational rural energy policy must first address the problem of how to ensure an adequate supply of firewood and other biomass fuels in the future, without causing unacceptable degradation of the rural environment (see Chapter 12). This is particularly important in view of the long period required for the replenishment of forests. Solutions to the rural energy energy problem based on the production and use of biomass are often characterized by economies of scale. Therefore, the planned cultivation of fuelwood plantations will become increasingly important, with the eventual possibility of producing sufficient wood per hectare of land, to support the needs of rural communities on a renewable basis. There are possibilities for fermenting agricultural crops such as sugar cane, to produce alcohol. Water-based biomass such as algae and kelp are also being investigated for their energy potential. Vegetable residues may be used together with human and animal wastes in biogas plants.

While centrally supplied R.E. grids will continue to expand wherever appropriate, decentralized electric power generation should play an increasingly important role in some rural areas through the use of mini-hydro plants and wind powered devices. Furthermore, hitherto neglected resources such as low grade coal deposits and agricultural wastes could also be used. The conversion of solar energy to electricity is being investigated through a variety of techniques, ranging from photovoltaic cells and conventional mirror concentrators to greenhouse type evacuated tubes and synthetic leaves which attempt to mimic the action of chlorophyl in plants. Other alternative technologies, especially for power generation, are described at greater length below.

11.2 New and Renewable Sources of Energy (NRSE)

General Review of NRSE

Systematic and steady progress has been made in the development of many new and renewable energy technologies, in recent decades. Nevertheless, their potential scope of application is still quite limited. In a recent study (IEA 1987), biomass, geothermal, ocean, solar and wind energy sources were divided into the four categories summarized in Table 11.3. The IEA study concludes that these energy sources can make a significant impact on existing commercial energy markets only after several more decades of technology development, requiring substantial financial support.

The following are indicative or benchmark costs for several typical NRSE (USAID 1988):

1. Wind systems for pumping - $250 to 500 per m^2 of rotor diameter.
2. Solar dryers - $60 to 400 per m^2 of collector.
3. Biomass alcohol - over $0.30 per liter.

More detailed descriptions and costs for electricity generation systems are presented below.

Alternative Electricity Generation Technologies for Rural Areas

The supply of electricity to feed a rural power network or supply isolated consumers may be drawn from the interconnected bulk supply grid or generated by independent power sources. The principal factors determining the choice among the various alternatives include: least cost, reliability and quality of service, hours of operation, and convenience of operation and maintenance.

The most common decentralised alternatives to central grid supply are:

1. Diesel autogenerators;
2. Small-scale hydropower plants;
3. Biomass based energy sources;
4. Windmills; and
5. Solar Photovoltaic systems.

Least cost comparisons between central grid supply and isolated sources are not easy to make because the quality of supply is usually much higher in the former case, and this advantage is very difficult to quantify in monetary terms. Thus while bulk supply is usually available on a continuous basis, isolated diesels may only supply power during certain hours of the day, and small hydel plants might also operate intermittently on a daily or seasonal basis, depending on the availability of water and storage facilities. Generally, the comparison of alternatives to meet limited service (e.g., only during the evening hours at relatively low reliability) will favour isolated energy sources, whereas central grid based supply will be the choice in situations requiring continuous and high quality service.

The familiarity of local technicians with the selected technology, the frequency and ease of operation and maintenance, and the availabilty and cost of spare parts, are also important considerations. For example, small diesel autogenerators might be the best choice for isolated villages, because the technology is so familiar and proven in most developing countries, even though the supply cost may be higher. Similarly, biogas digesters or small hydropower plants may be particularly attractive where a country has built up considerable experience and skills in the technology. Newer technologies like photovoltaics (PV) are inherently more reliable and maintenance-free, but unavailability of spares or unfamiliarity with servicing procedures could cause problems. For example, some recent trials resulted in a large number of failures of PV arrays, because the bolts anchoring the glass plates had been screwed down too tightly by untrained local technicians, resulting in cracking of the glass and exposure of the PV cells to weathering (World Bank 1982).

Table 11.3

Status of Renewable Energy Technologies in 1987

Economic (in some locations)

Solar water heaters, replacing electricity or with seasonal storage, and for swimming pools
Solar industrial process heat with parabolic trough collectors or large flat-plate collectors
Residential passive solar heating designs and daylighting
Solar agricultural drying
Small to medium photovoltaic systems
Small to medium wind systems
Direct biomass combustion
Anaerobic digestion (of some feedstocks)
Conventional geothermal technologies (dry and flashed steam power generation, high temperature hot water and low temperature heat)
Tidal systems

Commercial (with incentives)

Solar water and space heaters replacing natural gas or oil
Electricity generation with parabolic trough collectors
Non-residential passive solar heating and daylighting
Biomass liquid fuels (ethanol) from sugar and starch feedstocks
Binary cycle hydro-geothermal systems

Under Development

Solar space cooling (active and passive)
Solar thermal power systems (other than parabolic trough collectors)
Photovoltaic power systems
Large-sized wind systems
Biomass gasification
Hot dry rock geothermal
Geothermal total flow prime movers
Wave energy systems

Future Technologies

Photochemical and thermochemical conversion
Fast pyrolysis or direct liquefaction of biomass
Biochemical biomass conversion systems
Ocean thermal energy conversion systems
Geopressured geothermal
Geothermal magma

Definition of Categories

Economic. Technologies are well developed and economically viable at least in some markets and locations, for which further market penetration will require technology refinements, mass production and/or economies of scale.

Commercial (with incentives). Technologies are available in some markets, but are competitive with the conventional technologies only with preferential treatments, so that they still need further development to be economically competitive.

Under Development. Technologies need more R&D to improve efficiency, reliability or cost to become commercial.

Future. Technologies have not yet been technically proven, even though they are scientifically feasible.

Source: IEA, Renewable Sources of Energy, Paris, 1987.

It is very difficult to draw general conclusions regarding the relative desirability of the various options for several reasons. First, both the costs of technology and relative fuel prices vary frequently. Second, the suitability may change depending on the type of end-use, such as lighting, irrigation pumping and agro-industrial motive power, or even the specific crop to be irrigated. Nevertheless, a preliminary screening of rural areas may help to identify regions having certain characteristics where decentralised sources are likely to be more suitable.

Typical sets of such characteristics might include:

1. Abundance of alternative renewable energy sources, such as small-scale hydro or wind, remoteness from the central grid, and mountainous or difficult terrain.
2. Low population density, few and small scale commercial or industrial activities, and low domestic incomes with at most a few better-off households.
3. Fertile soil, availability of surface water or low water table, small farms, need for smaller mobile pumpsets.

Finally, we also note that the choice of technology is rarely absolute or permanent. Thus, prevailing conditions might favor the initial selection of a decentralized option for rural electrification (R.E.). However, over a period of years, load growth in the rural area and unrelated expansion of the central grid may make it feasible to eventually supply the rural electric system from the bulk power network. Thus the dynamic nature of R.E., implies that rural areas evolve through such stages of electrification, and this process must be recognized in long term project design and policymaking.

The great majority of nationally organised rural electrification programs are based on extension of supply from the central power grid. However, since alternative energy sources are important in certain situations, some of their principal technical and economic characteristics are discussed below. It should be understood that what is important are the principles by which technological alternatives may be compared, whereas the actual numbers given are for indicative purposes only.

Diesel Autogenerators

The generation of electricity using diesel engines is a mature, proven and widely used technology. Operating data from a variety of engines (most commonly four-stroke, medium speed, and two-stroke, slow speed types) are available for several decades, in a large number of developing countries, under widely different operating conditions (World Bank 1985).

With typical diesel generating sets in the 40 to 200 kW range, costs per kW installed vary from about US$800 for the smaller units, to under US$500 for the large units. Operation and maintenance costs per kW installed also decrease sharply as total capacity rises. While diesel plant may be cycled without difficulty, and plant utilization factors could range from 5 to 80 percent, greater utilization reduces the capacity charge component per unit of energy generated. The fuel consumption per kWh also tends rise sharply under low load operating conditions.

When continuous service is required, the sizes of the sets will have to be chosen to provide an adequate reserve margin (in the case of the loss of the largest unit), and also ensure that no unit is loaded below the operational limit of about 25 percent, under low load conditions. If only intermittent service is planned, considerable capacity savings might be realised, for example, by sizing the installation according to the load in the tenth year when the sets are likely to be replaced. For lighting loads, 5 to 6 hours service at night, and 2 to 3 hours during the day, would be adequate in most cases.

Small-scale Hydropower (SSHP) Plants

Hydroelectricity is still one of the world's major unused energy resources, with only about 20 percent of the total exploitable potential presently harnessed. Although a few developing countries rely heavily on hydropower, the third world as a whole is using less than 10 percent of its hydel potential -- the corresponding figure for the developed countries (over 30 percent), is much higher. The utilization of potential small hydropower sources in the developing countries, is even less.

From the operational viewpoint, the technology is relatively mature and well known. Small-scale hydropower (SSHP) may be defined in terms of the following three ranges (although this definition of ranges is not very rigid and there is also considerable overlap):

1. Microhydro - 0 to 50 kW.
2. Minihydro - 51 to 2000 kW.
3. Small hydro - 2000 to 5000 kW.

Small hydro sites are essentially scaled down versions of large hydro installations, and usually consist of dams, powerhouses, and penstocks, tied to a distribution grid. Minihydro sytems are basically pumps operated in reverse, using small diversion weirs and canals, rather than dams. The generators are housed in small structures which are like pumphouses, while the water is brought into the turbines through conventional-type pipes. Microhydro installations are of the same type, but much smaller. The turbines used are frequently centrifugal pumps operated in reverse.

Costs of SSHP range from as much as US$ 8000 per kW installed for remote micrhydro sites, to under US$ 500 per kW in the case of small hydro schemes, where certain economy measures are possible. Costs may be minimised by:

1. Encouraging local manufacture of turbines and generators;
2. Using local labour for installation;
3. Relying on manual voltage regulation; and
4. Simplifying or adapting already existing civil works.

The cost per kWh may vary from US cents 5 to 50, depending on a variety of factors.

The characteristics of the load and the hydro plant should be matched as well as possible, especially in the case of run-of-the-river schemes, where storage is unavailable. For any given level of installed capacity, maximising the energy generated will minimise the unit cost of energy supplied.

Biomass Based Energy Sources

There are a number of technologies that rely on biomass as the primary fuel source for generating electricity, including:

1. Gasifiers;
2. Biogas units; and
3. Dendrothermal power plants.

Gasifiers: This technology has been in use for many decades, and was much used during the second world war, where producer gas was generated from coal. The basic process involved is the pyrolytic gasification of wood and other carbonaceous matter, through partial combustion in a special vessel. The resultant output is drawn off as producer gas, consisting of about 25 percent carbon monoxide, 15 percent hydrogen, and other gases. It has a fuel value of about 15 to 20 percent that of natural gas, and may be burned in boilers designed for other fuels, or used in internal combustion engines (after appropriate filtration).

Wood and charcoal gasifiers are being tested and used in many developing countries. Their capital costs are in the range US$100 to 500 per kW, not including costs of preprocessing, sorting, conveying, handling, or storing the input fuel. Adding the costs of an engine to burn the gas, and generator to produce the electricity is likely to raise the total costs to around US$ 1000 per kW installed. Conventional diesel engines may be easily adapted to run on producer gas, sometimes with a little diesel fuel being used for starting-up. The power output is usually somewhat less than the original nameplate value. Unit sizes are in the range 5 kW to about 1 MW -- the performance of larger size units is not proven. A variety of other feedstocks such as coconut shells, rice husks, bark, straw, and similar residues, are being tested. However, further experience is required in these cases, because of problems (including excessive tar content, ash composition, and so on), associated with fuels other than wood or charcoal.

Biogas Units: A process that occurs in nature, involving the anaerobic decomposition of organic matter, is used to produce a combustible mixture of gases called biogas, that contains about 55 to 65 percent of methane. The biogas is produced in a digester or vessel usually made of sheet metal or concrete, with the fermenting material at the bottom, and the generated gas stored in the upper portion. Gas may be withdrawn under pressure from an outlet at the top, while the digested sludge (which is a valuable fertilizer) is drawn off from the bottom. Biogas production is mediated by the action of at least two main kinds of bacteria, and is sensitive to the ambient temperature, acidity, and type of feedstock used (animal waste or dung being particularly effective).

Both China and India have large biogas programs in rural areas. While biogas may be used in internal combustion engines to generate electricity, it is more frequently used for other purposes. There is a tendency for the more successful programs to be associated with wealthier rural families who have sufficient cattle and land to easily produce the feedstock necessary for the digester. The cost of a basic family sized unit is in the range US$300 to 500, which is comparable with annual household income. The dung and other material used in the digester are also likely to have an opportunity cost as fuels.

Dendrothermal Power Plants: Wood and other vegetable residues such as sugar cane, rice husks, coconut shells, wood shavings, straw, and so on, may be used in conventional boilers to produce steam, and thereby generate electricity. The technology is similar to conventional steam power plant tcehnology, and well proven. Considerable effort has been made recently in several countries, including the Phillipines and some of the Pacific Islands, to develop larger scale dendrothermal power plants. Strictly speaking, this term is associated with wood-fired boilers, but it is convenient to include other biomass fuels in the same category.

The costs of producing electricity are estimated to be in the range US cents 15 to 40, depending very critically on the economic value of the feedstock. Green plant material, which may contain over 90 percent water, must be pre-dried to ensure high combustion efficiencies. Maximum unit sizes that are operationally proven do not exceed a few megawatts. Besides, larger sized plants lead to significant costs and logistical problems associated with the growing and transport of wood. Thus for example, to supply a 1 MW plant would require about 1,500 hectares producing an average of 7 tons of wood per hectare per year. The long term viability of dendrothermal systems depends critically on the associated fuelwood plantations program (Sathaye 1987).

Windmills

Windmills have also been in use, not necessarily for electricity generation, for several hundred years. They are economically viable even now, more frequently for uses such as lift irrigation rather than for power production. The local wind regime is the critical factor, and generally, wind speeds in excess of about 5 metres per second are desirable. A wide variety of windmill designs are available, local manufacture of components can help to reduce capital costs. Off-the-shelf integrated and matched units, including windmills as well as generators, are available. In the 25 kW rated output range, costs are in the region of US$ 750 per kW installed, although machines under 10kW may cost almost twice as much -- per kW. Total supply costs may vary in the range US cents 10 to 40 per kWh, depending on the load factor. If the winds are intermittent or seasonal, other backup sources of power will be required.

Solar Photovoltaics (PV)

The most common technology for solar photovoltaic cells involve very thin slices of high quality silicon single crystals. Amorphous or non-crystalline materials are also being used increasingly. In areas having relatively high insolation rates, an array of cells rated at one peak watt (under ideal conditions) may produce about 5 watt-hours of energy per day. At present efficiencies of conversion, about 2 square metres of cell surface will be required to produce one kWh per day.

The costs of solar photovoltaic cells have been dropping steadily for the last two decades, and are currently around US$ 6 to 7 per peak watt. However, most applications require other components such as electrical controls, structural supports, and storage batteries (for periods when the sun is obscured) -- and the costs of this "balance-of-system" have not declined significantly in recent years. The total system costs may fall to about US$10 to 12 per peak watt within the next few years, providing output at a cost of about US cents 50 per kWh. At these prices, PV systems will be economically competitive only for specialised uses and remote locations such as telecommunications repeater stations in rugged terrain, that can be serviced only rarely.

References

Dawson, O. L., *Communist China's Agriculture: It's Development and Future Potential*, Praeger Publ., New York, 1970.

Earl, D. E., *Forest Energy and Economic Development*, Clarendon, Oxford, 1975.

Howe, J. W., Bever, J., Knowland, W., and Tarrant, J., *Energy for Developing Countries*, Overseas Development Council, Washington DC, 1976.

International Energy Agency (IEA), *Renewable Sources of Energy*, IEA, Paris, 1987.

Makhijani, A., *Energy Policy for the Third World*, International Institute for Environment and Development, London/Washington DC, 1976.

Makhijani, A. and A. Poole, *Energy and Agriculture in the Third World*, Ballinger Publ. Co., Cambridge MA, 1975.

Openshaw, K., "Woodfuel, A Time for Reassessment", *East African Journal*, Jan. 1977.

Revelle, R., "Energy Use in Rural India" *Science*, vol. 192, June 4, 1969.

Sathaye, J., "Rural Electricity in the Philippines: Planning Issues", *Energy Policy*, August 1987, pp. 339-51.

Singh, L. R., and Singh, B., "Level and Pattern of Energy Consumption in an Agriculturally Advanced Area of Uttar Pradesh", *Indian J. of Agr. Econ.*, vol. 31, July-Sept. 1976, pp. 157-164.

USAID, "New Directions for Renewable Energy Activities", Office of Energy, USAID, Washington DC, Feb.1988.

World Bank, "Solar Photovoltaic Systems for Agricultural Pumping", Energy Dept., World Bank, Washington DC, 1982.

World Bank, "Diesel Plant Performance Study", Energy Dept. Paper No. 21, Energy Dept., World Bank, Washington DC, 1982.

Chapter 12

BIOENERGY MANAGEMENT POLICY[1]

12.1 Introduction

The more than 2.5 billion people who live in the developing countries -- and constitute the majority of the world's population -- rely on biomass as their chief source of energy. Bioenergy or biomass energy consists of all the kinds of plant or animal matter which may be used as energy sources; typical examples include fuelwood, charcoal, agricultural residues, energy crops such as sugar cane, human and animal wastes, and muscle power (see also Chapter 11).

Bioenergy is basically energy stored from the sun. Plants convert (into biomass) a small fraction of the 170 million gigawatts (170 $\times 10^{12}$ kilowatts) of solar radiation incident on the earth's surface, through the rather inefficient process of photosynthesis. The conversion efficiency varies between about 0.5 and 2.5%.

About 10% of gross world energy supplies are obtained from bioenergy, of which the overwhelming part is fuelwood and charcoal. In many African and Asian countries, 60 to 90% of total energy is supplied from biomass. The United Nations has estimated that more than 100 million people, predominantly in the rural areas of the developing world, do not have sufficient fuelwood to meet their basic energy needs, while at least another one billion face actual or potential shortages.

The average rural household in a developing country needs at least 0.75 to 1 cubic metre of wood per year for cooking; this requirement may double or triple if fuelwood is also used for heating. The typical efficiency of domestic conversion of biomass into useful energy is extremely low -- usually around 5%; thus it affords considerable scope for improving energy efficiency.

Over-cutting and deforestation has reached alarming levels in many parts of the world. In addition to the immediate problems of inadequate local energy for the poor rural masses, potentially more disastrous ecological difficulties have also occurred. The Sahelian situation -- involving desertification, erosion, loss of watersheds, and the catastrophic collapse of the local biosphere's general capability to sustain human life -- is an extreme example.

In view of these serious problems, the UN Conference on New and Renewable Sources of Energy, held in Nairobi in 1981, identified six major steps to remedy the situation.

1. *Improving Existing Fuelwood Resources Through Better Management.* This includes giving a higher national priority to fuelwood problems and educating the population in elementary silviculture.

---

[1] Edited version of an invited paper presented at the Centre for European Policy Studies (CEPS), Brussels, Belgium in October 1985, and subsequently published as CEPS Working Paper No. 27, in October 1986.

2. *Creating New Biomass Resources, Such As Fuelwood Plantations, Community Woodlots, etc.* This would also require significant new resources to finance investments, education, and support services.
3. *Improving the Patterns of Distribution, Including Storage, Handling, and Intermediate Conversion (e.g., Fuelwood to Charcoal).*
4. *Upgrading the Technology.* This includes improvements in the efficiency of conversion at the end use (e.g., furnaces, cook-stoves, etc.), as well as intermediate levels (e.g., gasification). More applied research on bioenergy using technology as well as studies of locally adaptable, high-yield trees, should be carried out.
5. *Substitution of Bioenergy by Fossil and Other Renewable Sources Like Hydropower and Solar Energy.* Here the longer-term economic consequences and social acceptability would be important issues to consider.
6. *Rationalizing the System of Land Ownership and Utilization.* This would help to give people who collect fuelwood a stake in the land, thus providing incentives for better land use and biomass production.

While these general policy prescriptions are helpful, the fuelwood problem must ultimately be tackled at the local and national levels in order to be really effective. It is clear that a multitude of other problems and constraints also have to be taken into consideration before bioenergy management policy at the national level can be practically implemented.

One of the most important considerations is that a biomass problem cannot be considered in isolation, but must be analysed within the general socio-economic and energy-sector matrix within which it is embedded. Thus both the analysis and solutions must be:

1. *Holistic* -- within the context of the national economy;
2. *Realistic* -- based on the actual capacity of the government, especially the managerial, skilled manpower, and the financial and physical resources available; and
3. *Participative* -- with particular attention being paid to the design, implementation, and monitoring of programmes and projects to ensure maximum popular involvement, especially in rural areas.

In the following section of this paper, we will examine bioenergy management within the integrated national energy planning (INEP) framework discussed in Chapters 1, 2 and 4. This will be followed by a practical case study of a developing country (Sri Lanka), where this approach has been successfully used to formulate and implement biomass policy.

12.2 Bioenergy Management in an Integrated Framework

The concept of Integrated National Energy Planning (INEP) was presented in Chapters 1 and 2 and its practical implementation discussed in Chapter 4. In the INEP context, energy planning was broadly interpreted to denote a series of steps or procedures by which the myriad of interactions involved in the production and use of energy may be studied and understood within an explicit analytical framework. The many interactions and non-market forces that shape and affect the energy sectors of every economy have led decisionmakers in an increasing number of countries to realize the need for such an integrated approach.

Planning techniques ranging from basic manual methods to sophisticated computer modeling, have evolved over the years. Energy policy analysis involving the systematic investigation of the impact of a specific energy strategy or policy packages on the economy and society, at all levels was demonstrated via the case study in Chapter 4. Effective energy management techniques (which includes both supply and demand management) for the country studied in Chapter 4 (viz., Sri Lanka), were discussed using a selected set of policies and policy instruments, to achieve desirable energy and economic objectives.

While the conceptual framework for policy analysis and planning is integrated (to facilitate the formulation of broad energy strategies), the implementation process must involve maximum use of decentralized policy instruments and market forces to improve effectiveness. This would include an increased role for the private sector where appropriate. INEP provides primarily a conceptual framework for policy analysis and energy strategy formulation, while policy implementation should rely mainly on market incentives and decentralized competitive forces.

The development of the concepts and methodology of INEP and its subsequent application can be traced to the energy crisis of the 1970's. Before this period, energy was relatively cheap, and any imbalance between supply and demand was invariably dealt with by augmenting supply. The emphasis was more on the engineering and technological aspects. Furthermore, planning was confined to the various energy subsectors such as electricity, oil, coal, etc., with little coordination among them.

From the mid-1970's onwards, the rapidly increasing cost of all forms of energy, led by the world oil price, stimulated the development of new analytical tools and policies. First, the need became apparent for greater coordination between energy supply and demand options, and for the more effective use of demand management and conservation. Second, energy-macroeconomic links began to be explored more systematically. Third, the more disaggregate analysis of both supply and demand within the energy sector offered greater opportunities for inter- fuel substitution (especially away from oil). Fourth, the analytical and modelling tools for energy subsector planning became more sophisticated. Fifth, in the developing countries, greater reliance was placed on economic principles, including the techniques of shadow pricing.

Coordinated energy planning and pricing require detailed analyses of the interrelationships between the various economic sectors, and their potential energy requirements, versus the capabilities and advantages/disadvantages of the various forms of energy such as electric power, petroleum, natural gas, coal and traditional fuels (e.g., firewood, crop residues and dung) to satisfy these requirements.

As the following case study will show, it is essential that non-conventional sources, whenever they turn out to be viable energy alternatives, be an integral part of this framework. As previously mentioned, about 10% of gross world energy supplies come from biomass, with this fraction being much higher (often above 50%) in many developing countries. It is also important to recognize that changes in biomass supply and demand trends have impacts which range far beyond the energy sphere. The repercussions of deforestation in developing countries have been long recognized. These repercussions are both economic and environmental in nature. The economies of many developing countries are primarily agro-based. Consequently, while cutting down forests releases more land for agriculture, the overall ecological impact -- in the form of desertification, reduced rainfall etc. -- have tended to drastically diminish agricultural productivity. The consequences, especially in some African countries, are only too apparent.

The substantial market distortions, shortages of foreign exchange as well as human and financial resources for development, larger numbers of poor households whose basic needs somehow have to be met, and relative paucity of energy as well as other data, further exacerbate planning and policymaking in LDCs with regard to biomass resources. Many developing countries have maintained artificially low domestic prices for commercial energy products, even in situations where these products have to be imported, at international market prices. This practice has led to unsustainable economic burdens, and shifted resources away from productive areas of investment. Frequently, however, strong arguments for price subsidies have been made on the basis of minimizing the already severe pressures on a country's forest resources. Changing LPG or kerosene prices, for instance, could move many marginal users back to traditional methods of cooking based on fuelwood, or dissuade them from making the switch.

Such price distortions are exacerbated because fuelwood is frequently available at costs to the consumer which are only a fraction of their true economic cost. These situations prevail because of inadequate regulations or enforcement mechanisms on the one hand, and deep-rooted beliefs that forest reserves are free for the taking.

The need for an integrated approach to bioenergy management becomes quite apparent in view of these conflicting perceptions and objectives that are faced by most LDC energy planners. In Chapter 4, we discussed the overall planning framework developed for Sri Lanka using the INEP concepts described in Chapter 2. In the case study that follows, we will return to the Sri Lanka situation to focus in-depth on the fuelwood situation and its management in that country.

12.3 Sri Lanka: Overview of the Economic and Energy Situation

Sri Lanka, situated in the Indian Ocean, is a small island of 65,610 sq. kilometers in area which includes 959 sq. kilometers of inland water. The land area is compact, with a central hilly region. The rivers which spring up from this region (the most important of them is the Mahaweli Ganga), play an important economic role in providing hydroelectric power. Another major indigenous source of energy are the forests which have, however, declined from about 44% of total land area in 1955 to about 24% in 1981, mainly due to agricultural conversion and fuelwood use.

Sri Lanka is essentially an agricultural economy -- dualistic in nature. It consists of an export-oriented plantation sector with primary crops of tea, rubber and coconut; and a domestic or rural sector with the major outputs being rice paddy and other food crops -- essentially for local consumption. Tea, which is one of the major exports, shows a steady decline, as a percentage of total export value (as well as absolute volume), from 55.3% in 1977, to 27.2% in 1986. Rubber and coconut also show considerable declines; from 21.6% in 1970 to 7.7% in 1986 for rubber, and 11.7% in 1970 to 4.7% in 1986 for coconut. The policy of nationalization of the plantation sector in 1976 had adverse effects on production in the ensuing years, and the worst hit were the tea plantations. On the other hand, minor exports consisting of coconut by-products, spices, minor agricultural crops, precious and semi-precious stones, manufactured goods, minerals, and petroleum re-exports, had increased from 11.7% to 60.4% in the value of total exports, between 1970 and 1986.

In the past two decades, the Sri Lankan economy has passed through two distinct policy regimes, with consequent impacts on the energy sector. From 1970 to 1977, Sri Lanka was essentially a closed economy, with strict exchange control regulations and import controls. This was a period marked by low investments and low growth patterns; GDP grew at only 2.9% per annum on average; which was well below both the economy's previous performance of 4.4.% per annum in the 1960's and its inherent potential. One of the hardest hit sectors was the manufacturing industry -- due to the sluggish economy and the poor investment climate, investments averaged less than 16% of GDP during this period.

The oil price increase of 1973 had made petroleum, which supplies a third of the country's primary energy demands, a significant factor in the balance of payments. But strict import control measures and slow economic growth ensured that the burden of oil imports was manageable during the following years. At the same time the addition of new hydro capacity resulted in electricity supply exceeding demand, and thus helped to curtail the demand for oil. This period was marked by economic stagnation essentially due to the policies pursued.

With the liberalization of the economy in 1977, and the adoption of a market oriented development strategy, Sri Lanka's economy has shown considerable change. Most significant has been the ability to break the low investment and low growth pattern of the 1970-1977 period. Investments have grown from 14% of GDP in 1977 to an average of 28% in 1980-86, with growth being shared by both public and private sectors. However, this growth has not been accompanied by any substantial increase in national savings, implying little shift in domestic resources from consumption to investment. Most of the increase in investment had to be financed by drawing down international reserves, and by resorting to commercial borrowing. The real rate of growth since 1977 has averaged about 5.8%, which is all the more significant since this was achieved in a period of considerable international economic turmoil with high international inflation, doubling of oil prices and recession in the developed countries (which reduced demand for exports, and to some extent constrained aid flows). Further, the increased investment programs were accompanied by gains in employment.

Import liberalization and the decontrol of most prices provided an immediate boost to the manufacturing industry, which was the hardest hit sector in the 1970-77 period. Growth in this sector jumped to 7.8% in 1978 and averaged 5.2% from 1978-1985. The somewhat reduced growth in manufacturing since 1978 has been caused by the slow growth in capacity utilization and the low level of investment in the manufacturing sector -- due to easier, quicker and higher returns in other sectors like tourism, trade, and real estate.

Overview of Energy-Macroeconomic Relationships

During the past decade, international oil prices have twice risen sharply -- in 1973-74 and 1979-80. The overall increase was from under US$2 per barrel in the early 1970's to US$34 per barrel in 1980. Since then, prices have declined to below US$20 per barrel by 1986/87. During both oil shocks, the economic growth rate declined in industrial as well as developing countries. The oil importing developing countries (OIDCs) continued to be highly vulnerable to developments in the world economy, not only because of high oil import costs, but also due to shrinkage of export markets, official aid flows, access to international credit etc. Each downturn in the developed countries had corresponding adverse effects, especially on the OIDCs.

The impact of the first oil shock of 1973-74 was somewhat cushioned in the Sri Lanka economy due to a combination of factors. The strict exchange control regulations coupled with slow economic growth ensured that the burden of oil imports were manageable during the next few years. Though the oil import bill was a significant factor in the balance of payments, oil imports fell due to the prevailing economic climate. As previously stated, the turning points in the economy occurred in 1970 and 1977 with the change of governments and the economic policies adopted by them.

The first oil shock had no significant impact on GDP growth in view of closed economic policies that prevailed from 1970-1977, which protected the economy from external shocks. Table 4.3 (Chapter 4) shows that from 1973-77 the average growth rate of petroleum demand fell by 5.2%. This could be interpreted as a general response to the doubling of petroleum prices, in a difficult economic period.

The second oil shock of 1979-80 had much more severe repercussions than the first as would be observed from Table 4.3. With the liberalization of the economy in 1977, the growth rate of GDP during 1977-80 averaged 6.8%. The rapidly improving economic growth in this period resulted in an accelerated demand for electricity (which previously, during 1973-77, grew at an average rate of 4.7%), due to the low tariff structure and untapped potential markets. The demand was met totally by hydro-power. During 1977-80, without taking into consideration the power cuts that prevailed, electricity growth averaged 10.2%; this had a significant impact on the economy since the supply had to be supplemented by thermal generation. During the same period, demand for petroleum products grew at 7.2% compared to -5.2% in 1973-77. In the short-run adjustment period (1980-82) after the second oil shock, demand growth for both electricity and petroleum stayed high, at an annual 10.1% and 14.7% respectively, as the economy continued to expand. Since then growth rates have dropped significantly, particularly for petroleum (-6.7% in 1982-86), where domestic rupee prices followed the international price decline.

The marginal increases in the demand for commercial energy in Sri Lanka up to 1985 were directly linked to the size of petroleum imports, regardless of whether these increases took the form of higher electricity consumption or direct consumption of petroleum products. Thus after 1977, the combination of increased consumption and a doubling of oil prices resulted in a rapidly growing oil import bill. By 1981, the net oil import bill more than tripled and the proportion of export earnings devoted to importing oil rose from 15% to 39%.

The recent decline in world oil prices had little effect on energy demand since this dollar price decrease was offset by the exchange rate fluctuations (with the rupee declining in value against the dollar), thus keeping domestic oil product prices relatively stable.

Overview of Energy Supply and Demand

Energy Supply:

Sri Lanka has two major indigenous sources of energy -- hydroelectric power and fuelwood. The country's potential hydroelectric power is estimated to be in the region of 2300 MW, of which 1122 MW has already been developed, with 533 MW of this being contributed by the recent Mahaweli scheme. By the end of the current decade, over 50% of the potential capabilities would have been realized. Hydroelectric power is used primarily to meet base load energy generation, while gas turbines operate in the peaking mode and also provide spinning reserve. This pattern is expected to continue for at least the next five years.

Though reliable data on fuelwood supply is difficult to obtain, the estimates clearly indicate its precarious and unsustainable nature. Over the past two decades, incremental wood production -- from the natural regeneration of forests, agricultural residues and rubber replanting etc. -- has fallen far behind consumption, and today accounts for less than half the estimated annual consumption of around 5 million tons. The balance of wood supply has come mainly from the denudation of Sri Lanka's natural forest cover, which has declined by about 50% in the three decades since the mid-1950s.

The balance of the major domestic demand is met by oil imports. The crude oil imported is refined into other petroleum products which are either used in the domestic market or re-exported. Table 4.4 (Chapter 4) shows the main types of oil imports which are crude oil, kerosene, and auto diesel. Similarly Table 4.5 gives the consumption of electricity and petroleum products between 1975-1986.

Sri Lanka's energy supply pattern (1983) may be summarized as follows:

1. Fuelwood   -   67%
2. Oil (excluding power generation)   -   24%
3. thermal-based electricity   -   4%
4. hydroelectricity   -   5%.

Oil is the most important source in supplying useful energy or net supply (46%), with fuelwood at 38% and electricity at 16% (supplied by both hydro and oil) -- useful energy was calculated, based on end-use efficiency estimates of the different forms of energy.

After 1978, there was a substantial increase in the demand for all forms of commercial energy, which rose in aggregate at 8.8% per annum in the 1978-80 period, as opposed to a slight decline in the preceding 7 years. Petroleum consumption has grown even more rapidly, following the increase in demand for electricity in the post-1977 period -- which had to be met by increased thermal generation.

Sri Lanka has access to a variety of economically viable, non-conventional renewable energy resources -- solar, wind, biomass and mini-hydro -- which could be utilized to meet some of the country's energy demand in the medium term.

Solar Energy: Sri Lanka's location assures it of a relatively high and uniform level of insolation which could be harnessed for both water heating and crop drying. A very few households currently use hot water; the main market for these heaters will initially lie in the commercial and tourist sectors. The use of solar energy for crop drying is an important alternative to be developed, since tea and other crop processing industries consume over one million tons of fuelwood (or about 20% of total fuelwood consumption) per year.

Mini-hydro: While emphasis in Sri Lanka has been on large hydro power schemes, about 10 MW of small schemes (5 kV to 250 kV range) have been operating in the tea estates of the central region since 1925. However, these have been abandoned because of the availability of cheap and reliable electricity from the national grid. In addition to the rehabilitation of these existing plants, potential sites for mini-hydro schemes exist in the central hilly areas and in irrigation systems in the north central part of the island.

Other renewables: Apart from solar and mini-hydro, there are a number of promising renewable energy applications. These include generation of biogas from animal wastes, producer gas from rice husks and coir briquettes, wind energy for water pumping and electricity generation in isolated areas.

Energy Demand:

The energy demand sectors have been demarcated into four broad groups: 1. Industry/Agro-industry; 2. Transport; 3. Household/Agriculture; and 4. Government, Commercial and Others. The first three sectors (ie. industry, transport and households) account for around 99% of total energy demand in Sri Lanka.

The industrial sector accounts for more than 50% of electricity consumption, about 1/3 of petroleum consumption, and also 1/4 of the fuelwood used in the country. Fuelwood is an important source of energy for agro-industry in the rural areas, (e.g. tree crop processing). Eighteen large industrial organizations in the public sector account for 35% of total electricity sales; while ten large private companies are responsible for over half the sector's petroleum consumption.

The transport sector depends entirely on petroleum products for energy, and transport accounts for more than half the total demand for petroleum. Diesel is the predominant transport fuel (75% of the sales), which reflects the extensive public transport network, and also the policy of pricing diesel well below gasoline. As a result of this price differential, the proportion of diesel car registrations rose from 14% in 1978 to 35% in 1980. To reverse this trend, the government in 1980/81 raised the price of diesel to 60% of the price of gasoline, and increased the license fees of diesel cars to 3 times that of gasoline cars. Since then, the growth of auto-diesel consumption has been significantly reduced.

While per capita energy consumption in Sri Lanka is low by international standards and most households use energy for only cooking and lighting, the energy requirements in the household sector account for nearly half the country's primary energy consumption. The bulk of household energy requirements is met by fuelwood, which will continue to be the predominant source for the next decade. Even in 1986, only 13% of households had access to electricity, and the consumption of kerosene, which is mainly used for lighting, has been declining over the past decade in response to higher prices. The demand for energy in this sector will continue to grow with increase in the population and rising standards of living.

12.4 The Fuelwood Situation in Sri Lanka

The natural forest area of Sri Lanka has declined dramatically over the past few decades. By 1981, the natural forest cover was about 16,300 km² (or 24% of total land area), having declined to almost half the 1956 area of 29,000 km² (Munasinghe 1984). In the absence of major policy initiatives to reverse this trend, further declines can be expected.

Excessive consumption, waste, and inefficient use of biomass have contributed to the depletion of forest resources. Because most of the deforestation in Sri Lanka has occurred in the dry zone which is not heavily populated, domestic cooking needs are not the only major cause of deforestation. Rubber wood from plantations currently make up a large portion of the commercial fuelwood sold to households, especially in Colombo (the biggest market). In addition, most Sri Lankans do not purchase their fuel, so the market demand for domestic fuel is not great enough to have been the sole culprit for deforestation. In summary, the five main reasons for the drastic decline in Sri Lankan forest cover are:

1. Expansion of agricultural land. This is most often the "slash and burn" approach, with the felled trees being only partially utilized -- a very wasteful use of resources that provides poor agricultural yields and low financial returns (Pushparajah 1981).
2. Fuel for agro- and rural industries, e.g., tea, brick, tile, paddy, lime, rubber, coconut, tobacco, etc.
3. Commercial timber extraction (legal and illegal).
4. Domestic fuel use.
5. Forest fires.

A number of serious consequences can be expected from further losses in the forest cover. It was previously pointed out that fuelwood is the nation's principal source of energy and this situation will prevail for some time -- in 1983 fuelwood accounted for 67% of the primary energy supply, and 38% of useful consumption. However, if the forest cover declines much further, fuelwood shortages can be expected, with the result that fuelwood prices, especially in the urban areas, may rise dramatically. This, in turn, will cause many users to switch to electricity or imported petroleum products like kerosene and LPG for cooking needs. Second, the unchecked deforestation will inevitably lead to serious environmental consequences such as erosion and loss of watersheds, which in turn will have adverse effects on agricultural production and hydropower generation, respectively.

The remainder of this chapter analyses the worsening fuelwood problem, and describes policy options to address the issues involved. In the short- to medium-run, the National Fuelwood Conservation Program (NFCP) launched in 1984 seeks to rapidly replace the existing inefficient domestic woodstoves with more efficient ones in about 2.6 million households. The early launching of an accelerated reforestation program is also recommended (and has already been initiated partially) to supplement the NFCP in the medium- to long-run. These results are confirmed through systematic computer modelling studies.

The National Fuelwood Conservation Program

The more efficient and sparing use of present supplies of fuelwood is the only effective short-term measure available, until the long-term reforestation and silviculture programs begin to show results. Most of the households in Sri Lanka still employ the traditional hearth (consisting of 3 stones) or alternatively, the semi-enclosed hearth, for cooking. Although this is cheap and convenient, it is extremely wasteful of energy. Under these circumstances, improved types of fuelwood stoves are of great importance, since they provide significant potential for fuelwood conservation. In many developing countries including Sri Lanka, it has been demonstrated that considerable savings could be made by using such improved stoves. In fact, if widely used, such stoves could have a substantial effect on the demand for firewood.

Several local organizations like Sarvodaya, CISIR, IDB, State Timber Corporation and the CEB, have already made some efforts in the design or field testing of improved stoves. Experience gained by these organizations have proved valuable for future programs, although widespread dissemination was not achieved. Some of the constraints which have impeded progress in the past can be identified as:

1. Absence of systematic government support.
2. Lack of funds for implementation of extension programmes.
3. Absence of an institutional framework for wide-spread dissemination.
4. Designs unacceptable to users being disseminated.
5. Lack of women participating in extension programmes.
6. Lack of trained personnel.
7. Lack of general awareness of the need for fuelwood conservation, and the means available to aid conservation.

The Improved Cookstove Programme

The isolated efforts of individual organizations were not very successful in the popularization of improved stoves due to the problems mentioned earlier. In 1983, the Task Force on New, Renewable and Rural Sources of Energy (NERSE--described in Chapter 4) formed a working group to embrace all organizations actively involved or interested in fuelwood conservation. This step permitted proper planning and implementation of a long-run strategy, and also helped to work out the machinery for management and coordination of a programme of action (Munasinghe 1984).

However, it was realized at an early stage, that a single organization could not be expected to successfully perform all the activities required for a mass popularization and dissemination programme. Through the NFCP framework, it was found to be possible to make use of the existing institutional framework of participating organizations, rather than to set up a new (and redundant) organization. The existing organizations already had excellent extension services and community development programmes which could be successfully used in a stove programme. The NFCP provided crucial policy coordination, as well as supplementary technical expertise and other relevant assistance to these operating organizations.

More specifically, the National Fuelwood Conservation Programme (NFCP) launched by the NERSE Task Force is a course of action for widespread dissemination, that includes the following objectives:

1. *Sensitization*: People must be made aware of the need for fuelwood conservation and the availability of the means to achieve this end.
2. *Demonstration*: Effectiveness of the stove must be demonstrated to the satisfaction of potential users. This guarantees the demand for improved stoves.
3. *Production*: An adequate supply of stoves must be ensured to meet the demand. This would involve setting up of a network of centralized and/or decentralized stove workshops, employing local potters.
4. *Installation and Dissemination*: Installation of the Sarvodaya stove will have to be made in the home by the stove builders, while other models like the Cisirlipa can be centrally produced and sold in small shops (or retailed).
5. *Training*: This activity involves:
   a. Training of potters to make the pottery liner.
   b. Training of stove builders.
   c. Training of extension workers to promote the use of stoves and to provide technical advice.

6. *Follow-up*: This involves:
   a. Maintaining contact with the users and dissemination network, to find out incorrect methods adopted in installation and use, and to remedy them.
   b. Providing advice on suitable changes in future designs and procedures to be adopted in dissemination.
7. *Financing*: It is necessary to find funds to implement the objectives mentioned above. Although some organizations may manage to finance certain activities, the overall amounts available are likely to be inadequate. Therefore sources of finance as well as contributions in kind will have to be identified.

In order to reach most of the 2.64 million households in Sri Lanka, the NFCP consists of a phased campaign:

Year	No. of Stoves to be Disseminated	
1984	15,000	
1985	50,000	
1986	150,000	
1987	400,000	
1988	800,000	
1989	1,250,000	(Steady state value, assuming that each clay stove has a 2 year lifetime)

The NFCP was designed to begin slowly because of the need to train potters, build up production capability, and simultaneously create the demand. Careful coordination was required to prevent a situation where demand exceeded supply -- resulting in unfulfilled expectations, sub-standard and inefficient stoves, high stove prices, etc.

The benefits to be realized by introducing more fuelwood efficient stoves are summarized in Table 12.1. Details of economic and financial calculations are given in Annex A12.1.

Even though the traditional open fire is basically used for cooking, it also serves diverse purposes such as lighting, preserving food, preserving thatched roofs, reducing insect population etc. Therefore for successful dissemination, the design of a stove must take into account not only fuel efficiency but also a variety of end-uses. Flexibility in the use of a variety of bio-mass fuels is also important, since this is a major advantage of the open fire. Development of designs therefore required inputs not only from engineers and scientists, but also from social scientists, extension officers, production and marketing experts, and most importantly, users.

Production approaches differ too, depending on the design and the locality for which it is designed. Thus, different production strategies were devised for urban and rural markets. Even after suitable design (there can be many) and production strategies were identified, dissemination required consideration of a host of social and other aspects. Furthermore, many government and non-government organizations had to be brought together to provide the appropriate teamwork for successful dissemination.

In summary, the whole exercise of introducing improved stoves consisted of a series of complex activities for which no simple and obvious universal solutions were available.

Table 12.1

Benefits of Using Improved Wood Stoves

Note: Efficiency improvements = 20% greater than semi-enclosed hearth.
        Capital Cost of Stove   = Rs. 50.00

A. Fuelwood Saving Benefits

Number of Stoves	Fuelwood Saved (in MT)		NPV of Savings for 2 Years[a] (in Rs.)	
	After 1 yr.	After 2 yrs.	Savings to Nat'l Economy	Fin. Saving per family
1	0.6	1.20	1,702	Urban = 392 Rural = 79 Estate = 319
15,000	9,000	18,000	25.5 Million	
50,000	30,000	60,000	85.1 Million	
200,000	120,000	240,000	340.4 Million	
2,640,000	1,584,000	3,168,000	4493.3 Million	

B. Other Benefits

1. Reducing deforestation and its consequences.
2. Better job opportunities and income for potters and stove builders.
3. Improved safety, and improved hygienic conditions in kitchens. (Lower incidence of respiratory, skin and eye diseases generally associated with traditional stoves).

---

[a] For details see Appendix.

As indicated earlier, the NFCP was launched and coordinated by the NERSE Task Force, with the Energy Unit of the CEB acting as the central management group and orchestrating operations nationwide (see Figure 12.1). The strategy of implementation was to make use of the existing village level institutional infrastructure, primarily with the Assistant Government Agents (AGA's) acting as local coordinators who manage a network of promoters, stove builders and potters. Each person in the chain receives a financial incentive per stove installed. This approach not only avoided the necessity for a new organization for dissemination activities, but also permitted the use of the authority, experience and close relationship enjoyed by the existing institutions with the villagers. This is essential when introducing new concepts and activities. Moreover AGA's have access to and control over many village level organizations which have proved to be very valuable for the programme.

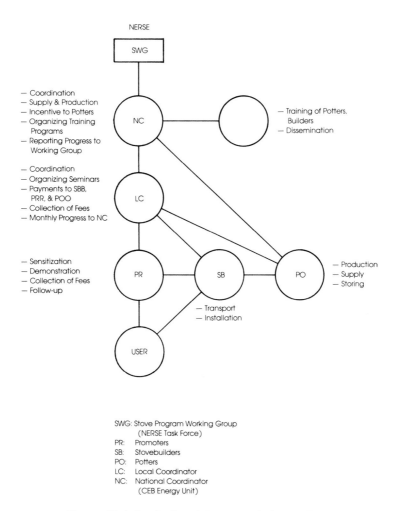

NERSE

SWG

— Coordination
— Supply & Production
— Incentive to Potters
— Organizing Training
 Programs
— Reporting Progress to
 Working Group

NC

— Training of Potters,
 Builders
— Dissemination

— Coordination
— Organizing Seminars
— Payments to SBB,
 PRR, & POO
— Collection of Fees
— Monthly Progress to NC

LC

— Sensitization
— Demonstration
— Collection of Fees
— Follow-up

PR   SB   PO

— Production
— Supply
— Storing

— Transport
— Installation

USER

SWG: Stove Program Working Group
 (NERSE Task Force)
PR: Promoters
SB: Stovebuilders
PO: Potters
LC: Local Coordinator
NC: National Coordinator
 (CEB Energy Unit)

Figure 12.1: Institutional Framework for NFCP

The programme was initially started in 5 key areas of the island: Kandy, Mahaweli (H area), Ratnapura, Hambantota, and Badulla (see Fig. 12.2 below), and subsequently expanded to other regions based on the experience gained earlier.

The Analytical Design

In order to assess the impact of policy initiatives in the fuelwood sector, a simple supply-demand balance model was constructed of the fuelwood subsector to the year 2010. Despite the obvious hazards of making projections over such long time frames, the fact that fuelwood plantations will produce only longer-term impacts, mandate such a horizon.

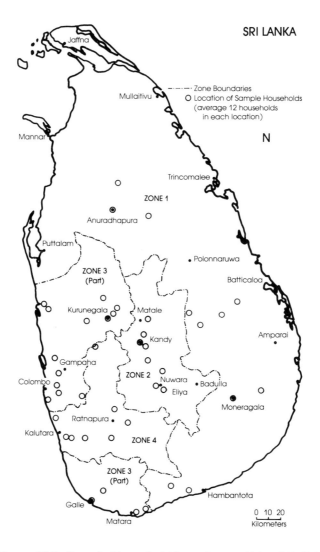

Figure 12.2: Sample Household Location and Zonal Definition

source: Wijesinghe (1984)

The basic approach is to estimate total fuelwood consumption based on current population trends and existing cookstove efficiencies, and then subtract the contribution from sources such as rubber wood, crop wastes, and those fuelwood plantations already underway. The balance is assumed to come from natural forest cover, either from the sustainable yield (the growth increment), or, should this source be insufficient, from actual felling. This permits an estimate of the area of the natural forest cover through time. On this calculation is superimposed, the impact of specific policy initiatives in the subsector, such as additional fuelwood plantation programmes, the introduction of improved cookstoves, or the increased use of charcoal. For reasons indicated below, some of the calculations must also be done on a regional basis.

Fuelwood Consumption

Despite the central importance of fuelwood to Sri Lanka's energy sector, data on the patterns of consumption remain poor. Until recently, the generally accepted figure for 1980 consumption was some 5.2 million tons per year, which was based mainly on theoretical calculations. In 1979, Bialy conducted what appears to have been the first scientific survey of fuelwood consumption in a village near Anuradhapura. The results indicated an average consumption of 50kg per household per week, which he extrapolated on the basis of 2 million fuelwood-using households, to 5 million tons per year. Bialy recognized the hazards of such extrapolations based on the results of a very limited survey of a single village, but his estimates were consistent with earlier studies.

Wijesinghe (1984) conducted a more extensive survey of 518 households in a stratified random sample that covered the entire island. Figure 12.2 shows the locations of the sample households, and the zonal definitions. The results indicated a much higher consumption figure than suggested by the earlier studies, with a 1981 island-wide usage estimated at 7.3 million tons (based on the 1981 population census results). Despite some limitations in the sampling design, these survey results are the best available, and could be used as a basis for planning.

Estimates of future consumption are subject to a number of uncertainties. The procedure adopted in this report is to base future consumption on a projection of total households (based on population growth), the assumption that the fraction of households using fuelwood remains at the 1981 level (based on the 1981 population census), and Wijesinghe's estimate of unit consumption per household (adjusted, as noted below, for the introduction of higher efficiency cookstoves).

Fuelwood Supply

Again, the most systematic estimate of the composition of the fuelwood supply is that of Wijesinghe. In addition to fuelwood from the natural forest, a number of other sources are available, notably crop wastes and rubber wood. However, as indicated in Figure 12.3, there are very sharp differences from region to region. Calculations based on the all-island averages therefore mask very significant regional differences, and the impact of particular policy initiatives (or their absence) will therefore also vary.

The Policy Scenarios

For purposes of analysis we define the following policy scenarios:

Case A: No cookstove program, fuelwood plantations based only on the current programs (see Table 12.2).
Case B: Cookstove program as presently envisaged by the NRSE task force, which calls for the targets for stove dissemination shown earlier.
Case C : As in Case B, but with a somewhat slower dissemination rate of the new cookstove; assuming here that adoption of the new cookstove by the bulk of households will be attained by 1995 rather than 1989.
Case D : As in Case B, but with the existing planting rate (for re-afforestation) extended through 2000.
Case E : As in Case B, but with an increase in the planting rate to 15,000 ha/year by 2000.

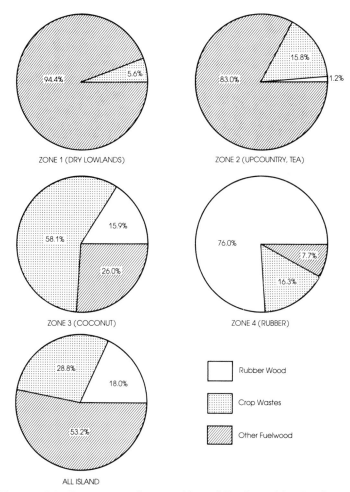

Figure 12.3: Percentage Composition of Fuelwood by Region

Table 12.2

The Current Plantation Program
(in 1000 ha)

	1982	1983	1984	1985	1986	1987	1988
USAID	5.24	2.14	1.81	2.64	1.64	1.64	N.A.
IRD	.81	.81	1.05	1.05	1.05	0.24	N.A.
CFP[1]	--	--	3.00	3.00	3.00	3.00	N.A.
Mahaweli	--	--	0.50	0.50	0.50	0.50	0.50
DoF[2]	--	--	1.00	1.50	1.50	1.75	2.00
Total	6.05	2.95	7.36	7.19	7.19	7.13	2.50

[1] Community Forest Project (Asian Development Bank)
[2] Government Re-afforestation Program (Forest Department)

For each of these cases, several model runs were made to reflect the uncertainty in some of the key parameters:

Efficiency of the New Cookstoves

As expected, this is one of the most important assumptions. Present expectations are that the improved stove designs will provide an efficiency improvement of 25%, thereby reducing the consumption rate per household from the present 2.3 tonnes/yr to about 1.8 tonnes/yr. Recent field evaluations of the stoves suggest that this is conservative, and that actual efficiency improvements may be over 35%.

Yield parameters

The calculation of forest loss due to fuelwood demands rests mainly on two parameters: the sustainable yield (tonnes/acre of standing forest), and the yield from clear cutting (tonnes/acre of forest cut). Even if these parameters were known precisely, the major problem is that much of the sustainable yield is available in areas distant from the population centers. In practice therefore, a substantial part of this yield may not be available, leading to increased pressures for felling in areas closer to the population centers. The sustainable yield is also a function of the climatic regime, and hence of the region of the country, estimated as follows:

Wet Zone	4.7 tonnes/ha.
Intermediate	2.0 tonnes/ha.
Dry Zone	1.6 tonnes/ha.

Since the bulk of the forest resource is in the dry zone, we vary the yield from 1.0 tonnes/ha to 2.0 tonnes/ha, in the national model. As one might anticipate, this proves to be one of the critical assumptions.

Analytical Results

Figure 12.4 shows the anticipated trends in total fuelwood consumption, including both residential and industrial demands, with and without the cookstove program. A 2% annual rate of growth of households is assumed (which may not necessarily correspond to the population growth rate, especially beyond the year 1995). The impact of the cookstove program is to provide an initial decline in consumption, followed by a resumption of the long term trend once the stoves are adopted throughout the population. Depending on the assumption made for the efficiency improvement over the traditional stove, current consumption levels are again reached by 1998 (25% improvement), or by 2006 (33% efficiency improvement).

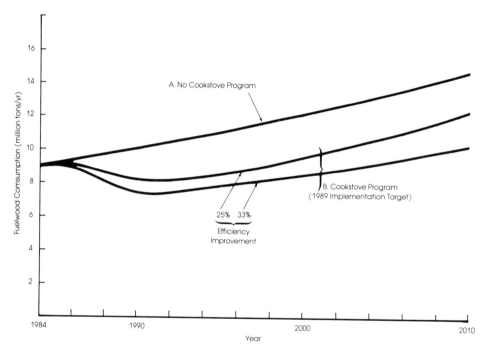

Figure 12.4: Anticipated Trends in Total Fuelwood Consumption

Table 12.3 shows part of a typical supply/demand balance, as produced by the fuelwood model, in this instance for Case B (with a 1989 implementation date for the cookstove program, and a 25% efficiency improvement). The full table has 28 columns, covering the years 1983 to 2010. For example, in year 2000, total consumption is 9.468 million tonnes (all figures in the tables are in 1000 tonnes). The current plantation program, agricultural wastes and rubber wood provide some 5.55 mt, leaving 3.913 mt to be provided by the forest. The forest area in 2000 is estimated at 1.257 million hectares, which provides an allowable cut of 1.257 mt. Therefore, the balance of 2.656 mt is assumed to be provided by clearing.

Table 12.3

Typical Fuelwood Balance (1000 metric tons)

	1995	1996	1997	1998	1999	2000	2001	2002	2003	2004	2005	2006
Total Consumption	8641	8797	8958	9125	9295	9468	9645	9825	10009	10200	10396	10596
Agricultural Waste	2709	2763	2819	2875	2933	2991	3051	3112	3174	3238	3303	3369
Rubber Wood	1311	1311	1311	1311	1311	1311	1311	1311	1311	1311	1311	1311
Current Plantation Prog.	1241	1439	2349	1047	1041	1253	1449	1869	720	523	628	719
Additional Plantations	0	0	0	0	0	0	0	0	0	0	0	0
Balance Needed from												
Forest Area												
Sustainable Yield for	3380	3284	2479	3892	4010	3913	3834	3532	4804	5128	5154	5197
Fuelwood Supply (tonnes)	1347	1330	1313	1303	1280	1257	1234	1212	1192	1161	1126	1092
Balance from Clearing	2032	1955	1166	2589	2730	2656	3834	3532	4804	5128	5154	5197
Area Cleared (1000 ha)	18	17	10	22	24	23	22	20	31	34	35	35

On the assumption that 1 ha provides 116 tonnes when clear cut, 23,000 ha will be lost in this year. Note that the area in 2001 reflects this loss (1257 - 23 = 1234); and thus the allowable cut in the following year is also reduced proportionately (see Figure 12.5 for the assumed harvesting patterns for *Eucalyptus Camuldulensis*, the species assumed for the fuelwood plantations.)

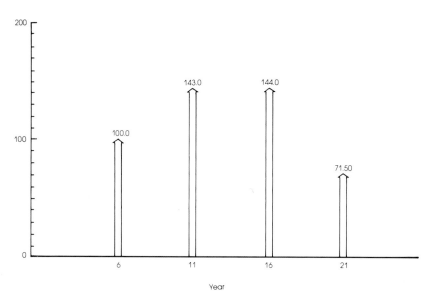

Figure 12.5: Harvesting Patterns for Eucalyptus Camuldulensis

This compounding effect of a forest loss in a particular year leads to the inevitable result of an accelerating rate of forest loss, as shown on Figure 12.6. To be sure, policy interventions in the 1990's would undoubtedly correct the severe deforestation projected in the absence of a cookstove program. As noted earlier, price effects may tend to offset deforestation once the forest resource is seriously depleted -- an effect by its very nature difficult to predict quantitatively, and therefore ignored in these calculations. However, what is clear is the fact that once severe declines begin to set in, the pace of deforestation accelerates, making interventions at a later time much more costly. It is certainly obvious from Figure 12.6 that the absence of a cookstove program leads to quite unacceptable consequences by the turn of the century.

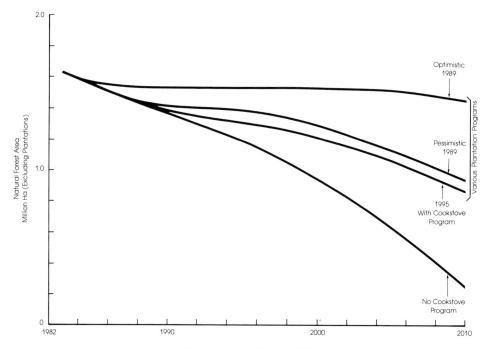

Figure 12.6: Movement of Natural Forest Area

The results of our two plantation program cases are shown on Figure 12.7. With the present plantation program extended through 2000 (Case D), significant forest losses will still begin to occur after 2000. It will take a plantation program of at least double the present planting rate (Case E), to reduce the rate of forest loss after 2000.

These simulations also point to the relationship between the cookstove programme and the plantation program. An accelerated plantation program in the absence of a cookstove program fails to arrest the rate of deforestation. Without the cookstove programme, even a plantation program of 5 to 6 times the present planting rate would fail to reverse this decline, because of the time lag between planting and harvesting, and because of the accelerating deforestation rate in the interval. It follows that both a cookstove and accelerated plantation programme should be initiated as a matter of some urgency.

Investment and Foreign Exchange Issues

A somewhat different way of assessing the impact of fuelwood plantations, and indeed of estimating the value to the nation of the forest resource itself, is to examine the opportunity costs involved. Every hectare of forest provides, on a sustainable basis, a certain amount of energy, which, if lost, must be replaced by petroleum product imports (Medema et al. 1981). Since the basic cooking needs of the population must be met under all circumstances, continued erosion of the forest area will require the importation of an equivalent quantity of petroleum product (or possibly coal), which in turn requires an additional foreign exchange outlay.

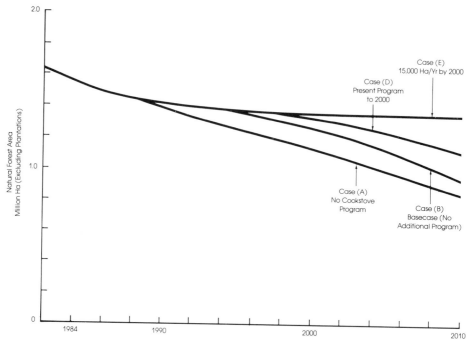

Figure 12.7: Natural Forest Area with Plantation and Cookstove Programs

Figure 12.8 shows the results of an analysis of the net present foreign exchange value of one hectare of fuelwood plantation. The assumed time pattern of harvesting is as indicated on Figure 12.9, from which we can calculate the energy value of the fuelwood harvest, and the useful cooking energy delivered (by accounting for cookstove efficiency). If the same amount of useful energy is to be provided by a petroleum product, one can readily derive the quantity of such a substitute, and its foreign exchange cost (see Appendix 12.1 for the details of these calculations). Of course, the value of the petroleum products displaced by the fuelwood is offset by the debt service obligation associated with the plantation investment.

To the extent that the natural forest would supply biomass needs not provided by fuelwood plantations, then obviously no petroleum product substitution is necessary. However, the discussion of the previous section indicates that a dwindling natural forest area will be unable to meet the demand, and hence the calculations presented here are valid. Figure 12.8 indicates a significant NPV over wide ranges of input assumptions; indeed, these estimates are conservative in that they do not consider the fact that the appliances which utilize petroleum products (LPG cookers and the like) may require additional foreign exchange, whereas fuelwood cookstoves are made from local materials.

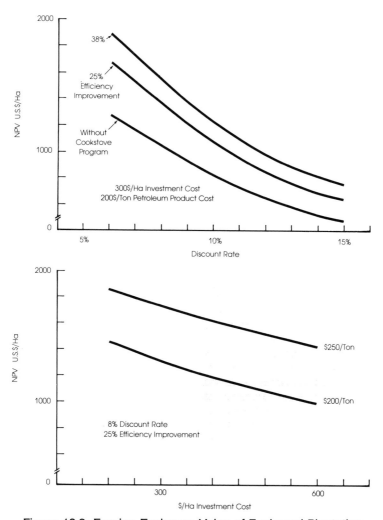

Figure 12.8: Foreign Exchange Value of Fuelwood Plantation

One of the more important points to emerge from these calculations concerns the relationship between the cookstove program and the foreign exchange value of the fuelwood; the higher the efficiency at which wood is utilized, the greater is the value of each ton of fuelwood (or, equivalently, for a given energy requirement, the less plantation investment will be required at higher efficiencies).

Figure 12.9 enumerates the year-by-year foreign exchange flows associated with a 5-year, 5000 ha/yr fuelwood plantation programme. Since the first harvest occurs in the sixth year, there is an increasing debt service burden in the short run. However, this is dramatically reversed in the sixth year. The long-term benefits of the plantation program are quite obvious, whatever the short-term impact.

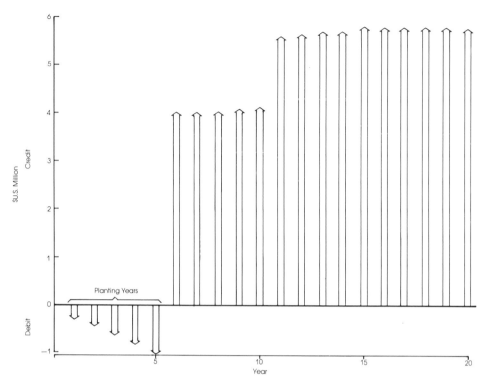

Figure 12.9: Annual Foreign Exchange Flows with Fuelwood Plantation Programme

12.5 Conclusions

Despite the great uncertainties in the data, the above analysis yields a number of conclusions that should shape the scope and urgency of the policy initiatives to be launched in the fuelwood sector.

1. Even under the most optimistic assumptions concerning the rate of household formation, the sustainable yield, and the potential contributions of non-forest sources to the fuelwood supply (agriculture wastes, rubber wood, etc.), a national cookstove program is absolutely essential. The consequences of not proceeding with such a program will be serious, with an accelerating rate of deforestation likely by the mid 1990's.
2. The speed with which the cookstove program is implemented proves to be of great significance. Delays in the widespread dissemination of the new cookstoves become increasingly serious, as optimistic assumptions are replaced by more pessimistic conditions. Thus, if the rate of household formation is higher than expected, or the contribution from non-forest sources is lower, the costs of delay

become greater. Since the probability of the most optimistic scenario considered here is small, the probable cost of delay is high.

3. Even an aggressively promoted cookstove program does not address the long term problem, because of the one-time nature of the efficiency improvement. As illustrated in Figure 12.4, while the cookstove program reverses the deforestation trend over the short term, by the mid 1990's, population growth will again put pressure on fuelwood supply. Therefore, the cookstove program buys time to initiate measures of a long term nature.

4. The breathing space afforded by a successful cookstove program must be utilized to put into place an expanded fuelwood plantation program. If serious problems are to be avoided in the early 2000's, by the early 1990's the plantation program should be at least double that currently underway (see Table 12.2). Because the growing cycle of even fast-growing Eucalyptus trees is at least 10 years, planning for such an expanded program should be initiated over the next few years if it is to be in place by the early 1990's.

5. It must be recognized that if such a plantation program is not initiated over the next few years, the possibility of another relatively low-cost short-term solution (such as the presently envisaged cookstove program), is no longer present. Today we can buy time for the plantation programs by promoting a stove design whose efficiency gain is large. To get the next increment in efficiency gain will be much more difficult, and in any event more costly.

6. The analysis presented here indicates that the long-term foreign exchange impacts of not proceeding with an enhanced plantation program are extremely serious. As the natural forest area continues to decline, and no longer serves as a fuelwood source, the costs of petroleum product substitution will place an additional burden on what is already a serious balance of payments situation at the national level, to say nothing of the impacts on the individual household budget.

7. All of the analysis presented in this chapter considered only the fuelwood demand. As noted in the introduction, it is well known that other demands (such as agricultural clearing and construction timber needs) place possibly an even greater strain on forest resources. Consequently, even if both the cookstove and plantation programs are implemented along the lines suggested here, there is no guarantee that the current deforestation trend can in fact be reversed. Therefore, these program elements must be viewed not only as part of the national energy strategy, but also as components of a much broader national forest and natural resource management strategy.

Appendix A12.1   Evaluation of Improved Fuelwood Stove[2]

In assessing the benefits of introducing the improved cookstove from a national viewpoint, an economic evaluation is first carried out to determine the least cost technology, i.e., the woodstove or the open hearth. For this purpose, shadow prices (or economic opportunity costs) are used to determine whether technology A (woodstove) is cheaper than technology B (open hearth). If technology A proves to be cheaper, a financial analysis is then carried out using market prices. This examines the feasibility from an individual's perspective, of using technology A instead of B.

Economic Evaluation

The open hearth which is referred to in this study (and commonly used in the urban, rural and estate sectors), is a semi-enclosed base made of clay (at negligible cost), rather than the simple three brick open hearth.

An average consumption of fuelwood of 2.98 metric tons(MT)/annum/family is assumed. It has been estimated that the new woodstove will reduce fuelwood consumption by approximately 20-30%. Thus three efficiency levels, viz. 20%, 25% and 30%, are considered, which correspond to annual usage by a family of 2.38, 2.24 or 2.09 MT, respectively.

The opportunity cost (value) of fuelwood is determined on the basis of kerosene displacement. This argument becomes increasingly relevant as fuelwood scarcity and overall deforestation progressively worsens. The kerosene equivalent is regarded as the upper bound on the economic value of fuelwood.

Assuming that 1 MT of fuelwood (FW) is equivalent to 0.19 MT of kerosene (see Note 1):

the value of 2.38 MT of FW   = 0.19 x 2.38 x 280 x 28.75
                               = Rs. 3640.20

where border price of kerosene = Rs.28.75/Imperial Gallon.

Corresponding figures for the other efficiency levels are:

25% efficiency of woodstove : Rs.3426.10
30% efficiency of woodstove : Rs.3196.65

The value of fuelwood consumed in an open hearth can be calculated in a similar manner.

Assuming a life of two years for the woodstove and a discount rate of 10%, the present value of economic costs over two years may now be computed. The results are summarized in Table A12.1.

---

[2] This appendix is based on an original study carried out by Sria Munasinghe and Shakuntala Gunaratne.

Table A12.1

**Present Value of Economic Costs for
Woodstove and Open Hearth
(all calculations on basis of representative family)**

		Woodstove		Open Hearth
Efficiency Level = 20%		25%	30%	--
Costs (Rs.)				
Capital	50	50	50	--
Fuel	3,640	3,426	3,197	4,558
Total PV for 2 Years	7,000	6,591	6,153	8,701
PV of Savings Using Woodstove	1,701	2,110	2,548	--
PV of Savings at National Level (Rs. million)[a]	4,493	5,572	6,729	--

[a] National saving = (PV of saving per family for 2 years) x (2.644 million households); also see Note 2.

Financial Evaluation

In the financial calculations, the costs incurred by an individual household are calculated using market prices, to compare technology A (improved woodstove) with technology B (open hearth).

The computations are similar to the economic evaluation and are summarized in Table A.12.2. Since the market price of fuelwood varies considerably in the three sectors of the economy viz. urban, rural and estate, the analysis is disaggregated on this basis.

Conclusion

It is evident from the economic evaluation that using the woodstove instead of the open hearth would result in considerable savings nationally. However, it is observed that the representative individual would have substantially less incentive to change to the new technology, especially in the rural sector. From Table A.12.2 it is seen that the net benefit of using the woodstove at an efficiency level of 20% is Rs.60 in the rural sector; Rs.206 in the urban sector; and Rs.310 in the estate sector, over a two year period. On the other hand, the woodstove entails a capital cost of Rs.50.

Since the potential saving from the national economic viewpoint is higher by an order of magnitude, the policy implication of popularizing the woodstove is quite obvious. One means of doing this would be to market the woodstove at a nominal price, ie. less than Rs.50 per unit.

Table A12.2

Present Value of Financial Costs for
Woodstove and Open Hearth
(on the basis of representative family)

	Woodstove			Open Hearth
Efficiency Level	20%	25%	30%	--
Costs (Rs.)				
Capital	50	50	50	--
Fuel:				
Urban	899	846	789	1,125
Rural	262	247	230	328
Estate	749	705	658	938
Total PV for 2 years:				
Urban	1,766	1,665	1,556	2,148
Rural	550	521	489	626
Estate	1,480	1,396	1,306	1,790
PV of Savings Using Woodstove:				
Urban	206	254	306	--
Rural	60	74	89	--
Estate	310	394	484	--

Note 1

Conversions:
1 MT of Fuelwood (FW)	=	0.4 MT of Crude Oil
1 MT of Kerosene	=	1.06 MT of Crude Oil

Thus:

1 MT of FW $= 0.4/1.06$
$= 0.377$ MT of Kerosene

It is assumed that:
The representative efficiency FW in cooking = 18%
The efficiency of kerosene in a cooking stove = 36%

1 MT of FW (useful energy)   = (0.18x0.377)/0.36 MT of kerosene (useful energy)
                              = 0.19 MT of kerosene (useful energy)

Note 2

Estimate of the total number of households using fuelwood:

Sector	Tot.no. of H.H.	% Using FW	No. Using FW
Urban	509,459	85.4	435,078
Rural	2,084,496	96.6	2,013,623
Estate	217,451	90.0	195,706
Total			2,644,407

Note 3

The price of fuelwood in various sectors of the economy is:

Urban: Rs.120 per cubic meter, ie., 377.60 per metric ton
Rural: Rs. 35 per cubic meter, ie., 110.10 per metric ton
Estate: Rs.100 per cubic meter, ie., 314.66 per metric ton

Cost incurred by an average family/annum for fuelwood consumption in each sector:

At 20% Efficiency	At 25% Efficiency	At 30% Efficiency
Urban 2.38 x 377.6 = 898.7	2.24 x 377.60 = 845.8	2.09 x 377.60 = 789
Rural 2.38 x 110.1 = 262.0	2.24 x 110.10 = 246.6	2.09 x 110.10 = 230
Estate 2.38 x 314.7 = 748.9	2.24 x 314.66 = 704.9	2.09 x 314.66 = 657

Open Hearth

Urban 2.98 x 377.6 = 1125
Rural 2.98 x 110.1 = 328
Estate 2.98 x 314.7 = 937

Appendix A12.2   Technical Assessment of Improved Fuelwood Stoves

CISIRLIPA: Single-Pot Chimneyless Stove

This stove, developed by the Ceylon Institute of Scientific and Industrial Research (CISIR), consists of two parts:
    (a) the firebox, and
    (b) the outer jacket which also doubles as the pot rest and pot surround.

It can accommodate a wide range of pot sizes and biomass fuels, and saves approximately 21% of the fuelwood compared to the semi-enclosed open hearth, and 30% compared to the 3 stone open hearth. It currently costs Rs. 32.50 to produce.

Summary of Test Results:

	Semi-Enclosed Open Hearth (Two sides enclosed)	Improved Hearth Single Pot (With clay jacket)
Water Boiling Test		
1. Wt. of water boiled (kg)	16	20
2. Wt. of fuelwood consumed (g)	1455	1455
3. Efficiency (%)	18.85	24.08
4. Time taken (min.)	115	128
Cooking Test		
1. Wt. of fuelwood consumed (g)	879	694
2. Time taken (min.)	80	80
3. % wood saving compared to semi-enclosed open hearth	–	21

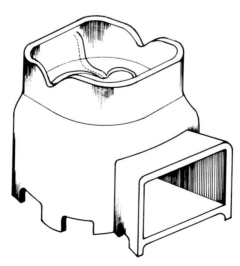

Figure A12.1: Cisirlipa

SARVODAYA: Pottery Liner Stove

This is a stove developed by the Sarvodaya Movement of Sri Lanka with the assistance of the Intermediate Technology Development Group (ITDG) of U.K.. The present design is the sixth generation of stoves developed. A large number of these stoves have already been installed by the Sarvodaya Movement and the Energy Unit of the CEB, in the Kandy District and Galnewa area (Mahaweli 'H' System). In these areas, the pilot projects were extremely popular, and most users have abandoned the traditional hearth. The demand created for more stoves could not be met within the limited scope of the pilot projects.

The Sarvodaya stove is a two-pot-hole stove, consisting of a pottery liner, insulated externally with a mixture of 4 parts clay, 4 parts sand, 2 parts ash and 1 part cowdung. It has a life span of 2 to 3 years and costs about Rs. 40 to produce.

Summary of Test Results: Comparison with Open Hearth (average of 48 tests)

Stove Type	Amount of Rubber Wood Saved Relative to Open Hearth	
	Water Boiling Test	Cooking Test
Open Hearth	0	0
Pottery Liner Stove (with Chimney)	-10%	-13%
Pottery Liner Stove (without Chimney)	-18%	-23%

(negative values indicate fuelwood saving)

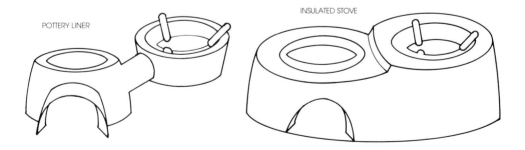

POTTERY LINER   INSULATED STOVE

Figure A12.2: Sarvodaya Stove

References

Bialy, J., "Firewood Use in a Sri Lankan Village - A Preliminary Survey", School of Engineering, Edinburg University, U.K., 1979.

Medema, E.L., C. Hatch and K. Christopherson, "Investment Analyses of Fuelwood Plantations in Sri Lanka", College of Forestry, Wildlife and Range Sciences, University of Idaho, Idaho, 1981.

Meier, P. and M. Munasinghe, "Implementing a Practical Fuelwood Conservation Policy: the Case of Sri Lanka", *Energy Policy*, vol.15, no.2, April 1987, pp. 125-134.

Meta Systems, Inc., *Potential for Fuelwood And Charcoal in the Energy Systems of Developing Countries*, Cambridge, Massachusetts, 1980.

Munasinghe, M., *The National Fuelwood Conservation Program (NFCP)*, Ministry of Power and Energy, Colombo, Sri Lanka, 1984.

Perera, W.R.H., "Some Thoughts on Social Agro-Forestry in Rural Sri Lanka", *Marga Quarterly Journal* (Sri Lanka), vol.8, no.1, 1985, pp.40-49.

Pushparajah, M., "Management of Forest Reserves", *Sri Lanka Forester*, vol.15, January 1981, pp. 21-24.

Soussan, J.G., "Fuelwood Strategies and Action Programs in Asia: Comparative Experience in Bangladesh, Indonesia, Nepal, Republic of Korea, Sri Lanka and Thailand", Report of a CEC-AIT Workshop (December 1984), Renewable Energy Resources Information Center (RERIC), Asian Institute of Technology, 1984.

Wijesinghe, L.C.A., "A Sample Study of Biomass Fuel Consumption in Sri Lanka Households", *Biomass*, vol.5, 1984, pp. 261-282.

Chapter 13

RURAL-INDUSTRIAL ENERGY AND FOSSIL FUEL ISSUES: THE CASE OF THAILAND[1]

13.1 Energy and the Thai Economy

This chapter contains a case study originally carried out during 1978-79, and involving Thailand -- one of the few rapidly growing developing countries of the world. Its average annual GDP growth rate was in excess of 7.5% during the last twenty years. Until now the country has been almost completely dependent on imported crude oil or refined products to meet its petroleum product requirements. Petroleum accounted for almost 75% of total energy consumption in 1979. However, the country has a number of indigenous energy resources that can be developed to reduce this dependence on imported fuels. Among them are substantial deposits of natural gas, lignite, hydro, and significant, but rapidly dwindling forest resources.

The key issues relating to this heavy energy import dependence and the policies designed to reduce it are discussed below. As will be seen, pricing policies play a prominent role. First, we examine a specific example of energy management involving fuel choices for the tobacco curing industry, which provides proof that energy users are more interested in total energy system costs and benefits than in specific fuel costs. This is followed by analyses of the economic costs of three fossil fuels: natural gas, petroleum products, and lignite. A final section summarizes some of the major changes that have occurred on the energy supply side in Thailand up to 1983 -- several years after the original work for this study was completed in 1978-79.

Thailand has a population of about 46 million people (mid-1979) and an area of 542,373 square kilometers. The largest concentration of people occurs in the Greater Bangkok area, which has a population of nearly 5 million (December 1978 estimate). Roughly 70% of the labor force is employed in agriculture, which contributed 26% of GDP in 1979, although its relative share has been declining fairly steadily. Per capita GNP was roughly US$490 in 1978, making Thailand one of the lower middle-income nations of the world.

The adult literacy ratio was estimated to be 84% in 1975. Regional differences in development are significant -- most of the manufacturing industry and much of agriculture (especially rice, cassava, and sugarcane) are concentrated in the central part of Thailand, around Bangkok and in the plains to the immediate north. The far northern and northeastern parts of the country are relatively poor.

The Thai economy has been undergoing a fairly steady structural transformation. The growth of cash cropping was followed by the development of an increasingly

---

[1] The first part of this chapter (on the Thai tobacco industry) is an edited version of a guest lecture presented at the USAID sponsored Energy Management Training Program for senior officials from developing countries, held at the Institute for Technology Policy in Development, State University of New York, Stonybrook, NY, in October 1979, and subsequently published in *Energy Systems and Policy*, vol.5, no.2, 1981, pp. 117-139 (co-author: Gunter Schramm). The second part (dealing with fossil fuel issues) is an edited extract from M. Munasinghe and G. Schramm, *Energy Economics, Demand Management and Conservation Policy*, Van Nostrand, New York, 1983, Chapter 10.

important manufacturing sector. For example, value added in manufacturing increased from 19.4% of GDP in 1975 to 22.0% by 1979. Future annual average growth rates are projected at close to 10%.

Parallel to the general structural transformation of the economy, there have been certain shifts in the relative importance of the major industrial groups, including a decline in the relative share of value added of the basic agroindustries (food processing, beverages, and tobacco), and an increase in the importance of textiles, rubber products, petroleum products and coal, and electrical machinery.

Thailand's recent economic performance has not been as good as the longer-term trends suggest. The following three items are likely to emerge as the country's major economic problems for the 1980s: (1) the balance of payments deficit, (2) inflation, and (3) the need to mobilize considerable financial resources (both foreign and domestic) in order to sustain economic growth.

The deficit of imports over exports increased from US$1.2 billion in 1977 to an estimated $3.3 billion in 1981. A key problem in the balance of payments has been the increase in oil prices. The ratio between petroleum imports and total exports fluctuated around 30% between 1975 and 1979; it was projected to rise to 44.6% in 1980 and 44.8% in 1981. Thus, oil imports were expected to become a more serious drain on scarce foreign exchange in the short run, until natural gas becomes available in 1982. However, after 1984, petroleum imports were projected to begin rising again. Petroleum consumption was forecast to total 13.9 million toe in 1981, 12.8 million toe in 1984, 14.5 million toe in 1987, and 15.3 million toe in 1990.

The country's energy situation is subject to a number of important trends and factors that require careful evaluation in the light of several potential, alternative policy options. Throughout the 1970s imported petroleum was the main source of its commercial energy supplies. In 1979 it accounted for 74.3% of total, and some 95.5% of total commercial energy consumption.

However, some major changes are expected to take place soon. Offshore natural gas is under development, and will reach Bangkok by the end of 1981. It will largely replace fuel oil now used in producing electricity. Furthermore, large lignite deposits are also being developed. Towards the latter half of the 1980s, therefore, most of the rapidly growing electric power demands will be supplied from gas and lignite-fired thermal plants, and to a lesser extent, by hydro.

Gas will also play an increasingly important role in the household, industrial and transportation sectors. Proposed natural gas based extraction plants will produce increasing amounts of LPG for household use, as a chemical feedstock, as a transportation fuel replacing gasoline, and for export.

Total investments in energy supply systems planned for the 1980s are estimated at US$6.8 billion (in 1978 dollars), an amount about equal to the country's total gross domestic investments in 1978.

Table 13.1 summarizes past trends in energy consumption. The four major categories of primary energy sources - lignite, petroleum, hydroelectricity, and non-commercial - contributed the following shares:

	1970	1975	1979
Lignite	1.9	1.9	2.2
Petroleum	65.7	70.4	74.3
Hydro[a]	2.0	2.7	1.3
Non-commercial	30.4	25.1	22.2

[a] includes net primary electricity imports, which are less than 5% of the total given for "Hydro."

Table 13.1

Internal Energy Consumption by Energy Source ('000 toe)

	1965	1970	1973	% ch.	1974	% ch.	1975	% ch.	1976	% ch.	1977	% ch.	1978	% ch.	1979
LIGNITE	45	147	137	57.66	216	0.46	217	17.05	254	53.94	117	46.15	171	101.75	345
PETROLEUM	2429	5061	8368	-2.91	8125	-0.13	8115	13.17	9192	12.18	10321	9.32	11283	4.16	11753
LPG	5	54	91	12.08	102	20.58	123	14.63	141	9.21	154	13.63	175	17.71	206
Gasoline[a]	328	789	1251	7.11	1340	9.77	1471	11.35	1638	11.17	1821	5.71	1925	0.62	1937
Kerosene	60	116	188	15.42	217	-14.19	186	42.47	265	-3.02	257	7.01	239	28.03	306
Jet Fuel	546	296	796	-19.23	643	16.95	752	2.39	770	-10.65	688	2.90	708	10.73	784
Gas/Diesel Oil	998	2083	2943	-4.18	2820	-2.95	2737	17.06	3204	8.86	3488	7.45	3748	12.35	4211
Fuel Oil	379	1331	2478	-2.22	2423	4.41	2530	10.43	2794	20.68	3372	12.69	3800	-0.11	3796
Crude Oil[b]	113	392	621	-6.61	580	-45.52	316	20.25	380	42.36	541	27.17	688	-25.49	513
PRIMARY Electricity[c]	72	152	175	28.57	225	36.0	306	6.53	326	-9.21	296	-30.41	206	-1.46	203
NONCOMMERCIAL[d]	N.A.	2343	2624	4.80	2750	5.27	2895	5.76	3062	5.78	3239	6.42	3447	1.22	3510
TOTAL	N.A.	7703	11304	0.10	11316	1.91	11533	11.28	12834	9.73	14083	7.27	15107	4.66	15811

Source: National Energy Administration of Thailand.

Notes: a Includes motor gasoline, aviation gasoline and some naptha.
        b For internal use by refineries
        c Includes net imports of electricity and hydro, except for 1979 which is only hydro.
          Net imports ranged from - 4000 toe in 1971 to 16000 toe in 1978.
        d Includes firewood, charcoal, bagasse and paddy husks.

It can be seen that petroleum consumption has become progressively more important while noncommerical energy was declining in relative importance. Energy consumption has increased an average of 5.8% per annum since 1973, with considerable fluctuations in this trend. Petroleum consumption has grown at about 6% per annum over this period (1977-79), and lignite and noncommercial energy consumption have each increased at approximately 5% per annum.

Lignite is produced domestically from three deposits: Mae Moh, Bang Pu Dum, and Li. The Mae Moh and Ban Pu Dum deposits are being mined for power generation and the Li deposits for tobacco curing. Some coal is also imported. A major expansion is underway at Mae Moh whose estimated reserves amount to as much as 650 million tons -- enough to support mine-mouth electric generating plants with capacities up to 2000 MW. Petroleum consumption increased 10-fold between 1960 and 1979, and roughly 95% of all commercial energy is petroleum based. The growth in the relative importance of petroleum vis-a-vis other commercial fuels has slowed somewhat since the 1973 oil price increases. In 1974 and 1975, the total amount of petroleum energy consumed actually declined. The shares of the major petroleum products in total petroleum energy consumption are shown in Table 13.2.

Table 13.2

Percent Distribution of Petroleum Product Consumption

	1970	1973	1975	1979
LPG	1.1	1.1	1.5	1.8
Gasoline[a]	15.6	14.9	18.1	16.5
Kerosene	2.3	2.2	2.3	2.6
Jet Fuel	5.8	9.5	9.3	6.7
Gas/Diesel Oil	41.2	35.2	33.7	35.8
Fuel Oil	26.3	29.6	31.2	32.3
Crude Oil[b]	7.7	7.4	3.9	4.4

[a] Includes motor gasoline, aviation gasoline and some naptha.
[b] For internal use by refineries.

The products which dominate the petroleum mix are gasoline, diesel, and fuel oil. Fuel oil is used principally for power generation and the gasoline and diesel mainly for transportation. Gasoline and fuel oil consumption each grew at an average rate of 7.6% per annum between 1973 and 1979, and gas/diesel oil at 6.4% per annum. The fastest growth among the oil products has been for LPG (14.6% per annum), mainly due to its low price relative to competing fuels. However, in 1979, LPG still accounted for only 1.8% of total petroleum product consumption.

Electricity consumption has risen quite rapidly over time. Table 13.3 shows absolute and percentage increases in peak power and energy generation. Between 1970 and 1979, the former grew at average annual rates of 13.0% and the latter at 14.6%. Thus, the annual system load factor gradually increased from 62% to an average of about 67%, during this same period.

Table 13.3

EGAT Generating Statistics, 1970-79

FISCAL YEAR	PEAK POWER GENERATION		ENERGY GENERATION		ANNUAL LOAD FACTOR (%)
	MW	%INCREASE	GWH	%INCREASE	
1970	748.35	17.28	4095.31	21.62	62.47
1971	872.70	16.62	4792.88	17.03	62.69
1972	1028.80	17.89	5711.15	19.16	63.37
1973	1199.30	16.57	6872.84	20.34	65.42
1974	1256.30	4.75	7258.62	5.61	65.96
1975	1406.60	11.96	8211.57	13.13	66.64
1976	1652.10	17.45	9414.48	14.65	65.05
1977	1873.40	13.40	10950.62	16.32	66.73
1978	2100.60	12.13	12371.67	12.98	67.23
1979[a]	2255.00	7.35	13964.56	12.88	70.69

[a] The 1979 load factor of over 70% was influenced by peak load restrictions.

Source: Electricity Generating Authority of Thailand (EGAT)

Table 13.4 indicates the sectoral composition of total energy consumption in Thailand for 1971 and 1977. The only significant change was the rising share of industry, and apparent declining share of all the other categories (including households). However, the latter's predominant consumption consists of traditional fuels, for which no reliable statistics exist. Therefore, statistical trends shown in Table 13.4 should be interpreted with caution.

Table 13.4

Total Energy Consumption by Sector - Percentage Shares[a]

SECTOR	1971	1977
Energy[b]	10.9	12.3
Industry	16.8	20.8
Transportation	23.2	24.5
Agriculture	6.7	6.5
Other[c]	42.4	35.9

[a] Excluding nonenergy uses.

[b] Energy consumption in energy sector is net of own use, losses and energy lost in thermodynamic conversion in power stations and refineries.

[c] Includes commerce, government, households and miscellaneous.

Source: National Energy Administration of Thailand.

The major user of petroleum products in recent years was the transport sector, followed by electricity (and water) and manufacturing. Annual average growth was most pronounced in the electricity sector with 15.2%, followed by the commercial and household sectors with 9.8%, and agriculture with 8.2%. Electricity consumption is dominated by industry with 64.1%, followed by the household sector with 20.2%, and commerce with 14.8%.

Little is known about energy consumption in sectors other than industry and transport. Because of the elimination of taxes on LPG, there has been an interfuel substitution within the transport sector. Taxicabs, in particular, are being increasingly fueled by LPG. While each of the domestic refineries has some capacity to produce LPG, much of it must be imported. LPG imports rose from 3.5 million litres in 1977 to 76.1 million litres in 1979. This still represented less than 5% of the total oil import bill, but preliminary observations indicated that the conversion rate to LPG had, if anything, accelerated in 1980. There is also an interfuel substitution occurring between gasoline and diesel, due to the availability of inexpensive diesel engines for small vehicles. Thailand has a relatively large domestic automobile assembly industry, which may enable it to be fairly responsive to change in domestic fuel costs.

13.2 Fuel Choice for a Rural Industry: Tobacco Curing

The Thai tobacco industry plays a small but regionally important role in the economy of the country. Tobacco-growing is concentrated in the four northern-most provinces, where soils and climate provide exceptionally favorable conditions. Flue-cured Thai tobaccos, particularly the Virginia leaves, are famous for their quality. Over 60 percent of total production is regularly exported, mainly to Western Europe, North America, and Japan. Demands have been particularly strong in recent years because Thai tobaccos have the lowest nicotine content in the world. Furthermore, Rhodesia (now Zimbabwe), Thailand's most important competitor was, until recently, strongly affected by the trade embargo.

While only about one-third of one percent, or somewhat less than 50,000 hectares of Thailand's agricultural land is devoted to tobacco-growing (see Table 13.5), the impact on national income, employment and export earnings are much higher. During the tobacco-growing season, about 275,000 farmers and farm workers find employment. A further 125,000 workers are required during the four-month curing season. Most of the tobacco is produced by small-scale farming units of two hectares or less.

Tobacco exports, almost all of them consisting of cured tobacco leaves, accounted for about 1.3% of total exports in recent years, while domestic tobacco product manufacturing represented somewhat more than 8% of the total value added of the manufacturing sector.

Overall, in terms of value added, employment creation, secondary (derived) industrial activities, and exports, the tobacco industry plays a far larger role relative to its use of agricultural land than any other agricultural product. Only the limited availability of suitable soils and appropriate climatic conditions prevent its further rapid expansion.

Table 13.5

The Tobacco Industry in Thailand: Some Comparative Statistics

Year	Area Planted Hectares	Area Planted as a Percentage of Total Agricultural Land	Yield (Dried) KG/HA	Total Production Tons	Total Value of Tobacco and Tobacco Products Millions U.S.$	Value of Products as a % of Total Value of MFG Output	Total Value of Tobacco Exports Million U.S.$	Tobacco Exports as a Percentage of Total Exports
1974	46,000	0.35	804	37,000	190	8.0	22.3	0.9
1975	47,000	0.34	915	43,000	230	8.8	28.4	1.3
1976	48,000	0.34	833	n.a.	250	8.3	35.0	1.2
1977	47,000	0.34	766	n.a.	300	8.3	46.2	1.3

Pricing Issues

Before analyzing the choice of fuels for tobacco curing, it is useful to review some key energy and shadow pricing issues. As described at greater length in the subsequent sections, energy prices for petroleum products, natural gas (presently under development), and electricity are government-controlled -- the former through regulated prices, the latter because the power companies are government-owned. Only locally traded woodfuels and coal are free from regulation. Thailand, fortunately, has avoided the pitfalls of heavily subsidizing petroleum prices in the wake of the 1973 OPEC price increases. However, while prior to 1973 petroleum products were heavily taxed and, thereby, made a substantial contribution to overall government revenues (about 8% of total government revenue in 1972), most of these excise taxes, except those on gasoline, were either reduced or completely eliminated, subsequently. Estimates for 1978 indicated that over 85% of all excise tax revenue on petroleum products would come from gasoline only. As a consequence, market prices for products such as low-speed diesel oil or kerosene compare favorably with those for other energy resources except lignite, as can be seen from Table 13.6. Compared to woodfuels, for example, low-speed diesel oil is somewhat less costly on a net heat content basis. Only lignite coal appears to be considerably lower-priced. The government makes no attempt to determine shadow prices for imported petroleum products and to adjust market prices accordingly.

Table 13.6

**Comparative Energy Prices,
Northern Region, Fall 1978**

Fuel	Local Price U.S.$	US$/ 10^6 kcal
Fuelwood delivered	6.00/m^3	$14.79
Lowspeed diesel	0.13/ltr	14.14
Kerosene	0.14/ltr	15.36
Lignite (from Li) delivered[a]	12.50/ton	3.11

[a] Assumes a net heat rate of 4,000 kcal per kg of (moist) coal.

Source: National Energy Administration of Thailand, and the tobacco industry.

The existence of protective barriers to trade in Thailand indicate that the local currency is over-valued -- thus foreign exchange has a scarcity value, and should be shadow priced (see Chapter 3).

If we use foreign exchange as the numeraire or unit of value, then this implies that on average, domestic market prices must be reduced by the standard conversion factor (SCF) of 0.79 (see Chapter 9), to compare these values with traded goods valued directly in terms of foreign exchange converted at the official exchange rate, i.e., for imports and exports measured at border (or international) prices. For shadow pricing the inputs used in the comparison of fuel costs, however, more specific conversion factors have to be used. Thus, using the same numeraire, the 1976-77 conversion factor for unskilled labor in the tobacco-growing northern areas was estimated at 0.32 and the lignite conversion factor was 0.52, based on the proportions of labor, capital, and transport used to produce and deliver lignite. These factors have been applied here to the market prices of the corresponding items, to measure the real economic costs of producing raw lignite coal and of using unskilled labor, respectively. The international price of diesel fuel was used directly since it is already in border prices.

While shadow prices may be used to evaluate energy decisions from a national perspective, private sector energy use decisions are being made on the basis of market prices, convenience of use, and reliability of supply. The same applies to energy users in the public sector, unless they are under direct orders to behave otherwise. Given the high real economic costs (or shadow costs) of petroleum imports, which often exceed transaction prices, constant vigilance is needed to evaluate any substantial deviation of economic from market prices that may lead to inefficient energy use decisions from a national point of view. Corrective action through changes in prices, taxes, or regulations must be taken when this occurs. The case of the Thai tobacco-curing industry provides a useful example of such differences in social and private costs.

Tobacco-Curing

The tobacco-harvesting and curing season lasts through most of the winter, from about November to the end of February. Two or three leaves are picked from each plant every five to seven days early in the season, and every ten to twelve days later on. The leaves then are brought to the curing stations, which consist of rows upon rows of two-story high frame and brick-sided curing barns. The capacity of each of these barns is about four tons of fresh leaves, which reduce to between 300 and 500 kg when cured.

Quality differentials of fresh-picked tobacco leaves are pronounced. This can be seen from the prices paid to farmers, which vary from US$0.03 (or Bhat 0.60) per kg., the legal minimum in 1978, to US$0.14 (B 2.70). The average price paid in 1978 amounted to US$0.08 (B 1.60).

Each of the barns is equipped with two simple firing boxes, which connect to concrete-lined baffles and then to large-diameter sheet metal pipes inside the barns -- the latter serving as heat exchangers. The firing boxes can accept a wide range of combustible materials. In recent years, the most important were firewood, charcoal, lignite, and low-speed diesel or fuel oil. Firewood and charcoal come from the surrounding mountain forests. However, available supplies are quite insufficient to meet the needs of the curing industry. The lignite comes from a number of open-pit mines to the south of the tobacco-growing areas. The most important source of lignite is at Li. Diesel or fuel oil is bought from local wholesalers at the government controlled price.

The major consideration in flue-curing of tobacco is temperature control. Ideally, temperatures are not allowed to increase at rates of more than one or two degrees per hour, and maximum temperatures must be carefully controlled to obtain a high quality product. The type of fuel used for the curing process has a major effect on the ease of such control. For temperature control purposes, firewood and diesel or fuel oils are far superior to lignite.

Cured leaves are hand-sorted into some 26 different grades. Grades depend in part on the original structure and size of the green leaves, but even more so on the subsequent curing process. If temperatures during the cure are too low, leaves will stay green; if they are too high, the leaves will turn brown and crinkle. Either way, they lose value. Depending on grade, export prices (in 1978) varied between US$0.50 to US$3.00 per kg (B10 to B60); the average price amounted to US$1.50.

According to industry sources, woodfuel provides the easiest temperature control, followed by diesel or fuel oil. Lignite, although it has been used extensively in recent years, is very hard to control and has a strong tendency to overheat. This affects both quantity and quality. For wood- or oil-cured tobacco, the fresh to dry leaves weight ratio is 7-8 to 1; for lignite-cured tobacco it is on average 9 to 1, a weight loss of some 15 to 20 percent compared to the former. Because the quality of the cured leaves is on average also lower, the value of the finished product from the lignite-cured shed is considerably lower; these differences may amount to between US$200 and $300 per barn load, or $0.50 to $0.75 per kg.

Use of lignite has other associated problems. Deliveries from the mine are unreliable; sometimes a truck will have to wait several hours to be loaded. The quality of the lignite supplied is poor. Only about 70 percent is useable because of excessive breakage and admixtures of clay. Stored lignite has a tendency to self-ignite, and the water content of the lignite usually is high. Because of the temperature control problem, overheating of sheds is frequent, leading to fires. In 1977-78 one curing station lost three barns due to lignite-caused fires. Because the lignite has a high sulfur content, baffles and heating ducts must be frequently renewed. With lignite as fuel, baffles usually last only one or two drying cycles before they have to be replaced.

Lignite firing also requires more personnel. One person can supervise the firing of two or, at the most, three lignite-fired kilns; with oil or diesel fuel, he or she can supervise six.

The Economics of Lignite Versus Diesel Fuel

Given all of the problems related to the use of lignite, it is not surprising that the tobacco industry is constantly looking for alternative fuels. One option offered by the government is the use of forests in remote, high mountain areas. Costs of access, cutting, and transport were found to be excessive. Another alternative under consideration is re-afforestation of overcut areas with fast-growing species, for the production of firewood or charcoal. Such schemes are under consideration, but would require a number of years for implementation and first harvest.

The only realistic short-term fuel alternatives are either lignite or some hydro-carbon fuel, because wood fuels are in increasingly short supply. Government officials in Bangkok expect the tobacco industry to expand the use of lignite greatly; they predict the use of some 300,000 to 350,000 tons annually. Such a quantity would be sufficient to cover the total energy requirements of the industry. Industry spokesmen believe otherwise, and they strongly resist government pressure to sign long-term, expanded contracts for lignite supplies. Instead, some are rapidly converting their drying barns to the use of diesel or fuel oil.

Lignite, at present prices, is by far the lowest-cost fuel (see also Table 13.6). This is clearly apparent from the data of Table 13.7, which indicate that the costs of lignite, delivered, per barn per year amount to only US$450 compared to US$1,325 for low-speed diesel fuel. However, the combined disadvantages of using lignite compared to diesel or fuel oil far outweigh the initial price advantage. Additional labor costs increase the total costs of using lignite by some US$100 per barn per year. However, the major disadvantages of using lignite are a result of the poorer quality and reduced quantity of output resulting from the use of this fuel.

Table 13.7

Fuel-Related Inputs, Outputs and Their Market and Economic Costs and Revenue in Tobacco Curing Per Barn Per Season
(1978 Costs and Prices; US$ 1.00 = B 20.00)

Item	Oil-Fired Curing Value or Cost at (US$)			Lignite-Fired Curing Value or Cost at (US$)		
	Quantity	Market Prices	Shadow-Priced[6]	Quantity	Market Prices	Shadow-Priced[6]
Uncured tobacco	37.5 tons	3,000	3,000	37.5 tons	3,000	3,000
Labor (curing only)[1]	60 man-days	72	22	144 man-days	172	52
Fuel, diesel, lignite	10,000 ltr.	1,325	1,257	30 tons	450	234
Sub-Total		4,397	4,279		3,622	3,286
Output, Cured Leaves	5.0 tons[3]	7,500[2]	6,873	4.2 tons[3]	5,250[4]	4,811
Remaining Margin[5]		3,103	2,594		1,628	1,525
Net Gain from Oil-Fired Curing		1,475	1,069		0	0

1 One laborer can handle 6 oil-fired barns simultaneously, but only 2-3 lignite fired ones; assume 8-hour days @ $US 1.20/day, 3 shifts per day, 120 days season.
2 This is the average selling price which includes sorting, packing, transportation, etc.
3 Ratio uncured/cured 7.5/1 for oil-fired and 9.0/1 for lignite-fired barns.
4 Average assumed selling price for lignite-cured tobacco is $1.25/kg ($1.50 for oil-cured).
5 The remaining margin contains a few fuel-specific costs for which no unit costs could be ascertained. Among them are costs of burners, valves, fuel tanks, or lines for oil or diesel, the costs of the concrete-lined baffles (see text), or of the coal-storage sheds.
6 The import costs of diesel ($1000) are evaluated at the border price, and the remaining $325 at the border price and the remaining $325 at the standard conversion factor (0.79). The shadow price or conversion factor for unskilled labor in northern Thailand is equal to 0.3. The lignite conversion factor is estimated to be 0.52 on the basis of labor, transportation, and capital goods inputs. The standard conversion factor of 0.79 is applied to the 40% of tobacco sold in domestic markets; the remaining 60% of exports are evaluated directly at the border price.

Source: Thai Tobacco Industry.

Overall, the value of output of an oil-fired barn in market prices amounts to an average of US$7,500; from a lignite-fired barn it is only US$5,250, a difference of US$2,250, or 30% of the value of output of the former. This differential dominates the initial cost advantage of lignite. The residual mark-up between selling price and fuel-cost related inputs plus raw tobacco is US$3,103 for oil-fired barns, but only US$1,628 for lignite-fired barns, a net difference in favor of the former of US$1,475, or 20% of the value of output.

It might be assumed that appropriate shadow pricing of the imported fuels versus the more labor-intensive lignite would substantially alter these results in favor of lignite. However, this is not the case, as can be seen from the economic data in Table 13.7. Evaluated at the appropriate shadow prices, the net advantage of oil-curing over lignite-curing is still about US$1,069, or 16% of the value of output of oil-cured tobacco. This stems from the fact that about sixty percent of the tobacco -- particularly the higher quality leaves -- is exported, and that the main difference resulting from the use of diesel oil is a large increase in the total value of output. This increase is larger than the increase in the shadow-priced economic costs of the imported diesel fuel. Hence, regardless of the magnitude of the foreign-exchange shadow coefficient, it is more efficient economically at prevailing fuel market prices to use diesel instead of lignite.

This conclusion, of course, holds only within certain fuel price limits. As import prices rise for diesel fuel, the financial as well as the economic advantage of diesel compared to lignite steadily shrinks. Assuming that all other costs and prices remain constant, the diesel import market price at which lignite is competitive with diesel is US$0.25/ltr ($39.75/bbl.) or $0.28/ltr at the pump -- a price that is 210% higher than the 13.3¢/ltr ($21.07/bbl.) used in the analysis. This translates into total fuel costs per barn per year of the $2,800, a cost sufficiently high to eliminate the advantage of the diesel. Evaluated in economic terms, the import price for diesel would have to rise to about $0.23/ltr (36.98/bbl.) until equivalence with lignite is reached. Hence, once diesel prices reach or exceed this level, policy measures such as taxes or direct fuel allocations should be introduced to force a switch to lignite, even though market prices still would favor the use of diesel fuel.

If these industry-supplied data truly reflect the average values of output and input costs, it is clear that the industry will continue to convert its curing operations from lignite to diesel or fuel oil as quickly as possible. For similar reasons it appears that, from a national economic perspective, the use of imported petroleum-based fuels is preferable to the utilization of domestic lignite, as long as their costs are below $37 per barrel and other costs remain constant in real terms.

Policy Alternatives

Other potential domestic fuel sources are wood or charcoal, crop residues, and natural gas. Wood is eminently suitable, but in short supply within a reasonable radius determined by transportation costs. Its costs on a heat-content basis are already as high as those for petroleum-based fuels (see Table 13.6). Some formerly forested land unsuitable for general agriculture is available in the region, for the establishment of forest plantations. However, even fast-growing species require at least six to eight years until harvesting can begin. In any case, it appears unlikely that sufficient land can be found to satisfy the needs of both the tobacco-curing industry and the competing and growing demands of households, commercial, and other industrial enterprises.

Experience has shown that locally available crop residues, mainly rice straw, are not suitable for tobacco-drying, because of handling and temperature control problems. Natural gas cannot be brought into the area because pipeline costs from Bangkok would be prohibitive. Shipping uncured leaves to the pipeline terminals near Bangkok would be equally impractical because of added transportation costs, product deterioration in transit, the need for constructing completely new drying facilities on high-priced land near Bangkok, and the difficulty of getting skilled temporary labor to cure and sort the uncured tobacco leaves.

This leaves the seemingly qualitatively and economically inferior lignite as the only major alternative fuel source. However, the conclusions derived earlier about lignite's various disadvantages apply only because, as utilized at present, it is a low-quality, unreliable and difficult to manage fuel. But lignite does not have to be utilized as mined. Technological methods to upgrade raw lignite into a more uniform product are well known and have been in use in other countries for many decades. These upgrading methods usually consist of washing, cleaning, drying, milling, and briquetting. The resulting product (in the form of briquettes), is of uniform quality, allows controlled burning, and is widely used by industry and households in lignite-rich countries. Although once disdained as an inferior fuel when fuel oil prices were $3 to $4 a barrel, lignite briquettes look attractive for many uses, when compared with oil at $20 to $40 a barrel.

Lignite briquettes of uniform quality and size would overcome the major objections against lignite use for tobacco-drying ie., the lack of control over the burning rate and, hence, the rate of temperature increase. Transport, storage, and handling costs for briquettes would be higher than for diesel or fuel oil, but these differences are minor compared with the cost differential between lignite and petroleum-based fuels on a heat content basis.

Conversion of lignite into briquettes would increase the costs of the fuel. In 1978, a small-sized briquetting plant based on the Li deposit was under construction, with a target production date of summer 1979 (Derek Industry of Synthetic Coal Co., Ltd). Its design capacity was 12,000 tons of briquettes per year, destined mainly for an acetylene plant and other local users. Total capital costs of the plant were estimated at US$750,000 and projected sales prices for the briquettes were $70 per ton.

West German manufacturing sources of briquetting plants estimate that the total installed costs of a highly mechanized plant at Li, for an annual capacity of some 500,000 tons, would amount to about US$103 million. Assuming a life expectancy of 30 years, capital cost charges for such a plant would be $24/ton at a real opportunity cost of 11%, and $62/ton at a market discount rate of 30%. For such a highly automated plant, labor requirements would be only 30 men per shift.

These somewhat sketchy cost estimates nevertheless indicate that lignite briquettes are likely to be a competitive fuel for the tobacco-curing industry. This can be seen from the data in Table 13.8, which estimate a range of briquette prices that would make them cost-equivalent with diesel fuels in real economic terms. The main assumption underlying the analysis is that lignite briquettes, because of their uniform quality, would provide the same controllability of barn temperature changes as do wood or petroleum fuels at present. Two diesel fuel prices were assumed. The first, of US$20 per barrel, represents the delivered, shadow-priced 1978 fuel costs as used in Table 13.7. The second, of $32 per barrel, approximates the average 1979 world market price. Several ranges of potential lignite briquette requirements were used. At present, average raw lignite briquettes would have a higher heat rate per unit of weight because they would be free from impurities and moisture, and have superior burning characteristics. On a comparative heat content basis, 10,000 liters of diesel fuel are equivalent to 15 tons of dried and clean lignite from the Li deposit (6,200 kcal/kg dry). However, the burning efficiency of briquettes may be somewhat lower than those of diesel fuel burners that blow the generated combustion gases directly into the heat-exchanger pipes. How much lower this thermal efficiency would be can only be established through field trials. Such data are not available at present; hence, three ranges of briquette requirements per barn per year have been shown: 15 tons, 20 tons, and 25 tons.

Table 13.8

Briquette Prices per Ton That Make Them Cost-Equivalent To Diesel Fuels in Economic Terms[a]

Delivered Diesel Price[b]	Quantity of Briquettes Required, per Barn, per Season (Tons)	Max. Allowable Economic Cost per Ton Delivered in Border Prices (Dollars)	Equivalent Market Price with Conv. Factor of 0.803[c] (Dollars)
$20/bbl. =	15	81.80	101.87
$12.57/ltr.	20	61.35	76.40
	25	49.08	61.12
$32/bbl. =	15	131.20	163.39
$20.08/ltr.	20	98.40	122.54
	25	78.72	98.03

[a] For underlying data see Table 13.7.
[b] Includes $3.25/ltr. (shadow-priced $2.57/ltr.) for domestic handling and delivery charges.
[c] Based on 80% cost share of manufacturing at a shadow-price of $0.86, 10% transport at $0.63, and 10% mining at $0.52.

At diesel costs of US$20/bbl., maximum allowable delivered briquette costs per ton in terms of border prices range from $49, if 25 tons are needed, to $82, if 15 tons suffice. In equivalent market prices they range from $61 to $102 per ton. At diesel prices of $32/bbl., which are more in line with post-1979 world market price levels, briquette costs per ton can range from $78 to $131 in border prices, and from $98 to $163 in market prices. At their lower bound these equivalent market prices are lower than the quoted market price of $70 of Derek Industry. However, a larger briquetting plant is likely to be more efficient so that, even in this extreme case, the briquettes are likely to be the more efficient alternative in both economic and financial terms. At all other prices, briquettes are clearly less costly than diesel fuel in economic terms. From a national point of view, therefore, every effort should be made to promote the use of lignite briquettes for tobacco-curing.

Unfortunately, the issue is not quite so clear-cut when the analysis is done strictly in financial terms, on the basis of market prices. Clearly, the results of the financial rather than the economic analysis will determine actual industry behavior, unless the government deliberately intervenes in the industry's decision process. Table 13.9 repeats the analysis of Table 13.8, in financial terms. At prevailing 1978 diesel fuel prices, maximum delivered briquette costs must be as low as US$53/ton if as much as 25 tons per barn per season are needed, or $88/ton, if 15 tons are found to be sufficient. The lower limit is below the quoted price of $70/ton from Derek Industries, the only existing briquette producer at present. At average 1979 diesel fuel prices of $33/bbl., however, the allowable briquette price range is more attractive -- from $83/ton for 25 tons per barn to $138 for 15 tons per barn -- substantially above the $70/ton Derek Industry price. Hence, if 1979 petroleum product world market prices prevail, and if domestic prices for lignite briquettes do not rise substantially relative to prevailing prices, briquettes are likely to be the more attractive fuel in strictly financial terms as well. This would obviously make it much easier for the government to persuade the tobacco-curing industry to switch to lignite briquettes; provided of course, that the technical assumptions about their suitability can be proved and that the needed investment capital and know-how for the production of qualitatively acceptable lignite briquettes can be found.

Table 13.9

**Briquette Prices per Ton That Make Them Cost-Equivalent
To Diesel Fuels in Terms of Market Prices[a]**

Delivered Diesel Price	Quantity of Briquettes Required, per Barn, per Season (Tons)	Maximum Allowable Cost per Ton Delivered (Dollars)
$21/bbl. = $13.25/ltr.	15	88.33
	20	66.25
	25	53.00
$33/bbl. = $20.76/ltr.	15	138.40
	20	103.80
	25	83.04

[a] Data based on Tables 13.7 and 13.8.

With an estimated demand by the tobacco-curing industry alone of between 120,000-200,000 tons of briquettes per year, this would result in a new industry with a value of output of some US$8 to $14 million. It would increase local employment, provide an opportunity for other users of heating energy to tap a new source of supply, reduce pressure on dwindling supplies of firewood and charcoal, and best of all, decrease dependence on hydro-carbon imports by approximately US$14-16 million per year.

For the Thai economy, this specific use of the lignite deposit at Li would mean that for a period of over 30 years a locally-produced energy product would replace $14 to $16 million of hydro-carbon imports per year. The present value equivalent of this switch-over would be between $122 and $139 million, evaluated at an estimated 11% opportunity cost of capital for Thailand. Considering that the foreign exchange costs of starting a briquetting plant to serve the needs of the tobacco-curing industry is likely to be in the $10 to $15 million range, this appears to be a worthwhile investment, indeed.

13.3 Natural Gas Costs and Pricing

Some time ago natural gas was discovered in the Gulf of Thailand. Overall reserves in early 1981 were estimated at more than 7 trillion cubic feet (TCF). The gas was found in two separate deposits, one explored by Union Oil Company, the other by Texas Pacific. Several other potential deposits were located but not explored at that time. The government has committed itself, through its fully-owned Natural Gas Organization of Thailand (NGOT), to build a gas pipeline from the nearest of those deposits owned by Union Oil to markets in and around Greater Bangkok. Negotiations with the owners of the second field, Texas Pacific, about delivery schedules, prices, and quantities, still had not been concluded by early 1982.

Under the terms of Union Oil's contract with the government, field prices started at a level of US $1.30 per million btu for the first 75 million cubic feet per day (MMCFD) and declined to a minimum of $0.67 for the last incremental block of an overall maximum total of 250 MMCFD that is to be supplied under the contract. At a delivery rate of 250 MMCFD, the average 1976 price amounted to US $1.05 per million BTU. However, prices were subject to various price escalator clauses so that current prices are higher. In early 1982, wellhead prices had increased to $2.20/MCF. Because 40% of the gas price is tied to Singapore fuel oil spot prices, overall gas prices could conceivably decline if fuel oil prices decrease.

The pipeline from the Union field was completed on time and delivered some 100 MMCFD of gas to Bangkok by early 1982. Projected gas utilization rates are shown in Table 13.10. About 90% of the projected demand was expected from EGAT-owned electric power generating stations. These were the existing, oil-fired generating plants at South Bangkok with an installed capacity of 1300 MW, and the Bang Pakong generating units 60 miles east of Bangkok, then under construction. The latter will reach a total capacity of 1,270 MW by 1983. Together, these plants were estimated to consume some 415 MMCFD by 1983, at an average heat rate of 9800 btu/kWh net of station use, and a heat value of 1 million btu/MCF of gas. An additional, 550 MW gas-fired thermal unit was planned for completion at Bang Pakong by 1984. This unit was projected to account for another 131 MMCFD of gas consumption, resulting in an overall demand of about 500 MMCFD of gas for electric power generation.

Projected industrial, commercial, and other natural gas uses were minor, by comparison. They were projected to be no more than 29 MMCFD in 1981, rising to 84 MMCFD by 1995. However, industrial demand could increase substantially if Thailand decides to proceed with a petrochemical complex based on natural gas as feedstock.

As described in Chapter 3, the economically efficient price for a fuel should reflect its marginal opportunity costs. In the following sections, we analyze three alternatives to help determine an appropriate economic pricing policy based on the marginal supply cost, the current replacement cost, and the future opportunity cost of natural gas. Clearly, the ultimate pricing policy will have to reflect other key social and political constraints also, but the scope of this study does not permit such detailed analysis.

Table 13.10

Natural Gas Supply/Demand 1981-1990 in MMSCFD (1000 btu/cf)

DEMAND/ SUPPLY Year	1981	1982	1983	1984	1985	1986	1987	1988	1989	1990
Electric sector demand	245	311	429	547	547	572	572	572	572	598
Industrial demand	26	29	32	35	39	41	44	46	47	48
Total gas demand	271	340	461	582	586	613	616	618	619	644
Total Union Oil and Texas Pacific gas supply	158	276	329	420	459	511	563	563	563	563
Supply/demand balance (deficit)	(113)	(64)	(132)	(162)	(127)	(102)	(53)	(55)	(56)	(81)

Source: NGOT

The Economic Supply Costs of Gas

The following cost categories should be considered in the evaluation of the marginal economic costs of natural gas: (1) The (foreign exchange) wellhead price paid to the drilling company, net of royalties; (2) the operation and maintenance (O&M) costs for each field; (3) the investment and O&M costs of the pipeline network needed to bring the gas to markets; (4) the investment costs needed to modify existing installations for use of gas instead of alternative fuels; and (5) the net differentials in operating costs, including differentials in fuel-use efficiencies resulting from the use of gas instead of other fuels.

Because of the possibility of developing the overall project in three distinct steps -- the pipeline to the Union Oil field, the interconnection to Texas Pacific, and, finally, the installation of additional compressors to boost pipeline capacity -- the marginal costs of each of these steps must be evaluated separately.

To Thailand, the immediate economic costs of on-site field developments are zero, because they are being financed by foreign-owned corporations out of their own funds. However, these companies expect to be compensated for their present investments through the flow of future dividend and interest payments, as well as depreciation charges only. These future flows of foreign exchange funds out of the country represent the true economic costs to Thailand, excluding retained earnings or depreciation charges reinvested in Thailand. They should be appropriately discounted to the present, and counted as part of the marginal economic costs of each project increment. The projected O&M costs of the fields should be appropriately shadow-priced (for the use of domestic resources) and these costs included in the present value of overall marginal costs.

The estimated financial costs of pipeline investment are about $575 million, consisting of US$395 million for the Union Oil connection, and US$180 million for the extension to the Texas Pacific Field (including initial compressor stations). Foreign exchange costs amount to about 75% of this total. If we apply the standard conversion factor of 0.79 to the remaining 25% (or $145 million equivalent) for domestic expenditures, the (border) shadow-priced real economic local costs are about U.S. $115 million. Therefore, the shadow priced total economic costs are about $545 million, which is quite close to the financial costs ($575 million). For convenience, we present the following results on gas transport costs in financial terms. The corresponding border priced economic costs are about 5% lower.

The underwater pipeline connecting Union Oil with the coastal terminal and overland route has been designed with a diameter sufficient for a total throughput of over 700 MMSCFD (34" diameter to the shore and smaller from then onwards, and with additional booster compressors). This specification anticipates the hookup with the Texas Pacific Field and the possible expansion of output.

It may be argued that the appropriate cost comparison should be based on a smaller diameter, less costly line, sufficient only to transport the projected 250 MMSCFD from the Union Oil field. This argument must be rejected because the average transportation costs of $0.52/MCF in such a smaller line would be higher than in a combined one. The average costs of a separate, 250 MMSCFD line from the Texas Pacific field would be U.S.$0.71/MCF. The combined line now proposed, with a total throughput of 500 MMSCFD, would result in average capital cost charges of U.S.$0.48/MCF, instead. Since an economically justifiable market for 500 MMSCFD is readily available, the combined line is preferable to two separate ones.

The average capital cost charges for the 250 MMSCFD supply from the Union Oil field alone using the larger capacity combined line, will amount to $0.65/MCF. The marginal additional cost for the extension to the Texas Pacific field would result in average capital charges of U.S.$0.31/MCF, assuming recoverable reserves of each field were equal to 1.5 TCF, 17 year life, 12% interest. In order to be cost equivalent to the joint line, the capital cost of the separate Union Oil line would have to be less than U.S. $310 million. In addition, the capital costs for increasing the capacity of the Union Oil field section to accommodate the Texas Pacific gas is about US$60 million or US$9.3/MCF at an average throughput rate of 250 MMSCFD from Texas Pacific. (Operating costs for the Texas Pacific field will be higher than for the Union Oil field because of the higher content of carbon dioxide and the need for pressurizing the gas). However, the doubling of throughput rates of the from Union Oil's field to markets would reduce the charges for the latter from $0.65/MCF, to the combined average of US$0.48/MCF for the pipeline system as a whole. If the Texas Pacific field's reserves actually amount to 3.5 TCF instead of 1.5 TCF as assumed in this analysis, the average financial pipeline capital cost charges would be reduced to US$0.43 per MCF.

As explained earlier, if we apply the standard conversion factor (0.79) to the 25% component of domestic capital expenditures, the average border priced economic capital cost charges for the proposed combined pipeline network would be US$0.456 per MMSCFD (or 95% of the financial cost of US$0.48) at a throughput of 500 MMSCFD and a total combined reserve of 3 TCF. If the total reserve was 5 TCF at an average daily throughput of 500 MMSCFD, (assuming an economic life of 28 years), economic costs would fall to US$0.407.

To arrive at the net delivered costs of the gas to customers, the costs of equipment conversion from fuel oil (or other, displaced fuel sources) to natural gas, must be added to the financial and economic costs of the gas. In the case of the South Bangkok power plant, for example, the capital conversion costs have been estimated at US$20 million. Given the projected gas utilization rate of this plant (an average of 257.9 MMSCFD for a 17 year period), these additional capital cost charges would amount to about US$0.03 per MSCF in financial, and US$0.029 in economic terms.

Another cost item which has to be added, arises from the reduction in the net output efficiency of the various powerplants and boilers when gas is used instead of fuel oil. These net reductions in output, for the electric powerplants, have been estimated to amount to 17.5% for the South Bangkok installations (units 1 and 2) of about 400 MW capacity. The time period over which these reductions are maintained is uncertain and will depend on the quantity of gas available for power generation. On a throughput of 500 MMSCFD, this loss of capacity is likely to be relevant for two years only.

While the overall analysis, so far, has been based on the assumption of constant real costs, it is likely that the relative costs of imported fuel oil and of the natural gas supplied from the Union Oil-Texas Pacific fields will diverge. Given the uncertainties surrounding future world market fuel oil demand/supply relationships, it is impossible to say whether fuel oil prices, in real terms, will increase or decrease. If they were to rise, then the real economic value of the natural gas would also rise, while its financial costs would decline in relative terms. This is so because the long-term price escalator clauses of the Union Oil supply contract (assumed to be duplicated in the Texas Pacific contract) depend only 40% on the world market price of fuel oil. The specific price escalator clauses of the Union oil contract are more complex and contain specific ceiling and floor price levels, and are weighted according to domestic, foreign exchange, and fuel oil price changes. Everything else remaining equal (i.e., no feedback effects of fuel oil price changes on the other relative prices that form part of the price escalator formulas), this means that for each percentage point increase in fuel oil prices, the gross field costs of gas increase by only 0.4%.

Of course, the opposite would be true if the world market price for fuel oil falls, since the fuel oil escalator price is tied to ex-refinery Singapore prices. However, the downward risk in economic terms is much lower than the upward one, because the economic cost of the gas is significantly lower than that of the oil. This means that gas would still remain the preferred fuel, even if fuel oil prices were to drop significantly below present levels. Hence, it can be concluded that, overall, the contractual terms of the price escalator clauses of the gas supply contract provide some potentially significant additional economic benefits to Thailand, that could be reaped without harming the gas field operators. On the contrary, the latter would make a windfall gain before taxes of some 40%, if fuel prices increase.

The Value of Natural Gas as Measured by Its Current Replacement Costs

The maximum economic value of the gas use in the two EGAT powerplants and in most industrial uses, is determined by the economic costs of the fuel oil that it replaces. For the time being, these uses cover some 95% of total projected gas utilization, so that the few other uses can be disregarded. However, for the second 550 MW Bang Pakong thermal powerplant (planned for completion in 1984), the relevant value may well be determined by the delivered cost of electricity from an alternative coal-fired powerplant at Mae Moh, because of the possibly lower costs of the latter compared to a fuel oil-fired powerplant.

The economic costs of the displaced fuel oil consist of the sum of the C.I.F. costs of imported fuel oil, plus domestic storage and delivery costs. Costs of imported fuel oil, in 1977, amounted to an average of B 1.63 litre (at the official exchange rate of US$1.00 = Baht 20.00.) Average fuel oil costs to EGAT for the South Bangkok plant were somewhat lower, amounting to B 1.58 in 1978. However, this was the result of the availability of lower-priced fuel oil from the price-controlled, domestic refineries. Delivery costs were quite small, amounting to between B 0.02 to 0.04 or an average of about, say, B 0.03/litre. Expressed in 1977 prices, this represented a total economic cost of B 1.66 per litre, or B 0.432 per kWh of electricity produced at an estimated consumption of 0.26 litres per kWh. By early 1979, actual costs had risen to about B 1.75/litre, or B 0.455 per kWh.

Imported fuel oil prices, rather than imported crude oil prices plus domestic refining costs, were the relevant measure of the economic costs, because Thailand had been a net importer of fuel oil in recent years. These imports were rising rapidly. Without additional refinery capacity, the availability of natural gas after 1981 was projected to reduce net imports of fuel oil for only one or two years. By 1984, total fuel oil demands were forecast to exceed existing domestic refining capacity once more.

Because Thailand is a price taker with respect to petroleum imports, future rather than current relative fuel oil prices (i.e., after adjustment for general inflation) should be used in estimating the economic costs of fuel oil compared to natural gas. Such prices are difficult to predict. However, one important aspect of this unpredictability is the degree of uncertainty or risk associated with importing such a vital ingredient of national productive activity. This type of uncertainty is absent in the case of domestic natural gas supplies (or all other alternative domestic energy sources such as lignite, for example). Therefore a special risk premium ought to be added to the estimated economic costs of imported fuel oil. Such risks premiums are quite commonly paid, directly or indirectly, by the main oil importing countries. (Examples are the elaborate and costly strategic oil reserve programs in the USA and various European countries, or the subsidized gasohol program in Brazil). However, while the basis for applying such a risk premium is quite rational, establishing its appropriate magnitude is a rather difficult undertaking. In one way or another, its value should be related to the potential net losses the national economy might suffer if prices rise suddenly, or if supplies are interrupted or reduced. Here, it is not possible to explore and discuss the many difficult issues that would have to be addressed in order to come up with such firmed-up estimates. However, a 10 to 15% premium appears to be reasonable, given the experiences of 1973/74 and 1979/80. Including such a risk premium of 10%, the economic cost of imported fuel oil is estimated to be B 1.93 per liter or 0.501 per kWh of electricity, on the basis of early 1979 prices.

The financial cost of imported fuel oil will be almost equivalent to the economic one (except for the risk premium) because of the use of the foreign exchange border price as the numeraire in the shadow pricing of imports, and the insignificance of domestic delivery costs.

Beyond 1983, it is possible that the appropriate marginal economic replacement costs of additional natural gas supplies used in the production of electricity may be represented by the prorated, appropriately shadow priced costs of electricity produced by new coal-fired, mine-mouth power plants at Mae Moh. Alternatively, there may still be other, not yet well-explored, coal deposits in the country, or there may be additional hydropower sites whose costs may make them appropriate candidates for estimating the maximum economic value of additional gas supplies. However, too little is known about these potential resources and their costs to use them for evaluation purposes here. It has been estimated that up to 2000 MW of thermal power generating capacity could be developed at Mae Moh. However, since 525 MW are already programmed for development at Mae Moh in any case, only about 1500 MW of potential capacity could be looked upon as an alternative to further natural gas utilization beyond 1983. At a 70% load factor, these 1500 MW of coal-fired capacity could replace about 245 MMCFD of natural gas.

The comparison of the real economic cost differential between additional natural gas or alternative coal utilization for electricity production, has to be analyzed in terms of delivered electricity costs per kWh, because of the differences in generating plant and transmission line investment costs, and the differences in O&M and fuel costs between natural gas and coal-fired powerplants. Coal-fired plants are more costly in terms of generating plant and additional transmission line investment and O&M costs, although they may have a substantial advantage in terms of delivered fuel costs on a btu basis.

The only other presently foreseeable alternative use of natural gas is in industrial applications -- as a fuelstock for chemicals, fertilizers, plastic, etc. On the basis of the rather high negotiated average prices per unit of gas from the Union Oil field, prospects for establishing such industries in Thailand are not great because of the relatively small domestic markets for end products (and consequent diseconomies of scale in the size of conversion plants), the inability to compete in export markets, and the likely availability (at relatively low prices) of such basic chemical feedstocks on the world market in the future.

The Future Economic Opportunity Cost of Natural Gas

The maximum economic value of the gas for use in the existing or committed EGAT power plants (that depend on the use of either oil or natural gas), as well as in most industrial uses, is determined by the economic costs of the fuel oil that it will replace. However, for the future (so far not committed) powerplants, the relevant value of the gas would be determined by the delivered cost of electricity from alternative coal-fired powerplants at tidewater, lignite-fired plants elsewhere in the country, or even one of the potential, large hydroplants along Thailand's borders. Judging by recent price trends for petroleum products, any one of those other alternatives is likely to deliver electricity at lower cost than fuel oil-fired powerplants. Hence, the present and estimated future oil price sets the maximum ceiling for the value of gas only for those plants that must use fuel oil over their economic lifespan, if natural gas is unavailable.

The second type of opportunity cost is given by the value of the gas in its next best future alternative use. These alternative domestic uses are limited. Sufficiently large markets simply do not exist to absorb the much larger proportion of the gas presently not allocated to EGAT's powerplants.

Therefore, the only other alternative would consist of exports. However, export markets (basically LNG, ammonia-urea or methanol gas derivatives) do not appear to be too attractive because of the substantial competition from other, lower-cost gas producers elsewhere, and the gas conversion costs. An LNG system for shipment to Japan, for example, may cost $2.50 to $3.00 per MCF. With landed gas prices in Japan of $4.50 to $5.00, the net-back to Thailand would be about $1.50 to $2.50, which is barely sufficient to cover the costs of production and shipment to a hypothetical liquification plant.

Hence, the domestic use of natural gas as a replacement for fuel oil appears to represent its highest foreseeable value. However, this does not mean that gas prices charged to users should be set equal to the present and future costs of fuel oil. The true present value of the gas should reflect its discounted future replacement cost, i.e., the cost of replacing it when the available deposit has been exhausted, or when other, high value uses start exceeding available supply (see Chapter 3).

To establish the present value equivalent of this future opportunity cost requires detailed information about future consumption needs, rates of use over time, prices, and costs of required infrastructure (additional pipelines, processing facilities, etc.). This information is not available. However, following the gas utilization projections for gas deliveries to EGAT after 1989, the user cost of the gas could be represented by the difference between the delivered future price of fuel oil and the future marginal costs of producing and delivering the gas over time, discounted to the present.

Thus assuming that the best alternative for additional gas utilization would consist of new domestic demands starting in 1990 which would have to use fuel oil instead, and that the real fuel oil prices would increase by 3% per year up to 1990, the gas depletion premium that must be charged in 1981 is $1.52/MCF. To this must be added the real costs of producing the gas, processing, and transporting -- assumed to be $2.45/MCF -- resulting in a total economic opportunity cost of $3.97/MCF in 1981. This price must be increased in real terms by 8% per year thereafter, in order to reflect the opportunity cost capital of 8%. In addition, of course, nominal prices must be adjusted to reflect purely inflationary cost increases.

If large additional gas deposits were to be discovered and no new economically equivalent or more valuable uses could be found for them, the depletion time horizon would be pushed back and the resulting depletion premium would decline (see Section 13.6). If additional gas uses were to be found without additions to known reserves, the depletion premium would have to be increased. This means that the prices and costs should be continuously reevaluated over time in the light of changing circumstances.

13.4 Petroleum Product Pricing

Traditionally, ex-refinery petroleum product prices have been determined by accounting costs because the various refinery products have joint production costs. Setting prices for individual products always involves a certain degree of arbitrariness. Depending on either willingness to pay principles (inelastic demand schedules) or other economic or social considerations, prices for some products may be increased, thus implicitly subsidizing others. In order to provide a flavour of the complexity and political sensitivity of oil product pricing, and the unpredictable dynamics of price changes, we first trace the evolution of these prices in Thailand during the 1970's.

Prior to the oil price escalation of 1973, oil products were subject to substantial excise taxes which ranged from 120 to 150% for gasoline, 60 to over 80 percent for jet fuels, and about 50 to 80 percent for kerosene and LPG respectively. For diesel oils, tax rates were much lower at about 24 percent, and for fuel oils, as low as 11 percent. Municipal and business taxes added another 13-14 percent to gasoline costs, 3-11 percent to jet fuel, 3-7 percent to kerosene and LPG, 7 percent to diesel fuels, and a modest 2 percent to fuel oils. In that period, petroleum excise and municipal taxes represented a significant amount of total government revenues -- for example, in 1970 they accounted for 8.6 percent of total revenues and for 1.2 percent of GDP. In terms of the value of petroleum imports, central government excise taxes alone amounted to almost 84 percent of import costs.

These relationships between product prices and taxes changed rather significantly in the post-1973 period. While ex-refinery prices were allowed to rise to reflect the higher market costs of crude oil, excise taxes were initially held constant in absolute terms, except for a relatively modest increase in gasoline taxes from 0.80 to 1.00 per litre. Municipal taxes were increased for all products in absolute amounts, but their share relative to ex-refinery prices fell for all but a few. Subsequently, most excise taxes were actually reduced. These adjustments represented an attempt by the Government to reduce the overall impact of the oil price increases on the economy. Excise taxes for LPG and fuel oil were all but eliminated. For jet fuels, they were reduced from the former B 0.33 per litre to 0.12 in 1977. For diesel fuels, taxes were raised slightly from B 0.12 to 0.14 per litre. Gasoline taxes were increased from B 1.00 to 1.10 per litre in September 1977, and to B 1.83 in March 1978. This increased gasoline taxes to about 75 and 84 percent of (1977) ex-refinery prices for premium and standard, respectively. However, these rates were still substantially lower than the 119 and 152 percent prevailing in pre-1973 days.

Three more price and tax changes were made in 1978 and 1979 (see Table 13.11). By July 1979, most ex-refinery product prices had risen by between 50 to 70 percent over 1977 levels, and excise tax rates had been increased to about 86 percent for gasoline, 12-13 percent for jet fuels, and to around 21 percent for middle distillates. LPG, previously untaxed, also faced a modest 8 percent tax. Only fuel oil remained essentially tax free. Municipal taxes were reduced to one percent of excise taxes.

The large world market price increases in late 1979 forced the Government once again to consider substantial price increases. Average crude oil prices had increased from $13.29/bbl in 1978 to $21.89/bbl by December 1979, an increase of 65 percent, while imported fuel oil had increased by as much as 89 percent. The Government, which had had to rescind an attempted price increase in electricity tariffs of some 56 percent in November 1979, had to pay heavy subsidies to EGAT because of the high fuel oil costs. Once again in February 1980, it attempted to raise petroleum product prices at the retail level, by 24-51%. At the same time the Government increased electricity tariffs by 38%. These increases met with overwhelming opposition in the National Assembly and among the public, and as a consequence, the Government was forced to resign.

The attempted petroleum price increases of February 1980 would have increased gasoline and other petroleum products prices to such an extent that the Petroleum Authority (PTT) could have placed about 20% of its revenues in the Oil Compensation Fund, which is used to cross-subsidize the power sector's fuel and diesel fuel consumption. In view of the political costs of the previous Government's energy pricing policies, it is not surprising that the new Thai government promptly reduced the announced retail prices of kerosene, diesel, and bottled gas in March 1980, by between 12-15% (see Table 13.11). This in turn reduced the revenues of the Oil Compensation Fund. For the balance of 1980, the government pledged to avoid further price increases.

One fundamental change was introduced in the excise tax system in 1979. Until 1978, taxes were levied in specified amounts per unit of product. Instead, this was changed in 1979 to a percentage tax on the retail value. Therefore, any increase in basic retail prices automatically increased tax revenues as well. Tax rates levied on retail prices as of July 1979 were 41% on gasoline, 15% on kerosene and diesel fuels, and 5% on all other products. For fuel oil the rate remained fixed at B 0.01 per litre and for jet fuel at B 0.30 per litre. The municipal tax for all products was set at 1% of the total excise tax revenues.

Table 13.11

Maximum Retail Price of Petroleum Products in the Municipality of Bangkok (Baht per Unit)

PETROLEUM PRODUCT	UNIT	1978 Mar 10	1979 Jan 31	1979 Mar 22	1979 Jul 13	1979 Jul 20	1980 Feb 9	1980 Mar 19
Premium gasoline	litre	4.98	5.60	nc	7.84	nc	9.80	nc
Regular gasoline	litre	4.69	5.12	nc	7.45	nc	9.26	"
Kerosene	litre	2.68	3.06	nc	5.12	4.20	6.71	5.70
High-speed diesel	litre	2.64	3.03	nc	4.88	nc	7.39	6.54
Low-speed diesel	litre	2.50	2.93	nc	4.71	nc	7.12	6.27
Fuel oil								
600 second	litre	1.66	1.86	1.90	3.04	nc	3.78	nc
1200 second	litre	1.62	1.79	1.83	2.93	nc	3.64	nc
1500 second	litre	1.61	1.77	1.81	2.90	nc	3.61	nc
LPG								
Size 12 kg	12 kg	66	nc	nc	100	90.0	132.5	114.5
" 14.5 kg	14.5 kg	79	nc	nc	121	108.9	160.0	138.0
" 15 kg	15 kg	82	nc	nc	125	112.5	165.5	143.0
" 25 kg	25 kg	123	nc	nc	193	173.7	261.75	225.0
" 45 kg	45 kg	221	nc	nc	348	313.2	471.25	405.0
" 50 kg	50 kg	245	nc	nc	386	347.2	523.5	450.0

Note: nc = no change

As can be seen from Table 13.12, excise taxes and customs duties on petroleum products which had amounted to 1.2% of GDP and 8.6 percent of total Government revenue in 1970 had fallen to 0.8 percent and 6.2 percent respectively, by 1976, owing to the Government's attempts to protect the economy from the effects of the higher world market price. The gradual but systematic increase in tax rates since then has finally brought about a significant reversal of these trends. In 1980, applying the new March 1979 prices and tax rates to NEA's projected total consumption for the year, excise taxes amounted to approximately 2.4 percent of estimated GDP, or double its share of GDP in 1970.

Suggested Economic Principles for Pricing Petroleum Products

The following four major factors must be taken into account to estimate the real economic, (as opposed to the financial), costs of petroleum products: (1) the shadow price for foreign exchange; (2) the shadow price for labour; (3) the effects of externalities; and (4) the derived effects (both costs and benefits) of petroleum product uses.

Table 13.12

Petroleum Product Excise Tax Plus Import Taxes as a Percentage of Total Tax Revenue and Total Petroleum Imports (in million Bahts) for Selected Years 1970–80

CATEGORY	1970 B	1970 %	1972 B	1972 %	1974 B	1974 %	1976 B	1976 %	1977 B	1977 %	1980[2] B	1980[2] %
Petroleum excise taxes[1]	1,066		1,382		2,496		2,207		3,080		15,929	
Petroleum import duties[1]	544		282		529		425		406			
Total taxes on pet. products	1,610	100.0	1,664	100.0	3,025	100.0	2,632	100.0	3,486	100.0	15,929	100.0
GDP	136,100	1.2	164,600	1.0	269,700	1.1	332,200	0.8	370,400	0.9	652,500	2.4
Total govt revenue	18,721	8.6	21,144	7.9	37,929	8.0	42,203	6.2	52,681	6.6	n.a.	---
Net value of petroleum imports	1,929	83.5	2,797	59.4	11,903	25.4	16,247	16.2	19,913	17.5	n.a.	---
Govt expenditures on highways	11,500	14.0	11,700	14.2	8,400	36.0	8,800	29.9	9,000	34.7	n.a.	---

Source: World Bank, Report No. 2059-Th, NEA

[1] Petroleum import duties are levied at the same rates as excise tax
[2] Based on NEA 1980 consumption estimates and tax rates of March 19, 1980. GDP estimated at 15.6% above 1979 in current prices.

As summarized in Section 13.2, the standard conversion factor is 0.79. This means that the shadow price for foreign exchange is 127 percent of the official exchange rate (or $1/0.79$ times greater). Thus on average, petroleum product imports should be priced in Bahts at a premium of 27 percent over their actual foreign exchange costs, in order to reflect the opportunity costs of foreign exchange. Also, all future interest, dividend and depreciation payments in foreign exchange made to foreign lenders and shareholders of petroleum production and distribution facilities should be evaluated at 127 percent of their actual Baht accounting values, to the extent that they are remitted abroad.

The net economic employment effects of petroleum use are difficult to evaluate. They are positive because petroleum importation, refining, distribution, and consumption, create jobs for people that may otherwise remain under- or un-employed. For these jobs, shadow wage rates below market prices are appropriate. On the other hand, the petroleum sector also draws on individuals with technical and managerial skills that are probably in short supply in Thailand, and who therefore, have foregone opportunity costs that are higher than their market wage rates. A premium above their wages, reflecting the net productivity of skilled labour in alternative employment, should be added to reflect this scarcity value. Furthermore, the use of petroleum-based energy is likely to replace less attractive alternative energy sources (fuelwood, animal power, etc.) all of which require labour inputs for their use. While probably less efficient (at least on a financial cost basis), these displaced energy systems also mean reduced employment, which is numerically probably greater than the new employment created by the petroleum-based technology. The immediate net effect may well be a decline in overall employment. However, indirect effects such as a greater productivity (in agriculture and transport, for example) may more than overcome these direct effects, because of increases in output and sales (including exports and net value added). Short of detailed and complex studies of these consequences, little can be concluded here about the overall net employment effects of petroleum product use.

Externalities of petroleum product use can be negative or positive. On the negative side, congestion and pollution costs are probably the most significant. On the positive side there are factors such as the greater mobility of the labor force, or the likely substitution of liquid fuels for firewood, thereby reducing the overcutting of timber resources and the resulting reduction in erosion.

Pollution costs, mainly through air pollution from the high-sulphur crudes utilized in Thailand, may be quite significant, at least in and around Bangkok -- especially since lower-sulphur crude oil such as that produced by Indonesia is not imported into Thailand because of its higher cost (about US$1.00 more per barrel in recent months). However, because of the well-known difficulties of economically quantifying the effects relating to health and human well-being, no attempt will be made here to measure them or to explore analytical methods appropriate for such measurements. This does not mean that such effects should be ignored in the future. Ultimately, studies ought to be undertaken to establish whether these effects are reaching dangerous levels for health, at least in such heavily polluted areas as central Bangkok.

Congestion costs (most of which are concentrated in the greater Bangkok area) consist of three major components. The first component is the additional amount of fuel consumed by vehicles held up by congestion. The second type of cost consists of the time lost by drivers and passengers, and the additional costs for less than optimal utilization of the vehicle stocks (the costs of waiting plus the costs of fewer ton- or passenger-miles per vehicle). Indirect consequences related to these inefficiencies are derived effects such as reduced productivity in plants, offices, warehouses, etc., from slower and less reliable deliveries. The third category of costs relates to the additional costs of traffic control and management. A further, potential cost may arise from higher accident rates. However, if traffic were to flow with less impediments, prevailing driving habits and higher speeds could well have the opposite result.

Without some detailed studies, little can be said about the economic magnitudes of these external economic costs. However, from casual observations of traffic conditions in Bangkok, it appears that congestion may well add at least 20-30 percent to driving time, fuel consumption, and reductions in vehicle efficiency in the greater Bangkok area. With, perhaps, two-thirds of Thailand's total passengers and one-half of its commercial vehicle stock operating in this area, such external costs are likely to be substantial indeed. Taken together, they may well exceed present retail gasoline and diesel prices by 100 percent or more. Sample studies might help to better estimate the likely magnitude of these costs. In addition, projections should be made for the future, given the rapid rate of increase in population and vehicle use, particularly in and around Bangkok. For example, National Energy Administration statistics indicate a 7 percent and 8.4 percent growth rate in total vehicle stocks in the municipality of Bangkok and the whole country between 1976 and 1977, respectively. Projections made by NEA to 1987 suggest annual average rates of growth of 5.8 percent for Bangkok, and 6.2 percent for the country as a whole.

13.5 The Pricing of Lignite

Lignite is a nontraded commodity. Owing to several unattractive attributes such as its difficult handling characteristics, tendency for spontaneous combustion, low btu content per unit-weight, and other factors, it can be used for little else but boiler fuel in power production. One exception to this rule may be the higher quality deposit at Li which can be utilized for tobacco curing (as discussed earlier in Section 13.2), or could become a useful fuel in the form of briquettes for a variety of industrial, commercial, and household uses.

The largest known lignite deposit at the present time is at Mae Moh. It is to be fully developed for power production by EGAT. The lignite can be produced by open-pit mining methods, and production costs are low. In 1978 average mining costs per ton of all lignite mines in Thailand were only $4.20/ton. Estimated 1984 mining costs for the expanded Mae Moh mining operation were about $10.20/ton. In the past, EGAT has based the cost of its lignite on the long-run marginal extraction costs, using established financial accounting procedures. However, because of the finite nature of the deposits, it has been argued that the relevant cost to be used is the replacement value.

At present, the replacement costs of the lignite committed to power production are not known with certainty. The most likely replacement will be additional lignite that has not yet been found. Some 50 lignite deposits have been encountered throughout the country, and at least one of them, at Mae Tip, appears to be several times larger than the Mae Moh deposits. However, little is known about the magnitude of reserves, likely costs of production, quality, etc.

The second most likely replacement fuel for lignite is steam coal from Australia. Its F.O.B. Australia costs have been estimated at between $30 and $38/ton. A detailed study of the value of Thai lignite in terms of its likely 1984 replacement costs based on Australian coal, were undertaken by consultants in the appraisal of the Mae Moh mine expansion project. The equivalent value of Mae Moh lignite, adjusted for differences in quality and net heat rates, power plant capital and operating costs, etc., was estimated to range between $13.20 to $15.90 per ton in 1984 prices. It was suggested that this cost should be used as the base for the transfer price of Mae Moh lignite to the powerplant.

This approach to the pricing of lignite is not appropriate. Allowance must be made for the fact that the lignite replacement will not be needed until some time in the future. In the case of EGAT's power expansion plans, new, major thermal plants are scheduled to come on line in October 1990. Thus, the user cost (or depletion premium) component of the lignite, committed today, and not available for future expansion, should reflect the present value of the difference in its marginal production costs and the costs of the replacement fuel, adjusted appropriately for differences in all other cost variables. Assuming Australian coal as the replacement fuel in 1990, the depletion premium in 1984 would amount to $1.35/ton. The transfer price to be charged for the lignite in 1984, therefore, should be $10.20/ton (the marginal mining costs), plus $1.35/ton -- for a total of $11.55/ton. The depletion premium must be raised by 8% per year in order to reflect its increasing value over time.

However, if additional new lower-cost lignite were to be found, the replacement cost as well as the time horizon of the depletion period would have to be adjusted accordingly.

13.6 Epilogue

Since this case study was completed in 1979 several important changes have taken place. The most significant one has been the very large increase in offshore gas reserves from about 3 million cu ft to some 4 trillion cu ft of proven reserves, and another 16 trillion cu ft of probable reserves, as of early 1981. In addition, Esso has encountered gas onshore, with estimated reserves ranging between 1 to 10 trillion cu ft. So large are the gas reserves now relative to potential domestic demands, that the government is seriously considering allowing Texas Pacific to commit part or all of its reserves to exports -- if a market can be found. Other important events on the supply side were the discovery of fairly significant crude oil reserves by Shell, which are projected to yield an annual production of some 500,000 tons by 1990. In addition, the proven reserves of lignite at Mae Moh now stand at 650 million tons, which is enough to sustain some 1,500 MW of thermal generating capacity.

These substantial increases in domestic energy resources have significant effects on the value of these reserves in the ground, i.e., via changes in the relevant depletion premia. As pointed out in Chapter 3, the higher the reserves are relative to projected demand, the lower the depletion premium becomes, because exhaustion is postponed. While in Thailand the effective demand for gas may increase above previously predicted levels, given recent plans for a gas-based petrochemical and fertilizer industry as well as an LPG gas extraction plant, prospective gas reserve/production ratios are still much higher than before. For example, if we assume that the reserve constraint becomes binding only after 20 years (rather than the ten years estimated in the earlier evaluation), the 1981 depletion premium falls from $1.52/MCF to $0.99/MCF. If the relevant time period extends to 30 years, the premium falls to $0.87 MCF. This, however assumes that real prices of fuel oil would continuously rise at 3% per annum -- not a likely assumption given the potential availability of alternative fuels. The foregoing has important implications for the assessment of the total economic costs of the gas (i.e., marginal supply cost plus depletion premium), and it may be economic to utilize the gas in lower-value uses for which it was considered too valuable before. Another important factor that reduces the economic costs of delivered gas is the extension of the economic life of the offshore pipeline. This reduces the unit transportation costs because of the greater throughput and the longer useful life.

Similar considerations apply to the valuation of the depletion premium for lignite, because the most likely replacement for lignite in the early 1990's is not imported Australian steam coal as postulated earlier, but either the extended reserves of domestic lignite or domestic natural gas. This, of course, reduces the applicable depletion allowance from $1.35/ton in 1984 to $0.67/ton (if the binding resource constraint is pushed back from 1990 to the year 2000).

The question whether these reductions in real economic supply costs for gas and lignite should be fully passed on to the respective energy users is a separate one, that must be decided on the respective merits of lowered energy consumption and production expenses versus higher governmental income or higher energy producer profits. This question has both income distributional and economic efficiency dimensions.

A further important change that is taking place is related to the availability, use patterns and economic costs of LPG. The wide divergence between domestic market prices of LPG and alternative fuels has made the former an increasingly popular fuel in the transport sector. In March 1981, the retail-level spread between gasoline and LPG prices was widened even further, from a ratio of 1.83 to 2.11 on a volume basis ($1.88/gallon for gasoline, $0.89/gallon for LPG). Not surprisingly, this led to a continuing increase in the demand for LPG which had to be covered by subsidized imports. In 1980, for example, total domestic LPG refinery output was 125,000 tons, while imports amounted to 115,000 tons, or 48% of total consumption -- the subsidies required are economically inefficient.

However, in 1980 the government decided to proceed with a natural-gas based, liquified petroleum gas project which will produce large quantities of LPG and other by-products. This gas separation plant is projected to produce some 460,000 tons of LPG by 1985, and 920,000 tons by 1990. Another 60,000 tons are expected to be added from increased petroleum refinery production. These levels of LPG output are so large that Thailand will switch from an LPG importer to a net exporter, at least for a number of years after the extraction plant comes onstream. Exports alone are not particularly attractive because of depressed LPG world markets resulting from the construction of similar, large extracting plants in the Middle East and elsewhere. However, if the LPG is evaluated in terms of its import substitution potential for gasoline, diesel and kerosene fuels as well as scarce domestic resources, the economic rate of return for the gas extraction plant is estimated to amount to almost 30%.

In light of the large but temporary surplus of LPG that will be created, strong marketing efforts are needed now to systematically introduce LPG into energy systems that are presently based on other more costly fuels. This may make the current net subsidies for imported LPG more rational, in a dynamic sense, because they increase market penetration -- thus preventing even larger temporary surpluses of LPG in the future that would have to be disposed off abroad at depressed prices.

It is interesting to note that now, LPG is also considered a serious contender for tobacco curing, substituting for the much higher-priced diesel fuels and kerosene used earlier, as well as for the inferior-quality lignites.

Overall, the lessons to be learned from these rather dramatic changes in the energy supply and demand balances of Thailand are that energy planning, demand management and pricing are subject to continuing and dynamic changes. As such changes occur, policy responses must respond quickly as well. However, this need for flexibility and adaptability must be balanced against the need for continuity and predictability of energy supplies and prices, in order to allow energy users to make rational decisions with respect to investments in long-lasting and costly energy-using equipment. Trading off these often conflicting goals are one of the important challenges facing energy planners and policymakers world-wide.

Chapter 14

ENERGY R&D DECISIONMAKING IN DEVELOPING COUNTRIES[1]

14.1 Introduction

Since the dawn of the industrial revolution, nations have increasingly relied on scientific and technological advances to accelerate their development and economic growth. Consequently, research and development (R&D) efforts that give rise to technological innovations are recognized worldwide as an important concern of governments. In the resource-scarce developing countries, identifying and targeting R&D policies in critical areas like energy is particularly important in order to maximize benefits derived from limited funds and skilled manpower. Accordingly, this paper seeks to develop a rational and systematic framework (as well as relevant criteria) for determining energy R&D policies and priorities in any given developing country.

Technology is defined here as all varieties of assets required for the production of goods and services, including:

(a) physical assets such as machinery, plant, tools, equipment, and intermediate inputs;
(b) non-physical assets such as designs, plans, models, patents, and know-how; and
(c) other skills such as management, technical services, and marketing.

Technological R&D, in particular R&D for energy, is understood to include all goal-oriented or purposeful activity by individuals or teams of specialists, to improve the state of the art. Not necessarily confined to pure scientific enquiry, it includes all the steps (such as engineering development and pilot projects or field studies) that help bring about widespread acceptance and implementation of new technologies.

In other words, the conventional distinction between scientific research (directed towards understanding phenomena) and technological R&D (oriented towards application of this knowledge) is not operationally relevant or helpful here. This point is particularly relevant to energy-related R&D activities in the developing countries. Typically, university or research laboratory breakthroughs in new areas such as solar and wind energy conversion will not yield significant benefits or have a measurable impact on the overall national energy scene until these basically small-scale units are commercialized and distributed extensively to potential decentralized users. In short, the ultimate implementation and dissemination of energy technologies must be an important and legitimate aspect of energy R&D policy.

Energy R&D policy analysis and formulation in a developing country should not be carried out in isolation - it must be consistent with overall technology policy, as well as national energy policy (Munasinghe 1980). Ultimately, energy R&D policies

---

[1] Edited version of a paper presented at the International Conference on Energy Research Priorities held in Ottawa, Canada, in August 1983; and subsequently published in *The Energy Journal*, vol.8, Dec.1987, pp.147-168.

and priorities must support the goals of national socio-economic development. Therefore, these priorities must be determined on the basis of an analytical framework that recognizes and addresses national development objectives.

Implicit in this approach is the idea that developing country decisionmakers should seek to guide energy R&D activities, because it is too important an activity to be left to itself, and some policy intervention is preferable to none at all.

In the modern world, expenditures on R&D are steadily rising, especially in the developed countries, with increasing emphasis on applications-oriented work. Energy R&D is no exception. For example, the U.S. federal government spent about US$ 16 billion for energy R&D during the five-year period 1977-81 (NSF 1983). In addition to the direct impact of this government activity, there was also a significant indirect effect through its influence on the behavior of private U.S. corporations (which have put up a roughly matching amount for energy R&D during the same years).

Some recent studies of research funding in western countries have sought to link resources devoted to R&D, and technological leadership. In this context, the industrial North (market and socialist economies), with a combined GNP of about US$ 5000 billion, spent about two percent of this amount on R&D in 1980. By contrast, the poorer South (the developing countries), with an income around US$ 1000 billion, devoted less than 0.2 percent of it to R&D -- a sum that appears to be quite inadequate to even begin closing the development gap between the poor and the rich nations (Salam 1982).

The foregoing amply illustrates that R&D has become a big business, especially energy-related R&D, following the two major oil crises of the last decade. If the developing countries are to compete successfully in the modern world, then a number of fundamental questions must be posed, such as:

(a) how much of scarce national resources should be allocated to this type of activity;
(b) how should energy R&D priorities be determined;
(c) how should this R&D activity be organized and conducted to be most productive; and
(d) whether energy R&D in developing countries is (or should be) fundamentally different from comparable activities in industrialized nations.

The remainder of this chapter is organized as follows. The next section sets out the rationale for guidance by the government in establishing energy R&D policy, and examines the various factors that should be considered in determining energy R&D policy in a developing country. The objectives of national energy policy which should help determine R&D policy are described in the next section, and their significance is discussed. A proposed framework for determining energy R&D policy in a developing country is then developed. The final section examines the potential and actual constraints and difficulties that could arise in the implementation of policy, followed by a concluding section which discusses the implications of the foregoing for setting energy R&D policy and priorities.

14.2 Elements of an Energy R&D Policy

Broadly speaking, two major influences that affect the allocation of manpower and funding for R&D may be identified. First, as discussed earlier, the needs of society and the perceived benefits of pursing a specific line of research will influence how

R&D priorities should be set. We will defer for the moment the important issue of how these judgments are made, whether by government or other groups. Second, the motivations and inclinations of the individual researcher will also play a role. This is based on factors such as a genuine desire for knowledge, personal advancement, financial gain, own capability, availability of facilities, moral conviction, etc. Although national objectives (most often determined by governments), should play the dominant role, the rights of the individual scientist must also be recognized, and an appropriate compromise struck between academic freedom and government direction. The nature of this balance will depend on the extent to which government funds such R&D.

Many of the most significant discoveries in science arose from seeming accident or the dogged and single-minded determination of the researcher concerned -- neither of which had anything to do with the ultimate benefit derived by society from these advances. Typical examples include the discovery of penicillin by Fleming, and the formulation of classical electromagnetic field theory by Maxwell. However, in the case of energy-related R&D in a typical developing country, there are several strong arguments for goal-directed activity that is relevant to the needs of society.

First, since financial resources (especially foreign exchange) and skilled manpower are scarce in the average developing country, the tradition of government intervention in resource allocation within the national economy is well established. Furthermore, both energy producing and using equipment tend to be capital intensive and have long lifetimes. For example, investments in energy may amount to as much as 50 percent or more of public investment expenditures in many developing countries (see Table 14.1). Energy supply projects are very often on a large scale and usually involve gestation periods of many years (e.g., hydroelectric dam, fuelwood plantation, etc.). Therefore, to use scarce resources efficiently, it makes sense for governments to determine energy R&D policies and establish priorities, rationally and systematically in a manner which is responsive to perceived national objectives.

Table 14.1

Estimated Annual Energy Investment As Percent of Total Public Investment During the Early 1980s

Over 50%	30-40%	20-30%	10-20%	0-10%
Argentina(60%)	Ecuador	Botswana	Benin	Ethiopia
Brazil	India	China	Egypt	
Colombia(65%)	Pakistan	Costa Rica	Ghana	
Korea(52%)	Philippines	Liberia	Jamaica	
Mexico	Turkey	Nepal	Morocco	
		Nigeria		
		Sudan		
		Portugal		

Second, energy R&D in a developing country is more likely to be productive if it is concerned with relatively less complex technological options based on fairly well-known physical principles (e.g., more efficient fuelwood cooking stoves that could have a significant impact on the majority of poor and rural third world citizens), or the adaptation and modification of more sophisticated technologies already developed elsewhere. Therefore, there is a better opportunity of making rational decisions regarding the future direction of energy R&D, based on current and reasonably predictable trends in technology and national needs. Thus there are many opportunities for adapting known energy technologies, processes and policies, to local conditions, thereby reaping significant benefits in terms of more efficient energy supply and usage. By contrast, in high technology areas characterized by significant R&D costs, uncertain payoffs, and rapid changes, it is prudent (especially for the least developed countries) to monitor developments in other countries and adapt such advances for internal application only at the appropriate time. This is particularly relevant when the costs -- on which the economic viability of the technology critically depends -- are expected to decline rapidly (e.g., photovoltaics).

Finally, there is evidence that consciously directed R&D has contributed significantly to productivity and profitability increases in industry (Griliches 1980, Mansfield 1968 & 1980a, Terkeckyj 1974). One study (Mansfield 1980b) indicates that long-term R&D is particularly effective in this regard. It has been shown recently that: (a) R&D contributed positively to industrial productivity growth and yielded high returns; (b) basic research was the most productive type of R&D; and (c) privately financed R&D appeared to be more effective than federally funded efforts (Griliches 1980). Although these studies are based on the experience of U.S. industry, they provide some support to the hypothesis that directed energy R&D in the developing countries could lead to increased benefits.

Next, we examine some of the most important factors to take into account when formulating energy R&D policies in a developing country. First, as indicated earlier, the R&D policy must be responsive to national development objectives in general, and overall energy policy objectives in particular. Second, it must be long-run and systems-oriented, where relevant (e.g., in the case of least-cost electric power generation expansion planning). Third, it should be integrated, explicitly recognizing not only the interaction among different energy technologies and substitution possibilities, but also the links between the energy sector and the rest of the economy. Fourth, (where necessary) energy R&D ought to be multidisciplinary, involving well-knit and integrated teams of engineers, scientists, economist, financial analysts, and sociologists. Such R&D teams would be capable of addressing a variety of issues ranging from problem identification and formulation to adaptation and wide-spread dissemination of the technology. Fifth, the uncertainty inherent in predicting the future must be recognized by adopting a probabilistic or stochastic approach, and a scenario-oriented analysis. Finally, the work should be realistic and recognize the practical constraints that are likely to hinder implementation of proposed energy R&D policies.

A noteworthy point is that research on energy demand-side issues is as important as the study of supply options. Energy R&D work should not be confined to supply technologies, but must also include such topics as demand management and conservation, and the impact on energy demand of various policy instruments like price, physical and legal controls, technical improvements, and education and promotion. In other words, the two options merit balanced treatment, since the principal objective of policymakers is to ensure adequate sources of energy to support future growth, and supply-demand imbalances can be redressed by adjusting either supply or demand, or both. More specifically, greater emphasis on demand-oriented research may yield significant benefits in many developing countries (see Chapters 6 and 8).

In the next section, we adopt the viewpoint of a developing country policymaker, faced with the problem of establishing energy R&D priorities. Accordingly, it is logical and convenient to begin by setting out the kinds of national energy policy objectives important to a typical developing country.

14.3 National Energy Policy Objectives and R&D Implications

The most commonly stated general policy objective of developing country governments is the promotion of socio-economic development and the maximization of the welfare of their citizens. Within this broad framework, it is essential, for operational purposes, to identify more specific objectives relevant to overall energy policy. Concerned individuals and groups outside the government should also have the right to provide inputs in establishing society's needs, and a participative approach to determining energy policy objectives is to be preferred. This is especially true where there is a natural bias among officials towards commercial forms of energy (like electricity and fossil fuels) used in urban-industrial areas, rather than the traditional and biomass-based energy sources more relevant to the majority of the population in rural-agricultural areas.

On the other hand, giving undue weightage to the opinions of sincere but single-minded advocates of various untried and often low-priority energy options, is very likely to be counterproductive. In the final analysis, a developing country's government must take the leading role in establishing national policy objectives (while consulting others), in order to avoid anarchy, and reduce duplication of efforts, and wasteful use of scarce resources. The importance of determining energy R&D policy, based on broader national goals and priorities, is recognized even in the market economies (IEA 1985).

Next we set out the different objectives of energy policy from the national viewpoint, and discuss their relevance for R&D. It must be emphasized that the relative weights attached to the many and often mutually inconsistent goals described below will vary widely among countries. This in turn will affect energy R&D priorities. Therefore, the order in which these objectives are presented do not necessarily reflect their relative importance.

Economic Efficiency

This objective seeks to maximize the net economic benefits of energy use, and efficiently allocate scarce resources, so as to achieve the highest possible growth rate of output. It implies that the technical efficiency of energy production and usage should be optimized, thus highlighting R&D efforts in areas like improving efficiency in end use, fuel substitution, loss reduction in energy supply, and energy conservation. The broader interpretation of this objective is that the supply and demand for energy should be tailored to maximize the net benefit to society represented by the difference in the value of total output and the cost of all inputs (including energy) used to produce this output.

This type of supply-demand management requires disaggregate analysis by energy source and type of use. It means that the structure and level of energy consumption is optimized through appropriate energy management policies, involving the coordinated use of all policy instruments. This include price and other financial incentives and penalties, physical and legal controls, technical improvements, and educational and promotional measures. Where sudden or chronic energy deficits occur, due to poor planning or unforeseen contingencies (like the oil crises or unusually poor rainfall), then systematic analysis can help to identify the most affected sectors of the economy. Thus the shortage can be rationed effectively, with minimum economic losses and disruption of output (Munasinghe 1979). On the supply side, the optimal energy mix must be produced at the least cost to the economy, requiring up-to-date knowledge of technologies and good planning and operation of energy systems. All these areas offer ample opportunity for fruitful research, especially on the demand-side, where very little operationally useful work has been done in most countries, and the data are also relatively weak.

The valuation of costs and benefits in the economic calculus must be based on so-called shadow prices which more correctly represent the true value of scarce resources, rather than on market prices that may be severely distorted in many developing countries. This point is discussed further below.

Basic Needs and Equity

Practically every government recognizes, in some form or the other, the right of all citizens to enjoy the benefits of certain essential amenities. Access to basic energy requirements is one of these "rights", with particular relevance to the poor and disadvantaged groups who often are unable to afford these services. This requires greater attention to R&D issues relating to biomass and integrated rural energy systems, rural electrification, energy consumption patterns among the urban and rural poor, expenditure on energy and affordability in relation to income levels, energy pricing policy and subsidy mechanisms, and methods of identifying target groups and avoiding undesirable leakage of subsidies (Munasinghe 1987).

While concern for the poor, and the satisfaction of minimum energy requirements are valid considerations, based on fairness and equity grounds, the mechanisms by which these issues could be addressed must be studied rationally. For example, it may be worthwhile examining the administrative feasibility of providing direct cash grants to poor rural families to purchase unsubsidized kerosene for basic lighting needs. This may be economically more efficient than directly reducing the price of this fuel in the market (say, well below the border or efficiency price). The latter policy is likely to lead to perverse effects, where the relatively better-off groups in society, such as industrialists and motor car owners, could use the cheap kerosene (mixed with more expensive diesel and gasoline), thus becoming the unintended beneficiaries of a public subsidy. In other words, more country- and consumer-specific research is required to identify the most effective package of policy instruments and to accurately target the benefits to low-income groups.

Energy Independence and National Security

This national goal emphasizes the need to develop indigenous energy sources, diversify the sources of imported energy supplied, and reduce technological dependence. It also raises issues relating to optimal levels for stockpiling fuels, and often runs counter to the economic efficiency objective.

The essential issue is the extent to which any developing country is willing to divert scarce skilled manpower, funds, and other resources, to achieve more energy independence, technological self-reliance and self-respect, and national security.

Mobilization of Financial Resources

As the production and distribution of energy becomes increasingly more expensive, the issue of raising enough revenue to satisfy the financial requirements of the energy sector also emerges. To ensure the efficient and uninterrupted delivery of energy to the economy, energy supplying organizations (which are most often government controlled in the developing countries), such as electric power utilities, oil and gas companies, coal mines, and forestry organizations, should earn enough revenues to meet their cash flow and investment needs.

The foregoing considerations suggest that R&D policy relating to energy supply options should be oriented (wherever possible) towards lower cost technologies with greater payoffs. For example, the development of some of the newer and more exotic technologies (such as ocean thermal energy conversion or OTEC), may appear glamorous, but is likely to impose a significantly greater financial burden on the limited funds available for R&D work (and also prove to be less effective), than more mundane efforts aimed at improving and disseminating relatively inexpensive energy-efficient fuelwood cooking stoves (see Chapter 12).

Research on pricing policy, taxation and public enterprise policy, the efficient management, planning and operation of energy supplying institutions, loss reduction, etc., should also be encouraged. The need to increase revenues may not be consistent with the economic efficiency objective, and will conflict even more directly with the goal of providing basic energy requirements to the poor, at affordable prices. However, it is possible to reconcile these apparently conflicting objectives, through studies that yield innovative energy pricing structures (Munasinghe and Warford 1982).

Finally, given the evidence concerning the beneficial results of applied R&D efforts, and the difficulty of persuading developing country governments to allocate adequate funds to support R&D work, it is appropriate to examine the possibility of encouraging revenue-earning energy producing institutions to earmark a certain modest percentage of their income for energy-related R&D efforts. Naturally, the amount to be allocated will depend on the expected returns to R&D, since diminishing returns will occur beyond a certain point.

Conservation and Oil Substitution

Energy conservation and substitution of other forms of energy for oil has become an important goal, especially for the oil-importing developing countries. Although this objective is actually a part of the economic efficiency concept (see above), it is worth identifying as a separate goal, because of its intuitive conceptual appeal to both decisionmakers and the energy consuming public. Furthermore, the short-run payoffs (reductions in the national oil import bill, and fuel savings) can provide the early impetus and sustained enthusiasm necessary to launch and maintain long-run efforts in energy management and indigenous resource development.

R&D efforts in this area should be responsive to several considerations. First, the coordinated use of policy tools for energy demand management and conservation is particularly important for successful policy implementation, as mentioned earlier. Second, in the case of commercial forms of energy like electricity and oil, maximum use ought to be made of the significant results achieved in the industrialized countries, especially with reference to the modern sectors like industry and transport. Many lessons learned in the developed nations can be quickly and easily adapted for use in the developing countries, with little or no modification. This is because the underlying energy-utilizing processes are the same.

Third, the conservation of biomass and traditional fuels should be given priority, since these energy sources (a) usually provide a large share of the gross energy inputs, (b) are often in short supply, and (c) receive much less attention than the commercial forms of energy (that appear more prominently in government budgets).

Fourth, energy conservation programs should always be subject to the overall economic efficiency criterion. Thus, plans that are not economically viable, where energy savings are achieved at the expense of an increase in overall system costs (i.e., the value of energy conserved is less than the corresponding increase in the costs of other inputs like capital, labor, and raw materials), should normally be rejected, unless there are other overriding considerations, like national security (Munasinghe 1983). In short, the blind pursuit of energy conservation as an end in itself, to the exclusion of all other considerations, must be avoided.

Other Objectives

Many other, more ad hoc, national energy policy goals can play an important role in various developing countries.

First, the government may set a high priority on eliminating dualism and other manifestations of severe inequalities within the economy. It would act on the ground that such phenomena might exacerbate social tensions and eventually result in major disruptions. The dualism may occur in several forms, including; (a) socio-cultural duality (i.e., an urban, foreign-oriented elite, versus a rural, tradition-minded peasantry); (b) sectoral duality (i.e., an industrial and commercial sector based on modern technology and organization, versus a traditional agricultural sector using labor-intensive methods and village organization); and (c) regional duality (i.e., highly developed areas, usually urban, versus poor and backward regions, usually rural).

Energy R&D policy should develop those options that provide greater benefits to the more disadvantaged sections of society, thereby reducing the duality. At the same time, care should be exercised not to pursue this goal at the expense of the energy needs of the modern, urban, industrial sector. Energy R&D policy must recognize that there is a very real trade-off in reducing disparities, between accelerating progress at the lower end of the scale on the one hand and levelizing or curtailing development at the top, on the other.

A typical example of this often arises with rural electrification (R.E.), where electric utilities that are scarcely able to adequately shoulder the burden of urban and industrial loads, are forced to undertake high-cost R.E. programs (which are politically popular, but not necessarily economically viable or well thought-out). A common outcome is that neither the urban nor rural customers receive satisfactory electricity services. This ultimately results in power failures and shortages that are disruptive and very costly to the national economy (Munasinghe 1987).

Another common government objective is to provide special support to certain privileged or priority sectors of the economy like import-substituting or exporting industries. One issue here is whether the economy would not be better off if these industries received cash grants or other financial support directly from the government, rather than subsidies or special services provided through the energy sector. In any case, specific studies and research may be required to determine the best supply and demand options for these consumers, in terms of the quantity, quality and price of energy. Once again, economic efficiency is a useful criterion to invoke. This means that overall net economic benefits arising from the increased productivity, international competitiveness, and output, of the privileged industry must exceed the subsidy cost of providing special treatment with regard to its energy supply.

We conclude this section by re-emphasizing that the national energy policy objectives discussed above are not necessarily exhaustive, and that the relative weights attached to them will vary from country to country. However, given the numerous and frequently conflicting goals, and the bewildering array of energy options available, the economic efficiency criterion provides a useful, common starting point for initiating the energy R&D policy-making process, as described in the next section.

14.4 An Energy R&D Policy Framework

Starting with a comprehensive list of topics for energy R&D, it is possible to select a subset of them, by rejecting those which are obviously unsuitable (e.g., small hydro R&D in a dry and arid country). Further preliminary screening could be done by classifying the energy R&D options in different ways.

Energy technologies could be classified according to their degree of sophistication (Boone 1983). R&D work in complex and high-technology areas of energy research being pursued by the developed or scientifically more advanced developing countries (e.g., nuclear fusion research, or very sophisticated energy-macroeconomic modelling) need only to be monitored by most LDC's. Eventually, acquisition of this high technology may become an issue. Meanwhile, options involving medium and simpler technology or policy measures are more promising candidates for immediate attention, depending on the resource endowment and needs of the developing country concerned.

Another useful classification is based on the availability of information. If access to data is restricted -- which often occurs in the case of commercially valuable proprietary technologies or models developed by multinational companies -- then it may be cheaper and quicker to purchase the information rather than duplicate it (e.g., petroleum or electric power technology). Where the relevant background material is freely available from universities, research institutions, or other sources, it may be easier for an LDC to launch its own R&D program.

The pre-screened subset of R&D options may be further analyzed in terms of possible R&D strategies to be adopted (Barnett 1983). First, a high-priority group could be identified, where the country should take a leading role in R&D, because of the importance of the work to national needs, and some comparative advantages in the local availability of natural resources, skills and knowledge. Second, information on some R&D options could be purchased from abroad if it is otherwise restricted and difficult, time-consuming, or costly to duplicate.

Third, it may be prudent to rapidly build up skills and capability in certain R&D areas where urgent national needs may soon arise, or an early technological breakthrough is expected abroad. Finally, in some cases, it would be sufficient to monitor energy R&D developments in other countries, for possible local application in the medium- or long-term future. Clearly, there is likely to be considerable overlap among the different categories discussed above.

After completing these preliminary exercises, a more comprehensive and refined analysis should be carried out. It should be based on the explicit evaluation of R&D possibilities according to the national energy policy objectives set out above.

The most convenient and logical starting point for developing such a systematic framework to determine energy-related R&D policies and priorities in a developing country, is the economic efficiency objective discussed earlier. The well-established, and widely-used, techniques of cost-benefit analysis (described in more detail in Chapter 9), are used in the model defined and explained below.

The Model

$$NB = B(R\&D) - C(R\&D) + B(IMPLEM.) - C(IMPLEM.);$$

where:

B(R&D) = the benefits of the R&D activity,
C(R&D) = the costs of the R&D activity,
B(IMPLEM.) = the benefits to be derived from the ultimate implementation of the R&D results, and
C(IMPLEM.) = the costs of implementing this R&D.

The items on the right-hand side represent present discounted values of benefit and cost streams that extend over a long period of time, usually encompassing the life cycle of the equipment and plant concerned (Munasinghe 1987). Thus:

$$B(R\&D) = \sum_{t=0}^{T} B(R\&D)_t/(1 + r)^t$$

where:

$B(R\&D)_t$ = the benefits of the R&D activity in year t;
T = the time horizon,
r = the intertemporal discount rate.

All costs and benefits are evaluated in terms of efficiency shadow prices or economic opportunity costs -- i.e., the value of these resources when they are used in the best alternative project. This implies that capital and operating costs are used net of taxes and duties, labor is valued at the shadow wage rate, and fuels are valued at marginal cost or the border price (if tradeable). The opportunity cost of capital is the recommended discount rate, usually lying in the range 6 to 12 percent for most developing countries. The reader is referred elsewhere for a more detailed explanation of the general principles of shadow pricing in developing countries and specific applications in the energy sector (Munasinghe 1979).

In general, considerable difficulties could arise in the estimation of costs and benefits. The cost elements may be somewhat easier to quantify. The easiest benefits to identify are those involving avoided costs due to energy savings, but some of the indirect benefits will have to be taken into account on a judgmental basis.

B(R&D) will usually consist of a direct component (e.g., from a pilot plant or demonstration project), as well as indirect benefits, such as the building up of research capability and skills of local staff that can have a positive influence on scientific and technological activity in other sectors. Although these indirect effects may be rather difficult to quantify, they could have a significant impact on a developing nation striving to build up a critical mass of researchers in order to achieve economic "take-off". The benefits of implementation, or B(IMPLEM.), include items like reduced energy costs, better quality of energy supply, more efficient use of energy, greater productivity or comfort, and so on, as well as related indirect benefits.

Both C(R&D) and C(IMPLEM.) will consist of the value of scarce economic resources (i.e., capital, labor, land, raw materials, and energy inputs) used up in carrying out specific activities. The costs of training local staff and acquiring know-how, and those imposed by external diseconomies (or externalities) like pollution, are also aspects that must be considered.

The benefits and costs of implementation are likely to be much larger than B(R&D) and C(R&D), particularly in the case of supply technologies involving capital intensive hardware. However, demand management options, like pricing, may require significant initial outlays to gather and analyze data, train skilled manpower, etc., while the costs of implementation could be relatively small. In any case, the benefits and costs of implementation will diminish in importance the further in the future they occur, because of the effects of discounting. Therefore, a higher discount rate implies that funds are scarce, and that the energy options with lower start-up costs and earlier payoffs will be favored.

Several factors must be borne in mind when extrapolating from the R&D stage to full-blown implementation (Love and Michel 1982). First, there are scale effects which usually result in economies. Second, technological advances could occur during the lengthy period prior to full implementation. Third, with the introduction of any new technology or policy measure, there is a typical learning curve which starts slowly, then accelerates rapidly, and finally saturates.

Ranking Procedure and R&D Strategies

On the basis of the economic efficiency criterion, the model seeks to first identify and rank the various energy R&D options, according to the net benefits (NB) to the economy, that each one will yield. In other words, the set of energy R&D projects that yields the highest total value of net economic benefits is selected, given a fixed level of investment resources. After this *preliminary* ranking is complete, then the portfolio of energy R&D projects is assessed in relation to each of the other policy objectives, and the final priority list is determined.

Several points are worth noting. First, the weights attached to the non-efficiency objectives discussed above will vary widely from country to country, and thereby affect the final outcome differently in each case. Second, where the data permit reasonably reliable quantification of net benefits, then this economic efficiency-related criterion could be used as a benchmark to judge the relative importance of the other objectives. Third, comparative advantage will affect the choice of energy R&D options selected. These special advantages might include the abundance of particular indigenous energy resources, geographic, climatic or demographic factors, and the availability (or lack) of specific types of skilled manpower and knowhow. Fourth, the considerable uncertainty inherent in making predictions of the future must be dealt with using the standard techniques of sensitivity and risk analysis. In general, R&D alternatives that are more robust over a wide range of scenarios (in the sense of consistently yielding significant net benefits), would be preferred.

14.5 Constraints and Problems of Implementation

This section looks at the constraints and difficulties that can hinder implementing R&D policy in a developing country. Overcoming these problems is as important a part of the energy R&D policymaking process as determining priorities. It is convenient to analyze the relevant issues in terms of two broad categories: lack of resources, and constraints on policy instruments and institutions.

Resource Shortages

Most developing countries are chronically short of both local financial resources and foreign exchange. Furthermore, R&D efforts are most often considered rather low priority, in comparison with the other major and politically sensitive problems (usually of a short-run nature) that frequently arise (Stewart 1978). Therefore, the search for funds to support energy R&D work is usually a difficult one.

The first priority would be to use whatever financial resources that are available as effectively as possible. In economic terms, this is equivalent to maximizing the net benefits of R&D, subject to overall budgetary and other constraints. The energy R&D prioritizing framework described in the previous section would go a long way towards meeting this criterion.

The second step should be to explore all possibilities for increasing the local contribution. The importance of energy R&D activities for the future growth of the economy must be stressed to the decisionmakers. These arguments will be all the more effective if they are perceived to have emerged from a rational and systematic procedure that is responsive to national needs. In addition to funds provided from the general government budget, it would also be prudent to look for other sources of innovative financing. As mentioned earlier, revenue-earning energy supplying institutions like power utilities, oil and gas companies, or coal mines could be requested to contribute to an energy R&D fund, especially if they are government owned. Special taxes may be levied on energy-related imports (e.g., crude oil), or locally sold energy services (e.g., gasoline or electricity). Finally, the banking sector should be encouraged to support R&D activities, particularly where there is a high probability of follow-up investments which have a good pay-off in the short-run (e.g., energy conservation, oil substitution, cogeneration).

The third possibility is, of course, foreign assistance. This means of supporting energy R&D work is especially important in projects requiring significant expertise or hardware from abroad. However, it raises several other issues such as excessive dependency, and pursuit of inappropriate technologies, which are examined later.

The lack of skilled manpower to undertake R&D work is another serious drawback in the developing countries. The problem of the brain-drain is most acute in areas where skills are in the shortest supply, because the personnel concerned are the most mobile and sought after by foreign employers, e.g., high-level technologists and managers.

As in the case of financial shortages, the first step should be to protect and effectively utilize the staff that is available. Salaries must be made as attractive as possible, and other fringe benefits (such as subsidized housing and transport) provided. Access to current information, in terms of recent publications, trips abroad to attend conferences and visit modern facilities, etc., is another often overlooked way of maintaining morale. The availability of up-to-date research equipment, particularly computer facilities, and recognition of the contribution that energy R&D is making to national development, will also contribute significantly to job satisfaction. Government authorities must be made aware that a relatively modest outlay, along the lines indicated above, would be extremely cost-effective by helping to avoid the much greater expenditures required for recruiting experts from abroad to replace the local staff who have left.

When maximizing the effectiveness of existing manpower resources, the contributions that can be made by universities and research institutions should not be ignored. Mechanisms to channel their efforts more usefully and provide incentives should be strengthened. A recent study in the U.S. indicated that although university research rarely generated new technology, it induced firms to spend more on R&D and also enhanced the productivity of such efforts (Nelson 1986).

The rapid building-up of new skills is the second and equally important priority, which is widely recognized by developing country governments, as well as bilateral and multilateral sources of foreign aid. At the outset, the types and numbers of staff required to carry out the proposed energy R&D programs must be determined as accurately as possible (Bailey et al. 1983). This should be integrated with any ongoing national manpower planning efforts. The following areas may be considered within the scope of the training program: basic research, design and development, system engineering, production planning and control, manufacturing engineering, teaching and skill acquisition, quality control and testing, post-installation servicing, economic and financial analysis and control, legal and socio-political aspects, and general management systems and procedures. In general, the preferred policy may be to encourage the growth of skills in areas where this could be done at relatively low cost (Cooper 1985).

Finally, efforts should be made to effectively use foreign manpower resources. Local people living abroad must be encouraged to return and make their contribution. Foreign experts and consultants should be employed judiciously. A special effort will have to be undertaken to ensure that those who are brought in from abroad work harmoniously with local staff -- especially where invidious comparisons may be made with regard to higher salaries or other expatriate privileges.

Institutional and Policy Constraints

One of the principal constraints encountered in implementing energy policy comes from lack of understanding and appreciation of the critical issues involved (UNCTAD 1981). To overcome this problem, mass educational and promotional efforts aimed at the general public should be undertaken, stressing the importance of energy issues, and the key role played by R&D policy. Appropriate changes could also be made in the educational curricula at all levels (i.e., primary, secondary, technical, and university). Within the government, bureaucrats and decisionmakers must be sensitized, and greater participation in the energy R&D policymaking process encouraged.

The chief institutional constraints arise from the fact that decisionmaking in the energy sector is often fragmented. Thus, there may be little coordination among the power utility, oil company, gas utility, coal supplier, and forestry agency, because they have evolved independently in the past, and are not even likely to fall within the same ministry. Therefore, the development of a coherent energy R&D policy cannot be separated from the integrated national energy planning process (see Chapter 2). In particular, policy coordination should help identify and orchestrate energy R&D efforts at various levels: national (e.g., planning commission or President's office), sectoral (e.g., ministries or economic sectors), and subsectoral (e.g., individual research institutions or line agencies).

Energy R&D capability could be strengthened by building up the following types of institutions: basic research, engineering design and consultancy, teaching and training, national standards and quality control, and investment promotion (UNCTAD 1981). Care must be exercised to avoid duplication and consequent waste, especially in areas of R&D which are considered popular or "fashionable". On the other hand, a certain amount of pluralism, and a modest degree of controlled competition, may be useful to maintain enthusiasm and ensure comprehensive analysis of the problem from more than one viewpoint. The government should ensure that there is adequate information flow among local institutions, as well as from abroad.

Next is the issue of cooperation. First, there must be enough coordination between the public and private sectors, within the developing country. Given that the government sector tends to dominate in most third world nations, it may be sufficient for public officials to clearly enunciate the national energy R&D policy, and expect the private sector to respond. Another crucial area of cooperation is the relationship of the developing country to multinational enterprises. The financial and technical aspects, as well as organizational forms and mechanisms, have been studied and described elsewhere (UNCTAD 1981, UNCTAD Secretariat 1983).

The last area of cooperation involves the interaction between a developing country and foreign governments or aid institutions. Such relationships could be very beneficial to energy R&D efforts. A developed country or multilateral agency could assist by either directly supporting R&D work in the developing country or by incorporating some of these activities within its own R&D programs. At the same time, it is strongly advisable for the developing country to clearly determine its own energy R&D priorities before establishing foreign contacts, and then firmly adhere to these chosen options. On their part, aid-givers must make a special effort to be sensitive to the needs of the developing country, and help its decisionmakers to articulate an effective policy (if it is lacking), rather than pursuing preconceived goals.

Clearly, unless each developing country makes up its own mind early enough, there is the risk of energy R&D policies and priorities being determined from outside, on the basis of the existing international trend or fashion (which may be quite inappropriate locally). Foreign consultants and experts can be a useful vehicle for technology transfer. However, foreign aid does involve large amounts of money, and so does R&D (as indicated above). Therefore, relatively unsupervised and unstructured assistance from abroad may be ineffective, and even worse, could tie up scarce skilled local manpower in fruitless and low priority R&D work. In other words, overseas cooperation is most beneficial when national policies have been clearly identified, and there is an adequate cadre of knowledgeable local technologists to interact with and manage the work of foreign experts.

14.6 Summary and Conclusions

This paper argues that the targeting of energy R&D policies and priorities is important for the resource-scarce developing countries. R&D is defined widely to include not only pure scientific enquiry, but also all steps leading up to widespread application of the results of R&D. The tradition of government intervention in determining energy R&D policy is well established even in market economies like the U.S., although implementation mechanisms may be different in developing countries. Energy R&D policy should be consistent with national energy policy and general technology policy. It should therefore be responsive to national energy policy objectives, and ultimately, to overall national socio-economic development goals.

Energy R&D policy in developing countries will usually be dominated by government, but a pluralistic approach that incorporates the views of other groups is desirable. Although pure research has made major contributions to human progress in the past, there are convincing arguments favoring government support and guidance of R&D in the energy area. These arguments include the effective use of scarce resources, successful identification of appropriate energy options to meet national needs, and the evidence of significant payoffs to R&D in the developed countries. Research on demand-side energy issues, including demand management, pricing, and conservation, is at least as important as work on technology-oriented supply options.

The best known general policy objective of developing countries is the promotion of socio-economic development and welfare. For operational convenience, it is possible to identify several more specific energy policy objectives within this broad framework. These goals include: economic efficiency, basic needs and equity, energy independence and national security, mobilization of financial resources, conservation and oil substitution, and other socio-political objectives and constraints. The implications of and trade-off among these often mutually inconsistent goals for setting energy R&D policies and priorities is discussed.

Starting with a comprehensive list of energy R&D topics, it is possible to determine a feasible subset of options suitable for a given developing country. The country's resource endowment and characteristics, as well as the characteristics of the technologies and measures, are used to carry out this first step.

After the preliminary screening, a cost-benefit model is used to further analyze energy R&D options. The efficiency shadow priced costs and benefits of carrying out R&D work, as well as implementation of the results, are included in the evaluation. The best set of energy R&D options may be determined, based on the maximization of the value of net economic benefits they yield, wherever this quantification is possible. The estimation of costs and benefits may be formidable task, and risk and sensitivity analysis should be used to cope with uncertainty.

This initial ranking, according to the economic efficiency criterion, is adjusted by systematically considering the impact of the other non-efficiency goals. The final R&D priorities will reflect the relative weights attached to the different policy objectives in the developing country concerned. The economic efficiency objective is not necessarily more important than the others, but provides a convenient starting point and quantitative benchmark against which the relative importance of the non-efficiency goals may be measured.

The principal constraints and difficulties which hinder the implementation of energy R&D policy include scarcity of financial resources, and skilled manpower, as well as policy and institutional inadequacies. Effective cooperation between the public and private sectors within the developing country, and between the country and multinational enterprises, is important. The developing country must establish its own R&D policies and priorities, and acquire self-confidence, in order not to be unduly, and sometimes incorrectly, influenced by foreign-aid agencies, consultants, and experts. Finally, further opportunities for South-South cooperation, regional cooperation among developing countries, and the possibility of setting up special international mechanisms or facilities, to support technological R&D (especially energy-related work) should be actively pursued. The funding of agricultural research through the CGIAR network is an useful example of such assistance in the past decade.

References

Bailey, J.C., P.M.S. Jones, J.P. Savage, J. Walker and E.H. Wignall, "Education, Training and the Transfer of Technology for Energy Producers in the Developing World," Twelfth Congress of the World Energy Conference, New Delhi, September 1983.

Barnett, Andrew, "Energy R&D Policy: Some Analytical Issues," Seminar on Energy Research Priorities, IDRC, Ottawa, August 1983.

Boone, Gerard K., "Dualism and Technological Harmony for Balanced Development", *Industry and Development*, Dec. 1983, pp. 51-73.

Cooper, Charles, "Policy Intervention for Technological Innovation in Developing Countries," Staff Working Paper No. 441, World Bank, Washington DC, August 1985.

Grilliches, Zvi, "Returns to Research and Development Expenditures in the Private Sector," in J.W. Kendrick and B.N. Vaccara, eds., *New Developments in Productivity Measurement*, NBER Studies in Income and Wealth, Vol. 44, New York, 1980.

Grilliches, Zvi, "Productivity, R&D, and Basic Research at the Firm Level in the 1970's," *The American Economic Review*, vol.76, 1986, pp.141- 154.

International Energy Agency, "Energy Technology Policy", OECD, Paris, 1985.

Love, P.E., and J. Michel, "The Selection of an Energy R&D Portfolio for the European Community," No. EUR 8049 EN, EEC, Brussels, 1982.

Mansfield, E., *Industrial Research and Technological Innovation*, NBER, New York, 1968.

Mansfield, E., "Technology and Productivity in the U.S." Conference on Post-war Changes in the U.S. Economy, NBER, New York, 1980a.

Mansfield, E., "Basic Research and Productivity Increase in Manufacturing", *American Economic Review*, vol.70, 1980b, pp. 863-73.

Munasinghe, Mohan, *The Economics of Power System Reliability and Planning*, Johns Hopkins University Press, Baltimore MD, 1979.

Munasinghe, Mohan, "Integrated National Energy Planning in the Developing Countries", *Natural Resources Forum*, Oct. 1980, pp. 359-73.

Munasinghe, Mohan, "Third World Energy Policies: Demand Management and Conservation", *Energy Policy*, March 1983, pp. 4-18.

Munasinghe, Mohan, *Rural Electrification for Development*, Westview Press, Boulder CO, 1987.

Munasinghe, Mohan and J.J. Warford, *Electricity Pricing*, Johns Hopkins University Press, Baltimore MD, 1982.

National Science Foundation, "Federal R&D Funding for Energy: Fiscal Years 1971-84," No. NSF 83-301, NSF, Washington DC, Feb 1983.

Nelson, Richard D., "Institutions Supporting Technical Advance in Industry", *American Economic Review*, vol.76, May 1986, pp. 186-9.

Salam, A., "Internationalization of Science in Developing Countries," Address to the IAEA Governing Board, Vienna, March 1980.

Stewart, F., *Technology and Underdevelopment*, MacMillan, London, UK, 1978.

Terleckyj, Nestor, *Effects of R&D on the Productivity Growth of Industries*, Washington DC, 1974.

UNCTAD, "Report and Recommendations of the Workshop on Technology Policies and Planning for Technological Transformation," United Nations, New York, January 1981.

UNCTAD Secretariat, "Major Issues in the Transfer and Development of Energy Technology in Developing Countries," Twelfth Congress of the World Energy Conference, New Delhi, Sept. 1983.

BIBLIOGRAPHY

Ahern John E., *The Energy Method of Energy Systems Analysis*, John Wiley & Sons, New York, 1980, pp.24-30.

Alessio, Frank J., "Energy Analysis and the Energy Theory of Value", *The Energy Journal*, vol. 2, no. 1, Jan. 1981.

American Physical Society, "The Efficient Use of Energy", US Government Printing Office, Washington DC, 1975.

Bailey, J.C., P.M.S. Jones, J.P. Savage, J. Walker and E.H. Wignall, "Education, Training and the Transfer of Technology for Energy Producers in the Developing World," Twelfth Congress of the World Energy Conference, New Delhi, September 1983.

Barnett, Andrew, "Energy R&D Policy: Some Analytical Issues," Seminar on Energy Research Priorities, IDRC, Ottawa, August 1983.

Bator, F.J., "General Equilibrium, Welfare and Allocation", *American Economic Review*, March 1957, pp. 22-59.

Baum, Warren C., "The World Bank Project Cycle", *Finance and Development*, The World Bank, Washington DC, December 1970.

Baumol, W.J. and D.F. Bradford, "Optimal Departures from Marginal Cost Pricing", *American Economic Review*, June 1970, pp. 265-283.

Beenstock, M. and P. Willcocks, "Energy Consumption and Economic Activity in Industrialized Countries", *Energy Economics*, vol.3, October 1981, pp. 225-32.

Beijdorff, A.F. and P. Stuerzinger, "Improved Energy Efficiency: The Invisible Resource", presented at 11th World Energy Conference, Munich, West Germany, September 1980.

Ben-Zion, Zilbfarb and F. Gerard Adams, "The Energy-GDP Relationship in Developing Countries", ibid., pp. 244-48.

Bialy, J., "Firewood Use in a Sri Lankan Village - A Preliminary Survey", School of Engineering, Edinburg University, U.K., 1979.

Boone, Gerard K., "Dualism and Technological Harmony for Balanced Development", *Industry and Development*, Dec. 1983, pp. 51-73.

Bos et al., "The Potential for Co-generation Development in Six Major Industries by 1985", FEA Report, Resource Planning Associates, Cambridge, MA, 1977.

Cano, R., "Argentina, Brazil and the La Plata River" in A. Utton and L. Teclaff (eds.), *Water in a Developing World*, Westview Publishing Company, Boulder CO, 1978.

Charpie, Richard A. and Paul McAvoy, "Conserving Energy in the Production of Aluminium" *Resources and Energy*, vol.1, September 1978.

Cooper, Charles, "Policy Intervention for Technological Innovation in Developing Countries," Staff Working Paper No. 441, World Bank, Washington DC, August 1985.
Dallaire, G., "Designing Energy Conserving Buildings", *Civil Engineering*, April 1974.

Davidson, R., "Optimal Depletion of an Exhaustible Resource with Research and Development towards an Alternative Technology", *Review of Economic Studies*, March 1978.

Dawson, O. L., *Communist China's Agriculture: It's Development and Future Potential*, Praeger Publ., New York, 1970.

De Backer, A. and K. Openshaw, "Timber Trends Study, Thailand: Detailed Description of Surveys and Results", FAO, Report No. TA 3156, Rome, Italy, 1972.

Earl, D. E., *Forest Energy and Economic Development*, Clarendon, Oxford, 1975.

Energy Research Group (ERG), *Priorities and Directions for Energy Research and Policy in Developing Countries*, IDRC-UNU, Ottawa, 1985.

Federal Power Commission (FPC), *The Methodology of Forecasting*, 1970 National Power Survey, Washington DC, 1970.

Food & Agriculture Organization (FAO), *Yearbook of Forest Products*, Rome, annual.

Food & Agricultural Organization (FAO), *Production Yearbook*, Rome, annual.

Fulkerson, W. et al., *Energy Technology R&D*, Oak Ridge National Lab., Tenn., USA, 1988.

Garfield, P.J. and W.F. Lovejoy, *Public Utility Economics*, Prentice-Hall, Englewood Cliffs NJ, 1964.

Gaskin, Gary and Julio Gamba, "Factors which Influence the Rational Use of Energy", presented at OLADE International Seminar on Rational Use of Energy in Industry, Lima, Peru, July 1983.

Grilliches, Zvi, "Returns to Research and Development Expenditures in the Private Sector," in J.W. Kendrick and B.N. Vaccara, eds., *New Developments in Productivity Measurement*, NBER Studies in Income and Wealth, Vol. 44, New York, 1980.

Grilliches, Zvi, "Productivity, R&D, and Basic Research at the Firm Level in the 1970's," *The American Economic Review*, vol.76, 1986, pp.141- 154.

Gross, G. and F. Galiana, "Short Term Load Forecasting", *Proc. IEEE*, vol. 75, Dec. 1987, pp. 1558-73.

Hall, D.O., "Bio-Energy Research -- A World Perspective", in *Bio-Energy '80 Proceedings*, The Bio-Energy Council, Washington DC, 1980, pp. 501-8.

Hannon, Bruce M. et al., "The Dollar, Energy and Employment Costs of Protein Consumption", *Energy Systems and Policy*, vol.3, No.3, 1979.

Harrold, Lloyd L., "Effect of Vegetation on Storm Hydrographs", Biological Effects on the Hydrological Cycle, Proceedings of 3rd International Seminar for Hydrology Professors, Lafayette, Ind., 1971.

Hartwick, J.M., "Substitution Among Exhaustible Resources and Intergenerational Equity", *Review of Economic Studies*, March 1978.

Heal, G., "The Relationship between Price and Extraction Cost for a Resource with a Backstop Technology", *The Bell Journal of Economics*, vol.7, Autumn 1976.

Hertzmark, Donald, "Joint Energy and Economic Optimization: A Proposition", *The Energy Journal*, vol.2, no.1, Jan. 1981.

Hotelling, H., "The Economics of Exhaustible Resources", *Journal of Political Economy*, vol. 39, April 1931, pp. 131-175.

Howe, J. W., Bever, J., Knowland, W., and Tarrant, J., *Energy for Developing Countries*, Overseas Development Council, Washington DC, 1976.

IEEE, "Load Forecast Bibliography, Phase I", *IEEE Trans. in Power App. Syst.*, vol. PAS 99, 1980, pp.53-8.

IEEE, "Load Forecast Bibliography, Phase II", *IEEE Trans. in Power App. Syst.*, vol. PAS 100, 1981, pp. 3217-20.

International Atomic Energy Agency (IAEA), *Nuclear Power Planning for Indonesia*, Vienna, 1976

International Atomic Energy Agency (IAEA), *Expansion Planning for Electrical Generating Systems*, Vienna, 1984.

International Energy Agency (IEA), *Energy Conservation*, Organisation for Economic Cooperation and Development, Paris, 1981.

International Energy Agency, "Energy Technology Policy", OECD, Paris, 1985.

International Energy Agency (IEA), *Renewable Sources of Energy*, IEA, Paris, 1987.

Johansson, Thomas B., B. Bodlund and R.H. Williams, *Electricity*, Lund University Press, Sweden, 1989.

Little, I.M.D., and J.A. Mirrlees, *Project Appraisal and Planning for Developing Countries*, Basic Books, New York, 1974.

Love, P.E., and J. Michel, "The Selection of an Energy R&D Portfolio for the European Community," No. EUR 8049 EN, EEC, Brussels, 1982.

Luenberger, D., *Introduction to Linear and Non-linear Programming*, Addison-Wesley, Reading MA, 1973.

MacAvoy, Paul, *Energy Policy*, Norton, New York, 1983.

Makhijani, A., *Energy Policy for the Third World*, International Institute for Environment and Development, London/Washington DC, 1976.

Makhijani, A. and A. Poole, *Energy and Agriculture in the Third World*, Ballinger Publ. Co., Cambridge MA, 1975.

Mansfield, E., *Industrial Research and Technological Innovation*, NBER, New York, 1968.

Mansfield, E., "Technology and Productivity in the U.S." Conference on Post-war Changes in the U.S. Economy, NBER, New York, 1980.

Mansfield, E., "Basic Research and Productivity Increase in Manufacturing", *American Economic Review*, vol.70, 1980, pp. 863-73.

Medema, E.L., C. Hatch and K. Christopherson, "Investment Analyses of Fuelwood Plantations in Sri Lanka", College of Forestry, Wildlife and Range Sciences, University of Idaho, Idaho, 1981.

Meier, P., "Energy Planning in Developing Countries: The Role of Microcomputers", *Natural Resources Forum*, vol.1, January 1985, pp. 41-52.

Meier, P. and M. Munasinghe, "Implementing a Practical Fuelwood Conservation Policy: the Case of Sri Lanka", *Energy Policy*, vol.15, no.2, April 1987, pp. 125-134.

Meta Systems, Inc., *Potential for Fuelwood And Charcoal in the Energy Systems of Developing Countries*, Cambridge, Massachusetts, 1980.

Ministry of Finance and Planning, *Public Investment Programme 1984-1988*, Government of Sri Lanka, Colombo, Sri Lanka, 1985.

Munasinghe, M., "Electric Power Pricing Policy", Staff Working Paper No. 340, The World Bank, Washington DC, June 1979.

Munasinghe, M., *The Economics of Power System Reliability and Planning*, Johns Hopkins Univ. Press, Baltimore MD, 1979.

Munasinghe, M., "The Costs Incurred by Residential Electricity Consumers Due to Power Failures", *Journal of Consumer Research*, March 1980, pp. 361-369.

Munasinghe, M., "A New Approach to System Planning", *IEEE Transactions on Power Apparatus and Systems*, vol. PAS-79, May-June 1980.

Munasinghe, M., *Energy in Sri Lanka*, SLAAS, Colombo, Sri Lanka, 1980.

Munasinghe, M., "An Integrated Framework for Energy Pricing in Developing Countries", *The Energy Journal*, vol. 1, July 1980, pp. 1-30.

Munasinghe, M., "Integrated National Energy Planning in Developing Countries", *Natural Resources Forum*, vol. 4, October 1980, pp. 359-73; also available as Reprint No. 165, The World Bank, Washington DC.

Munasinghe, M., "Principles of Modern Electricity Pricing", *IEEE Proceedings*, vol. 69, March 1981.

Munasinghe, M., "Third World Energy Policies: Demand Management and Conservation", *Energy Policy*, vol. 4, March 1983, pp. 4-18.

Munasinghe, M., "Energy Strategies for Oil Importing Developing Countries", *Natural Resources Journal*, vol. 24, April 1984, pp. 351-68.

Munasinghe, M., *The National Fuelwood Conservation Program (NFCP)*, Ministry of Power and Energy, Colombo, Sri Lanka, 1984.

Munasinghe, M., *National Energy Demand Management and Conservation Programme (NEDMCP)*, Ministry of Power and Energy, Colombo, Sri Lanka, 1985.

Munasinghe, M., *Rural Electrification for Development*, Westview Press, Boulder CO, 1987.

Munasinghe, M., Dow, M. and Fritz, J. (eds), *Microcomputers for Development*, National Academy of Sciences, Washington DC, 1985.

Munasinghe, M. and M. Gellerson, "Economic Criteria for Optimizing Power System Reliability Levels", *The Bell Journal of Economics*, vol.10, Spring 1979, pp. 353-365.

Munasinghe, M. and Walter G. Scott, "Energy Efficiency: Optimisation of Electric Power Distribution System Losses", Energy Department, The World Bank, Washington DC, 1982.

Munasinghe, M. and J.J. Warford, "Shadow Pricing and Evaluation of Public Utility Projects", Report No. GAS 14, Energy Department, World Bank, Washington DC, 1977.

Munasinghe, M. and J.J. Warford, *Electricity Pricing*, Johns Hopkins University Press, Baltimore MD, 1982.

Munasinghe, M. and C. Warren, "Rural Electrification, Energy Economics and National Policy in the Developing Countries", in *Future Energy Concepts*, Institution of Electrical Engineers, London, 1979.

National Science Foundation, "Federal R&D Funding for Energy: Fiscal Years 1971-84," No. NSF 83-301, NSF, Washington DC, Feb 1983.

Nelson, Richard D., "Institutions Supporting Technical Advance in Industry", *American Economic Review*, vol.76, May 1986, pp. 186-9.

Nicholson,W., *Microeconomic Theory*, Second Edition, Dryden Press, Hinsdale, Ill., 1978, Chap.4.

Office of Technology Assessment (OTA), *New Electric Power Technologies*, U.S. Congress, Washington DC, July 1985.

Openshaw, K., "Woodfuel, A Time for Reassessment", *East African Journal*, Jan. 1977.

Peck, A.E. and O.C. Doehring, "Voluntarism and Price Response: Consumer Response to the Energy Shortage", *The Bell Journal of Economics*, vol.7, Spring 1976.

Perera, W.R.H., "Some Thoughts on Social Agro-Forestry in Rural Sri Lanka", *Marga Quarterly Journal* (Sri Lanka), vol.8, no.1, 1985, pp.40-49.

Pindyck, Robert S., *The Structure of World Energy Demand*, MIT Press, Cambridge MA, 1979.

Pinto, Frank J.P., "The Economics of and Potential for Energy Conservation and Substitution", presented at 5th Annual International Meeting of IAEE, New Delhi, India, January 1984.

Prasad, N.R., J.M. Perkins and G. Nesgos, "A Markov Process Applied to Forecasting. Part I - Economic Development", IEEE Power Engineering Society Summer Meeting, Vancouver, July 1973

Prasad, N.R., J.M. Perkins and G. Nesgos, "A Markov Process Applied to Forecasting, Part II - The Demand for Electricity", IEEE Power Engineering Society Winter Meeting, New York, January 1974.

Pushparajah, M., "Management of Forest Reserves", *Sri Lanka Forester*, vol.15, January 1981, pp. 21-24.

Ramsdell, A. and K. Walton, "Basic Energy Statistics: A Global Perspective", in *Workshop on Energy Data of Developing Countries, Proceedings: Volume 1*, International Energy Agency, Paris, 1979, pp.33-44.

Ray, A., *Cost Benefit Analysis*, Johns Hopkins University Press, Baltimore MD, 1984.

Revelle, R., "Energy Use in Rural India" *Science*, vol. 192, June 4, 1969.

Rohrer, W.M. and K. Krieder, "Sources and Uses of Waste Heat", *Waste Heat Management Guidebook*, NBS Handbook 121, US Government Printing Office, Washington DC, January 1977.

Salam, A., "Internationalization of Science in Developing Countries," Address to the IAEA Governing Board, Vienna, March 1980.

Samii, M.V., "Economic Growth and Optimal Rate of Oil Extraction", *OPEC Review*, vol.3, 1979.

Sankar, T.L., and G. Schramm, *Asian Energy Problems*, Asian Development Bank, Manila, Philippines, 1982.

Sassone, P.G., "Shadow Pricing in CBA: Mathematical Programming and Economic Theory", *The Engineering Economist*, vol.22, Spring 1977, pp. 219-33.

Sathaye, J., "Rural Electricity in the Philippines: Planning Issues", *Energy Policy*, August 1987, pp. 339-51.

Schipper, L., S. Meyers and J. Sathaye, "Energy Demand in the Developing Countries", Report No. LBL-16260, Lawrence Berkeley Lab. Berkeley, California, June 1983.

Seneca, Joseph J. and Michael K. Taussig, *Environmental Economics*, second edition, Prentice-Hall, Englewood Cliffs NJ, 1979.

Shepard, R.W., *Cost and Production Functions*, Princeton Univ. Press, Princeton, N.J., 1953.

Siddayao, C.M., *Energy Demand and Economic Growth*, Westview Press, Boulder CO, 1986.

Singh, L. R., and Singh, B., "Level and Pattern of Energy Consumption in an Agriculturally Advanced Area of Uttar Pradesh", *Indian J. of Agr. Econ.*, vol. 31, July-Sept. 1976, pp. 157-164.

Soussan, J.G., "Fuelwood Strategies and Action Programs in Asia: Comparative Experience in Bangladesh, Indonesia, Nepal, Republic of Korea, Sri Lanka and Thailand", Report of a CEC-AIT Workshop (December 1984), Renewable Energy Resources Information Center (RERIC), Asian Institute of Technology, 1984.

Squire, L. and H. Van der Tak, *Economic Analysis of Projects*, Johns Hopkins Univ. Press, Baltimore MD, 1975.

Stewart, F., *Technology and Underdevelopment*, MacMillan, London, UK, 1978.

Sullivan, R.L., *Power System Planning*, McGraw Hill International Book Co., New York, 1977, Chap.2.

Taylor, Lester D., "The Demand for Energy: A Survey of Price and Income Elasticities", in: *International Studies of the Demand for Energy*, W.D. Nordhaus (ed.), North Holland, Amsterdam, 1977.

Terleckyj, Nestor, *Effects of R&D on the Productivity Growth of Industries*, Washington DC, 1974.

UNCTAD, "Report and Recommendations of the Workshop on Technology Policies and Planning for Technological Transformation," United Nations, New York, January 1981.

UNCTAD Secretariat, "Major Issues in the Transfer and Development of Energy Technology in Developing Countries," Twelfth Congress of the World Energy Conference, New Delhi, Sept. 1983.

UNESCAP, *32 Economic Bulletin for Asia and Pacific*, Bangkok, Thailand, 1981, pp. 46-62.

USAID, "New Directions for Renewable Energy Activities", Office of Energy, USAID, Washington DC, Feb.1988.

Walker, James M., "Voluntary Responses to Energy Conservation Appeals", *Journal of Consumer Research*, vol.7, June 1980.

Webb, Michael and David Pearce, "The Economics of Energy Analysis" *Energy Policy*, December 1975.

West Pakistan Water and Power Authority (WPWPA), Mangla Watershed Management Study, Lahore, Pakistan, 1961.

Wijesinghe, L.C.A., "A Sample Study of Biomass Fuel Consumption in Sri Lanka Households", *Biomass*, vol.5, 1984, pp. 261-282.

Wilbanks, Thomas, J., "Lessons from the National Energy Planning Experience in Developing Countries", *The Energy Journal*, Special LDC issue, vol.8, July 1987, pp. 169-182.

World Bank, *Energy in the Developing Countries*, Washington DC, 1980

World Bank, "Solar Photovoltaic Systems for Agricultural Pumping", Energy Dept., World Bank, Washington DC, 1982.

World Bank, "Diesel Plant Performance Study", Energy Dept. Paper No. 21, Energy Dept., World Bank, Washington DC, 1982.

World Bank, *The Energy Transition in Developing Countries*, Washington DC, August 1983.

World Bank, *World Development Report*, Washington DC, August 1983.